How to Manage Residential Property for Maximum Cash Flow and Resale Value

Fifth Edition

by John T. Reed

John T. Reed Publishing
342 Bryan Drive • Alamo, California 94507
925-820-7262 Fax 925-820-1259 E-mail: johnreed@johntreed.com
www.johntreed.com/realestate.html

To my son
Steven Tunnell Reed

OTHER MATERIAL BY JOHN T. REED

- Aggressive Tax Avoidance For Real Estate Investors
- Coaching Youth Football, 2nd edition
- Coaching Youth Football Defense, 2nd edition
- Distressed Real Estate Times—Offensive and Defensive Strategy and Tactics (Special Report or cassettes)
- Football Clock Management
- High Leverage Real Estate Financing (cassettes)
- How To Buy Real Estate For At Least 20% Below Market Value
- How To Buy Real Estate For At Least 20% Below Market Value, Volumes 1 and 2 (cassettes)
- How to Buy Residential Property (cassettes)
- How to do a Delayed Exchange (Special Report or cassettes)
- How To Find Deals That Make Sense In Today's Market (cassettes)
- How To Increase The Value Of Real Estate
- How To Manage Residential Property For Maximum Cash Flow And Resale Value (cassettes)
- How To Use Leverage to Maximize Your Real Estate Investment Return
- Office Building Acquisition Handbook
- Real Estate Investment Strategy (selected newsletter articles)
- John T. Reed's Real Estate Investor's Monthly (newsletter)
- Residential Property Acquisition Handbook
- Single-Family Lease Options (Special Report or cassettes)

For more information, see the order forms elsewhere in this book, call 925-820-6292

Thanks To

My wife, Marty Tunnell, for her proofreading…

My resident managers over the years: Marion T. Reed (also my Mom), Irv Welsted, The Stephensons, Vince and Pat Peterson, Lloyd and Evelyn Moore, Neal and Tammy Cowles, Pam and Steve Shockley, Bud and Clara Cameron, Ron and Linda Butler, Cecilia Pitcock, Harry Woods, Mark and Masheille DeRossett.

My advisors: William Nickerson, Leigh Robinson, Ro Freeman, Barry Conway, Mike Scott, Bob Bruss, Duane Gomer, Dave Hann, John Heintges, Tom O'Dea, Sam Plimpton, Ralph Bunje, Bob Goodman, Ira Serkes, Greg Crouch, Marc Goodfriend, Jane Garvey, Marty Rubenstein, Steve Patterson, and John Beck.

My fellow apartment owners: David and Suzanne Bloore, John Toraason, Frank McGinnis, Tom and Stephanie Kurkjian, Paul Meyer, Jim Sirbasku, and Chris and Vince Tobkin.

My former real estate employers: Bob and Dale Pritchett and Ted Fox.

Published by Reed Publishing, 342 Bryan Drive, Alamo, CA 94507 925-820-6292
Manufactured in the United States of America.
ISBN: 0-939224-42-9
Library of Congress Catalog Card Number: 98-067085

ABOUT THE AUTHOR

John T. Reed was a small-scale landlord for 23 years. He has been a real estate writer since 1976.

He has invested in New Jersey, Texas, and California.

He is the editor and publisher of *John T. Reed's Real Estate Investor's Monthly*, a national newsletter—and the author and publisher of ten books on various real estate investment subjects.

Mr. Reed has been interviewed about real estate by Morley Safer on *60 Minutes*, by David Hartman on *Good Morning America*, and by Larry King on *Larry King Live* as well as other television and radio programs. His analysis of real estate investing has appeared in *The Wall Street Journal, Newsweek, U.S. News & World Report, Changing Times, Money*, and various real estate journals.

His real estate experience includes single-family rental houses, duplexes, a triplex, and apartment buildings ranging in size from twelve units to over two hundred units. He has been resident manager of his own buildings and property manager for other owners.

CONTENTS

Introduction

Income and expenses

In a sentence, property management is the art and science of **maximizing the income** of a rental property while **minimizing the expenses and hassles**. But there's more to it than just raising the rent and replacing the sixty-watt bulbs with forty-watt bulbs. And not all investors have maximum return as their goal.

Some are interested in **pride of ownership**. That is, they regard their building as a proud possession. They want it to **look good**—to beam as tenants and others express their admiration. Pride of ownership owners earn lower rates of return than other owners—but then they earn a **higher** rate of "return" as far as pride goes.

Another goal which often goes along with pride of ownership is **hassle avoidance**. Simply stated, to avoid normal hassles in property management charge **low rents** and, if you have a manager, **pay him or her more than average**.

Resale value

I bought my first building, a duplex, in 1969. That was just about when real estate investing changed from an **income** business to a **growth** business. Used to be that rental buildings were considered income properties. They're still **called** that. But back in the sixties and earlier, they really **meant** it.

Just as you have income stocks and growth stocks in the stock market, you have income producers and growth properties in real estate. When I started, you bought rental buildings and such for the income they produced—what would now be called positive cash flow. If you wanted **growth**, you became a **developer**.

With inflation, who needs cash flow?

But in the early seventies, property values started to climb. My first duplex, which I bought for $14,000, had positive cash flow of $65 per month. That's with 20% down ($2,800) and a **twenty** year self-amortizing mortgage! If you have any experience with the current market, you know how fantastic that was. But that was no great shakes at the time. I worried that I had overpaid!

I sold that duplex five years later for $34,000. So although the before-tax cash flow was fantastic by today's standards, the **appreciation** return was even better.

I was not the only one who noticed. After 1970, real estate **prices** escalated dramatically—faster than inflation. But rents went up about the same as inflation. The median sale price of existing single-family homes was $23,000 in 1970 and $125,900 in 1998—a 447% increase. The Consumer Price Index (http://stats.bls.gov/news.release/cpi.t01.htm) was 38.8 in 1970 and 162.5 in 1998—a 319% increase. And the rent component of the CPI was 41.29 in 1970 and 170.7 in 1998—a 313% increase.

Increases from 1970 to 1998

Home prices	447%
Consumer Price Index	319%
Rents	313%

The reason prices of homes and multi-unit residential properties went up faster than rents was increases in building values. When you're earning a dramatic return from appreciation in value alone, who cares about cash flow? So investors began to think of residential rental properties (and non-residential income properties) as **growth** investments rather than **income producers**.

That meant they became willing to pay higher prices than the income warranted. Higher prices, in turn, meant that the mortgage payment was so high that the buildings did not make an operating profit—did not have positive cash flow.

With tax shelter who needs cash flow?

On August 13, 1981, President Reagan signed the Economic Recovery Tax Act of 1981 (ERTA) into law. It contained the Accelerated Cost Recovery System (ACRS) which allowed real estate investors to depreciate their properties using the 175% declining balance method over 15 years. That gave a first-year deduction of 12% of the depreciable value. Prior law would typically allow 125% declining balance over a 25-year life which gives a first-year deduction of 5%. (That could have been improved somewhat by component depreciation.)

ACRS was such a good deal that high-tax-bracket investors could earn a good return with **no** before-tax cash flow. The tax benefits and appreciation alone were enough.

So when appreciation rates abated somewhat in the early eighties, ERTA came along to give real estate investors another reason to not care about cash flow.

With*out* appreciation or tax shelter, you'd *better* care about cash flow

In the seventies and early eighties, the typical real estate investor started off with **negative cash flow**. He figured the appreciation and tax benefits would more than make up for it.

But high market appreciation rates ended in the seventies for most markets. And by the mid-eighties, most residential rental markets were overbuilt leading to **negative** appreciation rates. In other words, building values went **down**, not up.

And on October 22, 1986, that same President Reagan who gave us the **best** tax deal ever, gave us the **worst** tax deal ever—the Tax Reform Act of 1986. Among other things, it limits or eliminates real estate investors' ability to deduct rental property losses, depending upon the owner's non-real estate income.

A a result of the decline in appreciation rates—and **reversal** of appreciation rates in many cases—and the near elimination of tax benefits—real estate investors now want cash flow. That means, simply, that they want to buy buildings for a lot less than they paid a decade ago. By paying less, they get smaller **mortgages** which means smaller mortgage **payments** which means more cash flow.

And appreciation is no longer taken for granted. If you want appreciation now, you have to get it the old-fashioned way—by **earning** it. This book tells you how to manage for maximum cash flow and how to **make** the value of your property go up—as opposed to the old method of **hoping** it will go up.

Managing for maximum value appreciation

Do you manage differently when maximum value appreciation is your goal?

Not much. On buildings with one, two or three units, you worry more about the tenant's **housekeeping and cooperation** with showing the property to prospective purchasers than you do about maximum rent.

Otherwise, the things that maximize income and minimize expenses are the same things that maximize value.

The size of your operation

There are significant differences between managing a duplex and managing a 400-unit complex. If you read other property management books, you'll find that some are oriented toward the duplex owner; others toward the 400-unit owner. The authors tend to write about the size of operation **they** have at the time they write the book—forgetting that not everyone is at that point on the ladder.

I am going to try to keep the differences in size in mind as I write this book. So that I point out the different ways of doing things when I come to subjects where size makes a difference.

In addition to being biased toward 25- to 37-unit operations, I have no experience above the two-hundred unit level. I managed a two hundred-unit building when I was a property manager. And at that same time I ran other, smaller buildings and several non-residential buildings. So one of the reasons I'll not say a heck of a lot about running four hundred-unit complexes is that I've never done it.

How the size of the building changes the management

The main ways you change management techniques as you increase in size are in

- use of employees
- financial control systems
- extent of marketing effort
- economies and diseconomies of scale

Economies of scale are savings you get from being big. Like volume discounts on purchases. But there are also **dis**economies of scale. In fact, one 1978 study done in suburban Chicago found the following differences between annual per unit costs in 125-unit and 1,000-unit complexes

Category	125-unit	1,000-unit
Repairs	$193.40	$307.00
Payroll	217.15	291.10
Vacancy/collection loss	92.10	160.50
Supplies	18.50	52.25
Advertising	16.05	47.55
Legal	2.10	11.80

In today's regulatory and litigation environment, bigger businesses are increasingly burdened with litigation, regulation, and taxes that do not apply to mom and pop businesses. So bigger is not always better.

Geographical differences

There are also geographical differences in the way you manage buildings. **Climate** is one reason. You plow snow out of the parking lot in the north; but not in Texas.

Politics is another reason. I have never operated in a rent-controlled community. So I don't know a lot about how to maximize income and minimize expenses in rent-controlled towns. Owners who **do** own rent-controlled buildings will benefit from reading this book—but less than owners of free-market buildings.

Landlord/tenant laws

Rent control is not the only political influence on property management. There are also the many other landlord-tenant laws. In Texas, for example, you can confiscate certain personal property (like tvs and stereos) in the possession of tenants who have not paid the rent. In order to do that, a clause to that effect must be included in the lease and be underlined or in bold print in the lease. In most other states, such "landlord's liens" have long been outlawed.

In New Jersey, on the other hand, landlords have to give every tenant a "Tenants' Rights" booklet. It tells tenants all the ways they can sue their landlord and how much money they can get. Plus all New Jersey tenants have a **lifetime lease**—that is, they cannot be made to move except for "cause."

Since I have managed residential properties in New Jersey and Texas, I know both ends of the regulatory spectrum.

Bureaucracy

A lot of property management books are bureaucratic—lots of forms and reports for the resident managers to fill out. Even those by authors who are small building operators. The worst offender in this category is a book by the Institute of Real Estate Management (www.irem.org) called *How To Write an Operations Manual—A Guide For Apartment Management*. The very **idea** of an operations manual is bureaucratic.

Columnist Bob Bruss (http://fyiowa.webpoint.com/home/bruss.htm) criticized earlier editions of this book for not having enough forms. I can't fix that. I deliberately do not provide many forms because laws, regulations, and litigation climates vary dramatically from jurisdiction to jurisdiction and over time. Nowadays, the wrong word in a document you use can invalidate your lease or cost you your life savings in litigation. You must get your forms from an up-to-date local source like your state apartment association.

Management authors aren't the only ones who are bureaucratic. Many property owners and managers are too. One of my resident managers worked for a property management firm for a while. She told me they had her fill out a total of **fifty** reports each month—on a 33-unit apartment building!

Little bureaucracy in this book

I am **anti**-bureaucratic. My resident managers only filled out a **one** monthly report---an **income report** showing what money was collected for the month. When a tenant moved out, the managers had to tell me what, if anything, to deduct from the tenant's security deposit, but it's stretching things to call it a report. And my managers filled out the form printed on our petty cash envelopes every other month or so when they requested **petty cash**.

My approach to management is to hire good people, keep them fully informed on how the building is doing, require a minimum of reports, and talk to them on the phone a lot.

Actually, I sent more reports **to** my managers than I got **from** them. I sent them a **rent report** which is a computer analyzed version of the manual rent report they sent me. I sent them a deposit and vacancy loss report which are also computerized derivatives of the rent report the managers sent me. And I sent them a copy of the **cash flow statements** showing all income and expenses for the month.

By the way, I **used to be** more bureaucratic. I've learned from experience not to be. It's easier on the **owner** as well as on the manager. So expect to find my non-bureaucratic approach throughout the book.

Aggressive rent raising

I may be the biggest proponent of rent increases in the U.S.. For several years, I gave the speech on rent raising at the National Apartment Association (http://www.naahq.org) and California Apartment Association conventions. My approach can be summed up in one sentence: Every tenant pays **market** rent. That means new tenants, existing tenants, good tenants, long-term tenants, elderly tenants—**everyone**.

I am probably also the biggest proponent of **lowering** rents. There's less competition for that title.

Strict lease enforcement

I am a West Point graduate. That doesn't mean I do a white glove inspection of my tenants' refrigerator coils every Saturday. But I **do** require my managers to **strictly** enforce the lease. West Point is probably at least **partly** responsible for that. It's a strict place. And after adhering to its strict rules—and watching four thousand other guys do the same—for four years—one's idea of how well-behaved humans are capable of being tends to change.

Plus I spent a lot more years—23—being a residential property owner and manager than I spent being a cadet. And during that time, I've experimented with varying levels of strictness. I've regretted almost every time I've been lenient. So the strictness you'll notice in this book is about 80% from my experience in residential properties and about 20% from my West Point experience.

There are a couple of aspects to strictly enforcing the lease. Number one, you have to hold **yourself** to the same standards. Make the tenant in 106 pay his rent on time and pay the late charge if he doesn't. But don't expect to get away with that if he's been complaining about a ceiling stain for two weeks. You have to live up to **your** end of the lease too.

Number two, your lease and policies had better be **reasonable** to start with. And you or your managers should make sure the tenants **know of and understand** the policies. If I were going to put it in the form of a motto, it would be

We believe in reasonable policies, clearly explained, and strictly enforced.

"Landlord" and "tenant" or "owner" and "resident?"

Touchy-feely marketing is in now. You'll notice that I use the words "landlord" and "tenant." Most landlords and managers don't use those words anymore. They say "owner" and "resident." "Landlord," the reasoning goes, is an outdated word referring to landowners in feudal times. The words "landlord" and "tenant" conjure up images of evil Simon Legree demanding the rent from poor Little Nell.

I think the reason "in" managers and owners use the words "owner" and "resident" is because they don't like being unpopular. So they have become real estate "spin doctors." And they figure new words will make people forget how much they dislike landlords. I doubt it.

Being a landlord or property manager is like umpiring a Little League game. Ain't no way you're going to be popular. If you want proof of that, consider the Houston landlord who decided to let his tenants pay **no rent at all**. "God will provide," was his explanation.

Did the tenants love him? Nope. They were **angry** at him because the electric company turned off the juice and their air-conditioners with it.

Another problem with the words "owner" and "resident" is that they are not precise. One of the problems you often have as a landlord is that some of your **residents** are not **tenants**. That is, they moved in as someone's roommate without signing a lease or going through your screening.

"Owner" is OK as far as it goes. But since virtually all non-"owners" refer to rental building owners as "landlords," the word owner seems to suggest that the person you're talking about is someone **other than** the landlord. If you were talking about the landlord, they figure, you'd say "landlord."

I say "landlord"—and "tenant."

Overdone marketing

Saying, "owner" and "resident" is only part of a whole shtick of overdone marketing that's been going around for some years. For example, one of my managers was "shopped" by a manager posing as a prospective tenant. The shopper had been hired by the property management firm to check up on the manager. One of the shopper's criticisms was that the resident manager had failed to take the "most scenic route" to the vacant unit.

Gimme a break. It's a 33-unit building! How many routes can there be? That same property management firm would fire a resident manager on the spot if she were caught not wearing hosiery and high heels during business hours. Gimme another break. Neat, clean, and well-groomed is quite adequate.

A lot of owners and property managers try to convince resident managers that all vacancies are directly attributable to her smile not being wide enough or her makeup not being perfect enough or her closing technique not being professional enough. Baloney.

I want my resident managers to keep themselves and the building looking neat, clean, and well-groomed. I hope they're around a reasonable number of hours so that neither prospective tenants nor current tenants get many no-answers. And I expect them to be friendly and reasonably competent at answering the phone, greeting walk-ins, and showing apartments. But if they do all that and there's still a vacancy problem, it's probably **my** fault as owner—not the resident manager's fault.

So you'll find my marketing advice in this book runs to neat, clean, and friendly. But not to taking the "most scenic route" and putting Pillsbury cinnamon muffins in the oven.

Everything you do is marketing. A lot of owners and managers think you can make up for a mediocre product or mediocre service with super marketing. Not so.

Run your building well. Keep it looking good. Have a reasonably competent manager. And price it at market value. Do these things and you'll get your share of tenants. Even Sally the Supermanager can't make up for a poorly-run building, inadequate maintenance budget, or overpriced units.

The point of diminishing returns

Since I'm writing a book on property management, you might think my building is the most well-run buildings around. Spectacular to look at. Every maintenance request taken care of in minutes. And all that.

No way. There's a point of diminishing returns—in property management as in everything else. I wanted my buildings to look good. But they didn't knock your eyes out. Knocking your eyes out costs money. And the market will only pay for so much beauty. There comes a point at which everyone will agree your properties are so spectacular looking that they're worth the $700 a month you want. It's just that they can't **afford** such a spectacular-looking place.

Same goes for every other aspect of management. If you could investigate every facet of my building, I suspect you'd be favorably impressed. But you would not nominate me for the World's Greatest Building award. That's fine. I'm not **seeking** the World's Greatest Building Award.

I've met some owners who **are**. One architect comes to mind. And that's fine for them. But I'm too pragmatic to spend more money on the building than the return from the expenditure warrants.

The value of the owner's time

One of the important factors in the locating the point of diminishing returns is the value of the owner's time. I figure my time's worth over a hundred dollars an hour. So how much of it can I afford to spend trying to get the best possible price on vinyl?

When I first started, my time was far less valuable. And I roamed South Jersey saving money on vinyl remnants, buying gas ranges from the inner city guy who had the lowest prices, etc. Now **those** were well-managed buildings.

That made sense then. And **not** doing those things makes sense now. I try to encourage my **managers** to economize like that. And they generally do.

Property management books and articles rarely pay much attention to the value of the owner's time.

The owner's objective

People buy rental properties to get rich.

"Jeez! He said it right out loud!"

American businessmen, rental owners in particular, have been apologizing for, and almost denying, that they want to make a profit in recent years. "We only want a reasonable return," is the line you hear from apartment association leaders.

Baloney. Do you think I spent Christmas Day 1983 calling around Texas for a plumber to stop my burst pipe leaks for a "reasonable return?" Do I put up with tenants who carelessly stop up sewer lines, damage disposers, and put cigarette burns in my carpet for a "reasonable return?" Do I watch tenants break the lease whenever they feel like it but require me to absolutely adhere to every explicit or "implied" clause in it for a "reasonable return?"

You gotta be kidding.

Not a guarantee; just a shot at it

Tenants would protest that they were not brought into this world to make me rich. And I would agree with them. I don't claim that being a landlord **entitles** me to becoming rich. But I **do** want a shot at it. If there's a **possible** pot of gold at the end of the sewer backup, I'll put up with the trials of property management.

Besides, few landlords ever got rich from what **tenants** paid them. Landlords get rich from what **other landlords** pay them for their buildings. Tenants only provide the money the landlord needs to pay the bills until resale time—and the rent increases the landlord needs to justify selling the property for more than he paid for it.

How you get rich in residential properties

Property **management's** role in getting rich is to

1. Generate the income the owner needs to **pay the bills and mortgage payments** during the holding period and
2. Generate the income **increases** the owner needs to increase the building value and
3. Generate a portion of the return through **positive cash flow** especially after the first couple years.

How much is rich?

Rich is a net worth of one million dollars. As you increase your net worth **up** to that level, your life improves. You move to nicer, more adequately sized homes. You drive a nice car and take nice vacations. You can afford to send your kids to good schools. And you can afford to buy adult toys like a boat or even a plane.

Above a million dollars, about all you can do is show off. A ten-room house is better than a five-room house—if you **need** ten rooms. But a twenty-room house is **not** better than a ten-room house. Because hardly **any**body needs twenty rooms. A twenty-room house will impress your less affluent friends and relatives—but there will be rooms you don't enter for months at a time.

Not that you should **turn down** a twenty-room house. It's just that you ought not bust your back or take big risks to get one. Getting your net worth up to a million dollars is worth the hard work and risk of rental property ownership.

The two-phase career

Seems to me your career in rental property ought to have two phases: pre-million and post-million. In the pre-million phase, you take the risks and do the hard work necessary to earn the maximum rate of return—to haul your net worth up to a million.

In the **post**-million phase, you relax. If you've had it up to here with tenants—which is likely, you can do several things.

You can shift to the **hassle-avoidance management mode**. That means you allow your leverage (loans on the property) to drop down to the 30% to 40% of value range. That gives you a relatively low mortgage payment in comparison to your rental income. Which, in turn, means you don't sweat each month over whether you'll be able to make the payment or not.

The hassle-avoidance mode also involves letting your **rents fall behind market** value. Then you can take only the best new tenants, demand total lease compliance from your existing tenants, and have very little turnover. Rent-controlled owners are forced into the hassle-avoidance mode whether they want it or not. Finally, in hassle avoidance you get a **high quality manager**—and pay him or her an appropriate salary to keep them.

You can exchange your residential rental building for a less management-intensive property—like a net-leased nonresidential building. That's another form of hassle avoidance.

Or you can do as most real estate investors do---sell and live off the payments from the mortgages you take back. I am dead set **against** that course of action. But I won't go into it here. For details on why, read my books, *Aggressive Tax Avoidance For Real Estate Investors* and *How To Use Leverage To Maximize Your Real Estate Investment Return.* (www.johntreed.com/realestate.html)

'Compliance'

When I first got into the rental business, management journals contained articles about marketing and maintenance. In recent years, most of their articles seem to be about compliance. Today, the typical apartment association journal article warns, "New law such and such means that you will be subject to severe penalties if you do not comply by doing so and so." Bummer.

When I was in the Army, I couldn't wait to get out and be my own man. When I was in the Army I had to do dumb things like the universal government-employee practice of keeping a CYA file of documents needed to protect myself in case of bureaucratic infighting. In my last years as a landlord, I found myself again keeping a CYA file to protect myself from law suits and regulators. Owning or managing apartment buildings is now so regulated that it has become like working at a government job. Fortunately, that still is not as true of owning and managing rental houses.

Tenants and employees

Most of the new regulations and litigation revolve around landlord-tenant and employer-employee relationships. Some pertain to other things like toxic contamination.

You cannot eliminate tenants from your rental business—by definition. But you can reduce the number of them by buying higher dollar units. In other words, if you own a million dollars worth of apartments you will have more tenants than if you own a million dollars worth of rental houses.

You can eliminate employees. Basically by doing the same thing: owning smaller properties with fewer units per building. There are also many laws and regulations which kicks in at various levels of size which is stated in terms of dollars of income, number of employees, and number of units in the building. It used to be that getting bigger was desirable. Now, getting bigger in some ways brings you additional expenses and hassles.

Conclusion

Property management is a tough business. Ninety percent of the problems are caused by bad tenants. Rental property **ownership** is a **risky** business. If you buy a leveraged building, and fail to keep the income at least equal to the expenses, there's a good chance you will lose the building—and all the down payment and other money you invested in it. And keeping the income at least equal to the expenses is not easy.

The anti-landlord crowd condemn us up one side and down the other. They say we're a bunch of rent-gouging Simon Legrees. That we don't maintain our properties. That we steal security deposits. I've got an answer for all of them. Don't **tell** us the "right" way to run a building, **show** us. I have this fantasy in which a bunch of anti-landlord groups get together and buy an apartment building—to show us the "right" way to manage property.

A year after purchase, they find they have to send out a rent increase letter. They expected it would only be 2% or so. But, jeez!. Look at how the expenses went up. It'll have to be a **nine** percent increase. But the tenants'll understand. We'll just explain that the rent increase was necessitated by our expense increases. Sure, they'll understand.

And can't you hear them confiding that some of their tenants have taken advantage of their good nature. "*How so?*" we ask sweetly. "They don't pay the rent on time! And to be good guys, we gave them two-year leases. But they move whenever they feel like it—but we can't raise the rent for two years if they stay."

"*Isn't that terrible,*" we sympathize.

"Look, we wouldn't want it to get out that we asked you this, but how do you profiteering SOBs get people to pay the rent on time?"

"*We screen out applicants whose credit history is bad or whose income is too low. And we strictly enforce late penalties—including evicting chronic late payers.*"

"You mean the reason you don't rent to low income people is that they don't pay the rent? We thought it was discrimination. And late penalties and evictions—**we** can't do that. We said we were going to be **good** landlords."

"*Low income people with good credit histories do pay the rent—if the rent is correspondingly low. And as far as late penalties and evictions are concerned, you're welcome to use some other technique for getting them to pay on time. So far, however, it appears you haven't found one. Landlords know that some people respond to the carrot; some, to the stick. So you have to have both in your repertoire.*"

"But if we follow all your advice, we'll be doing all the things we've criticized landlords for."

"*And if you don't?*"

"We'll get foreclosed."

"*Welcome to the landlord business.*"

Something like that really happened

The April 2, 1992 *Wall Street Journal* (www.wsj.com) reported that something like my fantasy really happened in Chicago. A middle-class Baptist church there decided to help inner-city residents by buying and sprucing up a 24-unit apartment building.

Considering they only paid $22,000 or $917 per unit, including $12,000 in tax arrearages, you'd think it would be hard for them to lose. But they found a way.

They were denied a $302,000 loan because they did not have enough cash on hand to operate the building. They had to evict two drug dealers who also made the undesirable tenants list by virtue of not having paid the rent in six months. The evicted drug dealers promptly moved in with two other tenants in the same building and those tenants had to be evicted as well.

After those evictions, the building was only 46% occupied and six of the remaining tenants were not paying rent leaving a paid occupancy rate of just 21%. The rents collected did not even cover the heating bill.

A judge ordered the minister in charge to fix 49 housing code violations or be jailed for contempt. The taxes are still delinquent. A member of the congregation suggested that the church torch the building.

Arson is a felony. But torching might be an appropriate fate for their self-righteous, holier-than-thou attitude toward us "greedy landlords."

PART ONE: LEASING

1

Setting Rents

Fair market rental value

Your rents should be at **market**. "Fair market value," in building **sale** prices is defined as

The highest price a property will bring when exposed to the market for a reasonable period of time.

I would add that the "exposure" to the market must be **competent**. That is, if you just announce that the property is for sale by placing a 3 x 5 card on the supermarket bulletin board, it hasn't really been "exposed to the market." So fair market **rental** value can be defined as

The highest rent an apartment will bring when competently exposed to the market for a reasonable period of time.

'Rent gouging'

You've probably heard the phrase "**rent gouging**." The people who use that phrase would probably call me and most other landlords "rent gougers." I'd like to hear their definition of "gouging." I suspect they'd be forced to admit that "rent gouging" and "renting to the highest acceptable bidder" are the same thing.

Rent to the highest acceptable bidder.

By "acceptable," I mean a person whose credit history checks out. Someone who makes enough money to afford the rent—and who has a history of paying his or her rent and other bills on time.

'House gouging'

The liberals who self-righteously denounce landlords for "rent gouging" often own homes. And they **sell** their homes just like anyone else.

What do you suppose liberals do when it comes to setting the asking price for their home? Do they say, "Now what could a low-income person afford to pay for my home?" Do they think back to what they paid and their down payment amount and say, "Now what would be a **reasonable return** on my investment?"

When elephants fly.

No, they don't ask any of those questions. They ask their Realtor®, "What do you think I can get for it?"—with huge dollar signs in each eye.

'Gouging' and then some

In the typical case, the Realtor® says $75,900—and the liberal (or any other home seller) responds, "$75,900!! Are you crazy? Joe up the street got $89,000—and our house has a solar hot water heater. His didn't."

"Actually," replies the Realtor, *"I handled that deal. I know Joe **told** everyone he got $89,000. But he didn't. He **asked** $89,000. He sold for $81,000—and had to take back a mortgage at 6% to do it."*

In the typical case, Realtors® have a terrible time trying to get the seller to put a realistic price on their homes. Almost all sellers want significantly more than market value. I know. I used to be a real estate salesman. Look at any how-to book for real estate agents and you'll find a chapter on how to persuade the seller to drop his price to market value.

Aren't homes 'housing?'

In the debates about rent control, you invariably hear that we have a "housing shortage"—therefore we need to control the prices of apartments. Wait a minute. Aren't 1-family homes housing, too? In fact, 2/3 of the people in the United States live in owner-occupied homes. Only 1/3 live in apartments. So "housing" consists of two parts homes and one part apartments.

If we're going to control housing prices to solve the housing shortage, let's control home prices, too. Try advocating that and you'll be hanged from the nearest tree—by people who either advocate rent controls—or don't care whether rents are controlled. Matter of fact, you could go to the nation's most liberal, pro-rent control community and advocate controlling the resale prices of homes—and you'd **still** be hung from the nearest tree. Only they'd use a Volvo instead of a horse to hoist you up. A private citizen **did** urge house price control in Berkeley, CA in 1989. The furor was so great city council had to pass a resolution swearing they'd never consider such a thing.

Forget the guilt

You may be one of the many landlords who feels guilty about raising rents. **Quit** feeling guilty. When a liberal rent-control advocate sells his house, he gouges the eyeballs out of the buyer. "Whatever the market will bear," is his guiding principle. He couldn't care less about housing shortages, affordability, or "reasonable returns" on investment. Same thing goes for a tenant who's selling his car. He wants as much as he can get, period.

So don't let those hypocrites convince you that **you** should feel guilty about renting to the highest acceptable bidder. Not in the slightest.

When a **home owner** gets a fantastic price for his home, people say, "Great!" "He made a terrific investment." "He's a shrewd businessman."

But when a **landlord** gets a fantastic rent for his property, people say, "Rent gouger." "Excess profits." "Obscene profits." "He's charging whatever the market will bear." "Outrageous greed."

Above-market rents are their own punishment

I often read rent-control debate articles in the local *San Francisco Chronicle*. One of the phrases I see is, "If controls are removed, landlords will be able to charge whatever they want."

In a pig's eye.

The reporters need to make one slight change in that sentence. "If controls are removed, landlords will be able to **ask** whatever they want."

I **wish** we could charge whatever we wanted. It wouldn't be so hard to get positive cash flow if we could. But it doesn't work that way. I know from experience.

Like a cartoon character off a cliff

I raised the rent on a duplex apartment I owned once. Seemed reasonable. After all, I hadn't raised that tenant in three years—during a period of high inflation in the mid seventies. In fact, if we had had rent control in that town, I'd have probably been given permission to raise the rent three times in those three years.

But we didn't. So I just raised him. Thirty dollars a month as I recall. But remember this was the first increase in three years.

He moved. I put the apartment in the paper at an even higher rent. No controls, you know. So I could "charge" whatever I wanted.

Only trouble was, the prospects who looked didn't bite. So I lowered the rent to what I had asked him to pay. **Still** no takers.

I ended up lowering it to what he had been paying before I got an acceptable tenant. In the meantime, I lost two full months rent! In other words, I was **severely punished by the market** for trying to get **more than market value**. So not only did I not get to "charge whatever I wanted," my income from that apartment **dropped to zero**!

My raising the rent, in that case, was like one of those cartoon characters who runs off a cliff— then scrambles madly to get back.

Tenants set the rents

Tenants and other rent-control advocates say landlords set rents. Baloney. **Tenants** set rents. Landlords can only make a concerted effort to find out what rents the tenants are currently setting and raise their own rents to that level.

Landlords get the heat for rent increases because they are **messengers delivering bad news**. A rent-increase notice is nothing more than a letter informing the tenant that other acceptable tenants are willing to pay more for his apartment than he is currently paying—and that since the landlord is no fool—the existing tenant must either match the bids of his fellow tenants or move to a place which he feels represents a better value.

In fact, **my** rent increase notices actually **do** say something like that.

So the hatred directed toward rent-raising landlords is nothing more than yet another example of punishing the messenger for delivering bad news.

The Law of Supply and Demand

Rents, like all other prices, are determined by the Law of Supply and Demand. Not by landlords.

Rent control laws are attempts to repeal the Law of Supply and Demand. You can no more repeal the Law of Supply and Demand than you can repeal the Law of Gravity.

The mountains will crumble before tenants figure it out, but the tenant's best friend is the apartment **builder**. Because builders increase supply. And that either restrains rent increases or even causes rents to go **down**. If you don't believe it, look at rents in Texas in the mid-eighties.

And if politicians **really** want to reduce rents, they should encourage—or at least stop resisting—construction of apartments. That, too, will happen when elephants fly.

The three most important things in setting rents

The three most important things in real estate are location, location, and location. The three most important things in setting rents are market value, market value, and market value.

Landlord haters try mightily to make you feel guilty about charging market value. If you fall for it, you're a fool. Not a nice guy or a good guy or a generous guy. Just a fool.

How to determine market rental value

So how do you ascertain what fair market rental value is?

The standard answer is do a **rental market survey**.

I disagree.

I say, use your vacancies. **Only** your vacancies can tell you what your apartments are worth.

Market surveys

In a market survey, you visit the competition and see what they've got and what rent they get for it. It's typically done on a grid which lists the "subject property." That's **your** building. And it lists the five or six main competitors your building has.

Then it shows the size, number of bedrooms, amenities (pool, tennis court, etc.), appliances, who pays utilities, etc.—and the rents. Here's a sample.

Property	The Holly	Lakeside	Westwind	Cottonwood	
Rent 1br	$305	$315	$305	$310	
Rent 2br	$340	$350	$345	$345	
Sq. Ft. 1br	625	640	630	635	
Sq. Ft. 2br	800	825	790	830	
Rent/sq.ft. 1	$0.49	$0.49	$0.48	$0.49	
Rent/sq.ft. 2	$0.43	$0.42	$0.44	$0.42	
Utilities	sep. metered	sep. metered	sep. metered	sep. metered	
Sec. dep.	$100/$150	$100	$100/$125	$150	
Concessions	1/2 mo. free	1/2 mo. free	last mo. free	none	
Dishwasher	yes	yes	no	yes	
Wash/dry	hookups	laund. room	hookups	laund. room	
Frost-free	yes	some	yes	yes	
Drapes/blind	blind	drapes	drapes	drapes	
Fireplace	yes	no	yes	no	
Age	5	15	3	18	
Pool	yes	yes	yes	yes	
Balcony/pat.	Yes	No	Yes	Yes	
Lanscaped	Excellent	Poor	Good	Good	
Comments:	Nicer than ours in every way except location	Excellent location but mediocre in every other way	Great views from many units but out-of-way location	We should lower security deposit on 1 br to $100	

The basic idea is that if the other one-bedroom apartments in your area rent for $400 a month, **your** one bedrooms are worth $400 a month. There are two problems with that.

1. All rental properties are different.
2. The other landlords may be too low.

Comparables aren't comparable

When you do a rental market survey, you're supposed to compare your apartments to other, similar or "comparable" apartments. The other properties are called comparables or just comps. But all real estate is unique. Even within the same complex, every apartment is unique. It has a unique combination of orientation to the sun, distance to parking, view, relationship to noise sources, etc.

Apartments in other buildings are even **more** different. So comparables are never better than only **roughly** comparable. And I've seen many situations where apartments rented for much more than their comps.

'Invisible' differences

In spite of your best efforts to spot differences, a market survey may cause you to **under**estimate the rental value of your apartments. For example, you may decide that the Holly Apartments is the **most** comparable to your Greenbriar. They rent one bedrooms for $395, so you rent yours for $395. Then one day you mention to a tenant that the Holly is the most comparable. And the tenant says, "I'd never live in that dump."

"Dump?" you ask. *"Why do you say that?"*

"They've got a low class element there. If you want drugs, that's the place to buy them."

Drug dealers didn't show up in your market survey, did they?

Now you may feel the solution is to make a **better** survey and look for things like that next time. Nah. There are an **infinite** number of subtle differences between pieces of real estate.

It's better to just ask the tenants what your apartments or rental houses are worth—like this.

Ask

When you have a vacancy, ask more than you think you'll get. In effect, you're saying, "Prospective tenants, can I have your attention, please. I've got this apartment for rent. Will any of you pay me $425 a month for it?"

The prospective tenants will look (although usually not in a group). And give you their verdict. If an acceptable tenant says, "Yes," the apartment is worth **at least** $425. It might be worth **more**. You don't know because you didn't **ask** for more. Next time you have a vacancy, you should ask for $435 or $445—to make sure you can't get it.

Is it a fluke?

"What if only **one** tenant says it's worth $425? Isn't it possible he's wrong?"

"Yes. But you probably only need one right now. So don't look a gift tenant in the mouth."

Over the longer term, you're right. One tenant being willing to pay $425 may be a fluke. It may be that $415 is the actual fair market rental value. And this one guy who is willing to pay $425 is in a hurry or something.

So don't consider a rent level **established** until two or three acceptable tenants agree to pay it.

Suppose you only own a duplex?

Now if you own a duplex—with a one-bedroom apartment upstairs and a two downstairs—

waiting until two tenants have agreed to pay a certain rent is mathematically impossible. So what does a small-unit owner do?

You've got two routes. Number one, if resale value is your primary goal, you should be more concerned about the applicant's **housekeeping and cooperation** with showing the property to prospective buyers than with how much rent he or she pays.

Number two, if maximum income is your goal, you'll have to rely heavily on a market survey and less on what tenants tell you. With only a unit or two or three, you get few opportunities to obtain the market's opinion. You could ask for the moon every time you have a vacancy. Then crank it down until you get an acceptable tenant. But that increases the time it takes you to get a new tenant. And with no tenant, you lose money.

So in other words, it **is** hard to use your vacancies in a small building. The bigger building, the easier it is to use your vacancies to find out your rental value. But **all** building owners should use the vacancy technique as much as possible.

The other buildings may be too low

The other problem with market surveys is that the **other** landlords may be **too low**. In that case, using a market survey to set your rents is a case of the **blind leading the blind**.

In fact, if the vacancy rate in your area is less than 5%, the other landlords **are** too low.

Comparable buildings which are full

Let's say you decide the Woodhaven is a comparable building. You visit the building and get all the data on unit size, amenities, rent, etc. Then you ask their vacancy rate.

"Zero."

Now think about the underlying theory behind the market survey. A market survey is an artificial shopping trip by an owner or manager who is mimicking the behavior of a prospective tenant. In other words, the buildings listed on your market survey are the same ones a prospective tenant for your building is likely to visit. And the data you gather about unit size, etc. is the same data the prospective tenant will gather—although the prospective tenants are less formal about it.

But what happens when **you** visit a building with a zero vacancy rate is **different** from what happens when a **real** tenant visits that same building. When **you** visit, and identify yourself as a competitor, the manager tells you about her complex. But when a real prospect visits, that prospect is told simply, "We're full."

Full competitors aren't competitors

So the rent levels, unit sizes, amenities of **full** buildings are **irrelevant** to what your rents should be. Because the prospective tenants you want to rent your apartments will never **see** the apartments in a full building. In other words, you do not compete with the other **buildings** in your neighborhood. You compete **only** with the **vacancies** in your neighborhood.

There's a relevant old joke. Man asks a shopkeeper how much he wants for a hammer.

"$4.95."

"$4.95!" says the man. "The hardware store down the street sells the same hammer for $3.95."

"So why don't you buy it there?"

"Because they're out right now."

"Well, we sell it for $3.95 when we're out, too."

So if one of your tenants ever complains that her friend across the street (in a waiting list building) pays less for more, invite her to rent over there.

Keep raising til your vacancy rate passes 5%

Back to the larger buildings. All right, suppose you ask $425 and get it, then what?
"You ask $435 and $445 and so on."
"But when do you stop?"
"When your vacancy rate passes 5%"
Actually, it's a little more complicated than that. For one thing it's your **ninety-day moving-average vacancy rate** that counts.

The 90-day-moving-average vacancy rate

You can't make decisions based on your **daily, weekly, or even monthly** vacancy rate. It jumps around too much. You need about ninety days worth of vacancy rate for meaningful analysis. So you compute a ninety-day moving average.

Moving average is a high falutin' phrase. All it means is you calculate the vacancy rate for **the last ninety days—every** month. At the end of April, you calculate the vacancy rate for February, March, and April. At the end of May, you calculate it for March, April, and May. And so on. That's a ninety-day moving average.

It's dollars lost, not vacant apartments

And let's make sure you know exactly what a vacancy rate is. A lot of investors compute it by dividing the number of vacant apartments by their total number of apartments. The company that employed me as property manager was doing that when I arrived.

Incredible.

That's **not** the way to do it.

Here's the **right** way. You divide the **dollars** lost to vacancies by the **gross potential** of the property.

Gross potential

What's the gross potential? The total of the **contract rents** on the occupied apartments plus the **economic or street rents** on the vacant apartments.

What'd he say?

Contract rent is the rent specified in the lease. For example, if your one bedrooms are worth $425 but one is on a $405 a month lease with five months left to run, the **economic** rent on that unit is $425. But the **contract** rent is only $405. The **gross potential** on that unit is $405. Because potential is the contract rent if rented; economic rent if vacant.

Economic or street rents are what you could get for the apartment if it were vacant. Since your vacancies **are** vacant, you use economic rent on those. But economic rent is irrelevant if you're under a lease which states a lower rent. That's why you use contract rent on your occupied apartments.

You also use contract rent even if the unit in question is on a month-to-month lease. You can't claim the potential of that unit is economic rent until you either send out a rent increase letter raising the rent to economic rent—or it becomes vacant.

Your vacancy report

Here's a sample vacancy report on a five-unit building. Apartment A is vacant and probably worth $425. B through E are rented at the rents shown. A **was** occupied through the 12th of the month at a rent of $415. The tenant moved out.

Vacancy Report

Apartment	Potential	Collected	Loss
A	$425	$160.65	$264.35
B	415	415	0
C	405	405	0
D	425	425	0
E	400	400	0
Totals	$2070.00	$1805.65	$264.35

The vacancy rate is the vacancy loss divided by the potential or

Vacancy rate = Vacancy Loss ÷ Gross Potential =

$264.35 ÷ $2,070.00 = 12.8%

Your rents are probably below market

Unless you are in an overbuilt market, your rents are probably below market. A **lot** below market.

I have used the ask-more-than-you-got-last-time technique on my own apartments. And I've been surprised many times at how high the rents ended up going. Often in a short span of time like 90 days. In one building, apartments that rented for $180 when I bought the place were going for $250 within six months. That's a 39% increase! And since income properties' values are based on their incomes, the building value **also** increased 39% as a result. Since I put 25% down, I had more than doubled my money in six months.

How to make six million dollars in five months

I had lunch with a famous man once. He had taken one of my real estate seminars and invited me to his headquarters. I won't say his name here because he wouldn't want publicity for raising rents.

At his country club, he mentioned that he owned many apartment complexes and that all had waiting lists.

"Waiting lists!!," I said. "That means your rents are way too low!" (I'll tell you the signs of below-market rents later. Waiting lists are one of them.)

I proceeded to explain the keep-asking-more-til-your-vacancy-rate-hits-5% approach. And I told him forcefully that I was absolutely certain his rents were too low without even looking at the properties and the markets—if he had waiting lists.

It worked

Several months later, he told me he followed my advice. Rents in his multi-million dollar operation increased by an average of $70 per unit per month—from a base of about $250 per unit per month average. That's a 28% increase. Which again applies to the buildings' values as well as to the rental income. He had about twenty million dollars worth of apartments **before** he took me to lunch; about twenty-**six** million dollars worth five months **after** he followed the advice I get him at lunch.

Call me the Six Million Dollar Man.

And here I am giving you the same advice And you didn't even take me to lunch. Actually, I think that investor paid less for the lunch than you did for this book. But even if you only make ten percent as much money as he did, you owe me one.

Not just *one* success story

Later I made a speech to the Austin Apartment Association. In it, I told this story. At the break, a "delegation" came up and introduced themselves as property management employees of the multi-millionaire in question. He had heard I was making that speech and ordered them to attend. I asked if the story I had recited about raising the rents $70 a unit was accurate. They answered in a chorus, "You bet."

I also made a number of speeches on raising rents to the California and National Apartment Association conventions. After the first one, every time I spoke, owners and managers would come up to me and say, "My boss heard you last year and had us follow your advice. We raised rents an average $83 a unit. I thought he was crazy when we started. But it worked!"

Or "I heard you last year and decided to try that on one of my buildings."

"What happened?"

"I did it on **all** my buildings. I owe you eight hundred thousand dollars worth of increased value and $133,000 per year in increased cash flow."

"What did hearing my speech cost you?"

"It cost me a couple hundred to attend the convention."

"What's the best investment you ever made?"

"The ticket to that speech."

"You bet your sweet equity it was."

A Chicago reader of this book tried the raise-until-you-get-5%-vacancy trick in his buildings in 1987 and went up 25% from $400 a month to $500.

Low vacancy rates mean lost rent

Most landlords look at a **vacant unit** and see lost rent. I look at a **full building** and see lost rent. The difference is that most owners focus on the difference between 100% occupied and less than 100% occupied. **I** focus on the difference between market value and actual collections.

Owners and managers who focus on vacancy rates are vacancy wise and collections/building value foolish. Vacancy losses are peanuts. The money not collected due to low rents—and the building value not received on sale or exchange due to low rents—are enormous.

The most important advice in this book

My advice on rent raising is the most important advice in this book. I'll repeat it.

> *Keep raising the rent on your vacancies until your vacancy rate averages about five percent for at least ninety days. If your vacancy rate is **above** five percent, lower your rents after making sure that your marketing effort is not at fault. Raise all existing tenants to the same rent that new tenants are paying when they come up for renewal.*

The typical landlord who follows that advice will increase his vacancy rate. But he'll also increase his **collections—that** is the amount of money he takes in each month. And what's more important, he'll increase his **building value**. The typical owner who follows my advice will make thousands of dollars more in cash flow—and tens of thousands—even hundreds of thousands or millions more in building value.

Calculate your vacancy rate by unit type—if not by *unit*

If you have more than one of each kind of unit, you ought to break your vacancy rate down by unit **type**. For example, in one of my buildings, I used to have three kinds of units:

652 sq. ft. one-bedroom apartments,
706 sq. ft. one-bedroom apartments, and
two-bedroom apartments

When I calculate my vacancy loss, I do it on an **overall** basis—and **by unit type** and **by unit**. In other words, I know my vacancy rate on my **whole** complex—and on my 652 sq. ft. ones, my 706 sq. ft. ones, my twos, and on each apartment.

That's very important. Because a low overall vacancy rate might lead me to believe **all** my rents are too low. When, in fact, only the two-bedrooms are too low.

Experienced apartment managers and owners know that the popularity of unit types shifts back and forth. One month you can't **give** your ones away. A couple months later, you could rent a dozen more than you have.

You should raise and lower rents depending on vacancy rates. Vacancy rates vary according to unit type. So you need the vacancy rate **by type** to make your rent decisions.

'Near the woods'

The resident manager of a 75-unit complex I managed once said,
"We never have any trouble keeping the apartments in the back full."
Since we were having trouble keep the complex full at the time, I perked up.
"Why's that?"
"Those apartments back up to the woods. Tenants like the privacy."

Aha! So number of bedrooms isn't the only distinguishing feature in an apartment complex. Location in relation to positive and negative factors like woods or traffic noise can affect the value of apartments, too.

In that complex I discovered through questioning the resident manager, that we had three tiers of desirability. The apartments that backed up to the woods were the most desirable. Followed by the ones that backed up to another complex. Followed by the ones that backed up to other buildings in our complex.

A tiered rent schedule

So we adopted a three-tiered rent structure. A two-bedroom apartment, for example, would rent for one rent in the woods section, one rent in the other building section, and another rent in the remaining section. Thus were we able to **raise** rents on some of our apartments—even though we were in the midst of a vacancy problem overall.

You should check whether any of your apartments are more desirable than others on the basis of views and such. Then raise or lower the rents accordingly.

The classic example of this is a **high-rise** apartment building. In high-rises, there are often no two apartments alike. The rent goes up for each floor. And all the apartments on the floor have different views and orientations to the sun. The penthouse floor is worth more than the one below it—but by more than the difference between that floor and the **second** from the penthouse.

The problem is that many **garden** apartment complexes have more variations in desirability than the typical one- and two-bedroom rent variations suggest. In other words, many garden apartment complexes need tiered rent schedules somewhat like high-rise rent schedules.

Upstairs versus downstairs

Many two-story apartment building owners have different rents for upstairs and downstairs apartments. I did in one of my buildings but not the other. In addition to computing my rents by unit type, I also compute the upstairs and downstairs vacancy rates. In my Fort Worth building, I found that my average upstairs/downstairs vacancy rates over a 14-month period were:

Upstairs   29.49%
Downstairs   13.83%.

So I told the manager to charge $5 a month less for the upstairs apartments. But the upstairs continued to run a vacancy rate double that of the first floor.

Calculate your vacancy rate by unit

You should calculate your vacancy rate **by unit**. That is, you should calculate a vacancy rate for **each unit** in your complex. To make it meaningful, you need a twelve-month moving average. Don't let the phrase "moving average" throw you. It just means you calculate the average vacancy rate for the last twelve months, every month. For example, in April of '98, you'd calculate the average vacancy rate for the months of February '97 through March '98. Then in May of '98, you'd calculate the vacancy rate for March '97 through April '98 and so forth.

If it sounds like a lot of work, you must not have a computer. On a computer, you would simply have the computer calculate the vacancy rate for each unit (vacancy loss ÷ potential = vacancy rate. Then you copy the vacancy rate column and paste it over the appropriate month in a twelve-month spread sheet, which in turn calculates the twelve-month moving average. Like the tables on the next page. You can also accomplish the same thing with Quicken using the budget function.

The reason you calculate the vacancy rate for each unit is to look for **patterns** you might not see in the **overall** vacancy rate or even in the vacancy rate by unit **type** (e.g. near the trees). If you see such a pattern—either a unit or group of units with a consistently **high** vacancy rate—or a consistently **low** one—adjust the rent on those units accordingly.

My main point is listen to the market. Don't assume that you know what your apartments are worth—or assume that if the market says your one-bedrooms are worth $400 that every single one of them has the exact same value.

In theory, you should have a different rent for each unit—even in a garden apartment complex. The differing market rental values would reflect views, distance to parking, upstairs versus downstairs, etc. The rent differences might only be $2 or $3 a month in some cases. But they'd all be different. As a practical matter, you couldn't fine tune it that much. But you most definitely should scrutinize your vacancy rate by unit for any significant patterns. Doing this has enabled me to actually **raise** some rents in buildings which had high overall vacancy rates at the time.

Lowering rents

I've mentioned **lowering** rents several times. I suspect that most landlords have **never** lowered rents. Furthermore, most would vow that they never **will** lower rents. The very thought of lowering rents angers them.

I lower rents. I've done it many times. Matter of fact, it is those who are most aggressive at **raising** rents who are most likely to have to **lower** them.

If you were never turned down for a date when you were single, you probably didn't ask enough girls out. If you have few, if any, credit losses in your business, your credit policy is probably too conservative and costing you sales and incremental income net of the increased collection losses.

And if you've never had to lower your rents, your rent **increase** policy is too conservative. In other words, the harder you push, the more likely you'll push too far.

Lower rents equals higher income

Believe it or not, lowering your rents can often **increase** your income. That's right, I said increase.

Vacancy Rate Report

	A	B	C	D	E	
1	Rent Report For M		Apr-88			
2	Unit	Potential	Collected	Vacancy loss	Vacancy rate	
3	101	$400	$400	$0	0%	
4	102	$400	$358	$42	11%	
5	103	$375	$375	$0	0%	
6	104	$380	$380	$0	0%	
7	105	$400	$169	$231	58%	
8	106	$370	$370	$0	0%	
9	107	$400	$380	$20	5%	
10	108	$400	$400	$0	0%	
11	109	$375	$306	$69	18%	
12	110	$380	$380	$0	0%	

Just copy column E3 to E12 from this monthly spread sheet

and paste it over the April '87 column in the spread sheet
that calculates the twelve-month moving average...here:

	A	B	C	D	E	F	G	H	I	J	K	L	M	N
1	Year	88	88	88	88	87	87	87	87	87	87	87	87	
2	Unit	Jan	Feb	Mar	Apr	May	Jun	Jul	Aug	Sep	Oct	Nov	Dec	Avg
3	101	0%	0%	0%	0%	0%	100%	100%	22%	0%	0%	0%	0%	19%
4	102	0%	12%	0%	11%	0%	0%	0%	0%	0%	0%	0%	60%	7%
5	103	0%	0%	0%	0%	0%	0%	0%	0%	0%	0%	0%	0%	0%
6	104	0%	30%	50%	0%	0%	0%	0%	0%	0%	100%	0%	0%	15%
7	105	0%	0%	0%	58%	0%	0%	0%	76%	0%	0%	0%	0%	11%
8	106	0%	0%	0%	0%	0%	0%	72%	0%	0%	0%	0%	0%	6%
9	107	0%	0%	0%	5%	28%	0%	0%	0%	0%	0%	0%	0%	3%
10	108	0%	23%	0%	0%	0%	0%	26%	0%	0%	46%	0%	0%	8%
11	109	0%	0%	0%	18%	0%	0%	0%	0%	0%	0%	0%	0%	2%
12	110	0%	48%	36%	0%	0%	0%	0%	0%	0%	0%	0%	0%	7%

The formula for column D on the top spread sheet is =B-C (Microsoft® Excel spread sheet. Yours may difer.) The formula for column E on the top spread sheet is =D/B. And the formula for column N on the **bottom** spread sheet is =AVERAGE(B:M). When you copy each new month over the column for the same month a year ago, column N will automatically recalculate the new, twelve-month moving average for each apartment. The formula for cell N13 is =AVERAGE(N3:N12).

Owners of small properties don't need me to tell them that. For example, if a rental house owner puts his property on the market for $900 a month—and gets no takers—he lowers his asking rent. Eventually, he finds the market value and gets an acceptable tenant. When he does, his income goes from zero to $800 a month or whatever.

Apartment owners, on the other hand, have typically lost sight of that fact. For example, the owner of a 100-unit complex sees his vacancy rate go from 5% to 10%.

> *"It can't be my rents," he figures. "I've got lots of tenants in the building paying those rents."*

And indeed he does. But he is drawing an erroneous conclusion from the fact that those tenants are paying those rents. One robin does not a Spring make. Neither do 20 tenants paying $400 a month prove that your one-bedroom apartments are worth that much. If you have 36 one-bedroom apartments—and only 20 are occupied—your rents are too high. The 20 people who are paying $400 are doing so not because that's the market level. Rather they are paying $400 because of such reasons as:

- Happy and hate to move.
- Haven't paid attention to the market and unaware of drop in rents in the area.
- Out-of-it senior citizens whose rent is paid by children.
- Short-timers who plan to leave the area and for whom the cost of moving exceeds the rent savings over the period they expect to remain in the area.
- People who have special reasons to prefer your building, e.g., it's the only one from which they can walk to work, they need a garage like yours for their antique car

These people pay **more** than market rent. It would be nice if you could fill your building with such people. But you can't. And trying to do so will cost you a lot of money. Eventually, all of those people will move out. And few, if any acceptable tenants will move **in** as long as you have your rents above market level.

Your income will be maximized when you keep all your apartments at 95% occupancy. Not when

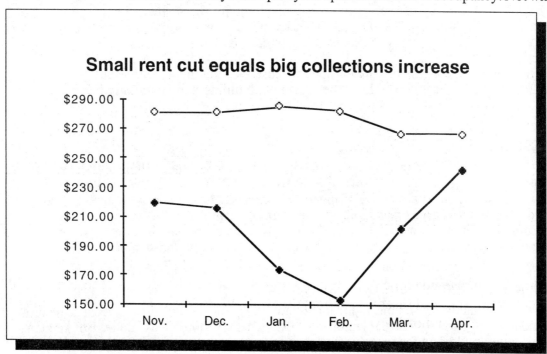

Small rent cut equals big collections increase

you get the maximum rent from a much smaller percentage of your units.

Here's an actual case history from my Fort Worth building. In February of 1987, my vacancy rate there jumped up to 45% overall. My collections fell to $153.07 per unit on average.

I cut the asking rents an average of 6%—and within two months my collections shot up to $242.71 per unit. That's a 37% increase in collections—as a result of just a 6% rent cut. Furthermore, if I had not acted quickly, my collections would have fallen **further**. Because when you ask **more** than market, tenants move out. Some move out more slowly than others. But eventually, they all move out.

The upper line on the graph on the previous page, is average asking rent per unit; the lower, average rent collected per unit.

Whenever your vacancy rate is greater than 5%, you need to lower rents. To tell **which** rents to lower, analyze your vacancy rates by unit. The vacancy problem may be confined to one type of unit—or one section of your property. But do **not** make the mistake of paying more attention to the few tenants who are willing to pay above-market rents temporarily than to the general market's clear message that you are too high.

Rent decreases pay an additional benefit. They can be used to get reductions in your **property tax assessment**, which, in turn, increase your property value.

Rent decreases versus rent concessions

Hardly any apartment owners will lower rents. But many **will** give rent concessions if their vacancy rate gets high.

Rent concessions are typically:

- One or more months **free rent.**
- Free **merchandise** like a microwave oven.
- Free **trips** to nearby resort areas.
- Free **tuition** (in college towns—with low state-supported tuition).

You get the idea.

I think rent concessions are goofy. First off, they are the mathematical equivalent of a rent reduction. Giving someone a $300 microwave oven is the same as giving him a $300 rent reduction.

Apartment owners give concessions for two reasons:

1. They think concessions are cheaper because they get them "wholesale."
2. They think the guy who buys the apartment building will be too dumb to ask whether concessions were given to obtain the rents.

Wholesale?

If you buy a bunch of microwave ovens, you do indeed get them wholesale. That lets you give a $300 oven for, say, $280. You save $20 over what a $300 rent concession would have cost.

But what if the applicant you're trying to snare **already has** a microwave oven? Well, maybe we should offer him a choice? Say a microwave oven or a color tv.

Problem with that is the applicant may already have **both**. And offering two freebies cuts the volume of each you buy in half. That, in turn, cuts the discount you're able to obtain.

And what if the tenant only stays a month?

It may be that the reason the applicant already has a microwave oven is because he just got one two months ago from his current landlord. He signed a six month lease there. But he plans to skip out to another building to get a color tv or free trip.

That's one of the main problems with concessions. You may give the tenant a concession, then find that he leaves after a month or two. A $300 concession is the equivalent of a $300/12 = $25 a month rent reduction over the course of a year. But that's only true if the tenant **stays** a year. If he stays just two months, it's the equivalent of a $150 a month reduction!

Why not put the concession at the END of the lease?

Many owners will say they have the solution to the tenant who gets a concession then skips out after only a couple months. Put the concession at the **end** of the lease.

They are correct to say that will prevent a tenant from getting a full concession for less than a full lease period. But it also reduces the drawing power of the concession. If your competitors offer **front end** concessions, you'll not draw tenants unless you match them—or give **bigger** concessions at the end of the lease.

If you insist on giving concessions, I recommend that you **do** put them at the end of the lease. Better yet, don't give concessions. Just lower your rent. If you like, think of it as a prorated monthly concession.

My experience in '75

In 1975, almost the entire country was overbuilt as far apartments were concerned—including the Southern New Jersey market where I was a property manager. Our vacancy rate in one building crept up to 20%. The boss was having fits.

He wanted to give concessions. A month's free rent or some such. I said I thought a rent reduction made more sense. He was horrified. "You never cut your price," he said.

"Why not?" I said.

Our one-bedroom rent was $195. Recently raised from $190. The boss wanted to give one month's rent free to people who would sign a year lease. I wanted to reduce the rent to $189—a six dollar rent reduction. My plan would cost $72 per year; his, $195.

Also, his would cost the full $195 even if a tenant skipped after only a month or two.

We tried the rent decrease

The boss finally agreed to let me try it my way. We did. We changed our asking rent in the model to $189. And when an existing $190 tenant came up for renewal, we sent them a rent **decrease** notice. That was fun.

The results? Our move-**outs** dropped to near zero. Move-outs had been the main problem. We were continuing to rent as many apartments in the model as before. The vacancy problem had come from our **renewal** success rate dropping. Within two months, our vacancy rate dropped to acceptable levels.

Truth to tell, I can't claim full credit for the turnaround. I suspect the rent decrease had something to do with it. But the apartment market is the result of many forces swirling around. Our 20% vacancy rate could have been a string of bad luck—and the fill-up a string of good luck. I **do** know that my solution was **cheaper** than the rent concessions would have been. And the boss acknowledged that.

So my rent reductions may not have filled the building up. But they surely saved us from the rent concessions.

Small decreases often enough

I've been amazed at the dramatic effect which very **small** rent decreases had on vacancy rates. I've lowered rents on several occasions. Most recently, $10 reductions on apartments renting for $400 to $500. That's only about a **two percent** reduction! Yet the six vacancies soon disappeared.

And in my 1975 experience, we reduced the rent $6 from a base of $195. That's only **three** percent.

So when I advocate rent **decreases**, I'm not talking 10 or 20%. You've got to get to market—wherever that is. But you'll typically only be about two or three percent **above** market if you do make the mistake of going too high.

Repercussions with existing tenants

The tenants who received the one dollar rent **decrease** letters loved them. But their neighbors did **not**. Particularly those who had recently come up for renewal and been **raised** from $190 to $195. As a matter of fact, the ones who had been raised to $195 were beside themselves with rage.

Their spokesman demanded an explanation. I told him we raised existing tenants to the same rent as the new move-ins. That when **he** came up for renewal, the new move-ins were paying $195. But when his neighbors came up for renewal, the new move-in rent had been lowered to $189.

He demanded a rent decrease. *"Why? Your lease renewed for a year at $195. Why should I let you pay $189. You sure as heck wouldn't let me **raise** you during a lease term. Why should we let you lower what we get?"*

The one-way street

"Also, you've been paying $190 for a year. Many of your neighbors have been paying $195 for months and months. How come you didn't call to get in on the $195 when we first went to that level?"

"I didn't know about it."

*"Oh, come on now. Are you trying to tell me you would have asked me to **raise** your rent to $195 if you had known others in the building were paying that much?"*

"It's not fair."

*"I'll tell you what's not fair. Tenants who think the lease is a one-way street. Tenants who want rent **decreases** applied to them **immediately** but who only accept rent **increases** at the **end** of their leases."*

That tenant organized a harassment campaign in which the tenants who got rent increases called us one after another for about twenty minutes to complain. That ended when we threatened to call the police.

'Where's my microwave oven?'

Another incident showed that similar problems with existing tenants can arise over concessions. I bought an apartment building in the Fall of '83. As all apartment buyers should, I sent a letter to each tenant. It stated their rent and security deposit and the expiration date of their lease. And it asked them to tell me if they had received any rent concessions like free rent or gifts like microwave ovens. Immediately, several tenants marched over to the resident manager's office and demanded to know why they had **not** received free rent or a microwave oven.

So whenever you give **any** tenant a rent decrease or concession, **other** tenants demanding the same is a possibility. It's probably best to offer the discount only to **incoming** tenants. Existing tenants rarely pay much attention to what newcomers get. Even when the rent is advertised in the paper.

But if you **do** offer the good deal to existing tenants, expect those who **don't** get it to complain. Tell them politely but firmly to buzz off. Applying "the customer is always right" principle to apartments would bankrupt you. That only works for retail merchants who see a customer sporadically.

Make sure your marketing is OK before lowering

You ought to charge fair market rent. If you're too low, that means rent increases. If you're too high, it means rent **decreases**.

Generally, your vacancy rate is the barometer. When it's **above** 5%, your rents are too **high**. When it's **below** 5%, your rents are too **low**.

But it's more complicated than that.

Your vacancy rate may be higher than 5% because your **manager** is never in the office to answer the phone or show apartments. Or because you're advertising in the wrong paper.

If your vacancy rate is too high because your manager's not around, a rent decrease would be **rewarding** the absence. Furthermore, a rent decrease will **fill the place up even though the manager's not around**.

Rents and vacancy rates are two sides of the same coin

Most landlords and managers think of rents and vacancy rates as two separate issues. Not true. They go hand in hand. Extreme examples illustrate the point.

I had two-bedroom apartments in Fort Worth which were worth about $335 a month (tenant pays electric). Do you think maybe it would be **real** easy to rent one of those apartments if I lowered the rent to $225? Do you think maybe my manager could tell everyone who called that she's showing it from 7:00 pm to 7:05 pm Thursday night only? Do you think maybe people would be standing twenty deep on Thursday night? Offering deposit checks without even seeing the apartment?

Darned right they would. In fact, that happened to me. In my early days.

Out of the market

My first two-tenants stayed a long time. I raised the rent a little while they were there. But **only** a little. When one bought a house and gave notice, I added $5 to his rent and called an ad into the paper. The first person to call was a friend of the ad-taker. Then a friend of someone in the editorial department called. Then the ad hit the streets.

You literally could not touch the phone down on the hook without it ringing. I told everyone to be there at 10:00 am Saturday. There were dozens of them. In fact, when I went up the steps with the entourage, I found that one guy was waiting **inside**. He had arrived early and asked the tenant to let him in. Dozens of people took one look at the apartment and immediately thrust deposit checks and filled-out applications at me.

Real estate genius

"Boy, am I a genius," I thought. "I bought this duplex and people are practically fighting to move in. A real estate genius, yes sir." Plus, there was almost a feeling of being the most popular kid in school. All these people were also being very **nice** to me—and **friendly**. I suspect I must have started to swagger a little.

My book-reading friends, **you** can accomplish the same thing. And you don't even need to own an apartment building. Just run an ad in the paper that you are going to give away $30 a month in cash on your front step on the first of every month. To the nicest ten people you find there. And you'll have a solicitous crowd just like I did that day.

Because that's exactly what **I** was doing—offering to give away $30 every month—in the form of below market rent. At least I figure it must have been about $30 a month.

Money *can* buy 'friends'

Folks, that mob of people being nice to me and shoving each other was **not** doing so because of my good looks—or my warm, wonderful personality—or my real estate genius. Far from it. They were behaving like that because I had lost touch with the market—and put my apartment on the market for far **less** than it was worth.

Knowing what I know now, I'd **immediately** recognize from such a situation that I had underestimated the market value of whatever I was selling or renting. And I would announce that I would **auction** the place off to the highest acceptable bidder. If I had made that announcement that day, all those warm, smiling faces would have turned to instantaneous frowns. And as the winning bidder was leaving the room, he'd have snarled, "I assume you're going to paint this place."

You see, real estate fans, money **can** buy friends. Allow your rents to fall below market and you'll find many friends among the tenants and prospective tenants of the world. It'll only cost you thousands of dollars per year in lost rent and **tens** of thousands of dollars in lost building value.

My first duplex

My first duplex had two two-bedroom apartments. The Realtor® who had the listing said he thought I could rent them for $150 each. I had thought $120. But he was a Realtor® and I was just a 22-year old kid.

I put one on the market for $150. All the people who came turned up their noses. "Is the owner going to do anything to it?" one asked. I told her no. Every single person who looked had an expression on their faces that said, "What a dump!"

I wondered if I had made a mistake buying it. (This is the exact same apartment which I just told you a mob wanted to rent later.) Then I tried $130 a month. People reacted differently. Now they looked at it **long and hard**. They spent long minutes staring at the rooms, the building, the neighborhood. But in the end, no one applied for it.

So I lowered the rent again to $120. Mind you, I had not done **anything** to the apartment or the building. Still the same place as when I asked $150. But the lookers! They were delighted. "Look at this, honey," one said pointing to the yard. Everyone who looked seemed to think it was a great place. And several offered deposit money. I rented it to one of them and they lived there for years.

Tenants travel in layers

Lesson learned: Tenants travel in layers. You've got your $150 tenants (those were 1969 rents), your $130 tenants, and your $120 tenants.

None of the $150 tenants said, "Your rent's too high." That's because they were just looking for a place to live. They were not real estate appraisers.

In fact, $150 was **not** too high in the sense that they had already decided that they could **afford** $150. Tenants do not appraise apartments as to their fair market value. Rather they decide what they can afford and look only in that price range.

But when they compared my apartment to the other $150 apartments they'd seen, it looked like a dump. That's because the other $150 apartments were worth about $150. Mine was only worth $120.

Try a lower layer

When I lowered the rent to $130, a new "layer" of prospects came by. They compared my apartment with other **$130** apartments they'd been looking at. Compared to those, mine was alllllmost as good. But not quite. That's why they looked long and hard. But didn't bite.

But when I got down to the $120 layer, I was showing the place to prospects who compared it to other $120 stuff on the market. It looked **quite good—in** comparison to the other $120s.

In fact, the place was probably worth $125. That's why the $130 layer didn't bite; but the $120 layer was enthusiastic. I know my marketing was not reducing the rent in that case because I was my own leasing agent then.

At the high end, nothing works

Back to my $335 Fort Worth example. I told you how easy it would be to rent the apartment if I lowered the rent to $225. Now think about what would happen if I raised the rent to $435.

My place was a nice 1970 building. It had wall-to-wall carpet, dishwasher, central air, one bath—the usual 1970 era stuff. And they were clean and well-maintained. But there were places in the neighborhood which rented for $435. They were:

• Brand new
• Had fireplaces
• Two baths
• Ceiling fans
• Built-in microwave ovens
• Washer/dryer hookups or actual appliances in the apartment
• 100 more square feet
• Cathedral ceilings
• Pool and tennis courts (I had a pool).

Do you think I'd have had much success trying to get $435 for my units when other places offered all of the above features for the same price? How about if I hired Sally the Supermanager and gave her an incentive bonus for leasing?

'Proven track record in soft market lease up'

I once saw an ad in the Texas Apartment Association newsletter. A property management company wanted a resident manager "with proven track record in soft market lease up."

What the heck is "soft market lease up?" Actually, we all know what they mean. But what, exactly, does this management company think is **different** about "soft market" leasing? Isn't there a **right way** to lease an apartment? Why should the right way **change** in a "soft market."

I don't believe in "soft markets." I think what normally is called a "soft market" is caused by the "soft heads" of the area apartment owners.

If your rents are fair market value, your building will have a vacancy rate of about five percent. If your vacancy rate is **above** five percent for more than ninety days, you've got a problem. It may be that your rents are OK, but your marketing effort is not. Or it may be that your marketing effort is OK, but your rents are not.

A "soft market" typically means a region-wide high (above five percent) vacancy rate. That, in turn, typically means that owners region-wide are trying to get **more than market value**. After all, it's not likely that every single manager in the region simultaneously and suddenly stopped doing her job.

How could all the **owners** simultaneously be above market? Because new apartments were built in the area—lowering the market values of the apartments the new ones compete with. As I write this, that is indeed the situation in most Texas markets.

Blame the manager

The manager that placed that "soft market lease up" ad is apparently one of the many who blame high vacancies on the resident manager. In the course of looking for a new manager recently, I came across an applicant who had been fired from an apartment management job she had for seven years. The reason: high vacancies.

The owner said, "I didn't think it was her fault. But my partners did and they pressured me to fire her."

The manager said, "I never had any trouble renting until they built several complexes in town (a smaller Texas town outside of any metropolitan area)."

I suspect that the market value of the building's apartments declined due to the amount of new apartments built in the area. And that the owners were unwilling to even consider that. So they fired a good manager—and tarnished her reputation in the process.

Musical managers

A lot of owners and property managers play musical managers. When the market is "strong," meaning their rents are equal to or below market value, they keep the manager and say what a good job she's doing. And when the market gets "weak," meaning the market value falls below the rent, they **keep replacing the manager until the recession ends**. Whichever manager happens to be in the job when the recession ends gets credit for filling up the building. And thereby acquires a "proven track record in soft market lease up."

In fact, all that happened is that the problem corrected itself. The new manager—the one who got credit for the lease up—may be the **worst** of the bunch. It's like hiring a succession of rain makers— and keeping the one who happens to be there when the drought ends. Or like playing musical chairs, and calling the one who happens to be next to an empty seat when the music stops a genius.

Owners are like tenants sometimes

Tenants like to blame rent increases on landlord greed. And landlords like to blame high vacancy rates (and other management problems) on their managers—both the resident manager and the property manager, if any.

That's more palatable than admitting that the value of their apartments has gone down. Mainly because when the value of the **apartments** goes down, the value of the **apartment building** goes down too.

For example, if apartment buildings sell for six times gross annual income in your area, a $10 per month rent decrease on a 100-unit building is a $1,000 a month decrease and a $12,000 a year decrease. Multiplied by six gives you a $72,000 reduction in building value!

But, my fellow owners, reality is reality. I know you don't **want** your building value to go down. But wishing won't make it so. Neither will firing and hiring a succession of managers.

Leasing is a team effort

Apartment leasing is a team effort. The team includes both the manager(s) **and** the owner. The manager covers the phone and the office for a reasonable number of hours each week. She also must be well-groomed, polite, friendly, and competent. And she has to put out a reasonable amount of effort. But that's about all the manager can do without the owner's help.

The owner has to give the manager the tools and other support she needs. And he has to give her a reachable objective. Not "*Impossible Dream*" rent levels.

Most tenants come not from new prospects but from **renewals** of existing tenants. But people tend **not** to renew if the owner lets the place run down. Or fails to spend the money necessary for the managers to respond quickly to legitimate maintenance requests.

I believe that many a manager has been fired not because the **manager** didn't do her job. But because the **owner** didn't do his—and blamed the manager.

Pressure to rent leads to bad tenants

If I put too much pressure on Sally the Supermanager to get impossible rents—she'll circumvent my credit standards. The place will fill up all right. It's just that the new tenants will be the kind of people who **don't pay the rent**.

There **are** some prospective tenants who will sign one-year leases in which they agree to pay $435 a month for my two-bedroom apartments which are only worth $335. Are they crazy? No. Their reasoning is quite sound. They don't care what the rent is because they don't plan to **pay** it. They shop around for places with **little or no credit screening**. And if you fail to **teach** your managers how to screen, and **motivate** them to do it, these non-price-sensitive folks will all move into your building.

And then you'll wish you never heard of the landlord business.

Vacancy and ease of renting change along a spectrum

Now I've told you that I can rent my $335 apartments for $225 with great ease. And I can't rent my $335 apartments at $435 (to people who will actually pay it) now matter how hard I try. So at $100 **below** market, it's incredibly **easy** to rent apartments. And at $100 **above** market, it's impossible. Obviously, those are opposite ends of a spectrum.

Somewhere in between, lies the fair market value. As I said, I suspect it was $335 in this case. At **any** rent level below the fair market value, it's easier to rent the apartment. The lower you go, the easier it is.

Waiting list buildings are a sinecure

That's why resident managers and property managers like buildings with waiting lists. The waiting lists indicate that the rents are below market. Probably **far** below. That means the resident manager can be away from the complex most of the time.

On the rare occasion when she has a vacancy (few move because they can't match the low rent), she simply calls someone on the waiting list. No sweat. She can be extremely selective because of the low rent. And once the tenant moves in, the tenant rarely complains—for fear of losing the good deal. Waiting list buildings management offices are **real** quiet. Because the manager is on a permanent "vacation" to an extent.

Everybody assumes 5% vacancy

Every investor and lender in the country **assumes** a 5% vacancy rate when doing projection—10% in some markets these days. Doesn't matter that you've been full for ten years straight. When you sell or refinance, the Realtors®, buyers, and lenders will all stick 5% vacancy rate in their figures.

That means you're paying for your low rents **twice**. Once when you lose the monthly income and property value which higher rents would bring. And again when the buyers and lenders subtract from your below-market rents the 5% vacancy loss that you never have because your rents are below-market. (Read that sentence a couple times if you have trouble following it.)

To paraphrase Confucius, "When five percent vacancy inevitable, relax and enjoy it."

Your low rents contribute to the 'housing crisis'

Every rent control law in the country claims to have been passed in response to the local housing "crisis." You know how they define a housing "crisis?" A vacancy rate of less than 5%.

Now **I** said a vacancy rate of less than 5% means your **rents are too low**. That applies to whole regions as well as to individual buildings. The vacancy rate in San Francisco was about 1% at one point. That meant the rents in San Francisco were too low. One **reason** they were too low is that San Francisco has rent control.

If a vacancy rate of less than 5% is the definition of a housing "crisis," I offer my services to every "crisis" area of the country. Here's my offer. Just put me in charge of rents in your city—and I'll have your housing "crisis" cleared up in about six months.

You know how, don't you? I'd **raise the rents**. And keep raising them until the vacancy rate was more than 5%. Matter of fact, I can give you any vacancy rate you want—as long as you give me control of the rents.

So being ignored by buyers and lenders is only one result of a full building. Another problem is that you are giving the rent control forces in your area ammunition. Your zero vacancy rate will be part of an overall statistic which they use to "prove" that your area has a housing shortage of crisis proportions.

'I won't pay it'

Many's the time I've raised an existing tenant's rent. The tenant got **angry** at the size of the increase and gave notice. Then I quickly rented the apartment for more than the old tenant had been raised to.

One of those was a law student and his wife. In the early seventies, he was paying $172 a month for a one-bedroom apartment. I raised him to $180 at the end of his first year. He was outraged. He gave thirty days notice immediately upon receiving the increase letter.

I put an ad in the paper offering the apartment for $185. It rented to the second person who looked at it.

About a week later, the law student called to say he had changed his mind. He had been out looking and couldn't find anything he liked.

"You can't change your mind. I already rented the apartment to someone else." I had sent him a letter I called "Owner's Acknowledgment of Notice" when I first received his notice. Here's what it said:

Owner's Acknowledgment of Notice

Dear _____

I have received your written notice that you will move out of apartment number _____ on _____ . Your notice must be written because some tenants change their minds and deny that they ever gave notice.

Once notice is given, we immediately try to rent the apartment to a new tenant. When we do that, we sign a new lease with the new tenant on your old apartment. The new tenant then usually gives notice to their landlord and makes moving arrangements. If the apartment in question were not vacant on the promised move-in day, we would be in trouble with the new tenant.

You must be out by noon of the date listed above. The apartment must be clean and every piece of your belongings and trash removed. We find that the

* Range,
* Oven, and
* Refrigerator

are the main problem areas as far as tenant cleaning is concerned. So please pay particular attention to those items.

Best wishes in your new home,

John T. Reed

A few weeks after the new tenants moved in, and the law student had moved out, he called again. "Do the new tenants like the apartment?"

"Sure. Why?"

"Well, we had to move in with my in-laws. We couldn't find anything like the old apartment in our price range."

I probably could have gotten $190 or $195 for the darned thing.

'Reasonable rents'

On another occasion, I had two one-bedroom apartments at $180 in a 36-unit building. During the five months or so since I had purchased it, we had gotten the street rents on one-bedroom apartments up to $240. So I sent rent-increase notices to the two tenants paying $180—raising them to $240. A 33% increase.

One tenant gasped—and paid it. "Took my breath away," was the phrase she used in talking to my resident manager.

The other tenant gave notice. We put the apartment on the market for $250, not $240. And rented it immediately.

If I had asked that new tenant who agreed to pay $250 why she selected that building, I suspect she would have said, "Reasonable rent." I say that because I used to ask that question on my rental application. And "reasonable rent" was the most common answer—even from tenants moving into units where the old tenant had moved out because of a large rent increase and the new tenant was paying **even more** than the old tenant had been raised to.

Why huge rent increases result in 'reasonable' rents

There are two reasons for that. One is that your existing tenants are out of touch with the rental market. Also, they believe what they want to believe. Namely that they are struggling to get ahead financially because of the landlord's greed. That's much more palatable than admitting that they can no longer afford the apartment. Or that their rent has been a bargain for the last year or more.

The other reason new tenants give "reasonable rent" as their reason for selecting your building is that it's **true**. New tenants are the world's most expert appraisers of apartment rental values. Because they've just recently been out looking at what's available.

They picked your building because it was the best one they saw given their needs and budget. By "best" I mean best value. All things considered:

* Rent
* Location
* Size
* Etc.,

your apartment was the best—the most reasonable rent given what the apartment had to offer.

You can't go higher than market value

Remember, landlords can only raise the rent up to what **another** acceptable tenant is willing to pay. Those 33%, $60 a month increases I sent out were not unreasonable. The **old rents** were unreasonable—unreasonably **low**.

All I did was bring them up to market. I delivered some bad news—a two-part message:

A. Other acceptable tenants are willing to pay more than you are paying now for your apartment
B. I'm no fool.

Most landlords have allowed their rents to fall behind inflation at one time or another. As a general rule, the rents in all those markets which have a vacancy rate of less than five percent have fallen below market.

Many Sunbelt markets have much **higher** vacancy rates. That's due less to the apartment owners' aggressiveness in raising rents than to the apartment **builders and financiers** aggressiveness in building them.

Raising existing tenants

Remember the three most important things in setting rents are market value, market value, and market value. That applies to existing tenants, too.

Many owners give existing tenants a break on the rent. For example, renewals pay $10 less than new tenants for the same unit. Bad idea. Terrible, actually.

One owner in an apartment association where I was an officer told me she never raised rents on existing tenants.

"Your turnover's pretty low, I assume?"

"Hardly ever have anyone move out," she said.

She might just as well have burned $100 bills every month!

Make sure the apartments are equal

Existing tenants should pay exactly the same as new tenants. One caveat there. The apartment the new tenant gets is often in better shape than the apartment of the tenant coming up for renewal. That doesn't mean you should give the old tenant a rent break. Rather it means you should fix the old tenant's apartment so it's the same as the new tenant's.

That can mean some whopping increases

Let's say you've been doing things he wrong way. Your apartment building is always full. But after reading this book, you got religion. You start raising rents and keep on until your vacancy rate is five percent.

If you're typical, you'll end up 20% to 35% above where you started. For example, apartments that were full at $300 a month my actually be worth $360 to $400. And the **new** tenants won't mind paying $360 to $400. "Reasonable rents," remember?

But some of the existing tenants are probably at $275 or $280. Most buildings have many apartments which are below the current street rents. Even when those rents are below market. So let's say you've found that the market value is $375. And Mrs. McGillicudy in 210 is paying $275. "Does Jack Reed really expect me to raise Mrs. McGillicudy from $275 to $375 in one jump? A $100 increase?! 36%!?"

"I do."

"But she's 91!"

"Raise her to $375."

"But she uses a walker!"

"I'm sorry anyone's in poor health. But since landlords don't cause health problems, there's no reason why landlords have any more duty than, say, other tenants, to subsidize people with health problems. Raise her to $375."

Retaliation

Many state laws make some rent increases retaliation, which is illegal. Generally, those laws permit increases which follow a general pattern throughout the building but prohibit increases that are higher than general increases and apply only to tenants who have recently filed complaints against the landlord or whitheld rent for repairs, e.g., Texas Property Code 92.057.

2

Signs of Low Rents

1. Waiting List

As I said earlier, waiting lists mean your rents are too low. Much too low.

If you have one vacancy, you need one tenant. Not two.

A waiting list means the number of tenants you have **exceeds** the number of apartments you have. What's the point of that? If you have, say, 35 units, why offer such a good deal that it pleases **40** tenants when you can only get **paid** for pleasing 35 tenants? If you raise the rents a little, two or three of those 40 will say, "Never mind, I'll live somewhere else." Raise it a little more, and another two or three will decide to live somewhere else.

Result? You make more money. And the five extra tenants you had live somewhere else—which is where they were living **anyway**!

Hold an auction

If you're selling one of something, and two people want it, you'd hold an auction. Wouldn't you? Why sell it to A for $100 when maybe B will pay $110? Why have a waiting list?

By the same token, why rent your apartment for $375 to A when B may be willing to pay $385 or more?

The hassle-avoidance mode

You may want to manage your apartments so as to minimize hassles. Waiting lists fit that approach. But let's qualify the low-hassle mode so we don't overdo the rent reductions.

Showing apartments is a hassle. Normally it takes **five showings** to get one tenant. That's called the **conversion ratio**. The conversion ratio is the number of leases signed divided by the number of showings. If it takes you five showings for each lease, your conversion ratio is 20% (1/5 = 20%).

Increasing your conversion ratio

If you are in the hassle-avoidance mode, you may want a higher conversion ratio to minimize the number of showings. Holding your rents below market value will do that. But don't overdo it. Keep lowering your rents until your conversion ratio is where you want it. Then raise the rents to keep pace with inflation. It's easy to overdo the rent decrease because after a point, you get the same high conversion ratio at all rents.

For example, let's say the fair market value of an apartment is $450 a month. If you lower rents to $425, you'll probably rent to the first or second person who looks at it—because they'll be comparing it to other $425 apartments, not the $450 apartments it's equal to.

And if you lower the rent still further to $400, it will still rent to the first or second person who looks at it. Same goes for $375. So in this example, you can get your low hassle by going to $425, $400, or $375. Obviously, $425 is the best low hassle rent.

Most owners and managers take *pride* in their waiting list

Many apartment buildings have waiting lists. And in virtually every such case, the owners and managers are **proud** of the fact that they have a waiting list. And these are people who have not consciously decided to adopt the hassle-avoidance (and lower rate of return) management approach.

They are proud of their waiting lists because they see it as evidence that their building is **highly desirable**. Evidence of what **great managers** they are. Evidence of what a brilliant choice the owner made when he bought the building.

Aaaaaaghhhhhhhhh!!!!

They're nuts

The owners and managers who are proud of their waiting lists are crazy.

If you want **me** to pat you on the back and tell you what a good job you're doing as an apartment owner, show me your **return on equity**.

That's return on **current** equity. The typical waiting list building has been owned by the same owner for more than a few years. **Recent** buyers can't **afford** to run buildings that way. Their higher mortgage payments force them to raise rents as high as they can.

Bloated equity

Because it's been owned more than a few years, the value of the building has gone up substantially. And the mortgage has gone down a bit. The result is 60% or more equity. With that much equity, the mortgage payments no longer put pressure on the owner to raise rents. So he doesn't. He's got **positive cash flow**. More than he's ever had before. So he figures he's doing **better** than ever before.

He's **not**.

A buildings with a waiting list has a terrible return on current equity. Because the **rents** are **low—but** the **operating expenses** (everything but interest) are the **same** as the operating expenses on a building which does **not** have low rents.

Low leverage increases cash flow. That's simple arithmetic. Increased cash flow allows you to get away with low rents in the sense that you still make a profit. But return on current equity—which is the only proper measure of investment performance—does not forgive the kind of stupidity or laziness which is manifest by low rents.

So the proud waiting list operators—who still have positive cash flow—are really proud of nothing but **lousy leverage** and **low rents**. Any idiot can produce positive cash flow if he has a low loan-to-value ratio. And any idiot can have a waiting list if he lets his rents fall below market value.

The owners and managers who take pride in their waiting lists are dingbats. They are the most incompetent and/or lazy apartment owners in the country. All you need to prove that is to compare their return on equity with that of a building with market rents.

I bought waiting list buildings

There's one time when I love waiting list buildings. When I'm **buying** the building in question. I salivate when I hear the words, "We have a waiting list." (I also check the rents against the market because many owners and managers lie about having a waiting list. Ask to see the waiting list. And call some of the people on it to see if they really would move into the building in question if a vacancy occurred.)

The reason I bought waiting list buildings is because their low rents depress the purchase price. That let me get the property on the cheap. Then I raise the rents to market—which increased the value of the building proportionately.

A building which truly does have a waiting list is probably 20% to 25% below market. If you can buy a building with rents that are 25% below market—then raised the rents to market—and you put 25% down—you just doubled your money. Probably in about six months.

2. Less than five percent vacancy rate

I've already discussed this sign of low rents at length.

3. Conversion ratio higher than 20%

I've already discussed this sign as well.

4. Low turnover

Your turnover ratio is the number of move-ins divided by the number of apartments you have. For example, if 34 tenants moved into your 38-unit building last year, your turnover ratio was $34/38 = 90\%$.

For the first four months of 1984, my 33-unit Fort Worth building had six move-ins. That's a turnover ratio of $6/33 = 18.2\%$. But since four months is only a third of a year, you need to multiply it by three to get the annual turnover ratio of $3 \times 18.2\% = 54.6\%$.

For the first four months of 1984, my 25-unit Dallas area building had fourteen move-ins. That's a turnover ratio of $3 \times 14 = 42/25 = 168\%$.

The Dallas turnover ratio is high because the seller had eleven vacancies a month or two before I bought it. Apparently he lowered his credit standards to fill it up before closing. Then again, maybe his credit standards were always that low. He collected 75 security deposits the year before I bought the place. I learned that when I went over the books. That's a $75/25 = 300\%$ turnover ratio!

Does 7.5% turnover mean low rents?

According to the Boston Rental Housing Association (www.boardplace.com/rha), the Spring 1987 regional turnover rate was 37%. But that same report showed Brookline, Massachusetts had a turnover rate of just 7.5%. According to what I've just told you, Brookline must have low rents, right? You're darn tootin' they do. Brookline had rent control from the early seventies into the eighties.

100% turnover is not as bad as it sounds

One hundred percent turnover sounds worse than it really is. A 37-unit building I owned from '78 to '83 had about 100% turnover. But it also had about six tenants who were there when I bought it and there when I exchanged out of it. The hundred percent turnover comes from a combination of long-term tenants who don't move at all and other tenants who move out after only a few months.

We require tenants to sign a six-month lease when they move in. But many people don't honor it. If we could spot them in advance, we'd have a lower turnover ratio. But if you tighten your screening to do that, you'd lose some good tenants and reduce the rent you could get.

300% turnover is not bad *per se*

I happen to be comfortable with 100% turnover. But there's nothing necessarily wrong with 300%. It's just that you and your managers have to work harder.

The tenants who violate their lease by moving out before the lease term is up also violate the lease in other ways. They pay late. They play their stereo too loud. They damage the apartment.

So more turnover also means more problems of **all** kinds. If you and your managers don't mind spending more time chasing slow payers, reprimanding misbehavior, and paying for damage, run your building at 300% turnover. Your rents will be slightly higher than those at a 100% turnover building. Not higher enough to make it worthwhile in my opinion. But they'll be higher.

That, in turn, will make the building more valuable—if the buyer is unable to spot signs of the high turnover when he looks at the property.

Running a high turnover building makes more sense in your youth. Your time is less valuable then. And cash flow and building value are your main goals. But as you get older and more successful, you neither need nor want the hassle.

5. Few complaints

You can often tell whether your rents are below market by listening to the tenants' "mating calls." Send out a rent increase letter and you will very probably hear the "mating call of the tenant who's paying market rent."

> *If I'm going to pay blank dollars for this place, I ought to be able to have blank fixed (repaired, replaced, upgraded, whatever).*

Have you ever heard that line? If you have, your rents, or at least some of them, are at or near market. When you demand market rents, tenants demand good service in return. That's fine.

The 'mating call of the below-market rent tenant'

Tenants whose rent is **below** market also have a "mating call."

> *Oh, I didn't want to bother you.*

You hear the mating call of the below-market rent tenant when you discover a maintenance problem in their apartment. One which they have **not** reported. When you ask why, the tenant replies, "Oh, I didn't want to bother you."

Case in point: A building I bought in 1983 had an efficiency apartment which rented for $180. When I inspected it prior to purchase, the tenant had just died. In the bathroom, there was a bad water leak. The tenant had rigged up his shower curtain to catch the leak and channel it into the bathtub. It looked far worse than it sounds—with lots of mildew, etc..

We rented that apartment—for $215. It rented after five or six showings.

Do you suppose the $35 a month rent break had anything to do with his not reporting that problem? What do you think the chances are that he'd have said, "If I'm going to pay $215, I ought to be able to have my shower fixed," if I'd raised him to that level?

The farther below market, the quieter the tenant

When tenants' rents are below-market, they will tolerate maintenance problems which a tenant at market will **not** tolerate. Because they're afraid to lose their good deal.

Sometimes they jury-rig a "repair" like that man did. Other times they do the repair themselves. Other times they just live with it.

One problem with this is that many of the problems are of the stitch-in-time variety. That is, they become much **more costly** to repair if the repair is **delayed**. So tenants tolerating lack of maintenance is not always a pure savings.

6. Tenants making capital improvements

Apartment owners install carpet in apartments. **Not** tenants. Same goes for cabinets. And shelves. And built-in appliances.

You say you've got tenants who have made expensive improvements to their apartments? Friend, your rents are too low.

When tenants are paying market rents, they do **not** make improvements to their apartments. At least not improvements which would be difficult or impossible to take with them when they move.

That includes:

- Wall-to-wall carpet
- Wallpaper
- Wall-mounted, expensive shelves
- Built-in appliances
- Cabinets
- Windows
- Doors
- Insulation
- Masonry
- Partitions (walls)
- Fixed heaters and air-conditioners
- Plumbing fixtures
- Electrical wiring
- Skylights
- Paneling
- Vinyl or other flooring
- Ceramic tile
- Shower doors

If any of your tenants are installing—or having this stuff installed—at their own expense, your rents are too low.

The reason should be obvious. When a tenant is paying market value—and wants something better—he moves to a better place. He sure isn't going to improve the greedy landlord's building for nothing.

Tenants who improve their apartment could move too. So why don't they?

Simple economics

Because they've got a good deal. It's pure economics. Let's say the tenant wants new carpet. She could ask the landlord. But tenants who are below market try to remain anonymous, remember?

Or she can pay to have it installed herself. New carpet costs about $600. It'll last five years if she takes care of it. That's $120 a year. Or the equivalent of a $10 a month rent increase.

She then asks herself the question, "Which is cheaper: moving to a place which has new carpet and paying the rent they charge—or staying here and paying $10 a month to a carpet store in addition to my current rent?"

If she chose "stay here," you know that your rent is below market by an amount equal to at least the monthly amortization of whatever improvement the tenant made.

The unwritten lease addendum

Like I said, it's simple economics. Tenants do not improve their apartment out of the goodness of their heart—or because they are "good" tenants. They improve it because it's cheaper to stay there **and** pay for the improvement than it is to move to a place where the owner has paid for it. Raise your rents to market and you'll **never** see another tenant capital improvement.

By the way, before tenants make such capital improvements, they usually tell you. And tell you in a way that says,

*Boy, am I the world's most wonderful tenant or what? I am about to make a tremendous improvement to your building **at my own expense!***

Then they ask for a two-year lease with **verbal** assurances that they can stay for at least five years without any "unreasonable" rent increases. They want assurance that they can remain throughout the life of the improvement—with no rent increases that would reduce the spread between market rent and what they've been paying.

In other words, they'll accept **cost of living increases** during the amortization period. They just don't want you to remove the subsidy they're receiving. The improvement doesn't make sense without the subsidy. Basically, the tenant tells you in no uncertain terms that in return for their improving the apartment, they expect you to continue to exercise "restraint" as to the rent.

What should you do? Replace the carpet or whatever **yourself—then** raise the tenant to market rent.

Sometimes it's not the rent

Turn three of the six signs of low rent I just gave you upside down and you have three signs of **high** rent. They are:

Three signs of high rent

1. More than five percent vacancy rate
2. Conversion ratio lower than 20%
3. High turnover

Concessions are another sign of rent that exceeds market value.

And then I observed the following phenomena in the high-vacancy-rate period in the Texas market:

The Office Hours Indicator

If the building's leasing office hours are	Its vacancy rate is
By appointment	less than 5%
10:00 to 4:00	5%
9:00 to 5:00	10%
8:30 to 6:00	15% +

The Security Deposit Indicator*

If the building's security deposit is	Its vacancy rate is
more than $200	less than 5%
$200	5%
$150	10%
$100	15%
less than $100	20% +

* The Security Deposit Indicator amounts may need to be adjusted for different markets. But the basic principle that landlords would rather cut security deposit amounts than rents when faced with vacancies applies everywhere.

When you have these signs, you should **lower** your rent—on both new tenants and existing tenants. But there's something else you should check when you have any of the signs of high rents. You may have a marketing problem. The three signs of high rents could be caused by:

- Dirty apartments
- Repulsive manager appearance
- Repulsive manager behavior
- Poorly maintained building or grounds
- Overly strict credit standards
- Too slow credit checking

and so forth. If you have any of these problems, fix them. They depress rental market values. Although I must note that lowering the rents will cause tenants to tolerate these problems. It's just more cost effective to fix the problems than it is to "bribe" the tenants to tolerate them.

It's *any*, not all

I learned a lesson about signs of low rents recently. You should be raising rents or taking other action like replacing your manager if you have **any** of the signs of low rents. You don't need all of them.

I suspected I needed to replace a manager. I couldn't raise rents because my vacancy rate was too high. But I had trouble getting the manager on the phone and such.

Sure enough, I had been focusing just on **vacancy rates**. When I looked at the **other** signs of low rents, they were all there. Low turnover. Tenants putting up with holes in the ceiling (I learned from the new manager). Vacancies filled by transfers of tenants from smaller apartments. Tenants painting their own apartments (I learned from the new manager.) Vacancies filled by people who were friends or relatives of those already living in the building (waiting list). I did not have a traffic report to compute the conversion ratio so I don't know it. I later had the manager send me a daily report which is a post card preprinted with questions about calls and visitors and preaddressed to me.

3

Excuses for Not Raising Rents

Excuses, excuses

I have made a number of speeches on raising rents. And written a number of articles on the subject. Afterwards, members of the audience have come up and told me why they do **not** raises rents as much as I say they should.

Over the years, I have heard all the excuses. There are six. Here they are. And here's why they're not valid.

1. 'I go easy on my *good* tenants.'

The underlying notion here is that good tenants are **rare**. Therefore, when you find one of these "gems," you must bribe them each month in order to keep them.

Baloney.

A good tenant is one who abides by the lease. Period. There is no useful difference between tenants who abide by the lease. In other words, there are not differing grades of quality once you get past the abide-by-the-lease criterion. Either the tenant abides by the lease or they don't.

What would differentiate a "good" tenant from a "mediocre" one? Do "good" tenants pay their rent **before** it's due? What good is that? And wouldn't practically every tenant in the building pay their rent early if you gave them a ten or twenty dollar a month discount for doing so? Which is what you're doing when you give "good" tenants a rent break.

Bad tenants play their radio too loud. Do "good" tenants surpass mediocre ones by never turning their radio on?

Good tenants are the only kind I have

To those who say good tenants deserve a break, I say, "Yeah. The break I give them is I let them live in my building. And I'm a good owner. That is, I abide by **my** end of the lease just as I expect the tenants to abide by their end."

Bad tenants, I reject or evict. Good tenants get accepted and renewed. There are no other categories.

Good tenants are not rare

GIs like to complain about mess hall food. Citizens like to complain about government. And landlords like to complain about tenants. But that ritual notwithstanding, most tenants are good tenants.

I was a landlord from 1969 to 1992. In that time, I owned and/or managed hundreds of apartments and dealt with even more tenants. Only a small percentage have caused me trouble that cost me money. Other owners who screen tenants carefully have had similar experience.

If good tenants (meaning those who abide by the lease) are **truly** rare in your operation. You're not screening carefully enough. Or else your building is in neighborhood where good **people** are rare. If the neighborhood is so bad that only **bad** tenants apply, screening won't help.

Bribes not necessary

You do **not** need to bribe good tenants with below-market rents to get them to remain in your building. You **do** need to hold yourself and your employees to the same standards you set for the tenants. Namely, living up to **your** end of the lease.

You need to maintain both the building and the tenant's apartment or house properly and promptly. You need to have reasonable policies. And your rent must not be **higher** than market value. But it need not be **lower** either.

Good tenants will pay market value. In fact, the minute a "good" tenant demands a "bribe" to remain in my building is the moment he stops being a good tenant in my mind. Good men give a fair day's work for a fair day's pay. And good tenants pay a month's fair market rent for a month's fair market lodging.

Incentive to stay already exists—moving expense

The tenants already have one significant incentive not to move. The **expense** of moving. The typical move probably costs $200 to $500 for a tenant. So why should you pay them an **additional** $120 to $240 (ten to twenty dollar a month rent break) for not moving?

Your *old* tenant is another landlord's *new* tenant

Many landlords are reluctant to raise rents on existing tenants. But hardly any have **any** bones about charging **new** tenants top dollar.

If one of your tenants feels the rent is too high at your place, he or she has to move somewhere else. And thus becomes someone else's **new** tenant. So it's not like if **you** won't give him a rent break someone else **will**. The other landlords will want as much or more than you're asking.

Rent raises bring a better class of people

One of the interesting things about rent raising is the way it changes the character of your tenants. If you raise rents more than about 10%, you move up to a higher layer. By raising your rent, you raise the **income** needed to qualify for the apartment.

People who make more money are generally better educated, more mature, more responsible, etc. And that's not just theory. In one building where I raised my rents around 40% in less than a year, the resident managers made the unsolicited comment that "a better class of people" were now applying.

That's because people tend to assume that your property is worth what you're asking for them. And people who make $1,500 a month generally want to live in $400 a month units. When your units were renting for $300, they didn't even **look** at them—because they were looking in the $400 rent range. By raising your rent to $400, you move into the group that they consider.

Of course, your property has to be **worth** $400 a month. Nobody will apply if they're not. But few $400 a month tenants will even **look** if you only ask $300.

New tenant often pays more and likes it better

Your existing tenants will not like having their rent raised. Even if you give them a ten or twenty dollar break. For one thing, they probably don't **know** you could have raised them more. And if you tell them, they won't believe you.

So your new move-ins are paying $400 a month for a one-bedroom. But to keep a "good" tenant, you only raise him from $360 to $380. He **loves** you for the twenty dollar rent increase, right?

No actually, he **hates** you—thinks you're a rent gouging S.O.B. And this twenty dollar rent increase is just further evidence of that.

Suppose you had raised him to the full $400 as I recommend. And he moved. A new tenant would move in paying $400. If you asked the new tenant why he chose your building, he'd say "Reasonable rent. I've been looking for a couple weeks. This is the best place I've seen for the money."

I know he'll say that because virtually **all** new tenants feel exactly that way about their new home.

So why give a ten or twenty dollar a month—$120 to $240 a year—break to some sullen, resentful jerk who hates you for not giving him a **forty** dollar break?

Mothers everywhere say, "You want something to cry about? I'll give you something to cry about." So if your tenants are going to hate you for raising their rent no matter how much you raise it, you might as well raise it **all the way to market**.

2. 'I can always raise it later.'

"I can always go up later."

Maybe. Maybe not.

You might get **rent control**. Many liberal cities already have it. Some other cities will probably get it in the future.

A number of states, in effect, prohibit cities from passing rent control laws. Does that mean owners there don't have to worry about rent control?

No. Those states could **change** those laws.

Nationwide rent control

The **whole country** could get it, too. Already had it. Twice. There were nationwide rent controls in World War II. And in the early '70s under President Nixon's wage-and-price-control program.

One of my fears is that some president will impose national wage and price controls—then lift them on everything but rents. A doctor from the country of Colombia was in one of my seminars once. When he heard me express that fear he said, "The government of Colombia did exactly that recently."

You may think it couldn't happen here. Wanna bet your life savings on it?

'Nice guys' finish last when rent control comes

Let's say you're a "nice guy." You don't raise your rents as much as you could. On average, you're about $40 behind the market at $360 a month.

The apartment owner across the street is a graduate of one of John T. Reed's rent raising speeches. He constantly raises his rents to keep them at market value. His apartments rent for $400 a month on average.

Then, your properties become rent controlled. The rent control law allows a 3.5% increase. That means you, Mr. "Nice Guy," get to raise your rents 3.5% x $360 = $12.60 a month to $372.60. (Under rent controls, rents usually are odd amounts as owners go for every penny.)

The "rent gouger" across the street also gets a 3.5% increase. Only in **his** case, that's 3.5% x $400 = $14.00 to $414.

Another year older and farther behind

So now you're getting $372.60 for an apartment which is the same as the ones Mr. "Gouger" is getting $414 for. "Nice guys" finish last under rent control.

Also, rent control is usually **forever**. You can count on one hand the towns which have gotten **rid** of rent control. Dozens and dozens of towns have it. Someone said of rent controls,

> *Rent control is like heroin: starting is euphoric, quitting is impossible, continuing is disaster.*

So not only do you get a smaller increase and fall farther behind Mr. "Rent Gouger" the **first** year. That pattern will repeat itself **forever**! With each passing year, the guy who kept his rents at market will get bigger increases and move farther ahead of you.

Rent control laws all have a base date

All rent control laws have a base date. You're stuck with whatever your rents were on that date. For all you know, **today** could be the base date of some future law affecting your property. Would you be happy living with all your **present** rents, adjusted for increases allowed by the rent control board, **forever**?

Typically, the base date is a date **before** there was any debate on the subject of rent controls. That's because debate on rent controls scares landlords into raising their rents to beat the law. If the lawmakers who pass rent controls did **not** choose a base date before the debate, they'd be encouraging huge, even **above**-market value rent increases to beat the deadline.

Sometimes the base date is the day before the subject was introduced in the legislature or city council. But often it's **retroactive**. Cambridge, Massachusetts, for example, passed its rent control law on November 8, 1972. But they picked a base date of September 1, 19**67**! **Five years** earlier!

That left Cambridge landlords zero opportunity to make up for lost time. (In the interest of full disclosure, the law said 1972 rents could be whatever they were on September 1, 1967 **plus 30%**.)

'I'll *gradually* get it up to market.'

I may not have made one aspect of raising existing tenants' rent clear. I'll make it clear now. When I say raise existing tenants to market rents, I mean in **one jump. No matter how far below market** they are.

A lot of owners say, "Well I couldn't do that. I've got some tenants who are eighty and ninety dollars below market."

Raise them to market—in one jump.

Here's an example. Let's say the market rent on your apartments is $400 a month. You've got one tenant who for various reasons is only paying $310. I say raise him to $400 next opportunity. Generally the next opportunity would be when it's been a year since that tenant's last rent increase.

"But," you protest, "that's a $90, 29% increase!"

"It sure is. That tenant's been getting away with murder."

The gradual approach

Let's say you decide to use the gradual approach to getting this tenant up to market. What size increase are you going to send? $20? $30?

Let's say $25 a year. And let's also say the inflation rate is 4%. Here's how your gradual approach would compare to my approach for the first four years.

Rent level	After 1 yr	After 2 yrs	After 3 yrs	After 4 yrs
Market	416.00	432.64	449.95	467.94
Your rent	335.00	360.00	385.00	410.00
Difference	81.00	72.64	64.95	57.94

At $25 a year and 4% inflation, it'll take you **eleven years** to get within five dollars of market. And then, twenty-five dollar increases would **never** allow to catch up. Because 4% of $625 equals $25. So after market hit $625, the inflationary 4% increases would exceed the $25 "catch up" increases.

Try $40 a month increases

If, instead of $25 a month increases, you try $40 increases, the progression looks like this.

Rent level	After 1 yr	After 2 yrs	After 3 yrs	After 4 yrs
Market	416.00	432.64	449.95	467.94
Your rent	350.00	390.00	385.00	410.00
Difference	66.00	42.64	19.95	-2.06

So if you hit your tenant with $40 increases each year for **four** years, you'll catch up to market **gradually**.

The reason for gradualism, of course, is to avoid making the tenant mad at you. A $90 increase like **I** advocate would really make the tenant mad, wouldn't it? Of course, **after** I send out that $90 increase the first year, I'd only be sending a $16 increase the next year. And a $17 increase the year after that.

You, on the other hand, would be sending out $40 increases **year after year**. The tenants will **love** you for your gradualism, won't they?

Like pulling off a Band Aid

Rent raises are like pulling off a Band Aid. They hurt. They hurt if you do it **slowly**. And they hurt if you do it **fast**. So you might as well get it over with as quickly as possible.

Furthermore, tenants start hating you at about the $5 or $10 level. So why bother differentiating between a $90 increase and a $40 increase?

The tenant will probably move in any event

Finally, whether you do it in one jump or four, your **current** tenant probably **cannot afford** the market rent. He simply does not make that much. And probably isn't going to in the foreseeable future.

So whether you raise his rent $90 all at once or gradually, he's going to move. That's another thing I've learned from sending out large increase notices. Not only does the character of the **new** tenants change. Many of your existing tenants will move.

Not because the apartments aren't **worth** what you're asking. They **are** worth it. It's just that many of your existing tenants don't make enough money to afford market rents at that building. So whenever you dramatically increase rents, you have to replace a large percentage of your tenants with new ones. Higher rents require higher incomes.

Sudden need

There's one more reason why the gradual approach does not make sense. You may not have as much time as you think. You may be **forced** to sell by an **emergency**. If the emergency is your **death**, your spouse may be forced to sell because he or she does not want to run an apartment building.

Emergencies that can force a sale before your gradual approach gets the rents to market include:

- Severe illness
- Death
- Job-related need to move
- Opportunity of a lifetime.

Emergencies, like rent control, can foul up your gradual time table.

3. 'I keep rents down on existing tenants to minimize turnover cost.'

This is the **scientific** excuse for not raising rents. Turnover costs money. The less turnover, the less cost.

As far as it goes, the argument is correct. Turnover does indeed cost money. But so do low rents.

And reducing turnover does indeed reduce turnover costs. And you **can** achieve lower turnover by reducing rents. There's no other way, assuming your building is generally well-managed to begin with.

But you must **net** the **savings** in turnover costs against the **lost revenue and building value** which results from reducing your rents to cut turnover.

How much does turnover cost?

Just what does turnover cost?

In the duplexes and triplex I used to own and operate, the only turnover cost was the cost of a classified ad and my time to show the apartment, screen the applicants, and sign the lease. I did not paint, clean, or any of that. Big complexes which run an ad continuously would not have any additional ad cost from a turnover.

The tenants usually did their own painting. I had a letter in which I offered to pay for the paint if they did the work. And I specified the colors they had to use. More about that later.

Cleaning cost paid by tenants

The tenants did the cleaning, too. I had a month and a half's rent as security deposit. That's a lot of money. When I made the move-out inspection, I required **clean**. And I do mean clean.

Then the **new** tenant inspected the place. I particularly directed their attention to the range, oven, refrigerator, and bathrooms. I made them sign a pre-move-in inspection check list saying the place was perfect except for items they listed. If they listed any cleanliness problems, I said, "How much money will you take to take care of that dirty oven (or whatever) yourself?"

"Fifteen dollars," was a typical answer.

"OK. I will take that amount out of the outgoing tenant's security deposit and give it to you and we'll call it clean."

So I had no cleaning turnover cost. Any cost was borne by the outgoing tenant—who had signed an inspection sheet saying that the oven was clean when he or she moved in.

Market determines how you handle cleaning, etc.

In my Texas apartments, we painted, shampooed, and cleaned **as needed** on turnover. That's because the Texas market is far more competitive than New Jersey was.

But I tell the New Jersey story to illustrate that turnover cost **can** be close to zero.

Now let's look at Texas turnover costs. As I said, we painted, shampooed, and cleaned as needed. Painting an apartment costs me $60 to $80 plus materials. My house painter said it took three to four gallons and 12 to 16 hours to paint an apartment. A Dallas make-ready company's price list says 22¢ a square foot to paint apartments. Shampooing cost me $25 to $35. Cleaning is about $20 to $30.

We didn't automatically do any of these things. We did them as needed. No painting at all if it was a recent move-in. Touch-up if there was some damage but still a recent move-in. And full painting when the old tenant was there for a long time. The idea was to get a **paint smell** in the air and take care of any **visible marks**.

Same with shampooing and cleaning.

In some towns, there are **laws** which require turnover costs like painting, shampooing, lock-changing, and so forth. If you have one of those idiot laws, you need to add them to your turnover costs calculation.

Turnover costs without turnover

You don't need turnover to have "turnover costs." If none of your tenants moved, would you **never** paint an apartment again?

Cleaning is about the only expense which occurs **only** on turnover. And security deposits take care of most of that. Painting is usually to correct "ordinary wear and tear." It's illegal to deduct for that. Although **not all** painting is for ordinary wear and tear. When the wear and tear is **extra**ordinary, security deposit deductions are proper.

But tenants who move out aren't the only ones with ordinary wear and tear. Long-term tenants also need paint.

So even if you could **eliminate** all turnover—which you can't—you'd still have painting costs. That means about all you can accomplish by reducing turnover is to **stretch out** the period **between** painting.

Some turnover is inevitable

You can only influence turnover slightly once you get below the 100% level. **Some** turnover is inevitable.

People die. They move to nursing homes. They get transferred. Fired. Married. Divorced. Evicted.

So what we're really talking about when you say you hold down rent increases to existing tenants is reducing the turnover rate from maybe 100% to maybe 40%. And what we're really talking about on reducing turnover costs is reducing the percentage of apartments which get a paint job from maybe 110% to maybe 50%. The paint percentage is higher than the turnover percentage because of long-term tenants requesting it be done.

50-unit example

Let's say you've got 50 units. To hold down turnover costs, you allow **renewals** to pay $10 less than market rents. And let's say that reduces your turnover from 100% to 70%. Let's further say that **three** of your existing tenants got a paint job each year. Now that you're reducing turnover, that'll go up to **four** per year.

At the end of year one, 70% of your apartments changed hands or 35 units. Figuring the average paint job at $110, that's turnover cost of 35 x $110 = $3,850. Plus you paint four existing tenants. Since the contractors have to work around the tenant's furniture, they charge **more**. Let's say $130. 4 x $130 = $520.

Total painting costs after reducing turnover are $3,850 + $520 = $4,370.

With*out* a turnover reduction policy

Now what would your painting costs have been with**out** a turnover-reduction policy?

With 100% turnover, you'd do 50 units—some more than once. 50 x $110 = $5,500. Plus you'd do three, not four, existing tenants at $130. 3 x $130 = $390. For a total turnover cost of $5,500 + $390 = $5,890.

Total savings due to your turnover reduction program: $5,890 - $4,470 = $1,420 per year.

What about the lost rent?

Now what about the rent you lost due to your $10 break. With 70% turnover, 30% of your tenants are paying $10 less than market. 30% x 50 units = 15 units. 15 units x $10 a month = $150 a month. $150 a month x 12 months in a year = $1,800 a year rent lost.

So you lose $1,800 in rent, and save $1,420 in turnover costs. That's a net **loss** of $1,800 - $1,420 = $380.

What about building value?

Don't forget the relationship between rent and building value. Apartment buildings often sell for six times gross. At that rate, losing $1,800 rent costs you 6 x $1,800 = $10,800 off your building value! And if buildings sell for eight, nine, or ten times gross in your area, the value loss would be greater.

Theoretically, the turnover cost savings would **add** to building value. But apartment building buyers tend to be far more sensitive to **rents** than to expenses. Most apartment buyers **reconstruct** the income and expense statement to one degree or another.

In other words, when you sell, you can **tell** them you have low turnover and therefore low turnover costs. But they'll believe you about as much as they'll believe 100% occupancy. Just as they always insert 5% vacancy, they'll insert their **own** estimate of turnover costs and ignore your experience.

To put it another way, apartment buyers and lenders **will** give you credit for the rent you collect when computing the building value. But they will **not** give you credit for the turnover costs you save. So why bother? Especially when there's a net $380 loss **before** you even take into account the effect on value.

Use your own figures

You may have disagreed with some of the assumptions I used in my figures on turnover costs.

Fine. Redo the calculations with your own figures. All I ask is that you not **assume** that you have a net savings without doing the numbers. And that you include the effect on **building value** of below-market rents.

Conclusion

Do **not** give existing tenants a break on rents to reduce turnover. Turnover costs are small to begin with. You can only influence them slightly with a small rent reduction. And the rent lost more than wipes out any savings. In terms of **building value**, the loss is orders of magnitude greater than any turnover cost savings.

4. 'I go easy on my long-term tenants.'

Many owners feel they have a duty to give long-term tenants a rent break. Often a substantial one. $20. $30. $50 or more per month.

Why?

Why would you owe a long-term tenant such a break? Or **any** break?

How long have you been paying **property taxes** to your town? Do **they** give **you** a break?

How long have you been buying groceries from your **grocery store**? Do they give you a break? Your **gas station**? Your **mortgage lender**? The **electric company**? Does **any** one you do business with give **you** a discount because of the number of years you've been buying from them?

I didn't think so.

So why should landlords—alone among **all** the businesses in the world—give long-term customers a discount?

They shouldn't. They **can't**. In the typical new owner situation, 100% of the rent goes right back out the door to pay for mortgage payments and operating expenses. If none of those creditors will give the **landlord** a discount, how can he afford to give the **tenants** a discount?

What's the theory?

What's the theory behind this notion? Do you feel the tenant "stuck with you through thick and thin?"

Gimme a break.

The reason your tenant has been with you a long-time is because each year the deal you offered was better than the guy down the street offered. Period. I have never heard of a tenant paying **above**-market rent—out of loyalty to her landlord—when she could have had a comparable place for less.

Your long-term tenants have not stuck with you through thick and thin. They've stuck with you through **thick and thick**. Slip them some **thin** and there'll be nothing but a pile of dust and a dirty oven where they used to live.

Poor maintenance

Some owners feel a debt due to the tenant's having tolerated some maintenance problem. Like an emergency that wasn't fixed as fast as it should have been. Or a problem that was **never** fixed.

I have a **simple solution** for that. Fix it.

Slow maintenance is poor management. Do not manage poorly.

Besides, I'll bet you the $30 a month rent break is costing you far more than the repair would have. Especially when you take into account the effect on building value.

When they receive my large rent increase letters, my tenants frequently demand this or that repair. If it's a legitimate request, we get right over to their apartment and fix it. To quote the old movie cowboys,

I don't want to be behold'n to no man.

Low rents are **not** the solution to poor maintenance. **Good** maintenance is.

'But I want *stable* tenants.'

A line I often hear is that going easy on the rent increases enable the owner to keep "**stable**" tenants.

What is a "stable" tenant? The opposite of an **un**stable tenant?

More to the point, what is the **value** of a stable tenant? Other than the turnover-costs argument discussed above, I know of no value to "stableness."

It **sounds** good. But that's all. A lot of the people who talk up "stable" tenants are simply managers who want to make their own jobs easier. They want that waiting list sinecure. With "stable" tenants, they're not bothered with annoyances like showing apartments or otherwise earning their pay.

5. The charity excuse

The charity excuse is my favorite—the one that really sets me off. Basically, it says that you shouldn't raise rent on a particular tenant to market levels because that tenant is deserving of charity. It may be a little old lady, or a struggling, pregnant young couple, or a guy who lost his job.

The primary charity case is the "senior citizen on fixed income." Matter of fact, that phrase ought to be hyphenated. Because you rarely hear the phrase "senior citizen" without the "on fixed income" attached to the tail end of it.

'Senior citizens on fixed incomes'

Fact is, hardly **any** senior citizens are on fixed incomes. In order to be on a fixed income, you'd have to be **ineligible** for social security and derive **100%** of your income from fixed annuities. A *Time* magazine study a few years ago sought the answer to the question, "Who is most hurt and who most helped by inflation?"

Time found the group most **helped** was senior citizens—because of the many cost of living and greater increases they had received in social security and other benefits.

Of course, the fact that senior citizens incomes went up due to inflation does not mean those incomes are **high**. Typically, they are **not** high. But let's analyze what, if anything, that means to landlords.

Charity in general

Charity is mandatory. You've heard the phrase, "I gave at the office." Well, we can all legitimately make that claim. We **did** give at the office—the IRS office. More than half the money you pay in taxes goes for "social programs." So like it or not, you've given thousands or tens of thousands of dollars to political charities—like social security—which is more handout than return of invested capital.

Whether you give to **voluntary** charities above and beyond government charities is up to you. A strong argument could be made that you've discharged any charitable obligations you had to society—and then some—through your taxes.

But most people, including my wife and I, **do** give more. According to the IRS (ftp://ftp.fedworld.gov/pub/irs-soi/93in21id.exe), the average charitable contributions deductions for various income groups in 1995 (the latest year I have figures for in 1998) are shown in the next chart.

Landlords' original sin?

Do landlords have some special duty to give more to charity than other people? That seems to be an underlying presumption in the rent-increases-are-uncharitable school of thought.

A landlord raises some little old lady's rent to market. Some tenant's rights guy shrieks like a wounded bull elephant. The landlord is greedy. He's cruel. He's heartless. Etc., etc.

The tenant activist denounces the landlord as the lowest of low life. And, in the process, dons the mantle of self-righteous champion of the poor.

What the average taxpayer gave to charity in 1995

Adjusted gross income	Contributions	Adjusted gross income	Contributions
$0-$15,000	$1,097	$50,000-$75,000	1,768
$15,000-$30,000	1,338	$75,000-$100,000	2,286
$30,000-$50,000	1,465	$100,000-$200,000	3,433
		$200,000+	16,882

Those are the national averages.

If a landlord rents an apartment or house for **less** than market value, he's making a monthly charitable contribution to the tenant. I would like to know why the **landlord** should be the one to contribute to that tenant? Why not someone else? Like the tenant activist, for example.

If he's so interested in the little old lady's welfare—so charitable himself—why doesn't **he** shell out the $40 a month? Or why not her butcher? Or her son? Or her brother? Or her car dealer?

How did landlords get saddled with the obligation to make substantial charitable contributions to millions of people who have business and other relationships with many non-landlords? Are we landlords born with some sort of original sin which we must atone for via charitable rents to our tenants?

Two questions to answer

When it comes to charity, you've got two questions to answer:

1. **How much** should I give?
2. **To whom** should I give it?

Seems to me the answer to the question, "How much," is **no more than the average guy** gives. In other words, no more than the IRS figures above.

And the answer to the "To whom" question seems equally obvious. To the most needy. Perhaps modified by the rule, "Charity begins at home."

In other words, if **your mother** needs financial help, and you can afford it, you should help her. If both your mother **and** one of your tenants needs help—and you can only afford to help one—help your mother. A tenant may be somebody else's mother, too.

Are your tenants the neediest?

Suppose your family does **not** need charity. You would then go back to the **most needy** answer to the "To whom should I give" question.

Are your tenants—even your most needy tenants—the neediest people in the world? Hardly.

If they're tenants in a normal apartment building or rental house, they must be reasonably healthy. You can find less healthy and therefore, needier people at a local nursing home.

And do senior citizens have a monopoly on need? What about the **children** with health problems in your community?

And why limit the search for the most needy to **your community**? Make it **nationwide**. Couldn't we find child burn victims, kidnapped children, cancer patients, accident victims, and so forth who's needs make those of your neediest tenants look trivial by comparison?

Or make the search **world**wide. There's no reason why you need limit your contributions to Americans in need. Go overseas and you can find whole peoples suffering malnutrition, political torture, curable diseases, earthquake victims, etc. Are any of your tenants more deserving of charity than starving Africans, for example?

So if charity is truly your motivation, this world contains an unlimited supply of people (and animals) whose needs would cause your neediest tenant to weep with gratitude for his or her situation.

More than on your spouse or mother?

You're probably giving a significant rent break to some of your tenants—because you haven't "got the heart" to raise them—due to some charity need you perceive. I want you to think about something.

You are probably giving that tenant or those tenants **more** per year than you spent on your spouse's Christmas **and** birthday **and** anniversary presents and on a year's worth of presents to your mother—aren't you?

Giving more to a **stranger** than to your loved ones. Does that make sense? For example, a $40 a month rent break is a $480 per year gift to the tenant. Did you spend that much on your spouse or mother?

Charity via rent breaks costs much more

If the difference between market and actual rent were **all**, it would be bad enough. but that's not the **only** cost.

Remember that anything you do with rents affects **building value**. I've used gross rent multipliers a few times to explain that. But since Easterners disdain gross rent multipliers, I'll illustrate it once with a capitalization rate.

A cap rate is the building's net operating income (rent minus operating expenses but before mortgage payments) divided by its value. For example, a building with a net operating income of $100,000 and a value of $1,200,000 has a cap rate of $100,000/$1,200,000 = 8.3%.

If you have four tenants getting an average charitable rent break of $35 a month, you've reduced both your gross and your net income by 4 units x $35 per unit per month x 12 months per year = $1,680 per year. Dividing that by the cap rate of 8.3% indicates a drop in value of $1,680/8.3% = $20,240.96!

So you **give** your tenants $1,680 a year in charity contributions. They **receive** $1,680 a year in charity. But it **costs** you $1,680 + $20,240.96 = $21,920.96 to give them that $1,680. Don't you think it would be wiser to charge market rent and write them a check?

'So I'll just tell the building buyer about the breaks I'm giving'

Many owners feel the rent breaks will **not** cost them on building value. Because they'll just explain to the prospective building buyer,

> *Oh, the rent on these four apartments is below market because I'm deliberately giving those tenants a break. One lost his job. Mrs. Cramer is 88. Mr. Wilbur had a hip operation. And Miss Wilson has been in the building for twenty-seven years.*

There are two problems with that. First, the buyer **may not believe** you. He may say,

> *When you get those apartments up $35 higher, I'll believe it. Until then, you get credit only for the rent you **collect**.*

In fact, most experienced apartment buyers ask the seller what his **collections** were for the most recent several months. And they expect to see **proof** of it.

The other problem is that the buyer may not want to play the **bad guy** any more than you did. Which building do you think he'd rather buy—yours where he has to raise these charity cases by an average $35 a month—or mine where everyone's **already** paying market rent?

Non-dollar costs: resentment

There are also some **non-dollar costs**. One is resentment. You give tenant **A** a $35 a month rent break for charitable reasons. Tenant **B** is less needy, you decide. But tenant B may disagree. In fact, tenant B may feel she's **more** deserving than tenant A.

Non-dollar costs: lack of market data

Remember I said the best way to measure the value of your apartments is to see what you can get for your vacancies. The more low-rent charity you give, the less turnover. The less turnover, the less opportunity to test the market value of your units.

When I had a smaller operation, I used to sometimes go for months without a move-out. That made me nervous. I wondered if the market had moved up in the interim. If it went on for very long, I would raise the tenant paying the least rent to a **new high**—higher than I'd ever got in a vacancy.

If he stayed, fine. And if he moved, at least I got a chance to see whether the market had moved. Since market value affects **all** your rents and your building value, making sure you're in touch with the market is worth losing a tenant every now and then if necessary. That only applies to **smaller buildings**. In larger buildings, you will always have at least some turnover. So you need not artificially instigate it.

Armies constantly probe. When opposing armed forces face each other, each needs to know where the other is at all times. That's why they send out reconnaissance patrols. The U.S. and Soviet military constantly send out air, sea, and land patrols to find out where the enemy is and what they're doing. In war movies you often hear the phrase, "Lost contact."

You, too, must constantly "patrol." That is, you must constantly challenge the market to turn down higher rents. If they don't, you raise them to the level the market **will** accept. Since charity cuts down opportunities to test the market, it may cause you to keep your rents in **all** your apartments below where they could be. That is very costly.

Non-dollar costs: attract more charity cases

Mrs. Jones broker her hip. She asks her landlord for a break on the rent citing the broken hip as the reason. He agrees. Mrs. Jones tells her friend, Mrs. Henrikson, what a nice guy her landlord is.

Mrs. Henrikson lives in **another** apartment building. She didn't break her hip. But she lost the sight in her right eye. That's worse than a broken hip, isn't it? She asks **her** landlord for a rent break. He says no.

Mrs. Henrickson tells her friend, Mrs. Jones what a no good landlord she has. And she adds,

Keep an eye out for a vacancy in your building. I should move there so I can have a nice landlord like yours.

The word gets around. Have you ever given to charity only to find your mail increasingly full of additional solicitations from the one you gave to as well as from other charities? Individuals don't exchange names and addresses of soft touches so formally. But the word gets around.

Give charitable rent breaks and the charity cases will be lining up outside your door. In one small town where I owned a building, a significant number of my senior citizen tenants moved to **one building** on the other side of town. The other owner was way behind market—as a result of his property manager and resident manager I suspect. All my charity cases moved there when I raised them to market. So now if **he** ever decides to go to market, he'll have an even higher percentage of sad stories to fight than he had when he started.

Rent control

You allow Mrs. Brownell's rent to fall $65 below market because you feel sorry for her. Rent control is passed. Her $65 below market rent is frozen at that level.

Mrs. Brownell dies. You rerent the apartment to a young couple. The wife is just out of medical school. The husband is an MBA. They are well able to afford market or even more. But you **cannot** charge them market. In fact, you have to give them the exact same $65 a month rent break that you gave Mrs. Brownell. Because whatever the rent was on the base date lives forever. The fact that Mrs. Brownell appeared to be a charity case and the medical couple do not is irrelevant. Your generosity is required to be **permanent**.

IRS may tax below market rents as gift

There have been a number of cases in which a tenant who got below market rent was held to have received **taxable income** or a **taxable gift**. Two involving corporations allowing stockholders to live rent-free were *Chandler*, 27 AFTR 172 and *Richards*, 24 AFTR 931. Those were not charity cases *per se*.

A minister in the Chicago area gave a tenant a substantial rent break and was forced to pay $400 in back gift taxes. I don't have a citation on that. I think I got it out of a *Wall Street Journal* Wednesday tax column in the late seventies.

But I **do** have a citation on a 1984 case. A taxpayer named Risicato was **not** allowed to deduct losses on an apartment he owned (*Risicato*, TC Memo 1984-238). The reason? The Tax Court said he failed to prove he had a **profit motive**. The evidence that he had no profit motive?

1. He rented the apartment to his mother. She **only paid the rent every now and then.**
2. Then he rented it to a stranger, but at a **below-market rent.**

The lesson? If you run your business like a charity instead of like a business, the courts may say that it **isn't** a business.

Give it to *your* tenants

I've got a suggestion for you. Instead of giving **your** tenants a charitable contribution in the form of below-market rents, give it to **my** tenants in the form of cash. Here's why.

Let's say in **your** building, you've got one tenant who you let pay $30 less than market. For charity reasons. You think she's poor and would have trouble paying market rent. That's a $30 a month gift.

If you continue to do that for one year then stop, the tenant will say absolutely nothing during the year and then will be **angry** about the $30 rent increase. In some cases, the local media may pick up the story and pillory you as a greedy, rent-gouging landlord.

Give it to *my* tenant

But if you give one of **my** tenants a **check** for $30 each month, you'll get these reactions.

First, the tenant will greet your initial $30 check with disbelief. Then when she finally believes it, she'll express boundless gratitude. She may even say,

Oh, I couldn't accept that.

Some tenants would **actually** refuse to accept it—saying they don't want to take "charity."

Surely, the tenant will invite you to **supper** before two or three months of receiving your checks have passed. The tenant, upon learning that you plan to do this every first-of-the-month will be sure to be home that day—to the point of turning down other invitations.

The tenant will tell others and there's a good chance you'll be written up in the local newspaper as a good Samaritan. Or even on TV.

And at the end of the year, when you inform my tenant that you'll no longer be bring the $30 around, she'll profusely thank you for all you've done and tell you she understands.

Identical gifts, opposite reactions

Those two situations are financially **identical** from the tenant's viewpoint. In both cases, a tenant gets $30 a month. But with **your** tenant, the gift is met with absolute **silence**. And the end of the gift, by **anger**.

With **my** tenant, the reaction couldn't be more different. Profuse **gratitude**. Invitations to **supper**. **Hero** treatment on the local news. And sadness, but more thanks, when it ends. Plus by giving it to **my** tenant, you avoid all the problems of lost building value, resentment, attraction of other charity cases, etc.

Give **your** tenant a one-year, $30 a month gift, and you're a **bum** for stopping. Give **my** tenant a one-year, $30 a month gift, and you're John Baresford Tipton (the guy who gave away million dollar checks on the TV series "The Millionaire").

The moral of the story? Charge **all** your tenants fair market value. And do your charity giving **elsewhere**.

How can you tell who's needy

Another problem with making charitable contributions to your tenants in the form of low rents is that you **do not know** whether the tenant in question is needy or not.

People can **prove** they make **at least** such and such amount. Tenants have to prove their income when they apply for an apartment. Home buyers, when they apply for a mortgage. You can prove you make **at least** such and such amount. But no one can **prove** they make **less than** any amount.

They can't prove it because they can't prove they aren't **concealing sources of income**.

Are you going to even ask?

If you had the guts to ask a tenant to prove he or she was needy, the tenant would probably tell you to drop dead. "My private affairs!"

The **government** has the right to ask for proof of need when someone asks for assistance. But you do **not** have any such legal right.

And even if you did, you wouldn't do it anyway, would you? I suspect 99% of all the landlords who make charitable contributions in the form of below-market rents do so on the basis of a **guess**. On the basis of appearances.

Money in the mattress

Not all senior citizens are poor. We've all read stories of old people who lived as if they were poor. Then, when they died, tons of cash were discovered in a shopping bag or mattress or hidden in the wall.

I'm not suggesting that such stories are the rule. Just that appearances can be deceiving.

One apartment owner I met was giving a substantial rent break to a woman in her eighties. When she was in her nineties, he decided to convert the building to condominiums. He felt especially bad about the lady in her nineties. So he offered her a particularly generous relocation bonus.

Turned out the lady in her nineties didn't move. She bought her apartment—for cash.

Another actual case

Both husband and wife were over sixty-five. Both were totally disabled years before retirement. Social security was their only income source. Would you raise them to market rent?

How about if you knew they were my parents? I own a $700,000 home in California. Prior to 1992, I owned apartment buildings in Texas. Would you forego hundreds of dollars of income and even more building value for someone whose children could afford to help them pay market rent?

Actually, my parents owned their own home before they died so they were not in need of charity. But the point is many a senior or other tenant who appears in need of charity has resources which are not apparent. It may be their own money salted away somewhere. Or it may be affluent relatives. Or government programs which they have not availed themselves of.

Too proud to take charity

Many landlords have had the experience of a tenant requesting, or even **demanding**, some rent break because of some hardship. Then, when the landlord suggested they seek help from a government or charitable organization, the tenant said,

What!? I don't take handouts.

I guess handouts from landlords don't count. Indeed, many tenants "too proud" to take government or charitable organization handouts think they're **entitled** to handouts from landlords.

Gall bladder operation

A tenant once called to tell me at length about her gall bladder operation and how much money it cost. When I asked what all this had to do with me she said angrily, "You're the landlord!"

I politely but firmly informed her that health-insurance companies, not landlords, pay for gall bladder operations. And that if she did not pay her rent (she had asked for a two month rent holiday—not postponement), she'd be evicted.

I average about one hardship story per month when I owned fifty-eight units. I say, "No" to all of them. If I ever said, "Yes," I'd get **more** than one a month in the future. Until I lost the building for non-payment of the mortgage, that is.

Did you ever *lower* rents for charity

The proper way to contribute to charity is by charging fair market rents and giving to charity separately. Confucius say, "Man who run business like charity may **need** same in future."

Now that I've said that, I'll tell you that I **don't believe** those landlords who claim charity is the reason they don't raise rents on tenants who appear needy.

I think it's lack of guts.

The reason I say that is I've never heard of a landlord **lowering** rents because someone appeared needy. Suppose you bought one of **my** buildings. All the tenants have been raised to market—including little old ladies on walkers, etc. Would you **lower** them?

You allowed some of your "needy" tenants to fall $40 below market. Would you send any of my tenants $40 rent **de**crease notices? Even the little 90-year old lady with the walker? I didn't think so.

If you wouldn't **lower** them for charity, isn't it apparent that charity is **not** the reason you fail to **increase** them?

Guts

You wouldn't **raise** Mrs. Simpson from $360 to $400—even though $400 is market. But you would **accept** $400 a month from her if **I** had sent out the increase notice **before** you bought the building.

Isn't it the same $40? The same $400? If charity is your reason, why are you willing to take the $40 in one instance but not the other?

Isn't it just that you don't want to be the one who delivers the bad news? You're afraid someone will accuse you of being a heartless S.O.B. if you send Mrs. Simpson a $40 rent increase notice.

So it's not the $40 you mind. It's the heartless S.O.B. accusation.

Want to be liked

Landlords want to be liked. If they raise rents, people won't like them. Especially if they raise rents on people who appear needy.

They say money can't buy love. But it **can** buy a phony, shallow, as-long-as-the-dollars-keep-coming love. That is what hundreds of thousands of landlords are doing. It's not that they're charitable. Just insecure.

They'll take money from a ninety year old any day of the week. What they **won't** take, **can't** take, is criticism.

People applaud generosity. Helping the needy. And generosity is the mantle many landlords wrap themselves in when they explain why they don't raise all of their tenants to market rents.

I believe they are motivated by cowardice, not generosity. A desperate fear of criticism. A pathetic need to be liked. A need so powerful it blinds landlords to the true, buying-love nature of their actions.

If you need to be loved by everyone you do business with, you're in the wrong business. It is the destiny of landlords, umpires, IRS auditors, and all other bad news deliverers to be **dis**liked. It comes with the territory.

Not having the guts to raise rents to market may not "kill" you financially. But spare me the "I'm-too-charitable" explanation as to **why**. When you start **reducing** rents on needy tenants, I'll buy the charity bit—and ask you why you're not giving the money to needier people.

Summary on the charity excuse

Landlords have no obligation to give more to charity than anyone else. If you want to give to charity, you should give cash to needy members of your **family—or** to the **most needy non-family** members you can find. I guarantee that not even the neediest of your tenants will fall into that category.

You have neither the right nor the ability—no one has—to determine which of your tenants is **truly needy**. Charity in the form of below-market rent costs you **more** than the tenant benefits because of the effect on your **building value**. Charity in the form of below-market rents gets you **no gratitude** whatsoever. Rent control may force you to be charitable long after the needy tenant has left.

Your other tenants will resent the charity you showed their neighbors. Your charity will attract other charity cases.

There is nothing immoral or even uncharitable about renting apartments to the highest acceptable bidder. Run your business like a business and make any charitable contributions a totally **separate** activity.

What about the needy?

I made a speech which included my feelings about the charity excuse for not raising rents at the

California Apartment Association Convention. The audience contained a couple representatives of a state government housing agency. After the speech, one of them confronted me in front of a group of apartment owners who had converged to talk to me.

Regarding the needy, she demanded, *"Do you care?"*

Liberals have no right to demand that I recite a "loyalty oath to caring" on command. Nor do they have a right to demand public disclosure of my contributions to charity.

As for my opinion on what public policy toward the needy should be, it is this. The "first line of defense" should be the **families and friends** of the needy. The second "line of defense" should be **voluntary charities**.

If government is going to do anything, it should be to pay a guaranteed, minimum, cash income to those who cannot be helped any other way. There should be no government housing or any other programs to help legally competent, needy people. **In**competents like mentally ill, alcoholics, children, and so forth, need more than cash.

If **any**one has a **duty** to help needy tenants, then **every**one does. Landlords have no more duty than any other segment of society to subsidize the needy.

It is a double standard of absurd proportions for a liberal who gives $1,500 a year to charity and pays $2,500 in taxes to self-righteously denounce a landlord who gives $5,000 a year to charity and pays $11,000 in taxes for not subsidizing tenants. The compassion on which liberals claim to have a monopoly consists almost entirely of giving away **other people's** money.

6. The rent control excuse

If I raised rents as much as you say, I'd bring rent control to my town.

That's the rent control excuse. If we avoid big rent increases, the politicians will not impose rent control. But if we raised rents as much as we could, we'll get rent control.

The first thing that's wrong with that excuse is that **self-imposed** rent control has a similar effect to **government** rent control. It keeps you from getting market rents.

Same thing goes for voluntary rent control urged by the state or national apartment associations or such voluntary controls as President Carter's Wage and Price Guidelines. If you comply with them, they have the same effect on your rent income as **mandatory** controls. The logic is like trying to persuade a mugger not to stab you because you plan to stab yourself.

Power, not morality

Rent control pushers say they're against "rent gougers." That they're in favor of landlords getting a "reasonable return." And that the landlords who oppose controls only do so out of greed.

That's a bunch of nonsense.

Rent control is nothing but a power play. If the pro-rent control forces in your town are more powerful than the anti-rent control forces, you'll have rent control. Period.

Rent control has nothing to do with greed, "gouging," need, or any of that.

Not for the poor

Rent control is supposed to help the poor, right? So how come there are only two rent control laws (in Los Angeles and Beverly Hills) which exempted **luxury** apartments?

And why do they have rent control in Palm Springs, California? But **not** in Detroit or Philadelphia?

I'll tell you why. Rent control is a way for tenants to get a bargain. Nothing more. Nothing less. What kind of tenants want a bargain? **All** kinds.

But not everybody gets what they want. Who **does** get what they want? People who know how to pull the levers of power. Namely **higher income people**.

The day San Francisco got rent control

They tried to pass rent control in San Francisco several times. It lost every time. Then a landlord named Angelo Sangiacomo raised all of his rents on the same day. I know because I was one of his tenants at the time. My raise was typical—55%. Sangiacomo was one of the biggest landlords in San Francisco. Most of his apartments were luxury high rise.

The building I lived in was 1000 Chestnut Street—a corner which is often used by movie and television crews to film scenes—because the cable cars go by the front door and there's a panoramic view of Alcatraz and San Francisco Bay. Every postcard rack in the city has a shot from that corner.

The parking garage is full of Mercedes and Cadillacs. Maids fill the building on weekdays. Dick Van Dyke was living there when I moved out. Liberace stayed down the hall one night while we were there. You'd pass the mayor in the lobby on his way to parties in the building.

When the **poor** people of San Francisco wanted rent control, they got nowhere. But when Angelo Sangiacomo raised the rent on the tenants in 1000 Chestnut Street and his other luxury building, San Francisco had rent control within three weeks. (By the way, I fought rent control and became very unpopular with my fellow tenants as a result.)

Doesn't that prove that rent increases bring rent controls?

You may cite San Francisco's experience as perfect evidence that rent increases **do** bring rent controls. I disagree.

San Francisco got rent control because it is a **left-leaning city**, Sangiacomo's tenants were particularly adept at using power, and because Sangiacomo made a **tactical** error.

I spoke to the California Apartment Association the Fall before Sangiacomo's March rent increase. I urged the audience to charge fair market. But I warned them to **never raise all their tenants on the same day**. I said,

You'll have instant tenants' union, rent strikes, and meetings in the lobby.

When Sangiacomo raised all 1500 of his tenants in one day, the Trinity Tenants Union formed (Trinity Properties was the name of Sangiacomo's company). I spoke out against rent control at a meeting in our lobby at which a rent strike was proposed. There was no rent strike because they got rent control.

How tenants react to large increases

When a tenant gets a large rent increase, he knocks on his neighbor's door and says,

Did you get one of these?

If the answer is, "No," he's just another guy who got his rent raised. The neighbor will sympathize. But he won't join any action because he doesn't want to trigger a similar or worse increase on himself.

But if the answer is, "Yes," the **two** increases will go to a **third** door and ask, "Did you get one of these?" And so it goes. Instant tenants union.

You should **raise one twelfth of your tenants per month**, ideally. That keeps the number of angry tenants to a minimum each month.

In some markets, like student and one-season resort areas, there is a single increase date—like August 31. The high annual turnover in those markets reduces the risk of tenant organizing somewhat. But student markets are high risk in general when it comes to rent control.

I believe that if Sangiacomo had heeded the advice I gave in my San Francisco speech six months before his increase, San Francisco would not now have rent control.

By the way, I understand he raised everyone so much so fast because he believed rent control would eventually win. He wanted to get his rent up before the base date was established. If he had followed my advice to constantly keep his rents at the level which produced a 5% vacancy rate, only small increases would have been necessary.

Rent control is a mugging

Rent control is a mugging of landlords by tenants usually abetted by their politician allies. Politically, tenants are bigger and more powerful than landlords. That's why nearly all rent control laws exempt three-unit or smaller buildings—to reduce the number of landlords who'll fight it. By controlling only four-unit or bigger buildings, the rent control advocates maximize the imbalance between landlords and tenants.

The driving forces behind rent control are:

- Class hatred
- Envy
- Leftist ideology, and
- The attraction of something for nothing.

The leaders use the rent control issue to advance their own careers or to simply go on an activist jag for its own sake. There is **no morality** involved. In spite of the fact that the rent control pushers proclaim themselves to be on the side of the angels.

'Economic racism'

Rent-control debates are a sort of "**economic racism**." Laws are supposed to prohibit certain **actions**. But **racist** laws only prohibit certain **groups of people** from engaging in actions which are legal for everyone else.

Southern laws requiring blacks to go to the back of the bus were not laws against the **action** of occupying the front of a bus. Rather they were laws against being black. Nazi laws prohibiting Jews from owning real estate were not laws against the action of owning a business. Rather they were laws against being Jewish.

And American laws prohibiting landlords from renting to the highest acceptable bidder are not laws against the action of accepting the highest bid. Rather they are laws against being a landlord. Just as Southern whites could occupy the front of the bus and Gentiles could own real estate in Nazi Germany, so can American tenants and homeowners sell to the highest bidder.

If "gouging" were against the law—and not just "**rent** gouging," the jails would be so full of home sellers there'd be no room for landlords.

So don't ever feel you're on the less noble side of the rent control battle. Rent control is an outrage. There is no nobility on the pro-rent control side.

Power, not increases

If rent increases bring rent controls, then you ought to be able to see rent increases in the statistics of cities which have rent control, right? Let's look.

Here's what happened in one city during the three years before rent control was imposed.

Year	1966	1967	1968
Rent increase	2.8%	1.0%	2.7%
CPI increase	2.9%	2.9%	3.6%

Every year, the Consumer Price Index went up **faster** than rents. The city's landlords should have gotten **medals**, right? That was Boston. They didn't get medals. They got rent controls. Mayoral candidate Kevin White ran on a pro-rent control campaign. He got elected and remained mayor until 1983.

Did "going easy" on the rent increases help Boston landlords stave off rent control? Nope. All it got them was **lower base rents**.

Another city

Here's another city.

Year	1972	1973	1974
Rent increase	3.6%	.8%	5.9%
CPI increase	3.3%	6.2%	11.0%

Did **those** landlords get medals for holding rent increases down? No. That's Washington, DC. They got rent control in 1974.

One more city

Now look at this city.

Year	1975	1976	1977
Rent increase	7.9%	11.8%	11.2%
CPI increase	9.1%	5.8%	6.5%

These landlords raised rents **more** than inflation in '76 and '77. They got rent control in '77 or '78, right?

Wrong. This is Houston. Never had rent control. And not coincidentally, Houston probably had the lowest rents in the nation during the eighties.

So why did Boston and DC get rent control in spite of **less**-than-CPI rent increases—and Houston did **not** get rent controls in spite of **greater**-than-CPI rent increases? Because rent control is caused by **liberals, not rent increases**.

Massachusetts and DC gave George McGovern his only electoral votes in 1972. He was the most liberal major party presidential candidate ever. Those areas voted for rent control for the same reason they voted for McGovern. They like that kind of stuff. They **don't** like it in Houston.

To avoid rent control, don't avoid rent increases, avoid left-leaning communities. There's a chapter on how to do that in my book, *Residential Property Acquisition Handbook* (www.johntreed.com/reibooks.html).

'Protection money'

If you charge less than market rents to stave off rent control, the rent you lose is "protection money." Big city candy store owners pay protection money to avoid trouble. And so do landlords who hold their rents down to avoid rent control. Using the threat of rent control to get below-market rents is a form of blackmail or extortion. And you know what they say about the wisdom of paying blackmailers.

Larry Levy is a prominent apartment manager in Connecticut. Regarding holding rents down to stave off rent control, he says he'd rather **fight strong**. Fighting rent control takes money. Holding rents down artificially is a massive "contribution" to the war chest of the **other side**.

If you want to use rents to fight rent control, charge fair market rents and give the difference to your local anti-rent control organization.

7. 'I'm making a profit.'

The last excuse I've heard for not charging market rent is the I'm-making-a-profit excuse. The owner has a positive cash flow. So he figures he doesn't **need** rent increases.

Without even looking at his books I can tell you he's earning a **lousy return on equity**. In today's market, positive cash flow comes partly from good management and mostly from lousy leverage.

Is the guy who won't raise his rents because of his positive cash flow a good manager? Heck, no! The first rule of good management is get your rents up to market. So I know without looking that his positive cash flow comes from lousy leverage. His loan-to-value ratio is probably 50% or less.

As a result of the combination of below-market rents and lousy leverage, that owner is getting a lousy return on equity. His positive cash flow divided by his current equity probably shows a return of about seven percent—or less. His tax benefits are shot because he's owned the property for more than four or five years.

He gets maybe a four percent appreciation per year if he at least raises his rents that much. Multiplied by the leverage of factor of two (assuming a 50% loan-to-value ratio), that appreciation gives him a return on equity of eight percent. Add that to the seven percent from cash flow and you have a total return of fifteen percent.

That's less than he could get investing in discounted second mortgages. Yet he's putting up with the extra hassles and risks of rental property ownership. Like I said, a lousy return.

The real reasons owners don't raise

Above are the seven excuses owners and managers give for not raising rents to market. The **real** reasons are:

- Fear of criticism
- Laziness.

I said I saw nothing wrong with the no-hassle approach to property management—as long as you recognized that you don't need to go overboard. If you want to avoid hassles, let your rents fall **a little** behind market. But if you're **lazy**, get into another line of investing—like discounted mortgages or some such.

Same goes for people who need to be loved by everyone they meet. The landlord business isn't for you.

Excuses for not *lowering* rents

I've just given you the seven excuses landlords give for not **raising** rents. But as I said in the signs of low rents chapter, there are also times when you have rents which are too **high**. When that happens you need to lower rents. Landlords don't like to do that. And here are the three excuses they give for not lowering rents.

1. 'There are only so many tenants to go around.'

Some landlords condemn rent cutting on the grounds that there is a fixed number of tenants. If one landlord cuts his rents, the argument goes, the other landlords will have to do the same. The number of tenants in the area will stay the same. But the amount of rent collected by the landlords in the area will go down. And the average vacancy rate in the area will stay the same. All the landlords will have accomplished by the rent cut was cutting their own throats. By "sticking together" and not cutting rents, the landlords will make more money.

That analysis is dead wrong. It contains a mistake that you should have learned not to make in Economics 101. The notion that there are only so many tenants to go around would be called "inelastic demand" in an economics class. In other words, demand for apartments and rental houses is constant at 30,000 units or whatever in your market.

That's incorrect. Demand for residential rentals is **elastic**. That means it expands and contracts as rents fall or rise.

If all the landlords in a market with high vacancies lower their rents, the amount of occupied space in that market will increase. Crudely speaking, it's called "undoubling." More precisely, tenants expand the amount of space they occupy.

Leaving home

When a one-bedroom apartment was $300 a month, Billy stayed at his parents' home where he paid just $150 board. He couldn't afford $300 a month.

But when the landlord dropped the rent to $250, Billy moved out to the apartment. He could afford $250. Here's the change in square footage occupied by Billy and his Mom and Dad.

Total square feet occupied by Billy and parents when he was at home: 1,500
Square feet **per person**: 1,500 ÷ 3 = **500**

Total square feet occupied by Billy and his parents after he moved out: 1,500 home +
    700 apartment = 2,200
Square feet **per person**: 2,200 ÷ 3 = **733.33**

Did the number of tenants increase? No. Did the number of square feet of occupied housing in the community increase? You bet. By 233.33 ÷ 500 = 47% for these three people!

Did the income of the landlord who got Billy go **down** as a result of the rent cut? Heck no! The apartment was vacant before. It now generates $250 a month. An **infinite** increase over the zero it previously generated.

The den

Bob and Mary live in a one-bedroom apartment that rents for $300 a month. The landlord gives notice that because of overbuilding and high vacancy rates in the area, he's lowering their rent to $250.

They could stay and put $50 in the bank each month. Or they could move up to a better apartment and keep paying their previous rent. They ask what you get for $300 a month under the new rent schedule in the same apartment complex. "A **two**-bedroom apartment with a fireplace," they're told. They're comfortable with $300 a month. Don't know offhand what they'd do with the extra $50 cash each month. And they've been a little cramped. So they move to the two-bedroom apartment. Here's the change in square feet occupied.

In the one-bedroom: 700 square feet ÷ 2 people = 350 square feet per person

In the two-bedroom: 850 square feet ÷ 2 people = 425 square feet per person

Any increase in the number of tenants? No. Any increase in the amount of space occupied? You bet. The landlord who previously had a vacant two-bedroom now has an occupied two-bedroom and a vacant one bedroom. And since the lower one-bedroom rent appeals to more people—like Billy above—it will fill up and the landlord's revenue from the two apartments will go from

$0 (two-bedroom) + $300 (one-bedroom) = $300 **before** the rent cut

to

$300 (2-br after) + $250 (1-br after) = $550 **after** the rent cut.

Other undoublers

Lower rents have numerous other effects which cause the occupied amount of space to increase:

- **Home ownership** becomes less attractive so people stay in or move to apartments or rental houses
- The area looks better to **companies** who want to relocate
- **Roommates** split up and get their own place
- Long-term tenants like businessmen on extended assignment switch to apartments.

Antitrust laws

Then there are the antitrust laws. Banding together to prop up prices violates federal Sherman and Clayton Antitrust Acts (www.stolaf.edu/people/becker/antitrust/statutes.html) and many state laws. Laws which carry Draconian penalties. Any landlord organization newsletter or magazine which carried a letter or article or comment in which refraining from cutting rents was mentioned could find itself looking down the wrong end of a civil antitrust suit or a criminal indictment.

Dissenters

If price-fixing agreements were legal, they still wouldn't work. I, for one, would refuse to go along. No doubt, many others would, too. And the cartel members who refused to cut rents would lose all their tenants to the dissenters.

The principle of substitution

Even if price-fixing were legal—and you could get everyone to go along—as OPEC did for a time—price-fixing still wouldn't work because of the economic principle of substitution. That is, people can always substitute product B for product A if the price of product A goes up.

With OPEC, by fixing prices at a high level, OPEC drove away customers. Instead of buying OPEC oil, people bought smaller cars, sweaters, day/night thermostats, insulation, etc. Result? The oil glut they thought we'd never see again.

By the same token, if landlords tried to hold rents up artificially, people would substitute home ownership, Murphy beds, mobilehomes, moving farther out in the country, moving to a lower rent region, and a dozen other things for renting the expensive apartments.

Just as OPEC drove part of its customers away forever (insulation, for example, **permanently** reduces a building's need for energy), an artificial propping up of residential rents would have the same effect—a long term reduction in demand for the price-fixing landlords.

2. 'But I have *plenty* of tenants paying the rents you say are too high!'

Tell a 50-unit apartment building owner that the rents in his 15% vacant building are too high and he's likely to say,

Baloney! I know $300 a month is not too high because I've got 42 tenants paying that amount right now.

Wrong. If you have 15% vacancy, your rents are too high. Over time, those 42 tenants who are paying too much will slowly wise up and move. Some of them would probably pay the too-high rent for years. But that's not reason enough to not lower rents. It's penny wise and pound foolish to suffer huge, unnecessary vacancy losses in order to avoid a small rent decrease in your still-occupied apartments.

Typically, you can fill a building with a high vacancy rate by cutting the rents only a **small** amount, like 3% to 6%. Simple math says you should do it. Here are the numbers on a 50-unit building with a 15% vacancy rate before a 6% rent cut and after that rent cut lowers the vacancy rate to 5%.

Before rent cut
42 occupied units @ $300 = **$12,600**

After rent cut
47 occupied units @ $280 = **$13,160**

Sure, some of the old tenants would have kept on paying the $300. When I lowered one tenant, she said she'd have preferred improved maintenance instead. (We fixed her maintenance requests.) But a 50-unit owner will make more money with a rent amount that pleases 47 people than with one that 42 people are happy with.

3. 'You never lower prices.'

Some landlords just believe that you never lower prices. It may be their ego won't let them. Or that they've glommed onto the notion that you never lower prices with unquestioning religious-type faith.

Wherever it came from, the idea that you never lower prices is simply wrong. The only way it could be right is if no one ever made a mistake on **initial** pricing and if market conditions **never changed**. Obviously neither of those describes the real world.

4

Advertising

Classified advertising

When you receive notice that a tenant is moving, you should place a classified ad. If you have so many rental units that you **always** have a vacancy or a notice, the ad should run continuously.

Some big complexes use newspaper **display ads**. A display ad is one with a photo or drawing, special type styles, logos, and all that. **Classified** ads have only words in standard type.

I don't believe in display ads. Here I'll remind you that biggest complex I ever managed was 200 units. It may be that 400-unit complexes **should** use display ads. But we did **not** need them in our 200-unit complex.

Display ads are **very** expensive. **Classified** ads in newspapers are cheaper but still too expensive. The Internet is about to blow them away. You can place huge ads for your vacancies on the Internet for little or no charge.

Wording the ad

Your newspaper classified ad should state the **bare facts** and no more. That means

- Location (neighborhood or town)
- Number of bedrooms (separate ad for each size may be best)
- Who pays utilities
- Special features like washer/dryer in each unit
- Phone number
- Whether furnished (if there's not a separate classification for furnished apartments)
- Important policies like no pets or adults only (where allowed by law)

Rent amount and **address** are optional. I like to include the rent to eliminate some phone calls. William Nickerson, author of *How I Turned $1,000 Into $5,000,000 in Real Estate in My Spare Time*, says a number of studies have shown that it's **best to put the rent amount in the ad**.

Although it's amazing how many people ask you the rent amount even when it's in the paper and they're calling with the ad in their hand. "Must see to appreciate" is a ridiculous line. That's the theory behind leaving off the rent. Although in some markets stating the rent in the paper just isn't done.

I also think it's a good idea to include the address. But some people like to screen tenants over the phone first. That may be sensible. In his book, *Practical Apartment Management*, Ed Kelley is very big on giving directions. And, he says most apartment ad directions are inadequate. People who try to follow them get lost. So he advocates very detailed directions and even to-scale maps if people still get lost. Note that Kelley manages huge complexes for the most part.

Internet ad

In the Internet, you generally get a large amount of space. Plus you can link to your own Web site where you have almost unlimited space.

Yahoo (http://edit.classifieds.yahoo.com) is one of the most popular Internet classified sections. It's free. Yahoo gives you a bunch of blanks which you fill out—stuff like address, number of bedrooms and bathrooms, and so forth. Yahoo gives you a lot more room than the typical newspaper classified ad. In addition, they let you link your classified ad to your own Web site. At that Web site you can put maps, pictures, floor plans, and so forth. The more information you give the better.

Yahoo has a few twists on the usual classified ad. For example, you can specify "Firm," "Best offer," or "negotiable" rather than state a rent. Here is the information you should put on the Internet about your rentals. If you cannot get it into the classified ad format itself, put it at your Web site.

Other Internet apartment-for-rent sites include www.rent.net, www.apartmentsplus.com, www.allapartments.com, and www.classifieds2000.com.

Information to put at your Web site

- map of your property and surrounding area
- interior and exterior photos of your property
- fill-in-the-blank copy of your lease
- fill-in-the-blank copy of your rental application
- floor plans of your units
- photos of neighborhood features
- fill-in-the-blank maintenance-request form
- directions to your property
- links to community organizations, schools, government
- your complex newsletter (if any)
- emergency-contact numbers
- your policies
- fill-in-the-blank employment applications
- links to other related sites
- local school information
- local crime information
- frequently-asked questions

Should you have your own Web site? Absolutely. It's now a necessity. How do you set up a Web site? Read the excellent book *The Non-Designer's Web Book* by Robin Williams and John Tollett. The basic idea is you need a modem ($100 device which lets a computer hook up to the phone lines), an Internet Service Provider (ISP, America On Line is the most famous. I use www.verio.com which costs me $45 a month), and a Web-authoring program (I use Adobe PageMill which costs $100).

You create pages for your Web site in your computer with the Web-authoring program then send them to your Web site over the phone. Anyone in the world can view your Web pages from their computer. After you set up your Web site, you need to register it with the main search engines. That is, you have to tell the search engines that your Web pages exist and their address. Do that at sites like www.submit-it.com or addme.com. The search engines then list your pages. Some read every word in your page periodically and remember them. If you do not register your pages, you have the Web equivalent of an unlisted phone number. If you register them, anyone in the world searching for a word or phrase that appears at your site will find you.

In 1998, a new Web language called XML is supposed to come out. When it does, you need to set up at least some of your apartment for rent Web pages in XML's standard format for rentals. XML will let prospective tenants search the Net by number of bedrooms, location, rent amount, and so forth. XML will likely kill off all other forms of apartment-for-rent ads.

You can get maps and directions into your Web site by linking to certain directories. For example, go to www2.switchboard.com and search for your own property. That will produce a map with a red pin labelled with the phrase or address you searched for stuck at your location on the map. At the top of the browser screen, you will find the address of that map of your property. Copy it by dragging your cursor over it. It will be too long to transcribe. Then paste it into your Web page as a link to the word "map." Because you are linking rather than copying the page itself, you do not need to get copyright permission to do this.

You can get some school information from www.2001beyond.com, www.nrs.com, or www.schoolmatch.com. You may want to link to one or more of those sites.

Test

You should fiddle with the wording of any classified ad you run. Change one word or phrase one week and see if it improves response. Ideally, you would do a **split run test**.

That means every other paper has a different version of your ad—but in the exact same position in the paper. Call one version A and the other B. You then ask each caller and visitor which ad they are responding to. By printing both ads the same day in the same position, you eliminate the possibility of mistakenly concluding that this week's ad wording was better than last week's ad when in fact the increase in traffic was due to better weather this week than last.

If your paper won't let you do a split run test, you might run two different ads the same day in every paper. And see which generates the most calls. Keep in mind that the first ad may pull better just because it comes first in the paper.

The ad that does best becomes your champion. Then, whenever you get an idea that might improve response, you do a split run test of the new ad versus the champion. If it wins, you have a new champion. If it loses, the old champion retains its crown.

Abbreviations

As a rule, you want to keep the ad as short as possible—to keep the cost down. Although there's no point in not filling every part of it if there's a minimum number of lines.

Abbreviations help you keep it short. But you have to be careful. Most people understand some abbreviations like br for bedroom—especially if it's in an apartment or house for rent ad and follows a number like 1, 2, or 3. But many people do **not** understand other abbreviations. A well-known Broadway play is called "6 RMS RV VU" mocking the typical efforts of landlords to save money by shortening words in the extreme in classified ads. Here are some examples I don't understand from the **Fort Worth Star-Telegram**.

"all appl."—Probably means "all appliances." But what does **that** mean? Does it have a microwave oven? A Cuisinart? "1-1"—One bedroom, one bath, I suspect. "wbfp"—"With brick fireplace?" "h/a"—"heat and air-conditioning?"

Maybe people in Fort Worth all know what these abbreviations mean. But I don't. And I doubt that the landlords running these ads are willing to write off all those moving in from out of town. So they probably ought to expand these abbreviations until they become understandable by all but a few.

Abbreviate where you can. But not so much that you fail to communicate.

Words to leave *out of* your ads

Do not use words in the ad which repeat the classification. For example, if you run an ad under "unfurnished apartments for rent," don't waste space and money with words like, "Available," "Apt.," and "unfurn."

And don't use words which are otherwise superfluous like "phone" in front of the phone number. Here are some examples of superfluous words from that same **Star-Telegram**.

"deposit"—Since requiring a deposit is the rule rather than the exception, leave it off. If you **don't** require a deposit, it's a special feature which you **should** include. But you should also have your head examined.

"appliances"—Gee, thanks. If it didn't have appliances, it'd be under "hotels," not apartments.

"complex"—That **could** be to distinguish a duplex from a complex. But who **prefers** a complex?

"leasing"—I'll bet that's why you have an ad under "apartments for rent."

No white space

There should be no white space in a classified ad. If you pay for three lines, you should **fill** three lines. When I was a real estate salesman, I made a grid which had a box for each letter I was allowed in our firm's three-line-house-for-sale ads. For example, one line of the one paper's classified ad columns is 24 characters wide. Looking at the paper, they apparently have a minimum of two lines. So I'd make a grid like this:

Then when I composed an ad, I'd fill in the grid **in pencil**. If the words I chose did not use all the space, I'd erase one or two and try another combination. The objective is to make use of **all** the space you're paying for. In that example, you have to **pay** for 48 characters whether you use them or not. So you might as well use them. You could also create this Grid on a computer spread sheet program.

Don't gush

Don't gush. That is, don't use subjective adjectives like "nice" or "exclusive" or "a lot to offer."

And don't exaggerate. It's OK to say "secluded" if it really is. If you exaggerate though, a perfectly nice place will **disappoint** prospects. There's only one way to do a good job yet still have unhappy customers. That's by **promising more than you deliver**.

Your apartments or rental houses are probably very nice in their own way. Fine. Tell the ad readers what you've got without exaggeration and they'll rent up.

If you exaggerate in some ways, you'll attract the wrong group of prospects. For example, if you advertise "affordable," but don't give the rent, you'll attract low-income people. Stating the rent would be a better way of conveying affordability.

Which paper?

You may have more than one newspaper. In my Dallas area building, the former owner advertised in the *Dallas Times*. One month, I asked my manager to try the local weekly paper.

We got **more** calls and visitors. And the ads cost **half** as much per month.

The point is to experiment with the various papers if you have more than one.

Your sign

I'm a great believer in signs. I also try to buy apartment buildings which have a high visibility location. "Secluded" apartment buildings may attract some tenants. But it's hard to get prospects to **see** the place.

One building I managed in New Jersey was way back in a single-family neighborhood. Nice place to live. But next to zero visibility. We had to rent sign space on nearby high-traffic roads to direct people to the complex. That's an extra expense you can do without.

What's worse, sometimes sign space is not available. Either the best property owners won't allow it. Or the property owners will allow it, but the city won't. So beware of hard-to-find buildings when you buy. A high visibility building is like having a free ad.

Permanent sign

Your permanent sign is the one that's up whether you have a vacancy or not. It usually just contains the name of your building—and maybe the street number, and a description of the kind of units you have. For example:

Holly Apartments
One and Two Bedroom

Should your small building have a name?

Large buildings nearly always have names. But many smaller buildings do not. Should they?

Generally, I think so. But I would not name a duplex or triplex. Maybe a fourplex. But when you get to five or six units, I think a well-chosen name can help and rarely hurts.

- I bought a twelve-unit once. It had no name. Just a street number. I named it "The Holly Apartments." And got good feedback about it from the tenants.

Names are highly subjective. So I can't pinpoint beneficial effects. But I **suspect** the name increased the value of the place—both for renting and for selling.

Changing the name

Other complexes I've purchased were named the Greenbriar, the Las Brisas, and the Fleur de Villa. I liked the Greenbriar and Las Brisas names and kept them. But I thought the Fleur de Villa was the pits. No two creditors spelled it the same way on bills. It was the:

- Flew de Villa, or
- Floor de Ville, or
- Fleur de Ville, etc.

Plus the language bothered me. "Fleur de Villa" means "flower of the village" in French. But most Americans are more familiar with the French word "Ville" than "Villa." And the correct pronunciation of "Fleur" is hard for Americans. That building is now The Cottonwoods. There are some cottonwood trees on the property. I also hate names made up from the first syllables of the owner's names. Like when Marvin and Joan buy a building and call it the "Mar-Jo Apartments." Ugh!

A not-so-hot name is one reason for changing. Another reason would be a **bad** reputation. For example, you might buy a building which is full of bad tenants and has a corresponding reputation. In that case, changing the name would be an appropriate part of a turnaround—along with getting rid of the bad tenants and posting an "under new management" sign.

How do you change the name? Just have the sign repainted. You should also file a fictitious or assumed name registration with the municipal or county government. In some areas, not doing that can prevent you from winning court cases against tenants—if the lease lists The Cottonwoods or whatever as the landlord. But in most cities, you don't have to ask anyone's permission to change the name. It's **your** building.

Sign design

Your main sign establishes the image of your building. A sign painted by an **amateur** says, "This is a sloppy building." A **professionally** painted, but unimaginative sign says, "This is your basic building—nothing special."

Since a quality sign is relatively inexpensive, you should have one. Signs draw the eye. A 30-square-foot sign is more important than, say, 30 square feet of siding.

Basics

Remember the sign's purpose. It should be **readable** to passers by. Both in cars and on foot. Cars are more important in most locations. That means the sign and its letters must be **large** enough to be seen and read by people driving by. That, in turn, means you can't put very much on the sign. The name of the building and the street number for sure. Maybe the number of bedrooms or the fact that it's an apartment building. You might need to say, "apartments," if the name does not include that word. "The Cottonwoods," for example, could be the name of a condominium.

Lighting

If the sign is not lit up, it's useless at night. So it probably should be lit up. Not that you'll have many **prospects** coming to look at apartments at night. But the sign also greets your tenants when they come home—and helps **their** visitors find the place. Do not put your own lights up if the sign is visible at night due to light from a street light or some other non-sign light. Check with your municipality. They often require a special permit for illuminated signs.

Letters

Avoid raised letters. Signs with attached letters are almost always vandalized—unless they are high up on a wall. Even then, birds nest in them. Or they get blown off.

This country is full of signs with letters missing.

Hol y Apa tme ts

says something about the management of the building. Signs like that turn off prospects and embarrass tenants. Repairing it only solves the problem until the next kid goes to work on the sign. I recommend that you stick to either **painted on or engraved** letters.

Type face

There are zillions of letter styles. And each makes a statement. When I bought the Greenbriar Apartments, their sign used English Times style letters with an extra extension on the leg of each R.

It looked something like this:

$$\mathcal{The}$$
GREENBRIAR

I changed it to this:

$$\mathcal{The\ Greenbriar}$$

How did I come up with the new version? I went to a local art supply store. They have a couple catalogs of all the type styles known to man. I leafed through them until I found the one I wanted. As I recall, I used the capital T and G from one style, and the lower case letters from another, similar style.

The store sold me a sheet of press-on letters of those two styles. I went home and pressed them on a sheet of white paper and I was in business. First, I sent the logo to a business card printer. They printed business cards for the manager. Then I sent a business card to the sign maker. And they reproduced the letters exactly on the new sign.

Getting the sign made

Sign making is an **art**. Whenever you need art, the best way to get it is to find something you like—and find out who did it.

My twelve-unit building had no name or sign. Just a pair of dime-store house numbers nailed to a couple of pillars on the front porch.

I knew I wanted a sign saying "Holly Apartments." But I wanted it to be a good one. So I looked around for a sign I liked. Finally, one appeared on a lawyer's office up the street. I went in, complimented them on their sign, and asked who did it. The secretary rooted around and came up with the sign painter's name.

I went to his shop and told him what I wanted. I don't have a picture. So I'll describe it as best I can.

'Wow!'

This was a colonial-period town in New Jersey. So I got a sign with a scroll-shaped top and bottom and milled spindles on each side. Milled spindles are like the balusters (vertical supports) on a stair railing. The words "Holly Apartments" were painted in black Olde English letters with a gold leaf trim line around each letter. Ditto the street number. And there was a green holly leaf with two red berries on it.

The sign painter put several coats of acrylic coating on it so it glistened as if it were freshly painted. When we were putting it up, a tenant came home. "Wow!" was her comment upon seeing it.

You don't have to be an *artiste* to get a "wow" sign. But like a Supreme Court Justice, you do have to "know what you like." Just scour the countryside looking for a sign you like. Then find out who made it, contact him, and ask his to do a similar sign for you. The more signs you look at before selecting one, the better your sign will be.

Engraved signs

At the moment, I'm partial to engraved signs. My Greenbriar sign was engraved. I got it from Southwood Corporation, P.O. Box 240457, Charlotte, NC 28224 800-438-6302 (704-588-5000 in NC). I recommend them.

They take your design, or help you with the design. In my case, they used an opaque projector to project my business card letters on to the sign. An opaque projector is one which allows you to project a book or other non-transparent item on to a wall or screen. That's how they match the letter style exactly.

Then they either sandblast or rout out the letters. Get their catalog to see what I mean.

Southwood, of course, is not the only sign company that does this. But they market actively to apartment owners. And don't let the fact that they're in North Carolina throw you off. The Greenbriar is in Texas.

Southwood and other companies can also make other signs which match your main sign. Like signs directing tenants to the manager's office, pool rules, hours, etc. Having them all coordinated is a good idea.

Mounting the sign

The mounting that holds the sign up is almost as important as the sign. The original Greenbriar sign was a piece of sheet metal mounted on two galvanized pipes. Two flood lights hung out over the sign on their metal electrical conduits. It looked as bad as it sounds.

We mounted the new sign on two white brick pillars—more or less matching the building's white brick veneer. And we installed two recessed flood lights **inside** the brick pillars. A tremendous improvement. Here are photos of the before and after.

Before

After

You find sign mounting ideas and contractors the same way you find sign painters. Look around for one you like. Beware, however, of **the Hong Kong Suit Syndrome**. That's where you combine a sign from "column A" with a mounting from "column B" and the result looks terrible. It's best that you see the whole schmear together beforehand. Because a sign that looks great and a mounting that looks great may **not** look great when combined.

Vacancy signs

Small buildings should have vacancy signs. To tell the world they have a vacancy. Larger buildings do **not** need vacancy signs, because they **always** have vacancies. Twenty to twenty-five units is about the break point where vacancy signs stop making sense.

If you have more than one unit size, you might want to have more than one vacancy sign. Or better yet, a sign with a changeable number. So you can put a one or a two or three in front of the word "bedroom." Your phone number might also be hung on the vacancy sign. That saves your manager from being bothered by calls when the building's full. But only **small** buildings (twenty-units or less) should be full for any length of time. So only small buildings should have phone numbers on temporary signs.

The vacancy sign could be attached by S hooks or those clips you use on a dog's chain or by some sort of drop-in-a-hole arrangement on top of the main sign. Only motels need "no vacancy" signs.

Sign budget

You ought to have a sign which costs about two-tenths of a percent of what the building's worth. For example, a million dollar building rates a $2,000 sign. That's not hard and fast. But I wanted to give you a rule of thumb to get those of you with overly cheap signs to take action.

Traffic report

You may want to make use of a traffic report. That's where you keep track of calls and visits by prospective tenants. It's the kind of bureaucracy I dislike. But if you're having a leasing problem, you may want to require it to pinpoint the cause. Or your resident manager may want to keep a traffic log for her own information. Here's my daily traffic report:

Cottonwoods Daily Report

Day of week: MONDAY   Date: June 24, 91

	Phone calls	Visit groups:		
Sign			Laundry take:	14.50
Referral			Leases signed:	
Newspaper ad	4	2	Move-outs today:	
Unknown			Other comments:	
Weather:	Hot	97°		
Applications received:		1		
Move-ins today:		1	– MASHBURN –110	

D. M. Manager
Manager's signature

To find out the source, ask the caller, "How did you hear about The Cottonwoods (or whatever)?" Often, for one reason or another, you won't get that information. Put those under unknown.

I deliberately left two extra blank lines under both phone calls and visits. That's because from time to time you try some other advertising medium. Or you get a prospect from an oddball source like the *Yellow Pages.*

You want to distinguish between phone calls and visits. Because a large number of phone calls which are not followed up by visits indicates a problem with finding the building, or telephone technique, or an exterior appearance which turns off would-be visitors, etc.

There's a line labelled "Weather" because bad weather affects traffic. And you won't remember what the weather was if you don't write it down. Mistaking weather-caused bad traffic for another problem can cause you to make a bad decision.

Yellow Pages

I don't believe in the *Yellow Pages* for apartment advertising. There may be some special situations where the *Yellow Pages* are important. But generally, they're not. That means you should have the **minimum listing**.

The *Yellow Pages* is a sneaky expense. They tell you what it costs when you first order the ad. But then it's buried in your phone bill forever after. That makes it easy to forget. Plus, they keep renewing it each year. You have to remember to tell them to stop.

Miscellaneous advertising media

Signs, classified ads, and the Internet are the primary ways to advertise apartments. There are also

- Radio and TV
- Real estate agents
- Rental services
- Bulletin boards
- Apartment guides
- Direct mail
- Contacts with key people.

Radio and TV

Radio and TV are very expensive. If they **ever** make sense, it would only be for filling many vacancies in a large complex. Like when a new building opens. Plus, you can be overwhelmed by the response to radio and TV advertising. Builders have run radio and TV ads in which an on-air personality promised to be at the Chateau Village Apartments (for example), only to find that the two leasing agents on duty couldn't begin to handle the crush of people who showed up.

Real estate agents

Do **not** let a real estate agent who normally sells houses handle leasing of your properties. I repeat, do **not** let a real estate agent who normally sells houses handle leasing of your properties.

You can tell them the importance of checking credit thoroughly until you're blue in the face. They will ignore you. They will ignore you even if they **agree** with you that checking credit is important. They will ignore you even if they swear on a stack of Bibles that they'll thoroughly check credit.

The reason is that leasing commissions are far **smaller** than house selling commissions. But the time required to do a proper job of leasing is not much less. Agents resent spending a lot of time for such a small commission. Where do they cut corners? On the credit check. The typical house-selling agent will turn over the key to an apartment or rental house to anyone who will sign a lease and hand over a check. When an agent who worked for a company I worked for did that—after she had **promised** to let me check the credit first—her explanation was, "But you don't understand. These tenants were in a hurry to move in." To which I thundered **my** reply,

> **No, you are the one who does not understand! Being in a hurry is a red flag sign of a bad tenant! And the ones you put in that rental house haven't paid rent since move-in!**

Why do agents rent at all?

You may wonder why agents do any leasing at all if what I say is true. To get **listings**. When it comes to the possibility of getting a listing, real estate agents can't say no. They'll send you a monthly newsletter for free. They'll give you a pumpkin at Halloween and a flag on the Fourth of July. They'll "help" you with renting properties. They'll even mow your lawn for free if you promise to give them a listing. But doesn't doing a lousy job mean they **won't** get the listing?

Maybe. The agent will typically claim they checked out the bad tenant. And blame the problems on the tenant. And many owners will buy that.

In addition, house salesmen simply don't know the rental business. So they don't **know** how to screen tenants. They may genuinely **believe** that the tenant's misbehavior could not have been prevented by better screening. (In most cases, it **can** be prevented by proper screening.)

Some real estate brokers employ agents who do nothing but lease. I have never used one. But they may be OK. Such leasing agents should acquire experience with **both** credit checking techniques and with bad tenants. And they never get house-selling commissions, so they don't resent the size of a leasing commission.

Apartment finding services

I have never used apartment finding services. Once, one of those services sent me a bill for a tenant we had accepted. I told them to drop dead—on the grounds that I had made no arrangement with them—and the applicant had not informed us that a commission would be due if we accepted him. The **tenant** might owe them a commission if he gave the service an exclusive right to represent him. But **I** didn't owe them anything.

I suspect they send similar bills to other owners and managers and occasionally find one dumb enough to pay it. That's not to say they're never entitled to a commission. If they do, indeed,
1. Find you a tenant, and
2. You either agreed to pay them in general, or
3. Were told a commission would be due prior to accepting the particular applicant,
then you owe a commission.

I will not recommend apartment finding services. Nor will I recommend that you **not** use them. Rather I will say that many seem to be successful businesses. And you don't get to be successful without rendering a useful service. I will also note that when these services first began, they gathered many complaints. Most commonly, that they were just reprinting newspaper classified ads.

If you have an apartment finding service, try them. If they do well by you, fine. If not, drop them.

Some people occupy positions which place them at prospective tenant bottlenecks. For example, many prospective tenants stay in motels while they are looking. It would be nice to have motel clerks referring people to your building. Ditto personnel officers of major local employers, college housing officers, military housing staff people, chamber of commerce staff, etc.

It would be nice to have them sending you tenants. But **how** do you do that? If you're Mr. or Ms. Personality, just asking them might be enough. Otherwise, they may ask, "What's in it for me?"

If that's the case, I'd forget it. You may want to **meet** key people if there are any in your market. Some markets have no such people. If your building doesn't always have vacancies, you should call the key people to tell them when you do. And you may want to keep them supplied with brochures.

Bulletin boards

If you can rent your units from bulletin board ads, your rents are probably too low. Again, you may have a special situation, like a rental building in a small college town where the main advertising medium is the bulletin board at the college housing office.

But generally, bulletin board advertising strikes me as something that would only work in extremely tight markets—where rents are below-market due to rent control or fear of rent control.

Apartment guides

Apartment guides are booklets. They are put together by companies who sell ad space in them. They are distributed to chambers of commerce, motels, etc. They are generally aimed at the affluent end of the market. At people transferring into the market from out of town.

For example, when a company moves its headquarters from New York to Dallas, those making the move would probably receive packets of information on Dallas. And those packets would typically contain an apartment guide booklet.

If they are effective, it is probably only for large complexes at the upper end of the rent range. Blue collar people do not get transferred, as a rule. As a general rule, I would **try** these thing once or twice if I had a large, up-scale complex. But I wouldn't expect much.

Salesmen typically try to sell you space in these. And they have a great line about how effective they are. But I'm skeptical. The problem is that they are rarely distributed as widely as the salesmen say. And they get out-of-date. So prospective tenants check the paper anyway.

Direct mail

I'm partial to direct mail because I use it in my book and newsletter publishing business. But I have never used it to **rent** apartments. (I **have** used it to buy and sell apartment buildings though.)

The basic idea behind direct mail is locating a group of widely scattered people with a distinguishing characteristic. For example, real estate investors. You could reach them with an ad in the paper. But the paper goes to many people who are **not** real estate investors. And the paper makes you pay for **all** the people they reach—regardless of whether they are your prospects or not.

I am **not** sure direct mail would help you find tenants, though. Virtually everyone who is **looking** for an apartment or rental house checks the classified section of the local paper. If you found that a significant number of your tenants were coming from a particular source—a source which you could reach more cheaply by direct mail than classified advertising, it might pay to use direct mail.

Direct mail might be cost effective if prospective tenants were not **seeing** your classified ad— because there so many in the paper that they didn't get to it. And direct mail might be cost effective if it inspired tenants who were **not** in the market for an apartment to consider moving. Tenants who are not in the market read their mail—but they do **not** read classified ads.

The company transferring its headquarters from New York to Dallas might be another situation where direct mail would be cost effective. You may have passed up paying for an ad in the apartment guide which they'll receive. But that doesn't keep you from sending your own brochure or letter to the company and/or its employees.

American Advertising (214-630-6767) in Dallas sent me a flyer which urged me to use direct mail produced and mailed by them to solicit tenants. They mail to a minimum of 5,000 targeted tenants. They target by ZIP code, neighborhood, and income.

The piece they've found most effective is either an 8 1/2 x 5 1/2 card or an 8 1/2 x 11 card folded down to 8 1/2 x 5 1/2. The card is glossy ("coated" to use printing terminology) and printed in two colors. It goes out bulk rate which was then 8.3¢ for a card like that. American Advertising's charge including postage was about $2,400 although they told me it varies.

You could save a lot of money doing it yourself. First, compile a list of mailing addresses of the apartments which are your main competitors. You could do that by looking at the complexes in question—or from reverse directories.

Then design a post card which tells your property's features. Print them and mail them. There are companies that do both printing and mailing in virtually every *Yellow Pages* under "Advertising— Direct Mail" or "Lettershops." Also, companies listed under "Mailing Lists" may be able to get you the appropriate lists more cheaply or faster than you can compile them.

Two hundred pieces is the minimum to qualify for bulk rate postage. Plus you need to pay an annual fee for a bulk rate permit. Printing two hundred 8 1/2 x 5 1/2 cards (one-color, two sides) would cost about $40. Adding postage of 200 x 8.3¢ (check current rates) each = $16.60. So not counting your labor of compiling the list and preparing the advertising copy to put on the cards, it would cost you about $40 + $17 = $57 to mail 200 post cards. Try it. If it works, you'll hear about it when you ask prospects, "How did you hear about us?"

In a building with a $50,000 annual gross income, you'd only need a $57 ÷ $50,000 = .114% improvement in your vacancy rate to break even on the 200-piece mailing. In a 10-unit building, that means 10 x 365 days per year = 3,650 apt. days x .114% = 4.16 days. In other words, you'd only have to rent **one** apartment **4** days sooner as a result of the mailing in order for the mailing to make sense.

"Now Leasing" banners are so cheap you probably ought to have one on any building bigger than about ten units. The last one I bought cost $18.22. That's from World Division, USA (800-433-9843). These are dark blue with day-glo red-orange letters. The banner is 3 feet by 5 feet and has metal grommets at each corner for hanging. They don't last forever but they are designed to survive the weather. They have other banners and pennants and all that.

Forget gimmicks

During the mid-eighties, I owned apartments in Texas. The Texas apartment market then was the worst in the U.S. since the Depression. Because landlord egos are intertwined with their rents, owners are extremely reluctant to lower rents. But the Texas market was so overbuilt owners had to lower rents. Eventually, they did. But only after they tried every gimmick in the book. Including:
- Huge helium-filled balloons
- Leasing agents dressed in rabbit suits handing out brochures at the supermarket
- 25¢ washers and dryers in the apartment complex laundry room
- "Burma Shave" type signs on the street in front of the apartment complex
- Vacations
- College tuition
- Gimmick lease clauses
- You name it.

Ultimately, they cut their rents. But they lost a lot of money they could have had during the anything-but-a-rent-cut period by wasting time with ineffective gimmicks.

Gimmicks are for those who believe in the **marketing-is-trickery** school of thought. That is, that the purpose of marketing is to trick people into doing things which they would not do if they had not been tricked. I am from the **marketing-is-education** school. That is, marketing is conveying information to prospective customers so that those for whom your property is the best value will recognize it.

I'm not looking for any good-guy award. I simply believe trickery does not work. Tenants are not idiots or strange beings from another planet who behave differently than you or I. They are just people who want to get the best place they can for their rental dollar. Use advertising to inform them about the value you offer.

Forbidden words

According to the California Newspaper Publishers Association the following residential rental ad words may be illegal: adults only, bachelor, bachelor pad, blind, Catholic, Christian, drinker, deaf, crippled, executive, female, male, no children, Oriental, number of people, one child, one person, white, mentally ill, older, private, senior citizen (except in certain all senior buildings), no play area. You also may not mention landmarks like Catholic schools which are used predominantly by one type of person. In response to this concern, HUD put out a list of OK words. It includes: mother-in-law unit, bachelor apartment, view, walk-up, jogging trail, walking distance, non-smoking, sober, wheelchair ramp, family room, and quiet. The courts may not agree with HUD on every word.

Photos and drawings, too

These rules apply to pictures, too. You must show all ethnic groups, ages, etc. in your ad pictures. If you leave out a group, it can be construed to indicate that you do not want that group. You don't need to have a picture of the United Nations and the handicapped in each ad. But over time, you better include everybody.

5

Leasing

The application

Step one is to fill out a credit application. The **manager** should fill out the application, **not** the would-be tenant. The manager should **interview** the applicant by asking for the information required by the application. The manager should write the applicant's answers into the blanks on the application. (Do not do this in the presence of other people. If the applicant is accompanied by a friend, ask the friend to absent himself from you and the applicant for a few minutes.)

A residential credit application has **more than one purpose**. Most people think it has only **one** purpose—to find out whether the applicant pays his rent on time and otherwise behaves himself. Wrong.

A residential credit application serves these purposes:

- Screen out bad tenants
- Skip tracing
- Notification in case of emergency
- Market research.

Manager fills it out

Don't give the application to the prospective tenant. If you do, he'll **leave blanks**. Especially in response to questions he doesn't want to answer. It's easy to leave blanks when you're filling out a form. But it's very **hard** to "leave a blank" when a human being asks you, "Why are you leaving your present residence?"

Also, it's easier to think of lies when you have plenty of time and you only have to lie on paper. For example, the true answer to, "Why are you leaving your present residence?" may be, "Because

I'm being evicted Wednesday." But the applicant who says that will almost certainly be rejected.

If he's filling it out at **home**, he'll probably say to a friend, "Hey, I'm being evicted. What do I tell these guys at the new apartment when they want to know why I'm moving?"

"Tell 'em the noise of the tennis court bothers you."

"Nah. How about if I tell 'em I live with you and you're getting married?"

"Yeah. That's a good one."

Harder to lie face-to-face

Now let's rerun that—only with the resident manager or leasing agent asking the question. The previous question on the Texas Apartment Association rental application is, "What's the expiration date on your local credit card?" Then, bang! "Why are you leaving your present residence?"

The applicant is ambushed. He's face-to-face with the manager and he has to answer **right now**. Hesitating will make the manager suspicious. So he tries to put his brain on an emergency lie basis. It comes out as stuttering and stammering. But if he gets to fill out the application himself—at home—the lie will come out smooth as silk.

Present and previous

Your application should ask for both present and previous landlord and present and previous employer. You want **both** present and previous landlord because the **present** landlord may **lie** to you to get rid of a bad tenant. If you think a fellow landlord wouldn't do that to you, you must be new to the business.

Previous employers are less important. The main thing you need on employment is a history of earning enough to pay the rent. And that history needs to be longer than a couple of months.

Is it really the landlord?

Bad tenants do not say, "Hi, I'm a bad tenant." They rarely admit they're being evicted. Or even their **real** present residence. Bad tenants must **lie** to you about their present landlord.

Most claim to be living with a **relative**. Or they give you the name of an uncheckable landlord. Like post housing on a military base. Or an address in the South of France.

Others give their landlord's name—or at least that's what they **say** it is. It may, **in fact**, be a friend or relative's name and phone number. Michael Keaton's "tenant from hell" character did that in the movie, *Pacific Heights*. (All landlords and managers ought to rent that movie.)

If the landlord he or she gives is a large complex, you should check the phone book or information to verify that the phone number is the really the apartment building phone number. The problem comes with tenant's who claim to be living in a rental house or duplex or other small building which would not have its own listing in the phone book.

Checking out a small landlord

Here are some ways to verify that the name and phone number the applicant gives are really his landlord.

- Look the applicant up in the **phone book**. His address in the phone book should correspond to the one he gave you.
- **Visit** the applicant at his residence—with**out** an appointment. If he's home, fine. If not, see if his name is on the mailbox or doorbell. Visits take time. So you or your manager probably won't want to do this very often. But it's only appropriate on a small percentage of applicants. And bad tenants take far more time than the visit technique.

- Check the landlord out in a **reverse directory**. A reverse directory is a phone book—only in phone number order instead of alphabetical by name. You look up a phone number, and it gives you the name and address. That doesn't tell you for sure that it's a phony. But most landlords live in single-family homes in the nicer section of town. If the reverse directory shows an apartment address, you have to wonder if it's really the landlord.
- Check out the landlord **on line**. There are numerous web directory sites: www.switchboard.com, www.555-1212.com, www.bigbook.com, www.databaseamerica.com, www.four11.com, www.yahoo.com/search/people.

What to ask the present and previous landlords?

- Is (Was) this person your tenant?
- Is (Was) he or she a good tenant?
- Did he or she pay the rent on time?
- Did he or she misbehave in any way?
- Would you rent to this tenant again?
- Did this tenant give you proper notice?

The employer

Applicants with inadequate or no income also lie about their employment. They play many of the same games they do in lying about landlords. Like giving you a buddy's name and phone number and saying he's the boss. Check out the previous and present employer the way you check out the present and previous landlords to make s-uer it really is an employer to whom you are speaking.

I know of one who had business cards listing himself as "vice-president" of a company. It was his own one-man company. When creditors or landlords called the company to verify his income, this man identified himself as the **president** of the company and told them the "vice-president" was a good employee and made $80,000 a year or whatever was required.

There are employers and there are 'employers'

Another problem is that some employers are honestly depicted, but aren't real employers **per se**.

One is **unions**. Many prospective tenants claim to be trade union members who work for many different employers. They get their work through the union. So they give you the union business office to verify their income.

Union business offices often lie for their members. The guy may have only worked an average of six hours a week in the last six months. But they'll say he makes $18 an hour and works steady.

Commissioned salespeople are another bogus employer category. Commissioned salespeople make zero, in many cases. Unless, that is, they succeed in selling something. But the salesperson's **boss** is also a salesperson. And probably spends a lot of time telling prospective salespeople what a great job they're offering. They tend to exaggerate how much the salesman will make—both to the new salesperson—and to themselves.

Don't let the "employer" of a salesperson tell you how much the person is **going to** make. Insist that they tell you how much the salesperson **did** make in the last year or more. Ask for W-2's or 1099's (income tax income statements). If they haven't been working long enough to have a W-2 or 1099, and they're commissioned salespeople, they don't really have a job.

In **transient** type jobs like bartender or lifeguard or Christmas tree salesman, short time-on-job renders the employment verification near worthless. Although short time-on-job does not **always** mean you should reject the applicant. For example, I rented my first apartment the month after I graduated from West Point. I was employed as an army officer for less than one month. But you can see that I wasn't a high risk.

Some people work for a **relative**. They **really** do. That's too bad. Because you cannot rely on a relative for an employment verification. Even if he **really** does work there. In that case, you need a **co-signer**.

Other ways to verify income

- Pay stubs
- Bank deposit records
- Letter offering job
- Income tax returns

You check the spouse's employment just as carefully as you check the main tenant. That's especially important if both incomes are needed to add up to enough money to meet your standards.

Your income standards

The old rule of thumb was 25%. The rent should not exceed 25% of the applicant's gross monthly income. Scratch that.

My rule is 33%. A California Supreme Court decision in 1991 said it was OK to have a 33% standard (*Harris v. Capital Growth*). The court approved that standard even though the landlords in question stipulated that the welfare mother in question could pay the rent. The opinion said such standards were "rational."

Can't set hard and fast standards

It would be nice if you could set hard and fast standards for tenants. But you can't. Often it's hard to get information even when you **have** the names and phone numbers of the correct people. Corporate bureaucrats in some companies refuse to give out employment or income information. Multiple calls never connect with the landlord you need to talk to.

Plus there are an infinite variety of situations. To a large extent, you have to play tenant screening by ear. That's not to say you can make leasing decisions on pure gut feel. You must do your best to talk to the landlords and employers.

But you have to do all this **quickly**. If you take more than a day or two to do your credit check, you may find that the tenant has rented somewhere else.

Often it comes down to a matter of judgment based partly on the information you gather and partly on gut feel.

Number of occupants standards

The Fair Housing Amendments Act of 1988 does not preempt local ordinances governing the maximum number of persons who may occupy a unit. If there is no local law, you may adopt reasonable standards as long as you do not unreasonably exclude families with children. On March 20, 1991, HUD General Counsel Frank Keating issued a memo to HUD regional directors. The memo said a two-person-per-bedroom limit will "generally" be considered reasonable. HUD still reserves the right to hassle landlords on a case-by-case basis even if the landlord has a two-person-per-bedroom limit. Although in 1994, talk was that HUD was going to rescind the two-persons-per bedroom limit and replace it with a minimum-square-feet-per-person limit.

Next of kin

Your application should request the name, address, and phone number of a person **not living in the apartment** or house to be notified in case of emergency. That serves the obvious purpose of telling you who to call if a tenant dies or suffers an injury which prevents them from giving that information. But it's more commonly used for skip tracing—locating former tenants who owe you money.

Deposit on application

You must collect **some** money when the prospect applies to be a tenant. Furthermore, you'd better collect **a lot**. That's just to **apply**. Why so much?

When I first started, I used to get $20. Then I'd check the applicant out, tell him he was approved, and look for him on move-in day. But often, he didn't show. I'd call and ask why. "Oh, we found another place."

"But that means you lose your $20 deposit."

"Yeah. We know."

I ran it up to $50. And **still** had no shows on move-in day. It's amazing the amounts of money people will walk away from these days.

One alternative to the $150 up-front deposit is the two-step deposit. You collect $50 or some such amount on application. But as soon as the tenant is approved, they must pay an additional $100 and sign the lease within 24 hours.

The basic idea is that you don't know whether you've really got a tenant until you collect about $150. And some even walk away from that.

The agreement as to the deposit money

Your rental application should contain an agreement and a line for the applicant's signature. That agreement should state

> The $_____ deposit made herewith will **not** be refunded if this application is approved. It **will** be refunded if this application is not approved.

If you use the two-step approach, your application agreement should also say something like this.

> Applicant agrees to sign the lease and pay an additional deposit of $_____ within _____ days of being notified of acceptance.

This agreement gives you the legal right to keep the deposit if you accept the applicant but he finks out on you. That's altogether fitting and proper. Because you take the property off the market from the time you accept the deposit until you learn that he's not coming. That typically delays the move-in date of the ultimate tenant—and costs you lost rent as a result. Keeping the deposit compensates you for that lost rent and administrative costs.

Nonrefundable credit check fee

In New Jersey, I charged a nonrefundable fee for checking credit. Only $8. But then that was the seventies. Plus I let the **manager** have the fee. If long distance calls were required, we charged $8 plus whatever the calls would cost.

I think that non-refundable credit check charge makes sense. Because applicants you reject cost you no lost rent. But they **do** cost you the time and money a credit investigation costs, but I didn't use the nonrefundable credit check charge in Texas. Because the market was too competitive.

No verbal options

Sometimes, prospective tenants look at a property—but decline to put down a deposit and sign an application. Then a week later they come back and find that the rent has been raised. They're outraged. "You told me $385!"

In effect, they are claiming that because you **quoted** them a rent, you are **obligated** to rent the place to them at that rent—that they have a binding, verbal **option** to lease at a fixed rent.

Baloney.

You or your manager should get into the habit of telling lookers who leave no money that the:

prices are subject to change without notice. If you put a deposit down, you lock in the rent we quoted. If not, and you decide you do want to apply, you may have to pay a higher rent.

In technica,l real estate terms,

We do not offer fixed-rent options to lease. And if we did, we would not give them away for free.

Compared to a bad tenant—

Ask my managers what my favorite rental management quote is and they'll say:

> **"Compared to a bad tenant,
> a vacancy is a delight."**

I pound that message into the heads of my managers repeatedly. The vast majority of owners give their managers a hard time about any vacancy. And owners **should** urge their managers to diligently work to rent vacant units. But they should never give their managers the impression that they **prefer** substandard tenants to vacancies. And owners should give their managers just as hard a time about bad tenants as they do about vacancies—so that the manager doesn't decide, "The owner **says** he doesn't want bad tenants—but he yells at me **more** about **vacancies** than he does about bad tenants—so I'll accept this not-so-hot applicant to get rid of one of the vacancies."

My other quote on that score is:

> **"When in doubt,
> leave them out."**

Credit-checking companies

I have used credit companies to check applicants. I stopped. For three reasons:

- Too slow
- Too sloppy
- Too little information.

You have to move fast when checking credit. One day. Two at most. Or you'll lose the applicant. Credit-checking companies that I've worked with took too long.

Also, they didn't give a rat's rump about accuracy. They are typically staffed by gum-chewing, work-long-enough-to-qualify-for-unemployment, minimum wage drones with double-digit IQs. They do the minimum required by their supervisors.

Finally, the national computer credit agencies like TRW often came up empty. And even when they had something, it was not a landlord or employer. Just a late credit card payment or some such.

If there's a checking bureau in your area, you might **try** them. But be quick to **stop** using them if they are too slow, sloppy, or sparse.

Solutions Publishing (800-255-6643) offers a credit-checking service via computer modem. If you have a computer and modem, you call a number they give you. The results of your credit check appear on your computer screen in seconds. And you can print it out on your printer. The system checks six credit services including the best-known ones. Initial fee was $249 in the Spring of '88. Credit checks cost $3.50 to $15 each with a monthly minimum of $10. Sounds worth considering. There are now numerous online tenant screening services. Go to an Internet search engine and type in "tenant screening" or "tenant credit check" for a current list of their Web sites. One example is at www.tsci.com.

The free, national credit check

Running a credit check through TRW or some such costs money. There's a way to obtain a facsimile of that check for free. Always ask the applicant this question, "Will anything negative turn up when I check you through the national credit bureau?"

One applicant answered, "Just my not paying my government college education loan."

I wasn't going to run any national credit check. But he gave me the information I needed anyway. I rejected him on the spot. The creep.

Nowadays, there is another free, national credit check: the **Internet**. Use an Internet search engine to search for the name of each of the prospective tenants. Search engines often ask **where** you want them to search. The answer is **everywhere**. For example, you can search for the tenant's name in news groups. Those are online discussion groups. One woman got into the habit of checking her dates on the Web. She discovered a guy she was dating was a flaming nutcake expressing all sorts of ugly radical views on Web news groups. You may discover that your prospective tenant has been bragging on line about taking advantage of his last landlord.

Lawyers as tenants

You may want to adopt a policy of not renting to lawyers if your state law allows it.

Does that sound strange? Read on.

For starters, it's probably legal in your state. You cannot discriminate according to race, sex, religion, etc., but **profession** is not on that list. In fact, in a 1976 New York State Supreme Court (a lower court in spite of its name) case, landlord Stanley Stahl (one of the 1985 "*Forbes* 400") refused to rent to an applicant—because he was a lawyer. The lawyer sued—and lost. Justice Edward J. Greenfield said,

> *There is nothing illegal in a landlord discriminating against lawyers as a group, or trying to keep out of his building intelligent persons, aware of their rights, who may give him trouble in the future.*

I don't think that was the reason.

My experience, and that of other landlords I've talked to, is that many lawyers are **contemptuous of the law**. Their **familiarity with** the law and the American judicial system breeds a **contempt for** the law. They know that the courts work slowly. And that there are dozens of anti-landlord laws they can use in any dispute—regardless of the merits of their case. Probably out of ignorance, non-lawyers are more respectful of both the law and the judicial system.

The 'mating call' of the lawyer tenant

Earlier in the book, I told you the "mating calls" of tenants with market and below-market rents. Here's a "mating call" I've heard from too many lawyer tenants:

I don't care what the lease says.

The average tenant **does** care what the lease says. He figures if he violates the lease, he'll get in trouble. He doesn't want to get into trouble.

I don't rent to people who "don't care what the lease says." I remember one applicant who declined my invitation to go over the lease before signing. I rejected her on the spot. There are only two reasons why a tenant would **not** want to go over a lease:

- It's **standard** and they've seen it before, or
- They plan to do whatever they want **regardless** of what the lease says.

In Texas, about a third of apartment owners use the Texas Apartment Association lease. So many tenants have seen it before. But in New Jersey, I used my own unique lease.

A tenant who does not care what the lease says should be **straightened out or moved out**.

Lawyers are high risk creditwise

People who extend credit—both landlords and lenders—generally are wary of lawyers. Not because they're dishonest or unable to make enough to pay their bills. But because, as a group, they are litigious. They pick fights knowing they often will win because of expense not merit.

Laymen tend to see much right and wrong in the world. Lawyers are trained to see gray virtually everywhere. Laymen figure they have to pay the rent every month. Many lawyers figure they have to pay the rent only if the landlord achieves perfection in maintenance standards.

According to the April 19, 1984 *Wall Street Journal*, the Golden Rule Insurance Company of Indianapolis, will not sell health insurance policies to lawyers. Because they sue more often than non-lawyers—and thereby drive up costs.

In another *Wall Street Journal* article ("Landlords' Verdict: Lawyers as Tenants Have Little Appeal" January 23, 1984), one New York landlord who **did** rent to a lawyer told why she regretted it—a tale of woe that would curl your hair.

That particular case was made much worse by New York City's incredible laws. But the basic point is still valid nationwide. That article quotes another New York landlord as saying, "Lawyer tenants are the worst." One of the most famous landlords in America told me the same thing—but did not authorize revealing his name.

Other Landlords

One last thought. You might also want to think twice before renting to **another landlord**. For the same reason. Landlords know that the wheels of landlord-tenant justice grind slowly—and that tenants have a formidable arsenal of legal weapons to use against landlords.

Many landlords who are tenants are sympathetic and would be **good** tenants. Like waitresses who are good tippers when **they** eat out. But there are plenty of **bad** landlords. And even the good ones can be dangerous. If I were someone's tenant, I'd be a good one. But I'd be the last tenant you'd want to cross. I know all about triple damages, warranties of habitability, "self-help eviction" laws, and all that.

Also, I had another experience that disgusted me with some landlords who were tenants. When the tenants in the affluent building I lived in all got rent increases, the tenants were up in arms and demanding rent control—**including the tenants who were themselves landlords**. Of course, **their** properties were outside of San Francisco and therefore not subject to the rent control they demanded. Indeed, some landlords who side with rent control advocates because they happen to be tenants in the rent control-seeking jurisdiction allow themselves to be paraded in front of the media. "See, even landlords believe rent control is warranted." Those same landlords obviously are vehemently opposed to rent control for the apartments they **own**.

Co-signers

Applicants fall into three categories:

- OK
- Not OK
- Don't know.

You **accept** the OKs. You **reject** the not-OKs. And you tell the "don't knows" that you'll accept them **if** they can get an acceptable **co-signer**. You do **not** accept a not-OK under any circumstances.

Don't knows

Who are don't-knows? Any tenant whose present and previous landlord and employer you cannot call—**for whatever reason**. Applicants have a zillion stories to explain why you can't check them out. But the stories don't matter. All that matters is that you not rent to someone you haven't checked out. Here are some sample stories:

- I've been living with relatives.
- I'm from out-of-town.
- Everything was in my husband's name.
- I lived on-post.
- My employer is on an archaeology expedition to the Yucatan. No phone.
- I've been living aboard ship.

Who as co-signer?

Any co-signer won't do. I required that the co-signer have a checkable credit history **and** own real estate in the same county as the rental building in question. At one location, the county line was nearby so we accepted property in the adjacent county, too.

If a don't-know applies, require a co-signer. But don't accept another don't-know—or even a not-OK—as co-signer. Getting **two** losers to sign the lease instead of one adds nothing to your safety.

In my early years, I asked an applicant to get a co-signer. The applicant was a bartender from out-of-town. So who's he bring? Another bartender from out-of-town. Wonderful.

You want a real estate owner so you can have a stationery target if there's trouble. If the tenant damages you in any way, you can file suit against the tenant and/or the co-signer. If you win, you can collect your court judgment by slapping a lien on the co-signer's real estate—or even forcing its sale.

How co-signers work

I have never been in court against a co-signer. But I have required many a tenant to get a co-signer. And even though I have never been in court against a co-signer, many a co-signer has either paid me or caused a tenant to pay me. Co-signers:

- Help screen out bad tenants,
- Encourage good behavior,
- Settle damage claims out-of-court,
- Can be forced to pay through court.

If a bad tenant with a good story applies, he'll probably fall into the don't-know category. If you require a co-signer, the bad tenant will either go elsewhere, or try to find a co-signer. Generally, only close relatives or friends will co-sign. And they tend to **know** whether the guy's a bad tenant or not.

As a result, they either tell the bad tenant to forget it. Or they agree but tell him in no uncertain terms that he'd better behave himself. Once the tenant moves in, reporting misbehavior which will result in a possible damage suit against the co-signer will usually inspire the co-signer to tell the tenant to behave. And if there's damage (financial or physical), the co-signer will usually either pay or convince the former tenant to pay.

As a last resort, you can sue. Typically, the tenant and co-signer lose because they don't show up. Then the court will give you the documents you need to file a lien on the co-signer's property. If you do that, interest accrues while you wait for him to sell or refinance. When he sells or refinances, the buyer or lender will nearly always insist that the judgment be paid off.

And in some cases, you can even force the sale of the property to get the money you're entitled to. (See "Execution Sale Superbargain" in the December 1990 and January 1991 issues of *Real Estate Investor's Monthly*.) Check your state law.

A chain is only as strong as its weakest link. If you do everything right—but don't make sure the signatures on the lease are legitimate—you've got nothing. Either make those signing the lease— tenants and co-signers—show you their drivers licenses—or make them sign the lease in front of a notary public. Do **not** let a tenant take the lease and have the co-signer sign it with neither you nor a notary as a witness. I required my managers to write the tenant's and/or co-signer's driver's license number under their signature.

The Fair Housing Amendments Act of 1988

The Fair Housing Amendments Act of 1988 changed discrimination law in two ways:
• Prohibits discrimination against handicapped and families with children
• Substantially increases the penalties for discrimination.

There also appears to be a bounty on landlords' heads as a result of the 1988 Act. I keep reading about people and groups who did not want to rent an apartment getting tens of thousands of dollars for catching landlords discriminating.

The definition of handicapped is probably broader than you think. It includes a disability that "is regarded" as impairing their "major life activities." The law does not say who has to "regard" the person as being disabled. Protected disabilities include: blindness, deafness, confinement to a wheelchair, AIDS, cancer, mental illness, and **former** drug or alcohol abuse.

You can only exclude mentally ill persons if they pose a **current** threat to the health, safety, or property of others. You may not even **ask** a prospective tenant if they have a handicap or if they ever abused drugs or alcohol in the past. You **may** ask about their ability to comply with the lease, previous rental history, and whether they **currently** use or sell illegal drugs. But if you ask **any** prospect those questions, you must ask **all** tenants the same questions.

Discrimination against a handicapped person is not just turning them down for an apartment. You are also discriminating if you refuse to make reasonable accommodations in your rules or if you refuse to let the handicapped tenant reasonably alter the building at his expense. You may make the tenant agree to restore the interior of the unit they alter to its original condition when they move.

Families with children includes pregnant women and persons in the process of securing custody in a divorce or adopting. Buildings which were intended for and are occupied only by persons 62 or older may discriminate against children. So can housing which has at least 80% of its units occupied by at least one person who is 55 or older and which provides significant facilities and services to meet the physical and social needs of older persons. You can**not** discriminate illegally temporarily to meet the 55 or 62 standards. Owner-occupied one- to four-family structures are exempt.24 CFR 100.10(c)(a). States often pass their own fair housing laws which one-up the federal version.

Disclosure

State and federal laws require various disclosures in residential leasing. There are also laws that specifically say you do not have to disclose such things as whether a previous occupant had AIDS or died from a cause unrelated to the property. (e.g., Texas Real Estate License Act § 15E)

6

Processing Move-Outs and Move-Ins

You should make a notice-processing check list. That's a list of the actions you and/or your manager take starting when a tenant gives notice and ending when the new tenant moves into that apartment or house. Here's the check list I used at one point.

1. Send acknowledgment of notice.
2. Call ad into paper (if it doesn't run continuously).
3. Place vacancy sign out (unless you're big enough to not use vacancy signs).
4. Start traffic report.
5. Notify tenant property will be shown in coming days.
6. Schedule return of security deposit.
7. Interview applicant to fill out application.
8. Applicant sign application.
9. Collect initial deposit.
10. Deposit money in bank.
11. Check credit (including co-signer, if any).

IF REJECTED
12. Notify applicant.
13. Return deposit. If it was a check, wait until it clears before returning.

IF ACCEPTED
12. Notify applicant of results. Request additional deposit and lease signing.
13. Take ad out of paper.

14. Take down vacancy sign.
15. Deposit additional deposit in bank.
16. Remind applicant to make arrangements with utilities if not supplied by owner.
17. Reproduce keys if necessary.
18. Tell new tenant move-in money must be cash, cashiers check, or money order. No personal checks.

MOVE-OUT OF OLD TENANT

19. Make move-out inspection. If significant damage, get witness and take photographs. Witness and owner or manager sign and date statement describing damage.
20. Schedule painting, repairs, rekeying, and cleaning as needed.
21. Return security deposit or send letter explaining why a full refund is not enclosed per local law. Bill old tenant for damage in excess of security deposit.

MOVE-IN OF NEW TENANT

DO NOT GIVE TENANT KEYS NOR PERMIT ANY MOVING IN UNTIL ITEMS 22 THROUGH 24 BELOW ARE COMPLETE.

22. New tenant and owner/manager have inspected apartment or house and signed move-in inspection check list.
23. All adult occupants and co-signers have signed lease in front of owner or manager or notary public.
24. Deposit and first month's rent have been received in the form of cash, cashier's check, or money order. No personal checks.
25. Give new tenant keys.
26. Deposit move-in money in bank.
27. File lease and move-in inspection check list.

Your check list will be different

If you use a check list for processing move-outs and move-ins, it will be different from the one above. Not just because of different management styles. But because of different building configurations, local market differences, and local law differences. In fact, the check list I used was different from this one. It had two additional items: Give tenant "Truth in Renting" and Federal Crime Insurance information—as required by New Jersey law.

Your check list should probably have all the items the one above does—**plus** other items which you add.

Acknowledgment of notice

You don't need to send a tenant an acknowledgment of notice. But it's a good idea. Here's one I used.

On [date], we received written notice of your notice to vacate your apartment on or before [date]. Since your lease requires that you give at least thirty days written notice and does not expire until [date], you will be responsible for payment of the rent through [date], or until the apartment is rerented, whichever comes first.

We will make reasonable efforts to rerent the apartment to a new tenant who meets our credit standards so that any vacant period is minimized.

*Your cooperation is essential to rerenting and is required by our lease. Your security deposit will be returned to you within thirty days after you move provided there is no damage other than ordinary wear and tear and all rent and other charges have been paid. Please do **not** ask for early return of your deposit.*

Please make sure the following are completed before you move:

1. All damage repaired
2. Range, refrigerator, and oven cleaned
3. Bathroom fixtures and shower wall cleaned
4. Apartment swept broom clean
5. All cabinets emptied and dusted
6. All keys turned in

Most apartment damage is done during moving. So please be careful. You will be responsible for any damage done by you or your movers to the hallways, building exterior or grounds as well as inside your apartment.

Upon receipt of your notice, we immediately placed your apartment up for rent. Keep in mind that as soon as someone makes a deposit on your apartment, we will be entering into a binding contract with that new tenant based on your vacating date. The new tenant, in turn, will be giving notice to his landlord and to movers based on your vacating date. So you cannot change your mind about moving once a new tenant is found and you must be completely out by noon on the date you gave in your notice.

Best wishes in your new home,

As you can see, this letter addresses many move-out problems.

• Lease-breaking,
• Cooperation with showings,
• Security deposit return,
• Cleaning,
• Damage,
• Moving, and
• Notice revocation.

Return of security deposit

Many tenants want to know if they'll get their security deposit back—and when—as soon as they give notice. The only answer you can give is to refer them to their lease.

Do **not** agree to give them all their deposit back before move-out. How can you until you've inspected? And a **pre**-move-out inspection is worthless. Because it's easy to cover up damage. Cleaning is not complete. And much damage is done **during** moving anyway. Plus there are problems which are invisible until after they move out. Like flea infestation from their pet (which pet you may not even know they have).

Don't let tenants talk you into refunding deposit before thirty days

When I was a beginner, I let a couple tenants talk me into returning their deposit before the end of the thirty days. In every single instance, I got taken advantage of. I mentioned that to one of my inexperienced managers the other day and she said she had recently done the same thing. "Never she vowed.

Dᴏ **not** agree to give security deposits back **before** move-out. And do **not** agree to give them back **after** move-out either. Not until the end of the thirty days. Why not right after move-out?

Because problems tend to surface a couple days after you give the money back. What problems? Fleas. Damage and dirt you overlooked on your first inspection.

Also, when you make the decision in the presence of the recipient, you are often influenced by them. The decision as to how much security deposit to return is best made **in private**—after several weeks have passed and the new tenant has moved in, if possible.

Take my word for it. If you give deposits back on move-out day, you'll regret it. And virtually all beginners make that mistake. The only answer to all security deposit inquiries is, "We will abide by the lease." Period.

Roommates

Roommates are a special situation. Some landlords insist that **one** of the roommates be the one who signs the lease and is "responsible." That's insane.

You must insist that **all** adult occupants sign the lease. If you rent to A and B, but only A signs the lease, what do you do if A moves out but B doesn't? You'd have a **resident** who was not a **tenant**. A resident who has not signed a lease and therefore is not bound by it. Theoretically, A is still responsible. But where is he?

And if B allows C to move in, you must insist that C apply to become a tenant. And if accepted, sign a lease.

Returning roommates' security deposits

Do **not** return security deposits to **one** roommate when he moves out. Only return a security deposit when they **all** move out. When C is substituted for A, A will often ask you to return **his** portion of the security deposit. No way.

You can't do a proper inspection, because B and C are still occupying the place. Tell A that return of his security deposit is between him and B and C. And tell C that once he signs the lease, he is responsible, along with B, for any damage done by A before C moved in. Otherwise, both B and C will blame all damage on A when they move out.

When they finally do all move out, make the security deposit return check, if any, payable to **all three**. That often drives the roommates nuts. Tough. Because if you start allocating it to one or the other, and there are any deductions, the guy you deduct from may say the other guy caused that damage. There's no way you can get involved in deciding who gets what. So you make it payable to all of them. Then **they** have to work it about among themselves.

Security deposit laws

Most states have stiff penalties for failure to return security deposits—or explain any deductions—within thirty days. Often, you can be made to pay double or triple the amount of the deposit—**plus** attorneys fees—**plus** $100 or some such.

So you must make sure you don't forget. You should make a note on your calendar. Or put the move-out inspection check list in your bill box.

Make-ready

If there is any smell in the apartment or house when you show it to prospective tenants, it better be paint. According to the April '85 newsletter of the Real Estate Investors Association of Cincinnati, the best product for getting rid of pet odor in carpet is "Love My Carpet" regular scent. Local carpet cleaning companies generally have techniques which they use to get rid of carpet odor.

Here are the items you generally need to clean to get a property ready to show:

- Front door clean or paint
- Steam clean carpet
- Clean all switch plates
- Clean frige—defrost and fix rubber sealing strips if necessary
- Clean out all light diffusers
- Eliminate all mildew on tub grout—recaulk as needed
- Clean or replace faucets as necessary
- Clean all air vent grates
- Clean or replace screens
- Check that drains are clear
- Replace all air-filters unless not necessary
- Touch-up or paint as needed
- Check smoke detector
- Check doorbell, intercom, and opener if applicable
- Replace windows as needed
- Check operation of doors
- Check operation of all locks
- Check operation of all security lights
- Keep doors locked (a Texas landlord lost a suit when a passerby was raped in an unlocked vacant apartment. *Nixon v. Mr. Property Management Co.*, 690 SW 2d 546).

Cash, cashiers check, or money order

When it comes to regular monthly rent checks, I prefer that tenants pay with personal checks. That reduces the risk that my managers will be robbery targets. And it reduces opportunities to embezzle or steal rent money by falsely claiming to have been robbed.

But move-in day is a whole 'nother smoke. Then I want **cash, cashiers check, or money order**.

Until you hand the new tenant the keys—or allow him to move anything in—you have **power**. After he moves in, your power is greatly diluted. All you can do is evict—which is like nuclear war. It's so drastic you tend not to use it until the situation gets drastic.

The *last* money you'll get

With very bad tenants, the money you get on move-in day is the **last** money you get from them. Once they get in, they never pay another cent. That being the case, you want to make sure that the money you **do** get from those very bad tenants is **real** money. Not a rubber check.

A friend of mine told me that you couldn't make money in residential rentals. He had tried it once. His first tenant moved in on a rubber check and never paid another cent. Took him several months to get rid of the tenant. I explained that couldn't happen to me because I accept only cash, cashiers check, or money order on move-in day. And he said, "Oh. I guess that would make sure you at least got **some** money."

Makes them go elsewhere

*It does **more** than that. It makes the hard-core deadbeat go elsewhere. Hard-core deadbeats live totally rent-free. They use rubber checks to move-in. Stay til they get evicted. Then move into another building with lax screening procedures.*

When they run into a landlord who doesn't discover their lies about landlords and job, but **does** require the first month's rent and security deposit in the form of cash, cashiers check, or money order, they say,

> *To heck with this place. Even if I don't pay another month, the landlord gets a month and a half's rent (or whatever) out of me. And he's probably the kind of guy who'll be down on me like a ton of bricks when I don't pay the first month's rent.*

So the requirement to pay in **real** money—combined with the fact that he knows many other landlords are easier touches—causes the hard-core deadbeat to look elsewhere. And that's just fine.

I **did** take personal checks for initial deposit money—if the move-in day was far enough away that if the check bounced I'd know **before** move-in day. And I would take a personal check for initial deposit money when there was only a week or so til move-in—but the check was drawn on a bank which was convenient for me to visit to cash the check. Do **not** take personal checks for any part of the move-in money unless you will know **before** move-in that the check is good.

Utilities reminder

Many tenants are renting for the first time. As a result, they don't think about arranging for utilities. I've had many a young couple or single person moving into a dark apartment in my buildings. They didn't realize until they arrived on move-in day and flipped the light switch that **they** have to make arrangements with the electric company to have electric service.

That's funny. But it can cause problems. One is that the tenant flips his light switch and figures the landlord screwed up. In his anger, he's liable to move elsewhere. Or waste management time ranting and raving at the manager until it penetrates his consciousness that it's **his** fault. Finally, moving in the dark can result in injury to the building and/or the tenant. And when people get injured, they tend to sue. You don't need that.

So as part of your acceptance notice, remind the tenant that they must arrange to have the electric and other utilities which they pay turned on.

Move-out inspection

All tenants claim that **all** damage beyond ordinary wear and tear was "that way when we moved in." That's why you have them sign a move-**in** inspection checklist.

Then when you find damage in the move-out inspection, and they recite the "mating call of the tenant moving out of a damaged unit," you can whip out a photocopy of the move-in inspection check list they signed.

"Well, yes, we **didn't** make note of that rip in the carpet when we moved in. But that was because we didn't **see** it until two days later."

Tough.

That's why your move-in inspection check list should have a blurb above the tenant's signature in which the tenant states something to the effect that

> *I have **thoroughly** inspected the above-named apartment and found no damage except what I listed above.*

When the moving-out tenant says they overlooked it on move-in, just point to the word "thoroughly" above their signature. That usually causes them to mutter some grudging acceptance of responsibility.

Must sign move-in inspection *before* move-in

Most tenants ask you to let them bring the move-in inspection check list to you several days **after** they move in. No way.

For one thing, you'll be bugging them for weeks to give it to you. For another, much damage is done **during** move-in. So if you don't get them to sign the move-in inspection check list **before** move-in, you will get stuck for move-in damage. And any damage done between move-in and the signing of the inspection check list.

That is an absolutely iron-clad rule—no move-in inspection check list, no key and no moving. If they protest, tell them to take all the time they like inspecting the place. But they absolutely cannot move in until they are finished inspecting and have signed that check list.

Files

You should have a manila file folder for each unit—not each tenant. Put all the documents relating to that unit in the file folder. Two-hole punch the top of the lease, move-in inspection check list, etc. Use Acco brand prong fasteners to attach them to the back of the folder. That will cause them to be in chronological order with the current or most recent tenant on top.

Required handouts

Local, state, and federal law requires landlords to give new tenants certain items. Generally the landlord must get a signed receipt for the items in question. The lease should contain the wording for that receipt. For example, in New Jersey, we had to give tenants a booklet about their rights. Starting October 1995, all residential landlords of pre-1978 buildings must give tenants an EPA Lead Hazard Information pamphlet and must inform tenants about lead paint in their building.

I and others recommend additional handouts like the Texas Apartment Association's Security Guidelines for Residents.

PART TWO:
OTHER INCOME

7

Cash Management

Handling money makes money

Landlords handle money each month. Unfortunately, **handle** it is about all most recent rental property buyers do. It comes in one door and goes out the other—to creditors.

But you can and should make a little money just from the handling. That's called cash management.

Stated simply, cash management means taking money **in** as fast as possible and paying it **out** as slow as possible. "Collect early and pay late," as one author puts it.

Interest bearing account

You should deposit money as fast as reasonably possible in an interest bearing account. And you should pay your bills **on time**, but not early.

Here's an example of **poor** cash management. Manager collects $10,000 in rents by the fifth of the month. Doesn't get to the bank until the 14th. Owner's bills are not due til the end of the month. But he goes ahead and pays them on the 17th. He gets only three days interest.

At 4%, $10,000 earns $400 a year. Or $1.10 a day. Had the rent been deposited on the fifth, and the bills paid on the 29th, the owner would have earned **24** days of interest instead of **three**. Actually, since the checks you write are not presented for payment to your bank on the day they're written, you'd get **more** days of interest. But let's stick with these figures for comparison.

$200 a year on a $10,000 monthly gross

A **good** cash manager (deposit on 5th, pay on 29th) would earn 24 days interest or 24 x $1.10 = $26.40 per month while a **poor** cash manager would earn only 3 x $1.10 = $3.30. For a difference of $26.40 - $3.30 = $23.10. In a year, that adds up to $23.10 x 12 = $277.20.

Won't make you rich. But you wouldn't ignore five $100 bills you saw laying on the street, either.

Actually, a poor cash manager probably wouldn't even earn $3.30. A poor cash manager probably wouldn't have the money in an interest-bearing account at all. Aaagh!

The bigger you are, the more important cash management becomes

Obviously, cash management is not for duplex owners. With maybe $1,000 a month coming in, the annual interest would only be $40. And that's only if the money were never out of the account. The daily rate would only be 11 cents.

On the other hand, if you manage two **hundred** units, not paying close attention to cash management should be **grounds for dismissal**. At an average rent of $300 a month, a 200-unit building brings in $300 x 200 = $60,000 a month. Daily interest would be 6 x $1.10 = $6.60. And the monthly benefit from 21 days interest would be 21 x $6.60 = $138.60—almost the equivalent of half of another apartment's rent!

Would you fire a manager who totally ignored one of your vacant apartments month in and month out? If yes, then you should fire a manager who ignores cash management on a multi-hundred unit complex.

Pay your bills on time

Don't get so carried away with earning interest that you fail to pay your bills on time. Good credit is worth far more than a couple days interest.

And don't ever get the idea that it's good business to pay **late.** You should always pay **"as agreed."** If the supplier gives you 30 days to pay, **take** 30 days. But **never** take 31.

Deposits, too

State law may dictate what you do with rent security deposits. If it gives you some leeway, you should put the money where it will earn the highest interest.

Some states require that you pay interest on tenant security deposits. That's a pain in the neck. I used to pay interest on tenant security deposits in New Jersey—before New Jersey law required it. The tenants did **not** appreciate it. After all, they were only getting about $6 a year.

But it was costing me over a hundred dollars a year. About the time I said, "to heck with it," New Jersey **required** us to pay interest. What's worse, they made us pay it **annually**. The bookkeeping cost more than the amount each tenant got.

Let the landlords keep the interest

The law ought to allow the landlord to keep the money. On the theory that it all comes out in the wash. Every nickel you **give** landlords in the form of tax breaks, interest income, or whatever removes a nickel's worth of pressure on rents. And every nickel of income you take away from landlords puts a nickel's worth of pressure **on** rents.

Plus, these laws put a significant—in relation to the tenant's annual interest check—bookkeeping expense on the landlord—which puts its **own** pressure on rents. So requiring landlords to pay interest on tenant security deposits is the **least efficient** way to get the benefit back to the tenants. Oh, well.

In the bank, not the drawer

The main message you need to get across is that checks and cash should be **in the bank, not the drawer.** Owners and managers need to know that a pile of checks represents interest lost every day. The bigger the pile, the more interest.

8

Laundry Income

Two percent of the gross

Laundry income amounts to one or two percent of the gross income in apartment buildings with central laundries.

There are three ways to handle laundry in an apartment building:

- Laundry room equipment owned by landlord,
- Laundry room equipment owned by concessionaire,
- Laundry equipment in each apartment.

Some buildings have laundry equipment in **some** units, but not all. They typically also have a laundry room.

Many new apartment buildings in the Dallas/Fort Worth area have laundry hookups and offer to rent the equipment for about $20 extra a month.

Concessionaire versus landlord owning

You should own the laundry equipment yourself, **not** have a concessionaire supply it.

I have done it both ways. Before I owned my own machines, I thought repairs would eat up all the income. I have now owned my own machines and found that the repairs expense was only 45¢ per apartment unit per month. And repairs and the cost of the equipment is all you get from the concessionaire.

When I computed my income form the laundry equipment I owned over a thre- and-a-quarter-year period it came out to $9.46 per unit per month gross and $7.07 per unit net after utilities and repairs expense. If I had a concessionaire with a 50/50 split, I'd only get $9.46 x 50% = $4.73 net before utilities. In effect, I'd have paid the other $4.73 for the repairs which really only cost me 45¢.

Overall, my machines paid for themselves in ten months. So I didn't need a concessionaire to relieve me of the burden of paying for the equipment. It's a fantastic investment. Why give it to a concessionaire?

As far as I can tell, the typical concessionaire split is fifty-fifty. That is, you get half of the gross.

Concessionaires will give you as little as you let them get away with. And some state the split formula in a convoluted way that **sounds** like you get the lion's share.

For example, in one building, my share was 10% of the first $10 per machine and 60% thereafter. Sounds pretty good, doesn't it? Unless each machine only grosses about $10.

I ended up getting about 50% on that deal. Although I came in after the ten year lease had run several years. Do not use concessionaires ever.

Laundry room renovation by concessionaire

Most concessionaires will renovate your laundry room free of charge. They'll put in new wall paper, panelling, paint, etc.—do a heck of a job—all free. That's to avoid losing you as a customer when the lease runs out. And to encourage your tenants to use the equipment.

What did I tell you in the chapter on rent raisin? Only tenants who pay below-market rent do their own renovations. Laundry concessionaires are tenants and these laundry-room renovations are the same as a residential tenant redoing your carpets at her own expense. Laundry-room renovation offers are an indication that the concessionaire is paying you below-market rent.

If your room needs it, and you have a concessionaire, ask them. They will also offer this as an inducement to get the contract to begin with. But better you should do your own renovations and get rid of the concessionaire.

Kickbacks

Concessionaires also sometimes offer kickbacks—maybe most of the time. When I was a property manager, one offered to pay me a "finders fee." People who **take** kickbacks are sleazeballs. And people who **pay** kickbacks are sleazeballs.

I told that concessionaire that he was a sleazeball, that I wasn't, threw him out of the office, and reported the offer to my boss. We continued to own the equipment ourselves.

There are a lot of kickbacks in the apartment business. You need to know about kickbacks for two reasons:

- Kickbacks equal discounts,
- Supervision of managers.

If concessionaires can afford to pay kickbacks to managers, they can afford to give the same amount to the owner in the form of a discount. Then it's not a kickback.

A kickback is a bribe paid by a supplier to get an employee or agent to betray the trust of his employer. The typical employer tells his employees or agents to get the **best possible price**. The kickback is to get your employee or agent to accept a **higher** price in return for the supplier's kicking back a portion of that higher price to the employee or agent.

If you ever catch an employee accepting a kickback, fire him or her immediately. I define a kickback as any payment or gift with a value of more than $25. In trying to get my business in a 25-unit building, WEB offered me $500 in cash as "additional decoration allowance." I don't know if they pay kickbacks. But you can see how much they're willing to spend to get the business.

Marketing, not profit

The main reason to have a laundry room is marketing, not profit. That is, if you **don't** have one, you'll lose tenants to buildings which **do** have laundry rooms. Unless you're right next door to a laundramat (or washeteria as they're called in Texas). In fact, if **I** owned a building within walking distance of a laundramat, I might close down my laundry room.

The expenses

Laundry concessionaires don't pay the expenses, you know. **You** do. You pay the:

- Utilities (gas, electric, heating oil, water, hot water) for heating and air-conditioning, lighting, washing, and drying,
- Cleaning the room,
- Mortgage on the room.

If you own the equipment rather than a concessionaire, you also pay the:

- Repairs,
- Cost of equipment.

The hassles

You also get the hassles. Refund hassles when the equipment doesn't work. Security hassles like getting rid of the punks who have started hanging around the room.

And if you own the equipment, you get the hassle of repairs and replacements.

The income

Your income is whatever you charge for washes and drys multiplied by the number of each. Typically, washes cost $.50, $.75, or $1.00. And a dry is $.10 or $.25 per time unit. You can adjust the dryer coin device to give various length time units in most cases.

If you have a concessionaire, the concessionaire sets the charge. Theoretically, that shouldn't be a problem. He wants to maximize the income same as you. Plus the concessionaire has much more experience. So he ought to know what's best.

When **you** set the amount, charge the amount which maximizes your income. There's some value to checking the "comps," the way you do on rents. In other words, go see what the nearest laundramat charges for a wash and a dry.

But don't feel you have to charge the same.

You have a convenience advantage

You have a tremendous **convenience advantage** over the laundramat. Typically, your tenants can **walk** to your laundry room. Maybe even without going out doors.

But to go to the local laundramat, they have to carry the clothes to the car, drive to the laundramat, wait at the laundramat instead of back in the apartment for the clothes to finish, then drive back to the apartment complex, and carry the clothes back to the apartment. The extra "commute" time is typically at least ten minutes. At the minimum wage of $3.35, that's worth $3.35/6 = $.56. A four-mile round trip at $.22 a mile would cost another $.88. It's hard to put a price on having to sit in a laundramat instead of being able to wait in the apartment. Let's estimate $2.00.

That means it might cost $.56 + $.88 + $2.00 = $3.44 extra to do the wash at the laundramat instead of the apartment-building laundry room. So it seems like you could easily charge $.25 more in your laundry room than the nearest laundramat. Maybe even $.50 more.

You may also have other advantages over the laundramat. Like security. Your laundry room should be punk-free. But many public laundramats aren't.

Of course, you have some **dis**advantages too. Like no change machine (they're too expensive). Maybe no Coke machine. No soap machine. Etc. But convenience is the main one.

Not losing any laundry business isn't the criterion

Tenants and resident managers complain about higher-than-elsewhere laundry charges. But talk is cheap. Pay more attention to how they "vote with their feet."

One of my managers complained about our machines being $.75 when the nearby washeteria was only $.50. "Where do you do your wash?" I asked her.

"Here. My husband takes the car."

In fact, the car is available to her many hours each week. If she really wanted to, she could get to the public washeteria down the street. But it's not **convenient**.

It's not what tenants and managers **say** about laundry charges that's important. It's what they **do**.

Plus, you don't have to keep every single tenant to come out ahead. An increase from $.50 to $.75 is a **50%** increase in income. You'll come out ahead as long as the number of loads done does not **drop** by 50%.

If, for example, the number of loads done per month drops from 200 to 166 when you raise the price from $.50 to $.75, you still make more money. Because 166 x $.75 = $124.50 is more than 200 x $.50 = $100. And that's just the **gross**. The **net** would improve even more because 166 loads use less utilities than 200 loads.

You should charge the amount which results in the **maximum monthly collections. Not** the maximum number of loads or tenants using the room or the minimum number of complaints.

How many loads?

According to WEB Service Co., the average tenant does **seven loads per month**. That'd get you $7.00 per unit per month if you charged $.50 wash and $.50 dry; $10.50 per unit per month if you charged $.75 each; and $14.00 per unit per month if you charged $1.00 each.

A 37-unit building I owned grossed $10.39 per unit in October 1983. We charged $.75 so we were quite close to the seven load figure of $10.50 for a $.75 operation.

That 37-unit was a concession. In my 25-unit, I own the machines. From January 1, 1984 through May 31, 1984, we grossed $996. Divided by 25 is $39.84 per unit. Divided by five months is $7.97 per unit per month. We charge .$75 wash and $.35 dry or $1.10 per load. So seven loads should yield $7.70. $7.97 is close enough.

My 33-unit worried me, though. It was a concession. They sent me a total of $363.06 from January through May of '84. That's $363.06 ÷ 33 ÷ 5 = $2.20 per unit per month. I got half so the total is $4.40 per unit per month. And the concessionaire charged $.75 wash and $.75 dry. That meant we were only getting about $4.40 ÷ $1.50 per load = 2.934 or **three** loads per tenant per month.

I switched concessionaires. Still got about the same amount.

An owner I know says he collects his own money and he averages **ten to twelve loads** per unit per month. So the seven loads rule of thumb isn't hard and fast.

Escaping concessionaire leases

Let's say I have convinced you not to let a concessionaire onto your property. Unfortunately, having the opportunity to say "No" to a concessionaire is rare. Usually, they come with the property when you buy it. That is, the previous property manager signed a long-term lease with the concessionaire in return for a bribe. Now you're stuck with that lease for the next seven years or some such. Or maybe the previous owner had no property manager, but he just assumed that because launhry concessionaires exist and sponsor many of the meetings of the local apartment association, it must be sensible to use them. So he let them in anew or renewed his lease with them.

The concessionaires work very hard to make their leases airtight. But you should still go over them with a magnifying glass looking for ways to escape. Remember that escaping from one of these leases raises your net income, which, in turn, raised your building value.

A judge let one of my readers out of a lease that came with the building on the grounds that the concessionaire's three-inch-square stickers on the machines were insufficient notice that the concessionaire had a lease on the laundry room.

Leases sometimes require the concessionaire to maintain the machines properly. You could try to evict him every time his machines were not working. If the concessionaire did, in fact, pay a bribe to the property manager to get the lease, it can be voided on that basis, if you can prove it. A judge or jury may buy that argument if you could just prove it was such a lousy deal for the owner that there must have been either a bribe or incompetence on the part of the manager. If you raise enough hell, a property management company may request the concessionaire to leave and they may comply to stay on the good side of their bribee for future deals at other complexes. Or the property manager may buy out the lease to end the dispute. Publicize your complaint at your local apartment owners meetings. (The association's paid staff will try to shut you up.) In general, make your account more trouble than it's worth to the concessionaire company.

˙If you just throw the concessionaire out, which is illegal, they can sue. That's rarely any fun for them. Plus they have an obligation to "mitigate their damages." You could concede that you broke the lease then argue that they had no damages because they were able to place the machines in another complex or that the machines were at the end of their life or some such. Many attorneys said that President Clinton should have offered no defense to Paula Jones law suit other than to argue that she suffered little ro no loss as a result. That would have saved him having to give the deposition which led to Monica Lewinsky and all that.

Utilities consumption

Here is the per-load energy consumption of washers and dryers according to Pacific Gas and Electric Company:

ENERGY CONSUMPTION

Equipment	Gas	Electric
Dryer	15 therms or 14.76 cu ft	3.75 KWH
Washer		25 KWH
Hot water (wash)	05 therm or 4.9 cu ft	1.6 KWH

The per load **water** consumption of washers is **35 gallons**, 8 of which are hot water, according to my local water company.

Gas costs far less than electric

Note the large amount of electricity used by electric dryers. I had electric dryers at the Greenbriar. I paid $.06357 per KWH there. At that rate, drying one load of clothes cost 3.57 KWH x $.06357/ KWH = $.227 or $.23. Doesn't sound like much.

But look at what the **gas** cost would have been with gas dryers. I paid Lone Star Gas $.06339 per therm. $.06339/therm x .15 therms = $.01. In other words, electric drying cost **23 times** as much as gas! But gas dryers cost about the same as electric dryers—not counting running a gas line to the laundry room.

The lesson? Use gas dryers. Or at least run the numbers before you choose electric.

Ditto the choice between electric **hot-water heaters** and gas. Heating water for ten loads costs 10 loads x 1.6 KWH x $.06357/KWH = $1.02 by **electric** hot-water heater and 10 loads x .05 therms x $.06339/therm = $.03 by **gas** hot-water heater. That's $1.02/$.03 = **34 times** as much!

What do we net?

Let's see how much I netted at the Cottonwoods—where I owned the machines and had gas dryers. I already told you the gross—$7.97 per unit per month.

Now the expenses. Here's what I paid for utilities there in '84:

Gas	$.49/100 cubic feet or $.0049/cu ft
Electric	$.59/KWH
Water	$.004/gallon

You get your **marginal** utility rate by calling the utility company. The marginal rate is the rate you pay on the **next** kilowatt hour or cubic foot or whatever. It's important to use the marginal rate rather than just divide the bill by the consumption because that average rate is typically depressed by lower rates on the first so many kilowatt hours. And the rate printed on the bill is usually a bit lower than what you actually pay due to tax and other charges.

So the seven loads run by my average tenant cost me:

Gas dry	14.76 cu ft x 7 x $.0049/cu ft	= $0.506
Gas hot water	4.9 cu ft x 7 x $.0049/cu ft	= 0.168
Wash electric.	25 KWH x 7 x $.59/KWH	= 1.033
Wash water	35 gal x 7 x $.004/gal	= 0.980
Total per tenant per month		$2.687

So my net per tenant was $7.97 income less $2.69 expenses = $5.28. That's not all profit, though. I had to buy the equipment, remember? And I had to pay the mortgage on the laundry room, the lights, cleaning, machine repairs, etc. Was I making a profit after all was said and done? I wonder.

So next time your tenants or manager complain about how much you charge for washing and drying, invite them to take over the laundry. They buy the equipment, maintain it, pay the utilities, and pay you a fixed rent on the room equal to that room's share of the mortgage, property taxes, and insurance. If they can count, they'll turn it down as uncompensated labor.

Minimum size building for laundry equipment

Obviously, you could not afford to put coin-operated laundry machines in a duplex. But how big does the building need to be to warrant coin-operated machines? I'd guess about **eight- to twelve-units minimum**.

I had concessionaires eager to put machines in my 25-unit building. They were going to put in two washers and two dryers. That's one washer and dryer set for every twelve units. A concessionaire put four sets in my 37-unit—one for every nine units. And that same concessionaire but three sets in my 33-unit—one for every eleven units.

In *Landlording*, Leigh Robinson (www.landlording.com) recommends not having a laundry room unless you have at least sixteen people or twelve bedrooms. In *Professional Apartmenteering*, the Multi-Housing Laundry Association (MLA, 1100 Raleigh Building, 5 W. Hargett St., Raleigh, NC 27601, 919-821-1435 www.mhla.com) recommends:

ancy type	Equipment
Lower and middle income	one washer per 20 bedrooms
Luxury	one washer per 25 apartments
Senior citizens	one washer per 40 apartments

And MLA recommends one single-load dryer per washer or one double-load dryer for every two washers.

Own it yourself?

In 1991, Sears Roebuck (Contract Sales Department) would sell you a coin-operated washer (complete with coin device) for $499. And a similarly equipped gas dryer for $425 ($395 for electric). Of course, there are other companies. In 1983, I paid $1,844 for three Speed Queen washers—$615 each. The Speed Queen salesman said his were more durable than Sears' equipment. As of 1991 the Speed Queens had been repaired a few times but they generally perked right along. So the durability claim appear to be valid.

These are the **before**-tax costs. **After**-tax, coin-operated vending machines like washers and dryers are unique in the residential rental business. They are the **only** residential items (other than new elevators) which are eligible for first-year expensing.

First-year expensing

Section 179 of the *Internal Revenue Code* used to say that you could **deduct** not depreciate the cost of coin-operated washers and dryers **in one year**. But they changed the law so you cannot do that anymore if the coin-operated washers and dryers are in an apartment building and owned by the building owner. Although an outside company could still use Section 179 first-year expensing on washers and dryers.

In 1998, there is an annual $18,500 limit on how much you can deduct under Section 179.

Used washers and dryers, too

Eligible taxpayers don't have to buy **new** coin-operated washers and dryers to be able to use first-year expensing. **Used** coin-operated washers and dryers are eligible too.

Counting the coins

If your operation is small and nearby, the **owner** should empty the coin boxes. You can buy cheap counters. In his book, *Landlording*, Leigh Robinson recommends the Nadex Coin Sorter and Packager Model 607 (Nadex Industries, 220 Delaware, Buffalo, NY 14202). It's not a piece of machinery. It's just a sort of pinball machine with no moving parts. You put the coins in the top, shake it, and they fall into tubes sized for each denomination—ready for inserting into those paper tubes you get at the bank.

Spot checks, counters, etc.

When you visit a building where the manager collects the coins, empty the box yourself once in a while. Then divide the amount you find by the number of days since the manager emptied the boxes. That'll give you a collections per day average. See how that compares to the collections per day average the manager has been reporting. If it's significantly **higher**, there is a good chance the manager has been skimming.

You can also **spot check** a concessionaire. When their man appears for his normal collection, ask him to count the money with you present. Again, if the total is abnormally high, you have reason to suspect skimming.

Concession companies also worry about skimming. They send out inspectors who count just before the regular counter arrives and/or put invisibly marked coins in the machines. Some concessionaires have counters on their machines. The owner or manager can read the counters and compare the loads count with the amount of money said to have been collected.

Security

I said earlier that I don't know much about managing 400-unit buildings because I've never managed one. I also don't know much about laundry-security problems because I've never had any to speak of. That's because I don't buy buildings in neighborhoods with security problems—on purpose. And the best advice I can give to you on the matter of security is follow my example.

But if you **have** a building with security problems, here are some suggestions. Some coin-mechanisms are harder to break into than others. You might try the better ones if you have a problem.

It helps to situate your laundry room or manager's apartment—whichever one is easier to move—so that the manager is generally aware of what's going on in the laundry room.

Locking the laundry room at hours when it cannot be monitored can help. Although that may reduce use by those who work odd hours. And thereby reduce income.

Collecting more often will reduce the burglar's take and your loss. Signs saying that the money is collected daily or whatever might help to get that message across.

You can get "coin" mechanisms which do not use coins. Rather they have **credit cards** which charge the tenant's account for each use. Then there's nothing to steal. Those

You can put lots of **windows** on the laundry room so the thief is more likely to be seen—and therefore less likely to try.

If the building is large enough, it might pay to assign an **employee there full time**. That will increase your take by having him or her make change also. Tenants sometimes go to laundramats because they don't have the change for your machines and need the laundramat's change machines.

Don't overlook security. One reader told me his laundry income went from $48 a month to $600 a month at a 66-unit building as a result of his eliminating theft.

Cleanliness

Your laundry room needs to be bright and clean to attract business. Or to avoid repelling it.

If your take seems low, an unattractive laundry room may be the reason. If you cannot figure out why the laundry take is low, try polling your tenants. Talk to some face-to-face. Or have your manager do this. And send a post card poll to all the tenants. Ask them whether they did their most recent load of wash in your laundry room or elsewhere. If elsewhere, ask why not in your laundry room.

Take what the tenants **say** in the poll with a grain of salt. They may sense that you'll cut the charges if they say the "right" thing. That is, they may **say** they always use the local laundramat when the truth is they almost always use **your** laundry.

Don't ask in your poll if the tenants think the charges are too high. I can tell you their answer right now—yes.

9

Garages

Rent garages, don't give them away

Residential properties often have garages. And landlords often throw the garage in along with the apartment or house for the same rent. That's usually a mistake.

The market for garages and the market for apartments or rental houses overlap, but they are not the same. In other words, not all tenants **want** a garage. Few will turn it down if it's free. But since they didn't want a garage to begin with, those same tenants would be willing to pay the same rent for the apartment or house with**out** the garage.

Let's say you have an apartment which rents for $400 a month and includes a garage. Tenants who don't want a garage may decide to rent the place. That means they'd pay $400 without the garage. A garage might rent for $40 or $50 a month. By renting the apartment to one tenant and the garage to another, you can often convert a $400 a month income to a $445 a month income.

Layout has to be right

The garage may be attached to the house. Or it may be in a neighborhood where cars may not be parked on the street overnight.

Some of these problems are correctable. Where you can correct the problem economically, you should. Like locking or walling off a door between a house and a garage. But if some local law or uneconomically correctable architectural problem prevents you from renting the garage separately, try hard to rent only to people who need garage space and are willing to pay extra for it.

Rent level

You set garage rents the same way you do apartments. The highest acceptable bidder. Check the in the area. Especially the miniwarehouses.

owners who rent one or two garages may rent them for far less than they could get. But miniwarehouse owners are usually more businesslike.

If the miniwarehouse has no vacancies, it's too low. Same as with apartments. So you should regard the rents on a **full** miniwarehouse as a subfloor when it comes to setting your rents. In other words, if the miniwarehouse out on the highway gets $40 a month for a 10' x 20' space—and they have no vacancies—you ask $55 for your 10' x 19' garage.

If **your** garages are full, raise your rents.

Marketing garages

The market for apartments and houses is anyone who works in a thirty or forty minute radius of your building. More in some parts of the country. But the market for a rental garage is much smaller. Typically only the immediate neighborhood.

A **sign** strikes me as the best way to market garages. Although some miniwarehouse owners I met in Hawaii told me the *Yellow Pages* was far and away their main marketing method and biggest expense. Note that miniwarehouses almost always locate on high visibility sites with high traffic counts. And they put up a big sign. There is now a Web site called www.selfstorage.net where miniwarehouse owners can advertise.

If you have only a few garages, you can get a Realtor's® sign and have it repainted. "Garage For Rent" and a phone number is all you need.

A very cheap **classified ad** in the local weekly shopper paper **might** be worthwhile. But it's probably a waste of money to advertise in a huge daily with circulation all over the metropolitan area. Remember that the immediate neighborhood is the only market.

Flyers

I pushed my manager at an apartment building with eleven garages to draw up a **flyer** advertising our storage spaces and garages. She had copies made and hand-distributed them to the adjacent apartment buildings. I also wanted her to distribute them to homes in the immediate vicinity. But she protested that they had all seen the "Garage For Rent" sign by now so why bother?

I still suspect that the flyer makes sense. It's cheap. And many locals may have driven by the sign without it registering. A flyer might get through. A flyer might also attract someone who had not thought about renting garage space. And therefore would not be looking in the classified section under "Garage For Rent."

Who rents storage space?

According to the book, *Self Storage*, storage tenants are about 70% residential and 30% commercial. Residential means people who rent apartments or houses or who own homes. Commercial means businesses who need extra space.

Most residential storage tenants are apartment dwellers. They need extra storage because apartments typically don't have very much storage.

Of course, your **own** tenants are your primary market. But the second most important market is tenants in other nearby apartment buildings. Followed by nearby homeowners and businesses.

Imitate the pros

"Imitate the pros" is a piece of advice I find myself giving often. In this case, it means visit a minwarehouse and see how they do things. Look at their **buildings, doors, leases, applications, procedures, policies**. How much do they charge for **security deposit**? What **lease** do they use? What **brand** of door (if yours need replacing)? What kind of **locks** do they use?

Ask the manager for a copy of the lease and application form. Try to get him or her to answer the other questions about how they do things. Try to establish a relationship in which you can call him or her when you have a question about your rental garages.

The book, *Self-Service Storage*

Even if you have one rental garage, you should get and read the book *Self-Service Storage* (Institute of Real Estate Management, 430 North Michigan Avenue, Chicago, IL 60611 apparently out of print. Get it from a library.). You may be thinking, "*I don't own a miniwarehouse. What do I need all this for?*"

The heck you don't. If you own just one rental garage, you have a miniwarehouse business with an annual income of over $500 and probably assets in the $5,000 range. For that you can't be bothered reading a $20 (or whatever) book?

Note the title of that book **used** to be *The Miniwarehouse*. The word "miniwarehouse" has gone out of fashion in the miniwarehouse industry. Scares neighbors too much when you want to build one. And the "warehouse" portion of the word conjures up images of huge facilities and thereby sails over the heads of many prospective tenants.

The Self Storage Association

There is a Self Storage Association (www.selfstorage.org). If you're just an apartment owner with a few garages, don't join. It's too expensive ($375).

The Self Storage Association sells a book called *The Self Storage Rental Agreement* ($29.95, members; $34.95, non-members). It explains in readable detail what should and should not be in your lease and why, including court citations. And it tells you how to present the rental agreement to the tenant.

Non-members can also subscribe to *Self Storage*, the association's monthly magazine, which is probably worthwhile even if you only own a few garages.

What's being stored?

Generally, you don't care what's being stored. Just make sure it isn't potentially harmful either to your tenants or your building. Also, make sure the storage tenant doesn't carry on activities that may violate the law or bother your tenants. Like working on a car or using the garage as a woodworking shop complete with electric heater and electric power equipment all plugged into **your** meter.

It's **storage** space, period. Not a factory or gymnasium or shop. And only storage space for **harmless** materials like snow tires, skis, furniture, boats, etc. Not for flammable liquids, explosives, leaky drums, etc.

I recommend that there be no electric including **no light**. "But how can people see at night?"

For one thing, they can come in the **day** time. If that's not possible, they can bring a flashlight or electric lantern. The authors of *Self Storage* recommend that the manager lend tenants a drop light on a fifty foot cord which can be plugged into an exterior wall outlet. Sounds like a good idea to me.

Otherwise, tenants will be plugging in heaters, freezers, and/or leaving the light on 24 hours a day.

Laws

Landlords are used to living with extremely onerous laws when it comes to tenants' rights. But as a general rule, the laws pertaining to storage tenants are much less onerous. For example, miniwarehouses typically **lock out** tenants who are behind in their rent.

Lock a tenant out of his **apartment** or house for non-payment and you're liable to end up in jail. A deadbeat's home is his castle. But a deadbeat's **storage garage**—that's another story. The law does not like to see people out on the street. But it's willing to be a little more businesslike when it comes to storage space rental.

Of course, you need to **check** the laws of your state before you take action against late paying garage tenants. Especially where the garage tenant is **also** one of your residential tenants. But you can generally expect to find much more even-handed laws when it comes to storage space.

Creating garage space

I'm a big advocate of "reducing the load factor." "Load factor" is a phrase which refers to wasted space in buildings. It's usually used regarding office buildings. And refers to unrentable space like lobbies, stairwells, elevator shafts, and common area rest rooms.

But residential buildings have load factors, too, sometimes. The building I own with eleven garages used to be eleven carports under one of the three buildings which make up the complex. The previous owner enclosed them and installed doors. Thereby raising their rental value considerably. A lockable garage rents for much more than an open carport.

I recommend that you stare at the blueprints of your property at length. Look over every part of the building for nooks and crannies which can be converted to rentable space. Like carports that can be converted to garages.

If you don't have any blueprints, make some. That is, photocopy your survey and draw in, free-hand, the walls as best you can. A rough "blueprint" is adequate.

I got a flyer from Group Management Properties Corporation (6060 N. Central Expressway, Suite 318, Dallas, TX 75206) offering "cash income from portable miniwarehouse units placed on your unused parking areas or vacant lot." A company called Frame Master (1113 Greenville Road, Livermore, CA 94550, 510-443-3161) also makes a variety of steel sheds. They're priced from $650 to $2,390 and you can spend more for additional features.

It doesn't have to be a garage

Space doesn't have to be as big as a garage to be rentable. Heck, consider safe deposit boxes—if you want an example of how small rentable storage space can get.

That same 25-unit building which has eleven garages also has four storage areas. Two are 8 x 10 rooms on the second floor at the dead end created by the stairwell. When I bought the place, one was rented for $10 a month. The other was the office.

The 'office'

Now they're **both** rented for $15 a month each. The "office" is now a desk in the manager's living room. The previous manager told me she thought it was "unprofessional" to not have a separate office. Call me unprofessional. That office generated $180 a year income as a rental—and no expense. Capitalize that at 9% and it means I've added $180/9% = $2,000 to the building value.

Do tenants run the other way when they learn that the manager's office is in her apartment? Not that I know of. What the heck. It's only 25 units. There are too many resident managers who manage their properties from the "fiftieth floor" even though they've only got a two-story building.

An office is a load factor. It produces no income. In a bigger building, you **should** have an office because the volume of traffic would prevent the manager's apartment from being a home. But I wouldn't think an office is necessary until you hit about 50 units. And even then, 10' x 12' ought to be enough.

Under the stairs

That building also had two under-the-stairs closets—both containing landlord property. My manager cleaned one closet out. And we rented it for $10 a month. Later $12.

Apartment building resident managers need storage. But not as much as most of them have. I know of one building where the resident manager used **two apartments** for storage! If one of my managers ever did that, she'd be shot at sunrise.

After renting out the office and the under-the-stairs closet, that building still has another under-the-stairs closet, the boiler room, and an over-the-stairs cabinet for storage of signs, lawn mowers, paint, etc.

Does it sound chintzy to be renting under-the-stairs closets for $10 a month? Doing things like that is the essence of the residential rental business. They add up. The non-garage storage space income when I bought the place was $10 a month. Now it's $15 + $15 + $10 = $40 a month. That's $360 a year in **additional** income and about $360/9% = $4,000 in additional building value.

Hazards in garage rentals

The Texas Apartment Association lists several often-over-looked pitfalls of renting garages. Starting a motor vehicle can **ignite** leaking gas from hot water heaters or fumes from oily rags.

Tenants also tend to store **flammable** materials like oil-based paint and gasoline in garages, and they tend to use garages to work with power equipment, including working on motor vehicles. You must prohibit such storage and activities both in the wording of your leases and regulations and in your policing of violations.

Tenants tend to violate apartment rules regarding nails in apartment walls and such. They are even more inclined to violate the lease regarding **modifications** of the garage.

In some jurisdictions, you must charge **sales tax** on garage rentals and pay that tax to the authorities. Tax generally does not apply when the garage is included in the apartment rent.

10

Forfeited Security Deposits

Not just incidental income

Almost every landlord derives at least part of his income from forfeited security deposits. But many regard it as a footnote on their income statement.

It averages about 2% of the gross.

That puts it in the same size category as laundry income. So you should pay at least as much attention to deposit forfeits as you do to laundry income. **More**, when you consider that forfeits are all **net**. Laundry income is only 2% of the gross **before** utility and other expenses.

Four ways to maximize forfeit income

There are four ways landlords maximize forfeit income. One of them is illegal, immoral, unethical, and generally stinks. That's keeping money when you're not entitled to do so. Don't do that. Landlords who do really honk me off—give the rest of us a bad name.

In twenty-three years in this business, including time as a property manager of other people's apartments, I have **never** been taken to court for not returning a security deposit—let alone **lost** such a case. I don't even recall many disputes which were settled with**out** a court.

That's not to say I don't get my share of tenants who think they should have received more. But they don't persist because we documented our case pretty well when we kept all or part of a deposit. That brings me to the other three ways to maximize deposit forfeit income.

The other three ways

The other three ways to maximize deposit forfeit income are:

• Have a high deposit,
• Strictly enforce the lease,
• Document your case well when you withhold.

Deposit size

The higher the deposit, the more deposit forfeit income you'll have. But there are three limits on that:

• The law,
• The market,
• Stronger tenant motivation.

In most states, state law limits the size of tenant security deposits. Comply with it.

In many states, the rental market is competitive. And one of the ways landlords compete with each other is on the total amount of money needed to move in. The higher the security deposit, the less competitive you are. So you don't want to run the security deposit up so high that the tenants you lose cost you more than the deposits you keep.

The more you have, the harder it is to keep

The **higher** your security deposit, the **harder** tenants work to get it back. In Texas, I used to get $150. Later as low as $100. Most of my tenants there broke their lease (failure to give thirty days written notice is the main violation) and thereby forfeited it. They didn't seem to care.

In New Jersey, I got one and a half month's rent security deposit (in addition to the entire first month's rent—no prorating for mid-month move-ins). That was the legal maximum. On a $300 unit, that's $450. My New Jersey tenants were **very** well behaved when it came time to move out.

They gave thirty days written notice, cooperated with showings while they were still there, worked hard to clean the place, and cleaned it and repaired it again if our inspection turned up any dirt or damage.

So the higher the deposit, the less likely the tenant will commit the offenses which entitle you to keep all or part of the deposit.

Documenting your right to keep it

Documentation starts with the **application form**. Some of the deposits you keep are from people who never move in. Your application should establish your right to keep the deposit if the applicant is approved but decides not to move in. I explained that earlier.

Then comes the **lease**. It must say when you can keep the deposit. And it must conform to state law on the subject.

Finally, comes **proving** the tenant violated the lease.

That's mainly a matter of keeping records. You should have a file on each unit. Whenever a tenant violates the lease, the proof should go into that file.

For example, written but too short notice. Preserve any evidence of the date it was given. The tenant may give 20 days notice. But back date the notice to show 30 days. If it was mailed, keep the envelope with the dated postmark. If it was handed to your manager or you, note the date received on it—so you can remember, mainly. A date written on the notice by the manager or owner doesn't **prove** anything. But it enables the owner or manager to speak with conviction in the event of a trial.

"I know I handed it to the manager on the first, your honor."

"Your honor, I know she did **not** hand it to me on the first. Because whenever a tenant hands me notice I immediately write the date on it. I've had too many tenants try to back date notices to **not** do that."

That's more likely to win in court than:

"I don't remember for sure, your honor, because it was six months ago. But I'm pretty sure the notice was only 20 days. We would have returned the deposit if it wasn't."

"But you aren't sure?"

"Pretty sure, your honor."

"And you, Miss Tenant, you're **positive**?"

"Absolutely, your honor."

Damage and dirt

The other main reason for deducting from security deposits is damage and dirt beyond ordinary wear and tear. Tenants will **always** swear that the previous tenant caused all damage and that the place *"is cleaner than when I moved in."*

Both statements are almost always lies. Or the tenant substitutes "facts" which favor his case whenever memory fails.

That's why you get him to sign a move-in check list **before** he moves in.

If there is damage, get at least one **witness** to join you or your manager in noting it. You should describe the damage in writing, date it, and both witnesses sign it. Then put that statement in the unit file.

Photographs can help. But often the damage is invisible or too hard to see in the photograph. Photographs are more effective as something to **mention** in the letter to the tenant threatening a lawsuit.

We have a statement of the damage signed by two witnesses and color photographs of the damage.

That's usually enough to convince them to run up the white flag.

But if you go into to court with **no** photographs and **no** witnesses other than either you or your manager, you'll probably lose. Because the tenant will typically have a friend or relative who will join him or her in swearing that the damage in question was not there on move-out day.

If there's only one of you, and no photos, you'll probably lose. But just one other witness should throw the battle to your side. Because the judge knows landlords and managers generally have better things to do than make this stuff up.

Not equal to a month's rent

I recommend that your security deposit **not** be equal to a month's rent. If it is, many tenant's will regard it as the **last** month's rent. In that case, you have **no** security deposit. Same goes for **multiples** of a month's rent like two months.

You'll have a far greater incidence of non-payment of the last month's rent if your security deposit amount equals a month's rent.

Strict enforcement

Most **beginner** landlords and managers are far too lenient about giving back security deposits. Many tenants will lean on you when they move out. Pressing you to promise to refund the deposit in full—and do it on move-out day. They need the money.

Your answer must be,

No. I will comply with the lease. That means we will inspect the apartment, check your file to make sure you don't owe us money like late charges from past months, check to make sure you gave proper notice and fulfilled your initial lease term. And we will send you *either your deposit and/or a letter explaining any deductions within thirty days (or whatever your state requires)—**not** on move-out day.*

If you don't do that, you'll be sorry. And I know that if you're a beginner, you **won't** do it. You let the first couple tenants sweet-talk or browbeat you into a premature and overly generous refund.

I'm only hoping that because I am warning you of this here that you will learn **quicker** than you would have had you not read this book. What I've said here, combined with the realization that, "I screwed myself out of $68 on that refund to Mr. Henderson" will cause you to wise up after two or three mistakes instead of a dozen.

11

Other Income

Vending machines

Apartment buildings sometimes have vending machines other than washers and dryers. When I bought it, the Las Brisas had a Coke® machine. I asked the seller how much revenue he got from it per month. He said, "None." *"So why is it there?"* "As a convenience to the tenants."

I had the manager call the company that supplied the machine and ask them if they would pay any rent for it. They said the volume was too low (33-unit building) and refused to pay anything. I told the manager to tell them to remove the machine and also told her to pull the plug on closing day. As I suspected, the vending company took their sweet time in removing the machine. They figured it was earning money while they delayed. Noooope.

A concessionaire I used told me a Coke® machine costs about $10 a month for the electric it uses. But Coca Cola® world headquarters in Atlanta told me their vending machines use an average of 3.9 to 6.9 KWH per day with an average of 6.4. At 10¢ per KWH, that's 10¢ per KWH x 6.4 KWH per day x 30 days per month = $19.20 a month.

One concessionaire I used said usage varies considerably from building to building. Generally, the **lower the income** of the occupants of the building, the higher their per capita usage of soft drink vending machines. He would not give a minimum size building that would warrant a Coke® machine. But after some months of having one at my 25-unit, he pulled it out for inadequate volume. Coca Cola® itself had one in my 33-unit—but they mumbled that the volume there is marginal. So I surmise that 30 to 40 units is probably the minimum to justify a Coke® machine—with extenuating factors like climate and outsider use lowering the mimimum in some cases.

An outdoor freezer on my electric meter

"What about the convenience of the tenants?" you ask. **I** don't have a Coke® machine. The nearest Coke® machine is four miles from my house. I supplied my tenants at that complex with central air-conditioning. I provided them with a refrigerator. I maintained a swimming pool for their use. And there was a shopping area within about 500 yards of the complex. So removing the Coke® machine shouldn't have caused anyone to suffer heat stroke.

If the concessionaire company had at least offered to pay for the electricity, I would have left it there for the convenience of the tenants. But I don't think I should have to subsidize tenants who forgot to buy Coke® at the grocery store or who can't be bothered to walk to a nearby gas station. Neither should you.

Furniture sales

I never intended it, but I seem to make money many years on furniture sales. Buildings I buy often have one or two furnished apartments for one reason or another. I sell off the furniture when that tenant moves. To do that, put an ad in the local weekly shopper newspaper. Or the big daily if there's no cheaper, smaller paper. One of my managers said his former owner had him take left-behind tenant furniture to weekend flea markets and sell it. The manager's compensation was to keep half of the proceeds. Call a used furniture dealer to see what they charge for similar items. And ask them to make you an offer on the stuff you want to sell.

Buying a building with its own furniture

Most stuff can be sold for something. Often more than you think. In fact, one technique for buying a building with little or no money down involves buying a furnished building and selling the furniture to get all or part of your down payment back. It's sort of the residential equivalent of a "leveraged buy out." *"But wouldn't that force you to lower rents?"* You ask.

Sometimes not. If the building is both furnished and under-rented, you can get rid of the furniture and keep the rents the same. Some tenants will protest. Some may even move. But if the rents are fair market value, the vacancies will fill up again without furniture.

Sell appliances, too

Sometimes you replace working appliances for cosmetic reasons. In my early years, I always replaced 21 inch wide gas ranges with 30 inch wide ranges. I thought the 21 inch style made the place look small and cheap. The old ranges were quite used but worked. I figured I'd have to pay someone to haul them away. But first I ran a shopper ad to see if there might be a chance to sell it. Somebody bought the darned thing. I sold a number of them over the years. People said they were for their basement or their second home. Amazing.

So as long as the appliance is working, you can sell it. And for pretty good prices, too. I kept raising the price I asked for my ranges. And never hit any resistance. I was up to about $100 in the early seventies—for a beat up old 21 inch gas range. Never did find out what the fair market value of a used gas range was. But apparently more than $100.

Cash before they load

The typical furniture or appliance buyer is a guy with a helper and a pickup truck. Make them pay you cash **before** they load it onto the truck. Before they even **pick it up** to move it outside. Because if they drop it and break it before they pay you, they'll probably not pay you at all.

And tell them there are no warranties. What they see is what they get. You usually have to demonstrate that it works. But you don't have to guarantee it for thirty days. And you should resist the impulse to do so.

Should you furnish your units?

I don't care for furnished units. But that doesn't mean you shouldn't be in that business. Here are some considerations.

If you rent furnished units, you must **inventory** the furniture at move-in and move-out. The tenant must sign the move-in inventory. And those inventories must cover the **condition** of the furniture as well as list each item.

First-year expensing on furniture

You may **not** claim first-year expensing on the furniture if you **own** the **furnished** building. But a **furniture rental company** *may* claim first-year expensing on the furniture which it rents either to you or to your tenants (Revenue Ruling 81-133).

That means rented furniture generates more tax breaks if it is **not** owned by a landlord. Although there's an $18,500 annual limit in 1998 so don't expect the furniture rental company to do flips. To the extent that the furniture leasing company can use the first-year expensing you should probably either lease furniture from or direct your tenants to a furniture leasing company.

Other advantages and disadvantages

Tenants for furnished properties are typically **more transient**. That means higher turnover.

Furniture gets **heavy wear**. And it gets **stolen**. One **advantage** is less damage to your walls during moving. Much damage is done by tenants' amateur moving men—typically three friends and a six-pack. If the furniture is already there, there's less to move in and out.

If you rent furniture, you'll need **somewhere to store it**. That's because some tenants have their own furniture. Others can **partly** furnish the place. As I said earlier, storage space which **you** use prevents you from renting out that storage space. That costs you money.

Marketing considerations

Often, when you have vacancies to fill, you get calls from tenants who want furnished units. It's tempting at those times to try it. Furnishing some or all of your units may be just the trick you need to fill those vacancies in a tough market. The market changes. The fact that you haven't needed furnished units to stay relatively full in the past doesn't prove that you don't need them now. You must remain flexible and in tune with the market.

Imitate the pros

Again I repeat my "imitate the pros" advice. If you're going to rent furniture, see how the pros do it. Visit a professional furniture rental outfit. Ask for copies of their **forms**. Ask about their **deposit** and **rent** amounts, **lease** terms. And their **credit** checking criteria and standards. Then run **your** furniture rental activities the way they do it.

Amenity fees

Amenities are things like swimming pools, spas, exercise rooms, and tennis courts. Some apartments include use of them in the rent. Others charge extra.

Charging extra is an administrative pain in the neck. A 200-unit building I managed had a swim club. We charged tenants to join. A fee which declined as the swimming season progressed. Those who joined got a badge to pin onto their bathing suit.

That was in New Jersey where state law required a life guard be on duty whenever the pool was open. (That's a shock to my Sun Belt readers, I'll bet. You guys ought to visit a New Jersey landlord some time to see how good you have it. A lot of New Jersey apartment pools are filled with dirt as a result of the life guard requirement.) The life guard collected the membership fees and evicted non-members from the pool area.

Swimming-pool-guest fees

We also had a guest fee. Swimming pool guests are one of the biggest pains in the neck ever invented to vex a landlord or his manager. **Tenants** tend to behave themselves fairly well at the pool. Because you'll evict them if they violate pool or any other building rules.

But what are you going to do if a **guest** violates pool rules? You can't evict them because they don't live there. About all you can do is call the cops. That's a hassle and a half.

At that 200-unit, one guest was asked to pay his fee. He said he'd pay in a few minutes. He didn't. When asked again, he said in a little while. Pleas to the tenant who accompanied him fell on deaf ears. "**I** can't force him to pay," the tenant protested. The guest was asked to leave which he grudgingly did after ignoring the request at first, then arguing. Ultimately, we collected that guest fee from the tenant who invited him. But only after suspending his swim club membership and threatening to evict him from the complex.

90% of the problems—

My Greenbriar manager asked me if we could outlaw all pool guests. I immediately agreed. He said, *"90% of our disputes with tenants are at the pool and 90% of those involve guests."*

Each year, we lost one tenant over that policy. The tenant would violate it. Be told to cease. Call me to protest ("It's my **sister** for Chrisakes!"). Then give notice when I backed up the manager. Bye bye. But that **one** problem was fewer than the more numerous problems we had when we allowed guests.

Should you have a pool at all?

It costs about $2,000-$3,000 a year to operate a pool without a life guard and about $6,000 a year to operate a pool with a life guard. To calculate your pool costs use this check list:

• supplies
• electric for
   light
   filter pump
   heat water
• gas to heat water
• water to replace evaporation and leaks
• Insurance (My agent tells me I pay $68 a year extra for having a pool at my 33-unit)
• Property taxes (the assessor may reduce your assessment if you fill the pool.)
• Permits
• Labor (cleaning, chlorination, repairs, life guard)
• Repairs (leaks, painting, pump replacement, resurfacing, etc.)

You may find the following useful:
   100 cubic feet of water = 748 gallons
   annual electric to run pool pump = 2,790 KWH

According to a study in the November/December 1987 *Journal of Property Management* (www.irem.org), 34% of tenants said they were unwilling to pay a penny extra in rent for a pool. About 45% said they'd pay $10 to $20 per month extra for a pool. I think the tenants were overestimating the amount they'd pay in that survey.

In an article I wrote in the December '86 issue of my *Real Estate Investor's Monthly*, I figured the pool was worth about $2.50 per month to the average tenant. That takes into account the fact that you can only swim three or four months a year in most markets and that the majority of tenants never set foot in the pool in the buildings I've owned.

At $2.50 per month, you need $2,000 ÷ ($2.50 x 12 months) = $2,000 ÷ $30 = 67 units to justify the $2,000 expense of a pool. $6,000 ÷$30 = 200 units if a life guard is required. Past president of the National Apartment Association, Ro Freeman, figures non-life guard pool operation costs about $3,000 and that the cutoff is 60 units. That means he assumes the tenants will pay $3,000 ÷ 60 = $50 per unit per year extra for a pool or $50 ÷ 12 = $4.17 extra a month.

There's a sure way to find out how much tenants think the pool is worth: charge them. If you can't come up with a fee that produces enough revenue to pay for the pool operation, close it.

Fees require toll-takers and enforcers

If you're going to charge fees, you have to have both toll-takers and enforcers. That is, somebody's got to be nearby to take the money. And somebody's got to evict those who got in without paying. In some cases, especially where you already have a life guard or tennis pro or whatever, that person can do toll-taking and enforcing duties. Although that's often easier said than done. The life guard's first duty is to save lives. Unless you're a big high-rise operation or some such, fees for amenities probably aren't worth the hassle. If you consider charging fees, look carefully at the expenses you'll incur before you leap.

Pay phones

You can allow the phone company to put a pay phone on your property in order to get royalties from the local company as well as from a long-distance carrier. I got a $12.44 check for the first twenty days I had the pay phone at my apartment building. Unfortunately, that was also the **last** check Southwestern Bell ever sent me. I've tried in vain to find out why.

Drug dealers have not been a problem. The phone company said if they were, they would rig the phone to only handle **outgoing** calls.

There are several phone companies you can select in most areas. Or you can own the pay phone yourself. Pay phones range from $600 to $1,300 last I checked.

Owning vending machines

You can buy **your own** new or used vending machines. I've seen some advertised for $1,599. I suspect owning them is a **bad** idea unless they are under the observation of your or your employee constantly. One break-in can destroy the machine. And break-ins are apparently common because many vending machines I see at apartment complexes have extra steel plates across their front.

Cellular tower space

In late 1995, Tom Kerr reported in his *Mobilehome Parks Report* (916-659-3381) that cellular phone companies would pay around $1,000 per month for a 25' by 25' pad for a cellular phone tower. Of course, you generally need a permit from the government to put one of those up. One landlord said to make sure you retain the right to rent to competitors of your first cellular tenant.

Location is important. But location in the antenna business is determined by things like centrality, altitude, and driving habits, not by normal real estate criteria.

Offer your tenants a cheap T-1 line

Most computer-literate people are poking along with 28.8K modems and champing at the bit for faster connections to the Internet. When they go to conventions, exhibitors typically use ISDN or T-1 lines to connect their convention computers to the Internet. Once you've seen a T-1 Internet connection in operation, you can't wait to get your own.

But when you inquire about a T-1 line, which is about 48 times faster than a 28.8 K modem, you learn that it costs about $1,500 a month. Ouch!

A computer-science student at Stanford, Mike Petras (415-947-0820), tells me he is working on selling hotels and apartment buildings on the notion of getting their own in-building Web server, tying it to the Net with a high-speed connection, and offering guests and tenants a much cheaper high-speed connection than the phone company. In other words, buy bandwidth in bulk at wholesale and retail it to your tenants for a profit. Petras suggested a 50-unit apartment building might spend $30,000 up front (for a server computer, wiring, and related equipment) and $1,500 a month to offer the high-speed connections to the tenants, who would pay $100 per month or more for the service.

I suspect this would work best in **non**residential buildings. Residential tenants of a certain type—young, highly educated, computer literate, working out of their home—would also pay extra for a high-speed connection. Recent college graduates especially would be prime candidates because they typically had T-1 or even fiber-optic connections in college and cannot believe the molasses speed of real world modems. But the average residential tenant would probably give you a "Say what?" if you offered him a T-1 line.

This is a very dynamic field. What you can do also varies considerably according to your location. Check your local phone companies to see what, if any, buy-wholesale-sell-retail deal you can work out. Keep in mind that the government is likely to pass laws restricting this the way they did with submetering of utilities in the aftermath of the "Energy Crisis." I normally recommend a three-year payback on capital expenditures. But in Internetland, three years covers two iterations of Moore's Law, which says that the price of computing power drops by half every 18 months.

The Toscanna, a new apartment complex built in Sunnyvale (Silicon Valley), CA in 1997, has "ultra-high-speed Internet connections." The units first rented for $1,150 to $2,770 and 25 of the initial 130 tenants agreed to pay $100 per month extra for the T-1 lines.

PART THREE:
<u>POLICIES</u>

12

Policies

All God's landlords got policies

A landlord is a bit like a lion tamer. He's outnumbered—by a group that has weapons superior to his (landlord/tenant laws)—but he's still got to maintain order. Policies are the definition of order. You ought to have:

- Reasonable policies,
- Clearly explained, and
- Strictly enforced.

So for starters, don't adopt a policy unless you have to. Some small owners imitate the pros by adopting the rules of a huge complex. That's a **bad** idea. The smaller the building, the more things can be run on a common sense basis. That's better than bureaucratic rules.

In the lease

I prefer rules, regulations, and policies be in the lease. But many owners have a separate sheet for such things. That's more cumbersome. And dangerous. In one Texas case, a landlord lost a suit in part because they had appended a rules sheet to the lease in which they said they had 24-hour security. The relatives of a tenant who was murdered used that against the landlord in court. The Texas Apartment Association lease the owner had used contained a clause saying the owner was **not** responsible for the tenant's security. Often, the professionally- prepared lease giveth protection from liability which the manager's rule sheet taketh away.

Office hours

Twenty-four hours a day, 365 days a year is the best policy for office hours. It's also too expensive. All daylight hours is probably the best, **workable** policy on office hours. Although smaller buildings like less than 50 units cannot afford even that.

In smaller buildings, you try to hire a manager who normally hangs around the house and let her play it by ear. Instead of a sign listing office hours, a smaller building might just have one of those "Be back at" signs with a clock face.

Except for the holidays when people tend to return home (Christmas vacation and Thanksgiving), holidays are prime rental days. But again, in smaller buildings, you'd be a slave driver to insist on always being open—and possibly be violating wage and hour laws.

Parking

Whatever you do, do **not** assign **numbered parking spaces** to tenants. You'll know you made a mistake the first night. A tenant will knock on your door and say, *"Someone's in my parking space."*

Now what are you going to do? Knock on every door in the complex looking for the violator? The best policy on parking is every man for himself.

Either prohibit the parking of boats, campers, and such—or charge extra. Prohibition is best. Those things detract from the appearance of the complex. And tenants can rent space for them at most miniwarehouse complexes. Also prohibit parking of **unregistered, undrivable vehicles**. Like a car up on cinder blocks. Or a car with a flat tire. That's the mark of a very poorly run complex.

Waterbeds

Used to be every landlord prohibited waterbeds because of all the weight—and the danger of leaks or spills. Turns out that the weight generally isn't a problem. And leaks are rare due to improved designs over the years.

On the other side, a disproportionate number of tenants are young. And waterbeds are quite popular with young people. And it's hard to stop tenants from having them. I have never allowed them. But my tenants have had them anyway. As far as I know, I've never suffered any damage due to a waterbed.

There is an extensive discussion of waterbeds, including a waterbed agreement, waterbed insurance, and all sorts of weight data in Leigh Robinson's *Landlording*. I have never informed myself on the subject. And, in twenty-three years, never found it necessary.

Pets

Fish are about the only pets I allowed. Although I have owned one building where the **previous** owner allowed pets. As you would expect, we had problems. Dog owners let their dogs out several times daily—neither accompanied nor leashed. The dogs do what they were let out to do. Usually on our lawn. And the maintenance man has to clean it up. We made it clear to those tenants that either the tenants will clean up the mess or they will find another place to live.

Here are some of the problems I've had with **illegal** pets.

I stepped into the first floor foyer of a three-story building I owned—and smelled the overpowering odor of a cat litter box overdue for cleaning. Turned out, that cat was on the **third** floor. When confronted, the tenant sang the mating call of all tenants who are caught with illegal pets,

It belongs to a friend. It's just here for a couple days.

Baloney. That's why the Texas Apartment Association lease says,

Resident will not permit anyone's pet, even temporarily, anywhere in apartment or apartment complex without owner's written permission.

I terminated that tenant's lease.

A tenant in a building I managed had a big dog. It urinated repeatedly on the carpet—we learned when she moved out. Also, when visitors came, she locked it in various rooms. Where it apparently spent the entire visit clawing at the door—hollow core birch veneer doors. Bye bye doors. How many times have you had to replace all the **doors** in a unit on turnover?

We sued her. She paid us all the money she owed. It helped that she was employed as a clerk in the court where we sued. "This is embarrassing to me in my job!"

"So pay for the damage."

"I will. But cancel that suit immediately."

"We'll cancel it when we receive the money you owe us in cash, cashiers check, or money order."

She paid that day.

That's incredible

It has been said that the Mayflower was the largest ship ever built—had to be to fit in the ancestors of all the people who claim their ancestors came over on the Mayflower. By the same token, any tenant who admitted that his dog or cat ever would cause problems could go on *"That's Incredible."* Tenants have the world's most amazing pets. Their dogs don't bark, or urinate or defecate anywhere but in a gutter two blocks away. Their cats' litter boxes never smell. Nor do their cats ever use their claws on anything but a scratching post. If you don't believe me, just sit in on any application interview where the prospect has a pet.

The behavior of tenant pets is all the more amazing when you consider that 100% of the dogs and cats owned by **home owners** bark, fail to wait for "walkies," scratch carpet, and remind their owners to clean their box by causing it to smell bad.

Forget the small pets OK policy

Many owners allow **small** pets. Forget it. They all do the things listed above. And some of them are still growing. And your **other** tenants will argue that a "70 pound Doberman is not as bad as a 20 pound pit bull," etc., etc.

Tenants complain that landlords adopt blanket policies rather than punish those who don't take care of their pets. Tenants of the world, try being a landlord for a while. If you allow **any** pets, other tenants will argue that they should be allowed to have **every** pet. It's not workable. Everybody understands a no-pets policy. A no-pets-over-20-pounds policy raises the questions:

- "Why not 21 pounds?"
- "Are German Shepherd puppies under 20 pounds OK?"
- "My boa constrictor is only 18 pounds. What's the problem?"
- "Are helium-filled, large dogs who are so ravenous from dieting that they're gnawing on the scale OK if they weigh 19 pounds, fifteen and three quarters ounces?"

Forget pets. Prohibit them in your lease. And terminate the lease of anyone who allows a pet in the place. Even if it's someone else's and only temporary and all that. Do **not** give them a week to get rid of it. Tenants **say** they'll get rid of pets. But they don't. They just try harder to hide them from you. And do not delay confronting the tenant. You or your manager should take action **the day you discover** the pet.

If you allow pets

Many of you will allow pets in spite of my advice. If so, you can and should get **extra deposit money and extra rent.**

Living in sin

It's none of your business.

Fair Housing Amendments

The Fair Housing Amendments Act does not apply to structures occupied by no more than four families if the owner occupies the structure as his residence. 24 GFR 100.10(c)(2)

Transfers from one unit to another

Make the tenant sign a new lease and put up a new security deposit on the new unit before they move. Then make a full inspection just as on any other move-out regarding damage and cleanliness. Return the old security deposit less appropriate deductions to the transferred tenant as you would with one who moves away from the building.

If you fail to get the tenant to sign a new lease, there is **no written lease** in effect. Apartment 101 is not the same as apartment 102. And if a tenant lives in 102, but you only have a lease from when they were in 101, you got nothing.

Number of occupants

The Fair Housing Amendments Act of 1988 prohibits discrimination against tenants with children except where:

- **All** the residents of the property are over 62, or
- 90% of the residents are over 55 and "**special services**" for seniors are provided.

You may not put families with children in one part of your property like all on one floor or all in one building of a complex.[24 CFR 100.70(c)(4)] Southern California Community Newspapers, a three-paper chain, filed bankruptcy rather than fight a lawsuit over their printing the words "adults only" in a classified ad.

If local law doesn't state a maximum number of persons per bedroom, you can adopt a "reasonable" policy. HUD's general counsel has said two will generally be considered reasonable. But lately they have indicated plans to change that to a minimum square footage standard. Most state laws allow more than two per bedroom. At one point, NJ said no less than 100 square feet per person—which would allow five or six people in the typical one-bedroom apartment. Texas says no more than three times as many adults as bedrooms.(TPC §92.010)

Storage

Do **not** provide free storage. Rent it. Never provide **common storage**. They did that at Harvard University housing I lived in. What a disaster. People would only store stuff they cared little about there. And when they moved, they often left it there.

The manager wanted to clean the place out. But how? Put a note on each piece of property warning that it would be removed in three weeks or some such? What if they didn't go down there for three weeks? But when they **did** go down for the property in eight weeks, they found it missing?

They ended up having to send multiple notices to every tenant in the building that the common storage was being phased out. And they had to store stuff in an interim location to make sure no one would claim it belatedly—and file suit.

If you provide lockable individual storage lockers, make them **secure**. Some owners divide individual storage lockers with nothing but 2 x 4s and chicken wire. No good. You should not be able to **see** what's in someone's storage locker. And chicken wire provides virtually no security. Security is the main issue in miniwarehouses. And the storage in your property is a mini-miniwarehouse, remember?

Antennas

Prohibit outside antennas.

Drapes

I provided drapes in all my Texas buildings (but not in the kitchen or bath). That's the market and the policy. In the buildings I managed in New Jersey, the **tenants** were required to provide drapes. That led to some problems. Our policy was the drapes must really be drapes, **not:**

- Sheets
- Aluminum foil
- Tents
- Blankets
- Newspaper

and they had to be white. We were constantly sending notices to tenants to get rid of their unauthorized drapes. If I were back in New Jersey, I **still** wouldn't furnish drapes if the market still allows that. I'd just keep after the people who were violating the policy. Drapes are expensive.

Don't allow different colors showing out. Different colors on the **inside** are OK. As long as the drapes are lined in white and show white outside. You **can** allow different color drapes—or even non-drape drapes in window which cannot be seen by other tenants or the public. But **only** there.

Do not allow non-drape drapes which can be seen. Makes the place look like Tobacco Road.

Abandoned vehicles

Get rid of abandoned vehicles as soon as you find them. Local law is often pertinent. Check it out before you touch the vehicle. In Texas, for example, you have to have signs worded a certain way in order to tow away cars. Cars are expensive. So you need to be very careful. Make sure you **strictly** abide by the law when having a car towed.

Disreputable vehicles

Make tenants get rid of disreputable vehicles as soon as you find them. Disreputable vehicles include those with:

- Flat tires,
- Major collision damage,
- No tires,
- No license or registration,
- Mechanical problems which render them undrivable.

Set a reasonable deadline—like a week—then terminate the tenant's lease if they don't comply.

Lease term

I recommend six months. Less than that and you're running a motel. I do **not** like **longer** leases either. Leases are a one-way street. They prevent you from raising rent or being able to rent the place to someone else. But tenants still move whenever they feel like it.

Tenant improvements to property

First, remember that tenants wanting to make expensive improvements are a sign of low rents. Raise them. Otherwise, you must exercise tight control over tenant improvements. When it came to painting, I allowed my New Jersey tenants to paint their units. (We painted between tenants in the big complexes I managed, but not in my own smaller buildings. In Texas, we painted as needed.)

I found young tenants did **not** know how to select paint colors. So I picked the colors for them. Landlords like white. But if you restrict tenants to white, they lose interest.

So I gave them a letter which listed the acceptable Sears Roebuck paint colors. Here they are:

- Jungle Moss Light
- Light Lemon
- Autumn Wheat
- White Tawny
- Avocado Heather Light
- Crystal Blue
- White
- Winter White
- Antique White
- Semi-gloss white for woodwork
- Bright White ceiling paint

These are all quite pastel. I warned the tenants that these colors would look too light in the **store**. But when they got them on the **walls**, they would look OK. Furthermore, I told them the colors which looked right in the store, looked **ghastly** on the walls. Beginners tend to buy colors which are too dark.

That's because in the store they see only a small swatch—and that's under dozens of fluorescent ceiling lights. When that same color covers a whole wall—and the only light is from a 60-watt incandescent bulb in a lamp, the color is too dark.

Workers compensation

Did you know that when a tenant paints his apartment or house and you give him some consideration for that, like free paint, or a rent discount, that he may come under workers compensation laws? That is, if he's in a car accident while on the way to the hardware store to buy a paint roller, and is injured, **you** could be liable on the grounds that he was working for you.

Lock-outs

Tenants often lose or forget to take their keys with them. Then they go to the manager and ask him or her to let them into their apartment. Often late at night. If I were the resident manager, I'd probably have no lock-out fee the **first** time it happened to a particular tenant. But I **would** charge tenants who locked themselves out repeatedly. As an owner, I did not set any lock-out policy. I left it up to my resident managers.

The lock-out fee, if any, should be large enough to discourage a repeat. But not so large as to encourage the tenant to **break in**. If you charge a high lock-out fee, the tenant may kick the door in or break a widow—then claim a burglar did it. Damage like that will cost you a lot to fix.

Noise complaints

Some leases have hours when stereos, musical instruments, etc., can be played. I prefer a common-sense basis. That is, "Don't disturb your neighbors."

If a tenant **does** disturb his neighbors, tell him to knock it off. If he disturbs his neighbors in a six-month period, terminate his lease.

"But what if we have a high vacancy rate at the time?" you may ask. Terminate him. High vacancy rates are caused by marketing failures and/or overly high rents, **not** by failing to allow tenants to disturb their neighbors.

Bad checks can sometimes be cashed

Texas Apartment Association legal counsel, Larry Niemann, wrote in an article in *Texas Apartments* magazine that you can sometimes force the tenant's bank to honor bad checks. This occurs when the tenant's bank fails to meet the "midnight deadline." The midnight deadline is a provision of the Uniform Commercial Code which says roughly that a bank must pay or return a check by midnight of the next banking day after they receive it. That applies whether the reason for not honoring the check is insufficient funds, closed account, or whatever (except forgery).

You find out whether the tenant's bank met the deadline by looking at the date stamps on the check when you get it back.

(In Texas, the citations are sections 4.104-5 and 4.302-3 of the UCC of the State of Texas. Your state may have different section numbers or have a different rule. The Uniform Commercial Code is generally in effect in most states.)

Death of a tenant or employee

If you are in this business long enough, one or more of your tenants or employees will die in your apartment complex. One of my managers died in 1987. A tenant died in 1990.

If the tenant lived alone, there are dangers. Mainly that the rent will go unpaid while the unit is unrentable because the deceased tenant's belongings are still there. And people often falsely accuse landlords and managers of stealing the deceased's property. The property in question may not have existed let alone been stolen. Or the accuser may be the thief.

Here's a check list based in part on an article Larry Niemann wrote in the Spring '86 *Texas Apartments*.

- Notify the authorities like the police or rescue squad and coroner.
- You and a witness must accompany anyone, including the above folks, who goes into the unit, to prevent theft.
- Change the locks. The deceased may have given the key to a friend or relative who may steal and blame you.
- The estate is liable for the rent after death until the unit is vacated. If your state allows you to confiscate property for nonpayment of rent, you can confiscate the deceased's property for that purpose. Always make sure you comply with the procedures required by your state and that you have a witness who also signs an inventory of what you removed.
- Evict the estate using the normal procedure if they breach the lease—most likely by non-payment of rent.
- Your application forms or leases should say whom you are authorized to turn the property over to in the event of the tenant's death. If they don't—or if someone other than the person named by the deceased tries to remove the property—be very careful who you let take that property. Check with a local real estate attorney if you are in that situation.

In the absence of clear instructions from the deceased, releasing the property is an **extension of credit**, in effect. Because if you release it to the **wrong** person, you could have to pay for it. So use the same kind of credit procedures you apply to leasing. Like a **written agreement** including an inventory between you and the person taking the property in which they indemnify you against claims by someone else who says the property is theirs. Then keep in mind that a written agreement is no better than the people who sign it. Try to get a local co-signer or bond or some such if there is a question about your ability to enforce the indemnification agreement against the person you give the property to.

Evictions

Maybe I'm just lucky. But in 22 years as an landlord—including a year as a property manager—I have never evicted anyone in the sense of having the sheriff remove their belongings. I have **filed** about eight eviction lawsuits. But only two people ever showed in court. One came to point out an error in the complaint. (He was a drug dealer and professional deadbeat.) Several days later, we filed again and he disappeared. The other tried to pull a *Pacific Heights* but was too dumb. Disappeared is what all the other people did, too.

But I am assured there is such a thing as an eviction. If you need to do one, I refer you to such books as:

• Leigh Robinson's *Eviction Book for California* ($14.95 plus tax and $2.00 for shipping ExPress, P.O. Box 1639, El Cerrito, CA 94530)
• *The California Rental Housing Reference Book* ("The Gold Book"), California Apartment Association, sold through local chapters
• *The Texas Apartment Association Red Book*, sold through local chapters.

I presume and hope that other apartment associations publish up-to-date reference books on local and state laws pertaining to evictions and other situations. The Fall, 1986 issue of *Texas Apartments* magazine had an article by Texas Apartment Association Legal Counsel, Larry Niemann you might also want to get. It contained, in effect, a fill-in-the-blank script for the resident manager to read to the judge at eviction trials. This would be appropriate either if the resident manager or an attorney handles the eviction. Niemann says the judges will love you for using such a check list.

Utility turn off

It's illegal in most places that I'm aware of to turn off the tenant's utilities for nonpayment of rent. But In Texas, at least, we can do it if the landlord pays for the utility in question. If your state allows that, just make sure you comply with the notice requirements. We used this in my master-metered Texas building when someone is a couple days overdue. Worked pretty good. Maybe that's one reason I haven't had any evictions.

Landlord's lien

Landlord's liens, which are not allowed in most states, enable you to confiscate such property as stereos and tvs from the apartment or house of a delinquent tenant. We use this at times. I always have my manager take an adult witness and have them both sign an inventory of what was taken. Do **not** tell the tenant where the property is stored. They are likely to break in and take it.

Tenants whose property has been confiscated invariably utter the Mating Call of the Landlord's Lienee:

But you don't understand. It wasn't **my** *whatever. It belonged to my [friend or relative].*

If the property does, in fact, belong to someone other than the tenant, you have to return it. The key word in the law is "**know.**" When you "know" the property belongs to someone other than the tenant, you have to return it. [Texas Property Code, section 54.042(13)]

Make sure it is properly printed in your lease where permitted. In Texas, it has to be underlined or otherwise emphasized to be enforceable. Also, make sure you leave the proper notice as you remove the property. If you plan to confiscate the property while the tenant is **in** the unit—which I do **not** recommend—you'd better take **lots** of witnesses—and maybe a video camera with lights and operator. The Texas Apartment Association *Redbook* has a two-page checklist of recommended landlord's lien procedures.

Maintenance requests

Insist that they all be in writing. My managers did not and the judge held that against us when he awarded a former tenant $80,000 in a negligence-leading-to-rape case.

File destruction

If you destroy old files, it is important that you have a **uniform** policy. Because if you destroy some files and not others, it will look like you destroyed adverse evidence in the event of litigation.

At the very least, you must not destroy files until permitted by law. Some states have specific laws which pertain to how long specific files must be retained. Also, you'd better not destroy any files until after the statute of limitations has run out on the issues in question. For example, in Texas, there is a two-year statute of limitations on personal injury suits.

One reason to destroy files is to avoid onerous discovery. Opposing attorneys will often demand that you go through and produce huge quantities of documents—not because they want the documents—but rather just to jerk you around and run up your attorney's fees. On the other hand, old files can be invaluable in **winning** suits or reducing the size of settlements or judgments. If you are doing the right thing, preserving files to prove it is probably the best course of action.

Cash

Receipts are required by law in some states, e.g., Texas Property Code § 92.010. If you receive more than $10,000 in cash in one year from one person, like rent on an apartment that rents for $835 a month, you must report it to IRS on their Form 8300 (31 CFR 103.11). Cash includes cashier's checks, bank drafts, travelers checks, and money orders. [IRC §6050I Proposed Reg. 1.6050I-1(c)(ii)(b), IR 91-62]. There are both civil and criminal penalties for failure to comply.

Safety representations

Time after time in recent years I have read of landlords losing multimillion dollar lawsuits because their employee or an independent contractor they used said something or was accused of saying something about the property being safe. You and your employees should say nothing about security. Anything you say can and will be held against you in a court of law.

Required posters

In dictatorships, like the Soviet Union or Nazi Germany, they always had signs all over telling people what to do. With more and more government involvement in the apartment business, apartment lobbies are looking downright totalitarian. The federal government can now fine you up to $7,500 for not putting up the following posters: Employee Polygraph Protection Notice, Federal Minimum Wage Act Posting, OSHA poster, and an EEO poster (29 USC §215). States have another list of posters they want and their own separate penalties for not putting them up. California currently wants six state posters up and fines you up to $1,000 for not having them. (Labor Code § 6431, 1199) Of course, the list of posters grows longer constantly. Join your state apartment association to keep up with these laws.

13

The Lease

One-way street

The lease is a one-way street in the minds of most tenants and judges. It obligates the landlord, but not the tenant. So you don't have a written lease to keep the tenant in the property until the end of the lease term. Rather, you have a written lease because if you don't, the state imposes its own lease in the event of a dispute. The state's lease is much more favorable to the tenant than the typical written lease.

Minimum requirements

A lease must have at least the following elements to be legally valid:

- Names of the landlord and tenant,
- Rent amount,
- Address of the apartment or house being rented,
- Starting and ending dates.

Some states have extensive laws as to what may or may not be in a lease. And in some cases, if you include an illegal clause, the **entire** lease is invalid. So you have to be careful about what you put in.

Lease forms

In New Jersey, I wrote my own lease. In fact, I typed out the entire lease every time I rented an apartment in the early years. The advantage was that I knew the lease cold. Later, I had a printer make a hundred copies with appropriate blanks.

Stationery stores sell lease forms. Don't use them. They're typically long on fancy lettering and short on the clauses you need.

Apartment association leases

If you have a strong apartment association in your state, they are almost certainly the best source of lease forms. I always used the Texas Apartment Association lease since I first invested there in 1978.

Why apartment association leases are best

The leases prepared by strong apartment associations are excellent because they typically have an attorney who specializes in landlord/tenant law. Part of his job is to monitor court decisions and new statutes and modify the lease as necessary. He should also make changes whenever the members of the association report practical problems with the current wording of the lease.

Owners of single-family rental houses should join the apartment association and use their leases—perhaps adding a few clauses that are pertinent to houses.

If you don't have a strong apartment association

If you are in an area which does not have a strong apartment association, find a strong landlord/tenant **attorney**. Ask some of the largest apartment owners in the area who they use. See which attorneys are filing the most evictions in the local courts. Ask the state bar who, if anyone, is making speeches on landlord/tenant law at their next convention—or their last one. Ask your state legislators' offices what attorneys have testified on behalf of landlords regarding landlord/tenant laws in the state legislature recently. What attorneys have represented landlord interests in drafting recent landlord/tenant laws?

Word processor leases

If you have a computer handy, put your lease in it and print several copies every time you need them. The computer will make it easy to modify the lease—not only when laws require changes—but when you discover practical problems unique to your property—like prohibiting tenants from parking on the lawn—or from putting out the trash in paper bags.

Owner's name on the lease

Leases have a blank for the owner's name. If the apartment building has a name, the manager or owner often writes the **building's** name in the owner blank. That's OK **only if** you have filed a fictitious or assumed name statement with the local government. A tenant may be able to invalidate the lease or an eviction filing or other lawsuit if you list the apartment building name and have not registered it.

Apartment number

The apartment number must be correct and current. This is mainly a problem if a tenant transfers from one apartment to another. A lease with the wrong or an out-dated apartment number is waste paper.

Permitted use

Prohibit any use other than private residence. Running businesses that generate traffic or extra

Prohibit any use other than private residence. Running businesses that generate traffic or extra occupants causes extraordinary wear and tear on the property. And may put you in violation of **zoning**. The typical problem is a tenant who wants to operate a day-care center. Your answer must be no.

One rental house owner I know called me for advice. A neighbor of the house had called to say that the tenant had cut a **new door** in the house! Turned out the tenant wanted to operate a day care center—in direct violation of the lease—and needed a separate entrance to meet California certification requirements.

The landlady asked me what she should do. "Throw them out and sue for damages!" I said. *"But they're good tenants,"* she protested.

"Good tenants!?" I said. "Are you crazy!? They just did a thousand dollars worth of damage to your house—in direct violation of the lease—and kept it secret from you—and you call them good tenants! What would they have to do for you to call them **bad** tenants?"

The lengths to which some landlords go to avoid confrontation with bad tenants blows my mind.

Some businesses, like my writing and publishing out of my home, are so innocuous that they should not be banned. In fact, such people **enhance** security. So don't ban all home businesses. Only those which cause zoning violations, extra wear and tear, or disturb the neighbors.

Who gets to live there

Your lease should name all the people—including children, mothers-in-law, etc.—who will be living in the property. The reason is you don't want a mob—or anyone you haven't checked out. You should limit occupancy to as many as local, state, or federal law permit.

Visitors

Tenants must have the owner's written permission for overnight visitors who stay more than blank days or more than twice that many nonconsecutive days in one month.

If you spell out who's living in the unit, the tenant could get around that clause by saying a new roommate is "just visiting." By defining acceptable visit durations in a reasonable fashion in the lease, you restrict their ability to use that dodge.

Subletting

Require your written permission for any subleasing.

Term

I recommend an initial term of six months, followed by automatic month-to-month renewals. Remember that the lease is a one-way street. It prevents you from raising the rent. But it doesn't prevent the tenant from moving whenever he or she feels like it. (Technically, it does. But as a practical matter, the tenants ignore their obligation.) So you want the shortest possible lease—without allowing stays so short you're running a motel. Do **not** make tenants sign a new lease every year. Make sure you lease has an automatic extension clause. New leases are a waste of time and money unless they contain important up-dating of terms.

Notice

You should require at least thirty days written notice. Sixty is better. And it must be **written** notice. If you accept verbal notice—rent the place—and the old tenant does not move out—you've got a problem.

Also, the notice must state a **definite** move-out date. Vague notice that, "We plan to move this

Notice doesn't count until it's **in writing** and states a **definite date**.

Rent, due date, late charge

The lease should state:

- Monthly rent
- Due date
- Late charge
- Form of payment
- Place of payment
- That the rent is paid **in advance.**

Most leases have **grace periods**. That's dumb. If you say the rent's due on the first, and give a five-day grace period, you're really saying it's due on the fifth of every month. Why is it any easier to pay on the fifth of every month than on the first of every month? The rent's due once a month either way. How are you being a nicer guy to give the grace period? You're not. Grace periods are stupid. All they do is make the due date vague. That's bad. Do **not** give grace periods.

Late charge

You **must** have a late charge—to discourage late rents. Do **not** view late charges as extra income like laundry money. One small building I bought showed over a hundred dollars a month in late charge income. The seller wanted me to capitalize that income and pay more for the building because of it. I was inclined to pay **less** for the building because I'd have to get rid of those scuzball tenants. As indeed I did after closing.

A properly-run building has very little late charge income. Late charges in my two buildings averaged .23% of the gross income over one four year period. That's **point** two three percent. If you have higher late charge income, tighten up your tenant screening and lease enforcement.

Your late penalty should be as high as the law allows. Exceeding the legal limit may be construed as usury. Also, there should be a **per day** charge for each additional day of lateness. Otherwise, once a tenant is late, they'll figure "why hurry?"

'Discount' for on-time payment

Instead of a late charge, a lot of landlords give a "discount" for on-time payment. The landlords and property managers who do this typically claim it's the greatest idea since round wheels. It's not. It's just a late charge in discount's clothing.

You wouldn't advertise the undiscounted rent. But when you ask the tenant to sign the lease it says the rent is higher than you advertised. You then explain the discount for on-time payment brings the rent down to the advertised level. But the bait-and-switch aspect of having one rent in the ad and another in the lease is a turn off and could even be illegal or jeopardize enforcing the lease. I suspect judges are a little put off by the discount instead of a late charge on the grounds that it seems like you're trying to put something over on someone. Rules number one and two of my Reed's Rules of Real Estate Finance are "Simple is better than complex" and "Familiar is better than exotic." That's a good rule to apply to leases, too. Late charges are simple and familiar. Discounts for on-time payment are less so.

Due date

Make all the rents due the **first** of the month. I started out making the person's move-in date their monthly due date. If they moved in the eighth, their rent was due on the eighth of every month. That

Due date

Make all the rents due the **first** of the month. I started out making the person's move-in date their monthly due date. If they moved in the eighth, their rent was due on the eighth of every month. That was OK until I got 20 units. Then it drove me nuts. So I switched everyone to the first.

Semi-monthly and weekly rents

As the Texas market collapsed, I found it necessary to agree to semi-monthly and weekly rent collections. That's a pain. But it beats vacancies. Although such tenants tend to chronic delinquency.

If you allow tenants to pay more than once a month, charge a **premium** for the privilege. I recommend your semi-monthly and weekly rents be calculated by the following formula:

Semi-monthly rent:	110% x monthly rent divided ÷ 2
Weekly rent:	120% x monthly rent ÷ 4.3

For example, if your monthly rent is $350, your semi-monthly and weekly rents would be

Semi-monthly rent:	110% x $350 ÷ 2 = $192.50
Weekly rent:	120% x $350 ÷ 4.3 = 97.67

Round off to the nearest dollar. Weekly rentals may bring your building under hotel/motel regulations. Check your local and state laws.

Mail payments

When I first moved to California, I still owned twenty units in New Jersey. I had those twenty tenants mail their rent to me in California. Using the mail forced me to establish criteria for deciding when the rent was late. I chose this wording.

Rent will be considered late if received by the owner after the first and not postmarked at least three Postal Service working days prior to the due date.

Returned-check charge

You ought to have a charge for each returned (bounced) check a tenant gives you. In many cases, your bank will charge you for depositing it. Your charge should cover that charge plus the hassle.

In most areas, writing a bad check is a **criminal**, not civil, offense. Most other landlord/tenant disputes are civil. When someone breaks a criminal law, you can call the **police**. The police can get warrants for their arrest, read them their rights, take them "downtown," "book 'em" (not for "murder one" though), and all that. A lot of tough guy tenants have an attitude adjustment when confronted by a police officer.

A returned check is also a late payment. So charge the late penalties—both initial and daily.

Keep it in the file

Sometimes tenants who owe late penalties don't pay them. But they do stop paying late. In those cases, you probably don't want to evict the tenant. But neither do you want them to get out of paying the late penalty.

Write the amount they owe and put it into their lease file so that you'll see it when it comes time to return their security deposit or transfer the security deposit to a new owner.

Partial payment

If local law permits, include a clause which says you can accept partial payment without losing any rights to the rest.

Form of payment

Get cash, cashier's check, or money order on **move-in day**. Thereafter, personal checks or money orders are better than cash because lots of cash is a temptation to embezzlement or robbery.

But if a tenant pays me with a bad check, I sometimes insist that they pay their rent in the future in cash, cashier's check, or money order. Your lease should give you the right to do that.

Some leases prohibit cash payment to deter employee theft. In fact, an increase in the amount of cash deposited should cause you to become suspicious of your manager and question him or her about it.

Proration

Prorate the **second** month's rent, not the first. If you prorate the first month's rent, the tenant can move in toward the end of the month on little more than the amount of the security deposit. Remember I told you that the move-in money is sometimes the **only** real money you ever get from a tenant.

Example: Tenant moves in on the 25th of March. The rent is $300. But since you prorate the **second** month's rent, you get the full $300. That covers the tenant from March 25 through April 24th. On April 25th, the tenant owes six days (April 25th through 30th) x $300/30 days = 6 days x $10 per day = $60 rent in April. Then on May first and the first of every month thereafter, he owes you the full $300.

By prorating the second month's rent, you make sure the move-in money is always the security deposit plus one month's rent. That's enough money to send some of the deadbeats—who would try to move into your building to someone less careful's building—which is a far better place for them than **your** building.

Furnished or not

The lease should say whether the unit is furnished or not. If it is, there should be an attached inventory and signed inspection sheet saying whether the furniture had any nicks or scratches or other damage at the time it was rented.

Who pays which utilities?

Spell out who pays which utilities. Also require the tenant to keep the **heat on** to at least 50 degrees 24 hours a day n the winter to prevent frozen pipes (which burst and flood the place when they thaw).

If any utilities other than the tenant's are on the tenant's meter, either rewire the place or tell the tenant in the lease. People will often accept a minor extra charge if you tell them **in advance**. But if you do **not** tell them and they find out on their own, look out!

My first duplex had a central heating boiler. It was fueled by oil which I paid for. But it had a little blower motor which had to be on someone's meter, so the previous owner had put it on the first floor tenant's meter. I had never thought about the blower's electric.

Then one day, the first floor blew a fuse and the tenant noticed the heat went off. Then he discovered the blower motor for both units was on **his** meter.

He asked me to install a third owner's meter just for the blower. I looked into it and found that the cost of doing so was quite high—and the amount of electric the blower used was negligible—so I refused. Nevertheless the tenant complained for years. And when I sold the property, he immediately persuaded the new owner to separate meter the blower. I'll bet if I had told the tenant about the blower **before** he moved in—at a time of severe apartment shortage—he'd have probably said, "No problem," and never thought about it again.

If you pay the electric, limit the appliances the tenant can have to prohibit freezers and electric space heaters and such. Tenants who insist on such extras should pay a surcharge.

Subordination

The lease should contain a clause stating that the lease is subordinate to existing and future mortgages placed upon the property.

No alterations

The lease should require written permission for any alterations. Among the alterations I've heard of are new doors installed by the tenant to qualify the property as a day care center and walls painted black for psychedelic light use.

Picture hanging

They're going to do it whether you allow it or not. So just limit the number to about two per room and require them to repair the holes. Note that tenants sometimes "repair" them with white toothpaste. That doesn't work.

Locks

The landlord and resident manager should have a key to every door in the building. That means the lease must prohibit tenants from installing or rekeying locks and not giving the owner or manager the key. One reason is emergencies. Like water coming out of the apartment into another apartment.

Prohibit lock installation without your written permission. But check your local law on the subject. Some jurisdictions allow tenants to change locks without landlord permission. Make sure your lease conforms to local law. State and local laws are increasingly detailed on the kind of locks you must provide and on rekeying on turnover.

Reasonable wear

The lease should contain a clause in which the tenant agrees to allow no damage to the unit beyond "ordinary wear and tear."

Tenant's guests

The lease should make the tenant responsible for the behavior of his guests if permitted by state law.

Owner not liable for certain injuries or damages

If your state law allows this (Texas does to an extent), by all means include it. If it invalidates the lease, as it would in some states, do **not** include it.

Insurance

Urge the tenant to carry **contents** (home owner/tenant insurance policy) insurance. Tenants' belongings are **not** covered by the landlord's hazard insurance. Although many tenants **think** they are.

When the tenant suffers a loss, they typically ask for reimbursement. When told they aren't entitled to any, they often talk to a lawyer. He or she will tell them that they can only collect from the landlord if the landlord was **negligent**. The landlord's liability policy usually covers negligence claims against the landlord.

The tenant and the attorney then try to find ways to say that the loss was caused by the landlord's negligence—even if it wasn't. And they sue you. If, however, the tenants had home owner/tenant insurance, they would just file a claim with their **own** insurance company and the thought of suing would probably never occur to them.

Repairs

The lease should give the owner reasonable time to make repairs when something breaks down. When a Texas **home owner's** air-conditioning breaks down, he gets it fixed as quickly as possible—but he tries to get it done for a reasonable cost, too. And if that takes an extra day, well he'll buy some extra lemonade and sit in a tub full of cold water in the meantime. But when a Texas **tenant's** air-conditioner breaks down, he wants it fixed RIGHT NOW! Until it's fixed, he wants to be put up at a motel at the owner's expense.

Baloney. Comply with the reasonable time clause in the lease. Do not put people up in motels. Virtually everyone puts up with a lack of air-conditioning for a day or two when a break down occurs. I have at my home a couple times. Tenants are no better than the rest of us.

The repair clause should also give the owner the right to enter the unit during reasonable hours, turn off utilities, and do work there as needed. Require that all maintenance requests be in writing.

Tenant damage

Aside from moving damage, tenants do a lot of damage with **water**. Namely leaving the windows open when it rains and putting things in drains which stop them up. Tenants generally recognize that open windows are their fault—unless you failed to get them to sign a move-in check list—in which case they will say about the water damage, "It was like that when I moved in." But tenants tend to think **drain stoppages** are the landlord's fault.

Wrong. A drain has no moving parts. It's nothing but a **hole**—a pipe. It does not malfunction. It only stops up. And then only when someone puts something improper into it. That's why drain stoppages are the **tenant's** responsibility.

That's one reason why your insurance policy probably **excludes** drain stoppages. Ask your insurance agent if that's true in your policy. If the tenant stops up a drain and the carpet is ruined as a result, it is typically **not** covered by insurance.

Make the guilty tenant pay for drain stoppages and their resulting damage. Give them a week to come up with the money. Sue them in small claims court if they don't. Make sure your lease requires the tenant to pay for drain stoppage damage which they cause.

Obstruction and external storage

The lease should prohibit tenants from using common areas (halls, sidewalks, parking lot, etc.) for personal storage. It's dangerous and unsightly.

Trash and garbage

The lease should say where trash and garbage must be put. And in what kind of containers if appropriate.

Parking

If local laws require it, the lease should give the owner the right to exert reasonable control over the complex's parking areas.

Rules and regulations

The lease should give you the right to promulgate rules and regulations and to change them. **Be careful**, though. As I mentioned earlier, a property management company in Texas got zapped to the tune of millions of dollars by putting a statement in rules and regulations about "24-hour security guards."

A tenant was killed. Neighboring tenants heard the scuffle and called the security guards. But the guards were not allowed to get involved and called the police. The jury felt the **delay** in calling the police was responsible for the death. And that the delay was caused by telling the tenants to call the security guards—but not warning the tenants that the security guards could not get involved in violent situations.

In other words, a well-written, protective lease can be **wiped out** by a set of well-meaning but incompetently drawn rules and regulations. You should have a landlord/tenant attorney check any written communication you send to the tenants for language that can be used against you in the event of injury.

Pets

Prohibit them. If you fail to follow my no pets admonition—and I know those of you who are beginners will think it's unreasonable to prohibit pets—at least get a large extra security deposit. If you prohibit pets—but buy a building which already has pets—raise the security deposit of the tenants who have the pets as soon as their lease permits. If they don't pay the extra security deposit, terminate their lease if local law permits. State that you'll not be liable for injury to pets who have to be removed by landlord unless the injury was due to the owner's negligence and that the tenant will have to pay for kenneling if required.

If you allow pets, you'll be sorrrrry. Don't say I didn't warn you.

Owner's right to enter the unit

The lease should give you the right to enter the unit at reasonable times for reasonable purposes. Furthermore, those hours and purposes ought to be spelled out in the lease. Here's the clause I had in my New Jersey lease.

The landlord or his agents may enter the premises at any time to make emergency repairs or between nine AM and nine PM to inspect, repair, and maintain same, or to show the premises to any prospective tenant or buyer or loan or insurance agent either by appointment or by use of a key when the tenant is away.

If I were using a self-drawn lease again instead of the Texas Apartment Association leases I now use, I would specify that no more than thirty minutes notice need be given. And you might add the words, "or by other means if locks have been changed in violation of the lease" after the word "key."

Important in small buildings

This clause is especially important in **one-, two-, and three-family buildings**.

I was a residential rental property owner and manager from 1969 to 1992. I also spent two years as a real estate salesman. While I was a real estate salesman, I noticed that we had many houses and duplexes for sale which were occupied by tenants. Most tenant-occupied properties were difficult to show. Because the tenants would set up all sorts of restrictions.

You can only show it between 7:00 pm and 7:30 pm on weeknights—and then only if you make an appointment two days in advance.

Plus, I noticed that my tenants would try to make the same demands on me. Having your place ready to show is a pain. But it's unavoidable. And if a landlord lets tenants get away with these restrictions, he's letting them take the property off the market.

Gotta have the clause. Gotta enforce it, too.

You gotta have this clause. But that's usually not enough. When the time comes to show the place, the tenant has forgotten about the clause. Plus, they really didn't understand how bothersome showings can be when they signed it. So now they balk at abiding by the clause.

Damn the balking, full speed ahead.

One of my tenants protested fiercely when I announced the property was up for sale and we'd be showing it. "I have valuables in there," he said. "You can only show it when I'm home."

"Baloney!," I told him. "I rented you an apartment, not a safe deposit box. Get your valuables out of there while it's for sale."

Turned out he had an illegal cat. The "valuables" line was phony. He just wanted time to hide the cat.

Deliberate non-cooperation with showings

As a real estate salesman, I saw many situations in which the tenants were deliberately piling on the restrictions—and not answering the phone or door—to prevent the house from being shown at all. They weren't concerned about inconvenience. They just didn't want to move—or pay more rent. If your tenants behave like that, come down on them like a ton of bricks.

You're worried about the new owner making you move or pay more rent? Well, I'll give you something more immediate to worry about. The old owner. If you don't allow showings in accordance with the lease starting immediately, I'll evict you right now. And sue you for damages to boot. Clear?

If they still won't cooperate, start taping the phone calls you make to them. And videotape what happens when you arrive to show the place. (Hey, it's a tough business.) Even the most recalcitrant tenants will begin to get the message at that point.

If you tape their phone calls, you must **tell** them that you are doing so **before** you turn on the tape recorder then **repeat** that you are taping the phone call with their knowledge and consent and get their acknowledgment of that fact **on the tape**. It's important that you do this. In Massachusetts, it's a **felony** to record a phone call without the consent of the parties being recorded. And it can make your tape inadmissible whether it's a crime or not.

How do you tape a phone call? I got a very inexpensive Archer Telephone Recording Control from Radio Shack. It plugs into the wall jack and the phone wire and tape recorder plug into the Archer device. You also need a cassette recorder or some such.

Do **not** let the tenants prevent you from showing your property. That's outrageous behavior which can easily cost you thousands of dollars. Ignore them if your lease and local allow.

'Boiler Plate'

"In the event litigation is necessary to enforce this lease, the losing party will pay the prevailing party's court costs and reasonable attorneys fees. Although if this clause is never enforced against the **tenants** in your area, better leave it out. Tenant will pay all collection agency fees incurred by owner in connection with monies due under this lease.

"Neither party is relying on any statements or representations other than those specifically set forth in this lease.

"The words 'Landlord' and 'Tenant' in this lease shall be construed to mean both singular and plural, and to mean not only the herein designated, but also his, her, their or its respective heirs, executors, administrators, or successors as the case may be.

"Time is of the essence of this lease.

"The tenant will not share in the proceeds of any condemnation action."

Who owns it

Your state may require you to tell the tenants that you own the building and how to get in touch with you. New Jersey did when I owned there. Texas does now (TPC 92.201) Make sure you comply with that law. Furthermore, you should tell the tenants how to get in touch with you even it the law does **not** require you to do so. Put your name, address, and phone number in the lease so there can be no denying that you gave it to them. I put my title, name, home address, and home phone number on the outside wall of the office.

Return of security deposit

There's usually a state law about security deposits. Make sure your clause complies with it. If you have any leeway, give yourself thirty days to either return the deposit or say why you aren't.

New construction

If you are building the property—and signing leases for not-yet-completed units—make sure you give yourself an out in the case of construction delays.

Transfer clauses

A transfer clause allows the tenant to move if he's transferred by his employer. Do **not** put such a clause in your lease. Why should you?

The vast majority of tenants know about when they are due for a transfer from the time they arrive at their current job. That applies especially to **military** people. I was in the army for four years. Military people imply to landlords that orders transferring them were a bolt from the blue. Baloney.

When an employee is truly transferred unexpectedly, the **employer** should pay for any unexpired lease obligations. In one case, a tenant of mine who worked for IRS was transferred on short notice. When I demanded payment of the remainder of the lease, he passed my letter on to the IRS. And they paid it. (No, I did not get audited as a result.)

'Ordered' to Kansas City

One navy officer tried to get out of a lease containing a transfer clause at a property I managed by showing me his orders. They were separation-from-the-service orders. He was getting out of the navy. And the orders authorized him to separate in Kansas City. The building in question was in New Jersey.

He showed me the orders and yelled, "You see these! They're **orders**. Ordering me to Kansas City (pointing at the Kansas City mention on the orders)!"

Lieutenant, you're a liar. Those are separation-from-the-service orders. You are voluntarily getting out. And when you get out you're authorized travel money from the

*Philadelphia Navy Yard to Kansas City—because Kansas City is either your 'home of record' or the location at which you entered the navy. No one's **ordering** you to go to Kansas City. Do you think you're the only one who was ever in the military?*

Turned out he had bought a home not far from the New Jersey apartment building where he was trying to break his lease.

Landlord's lien

A landlord's lien or baggage lien is the right to go into a tenant's apartment or house and confiscate the property of a delinquent tenant. That's allowed in Texas. I presume there are a few other states that allow it as well. But it's ancient history in most areas.

If your state allows landlord's liens, make sure you have the enabling words in the lease. In Texas, the words authorizing the landlord's lien have to be underlined or in bold print.

Remember that you can only take certain things like stereos, tvs, etc. Make sure you take an adult witness and that both you and the witness sign an inventory of what you took. Also comply with the requirement to tell the tenant what you took and why (by leaving a note in Texas). Do **not** tell the tenant where the property is stored if you can avoid it. They may burglarize the property in question to get it back.

Abandonment

Define abandonment in your lease if your state law doesn't. Check before you make up your own.

I suggest defining it as five day's absence when the rent is unpaid. If you **don't** define abandonment, you may find the place empty except for some battered furniture, old clothes, and trash. Because it's not **completely** empty, you are worried that you might get in trouble if you remove the furniture, etc. and rent it to someone else. So you waste time and money "evicting" the furniture, clothing, and trash.

Whenever an apartment or house is abandoned—and there's anything left behind—remove the stuff with an adult witness and each of you sign the inventory. Then store the stuff in a safe, dry place for 30 to 60 days while you try to find the owner. Your state law may have a specific procedure. Then you can sell the stuff at a flea market, sell it through an ad, or junk it. Be careful. Because tenants sometimes reappear and claim the stuff was extremely valuable because it's antique or art or an heirloom or whatever. If you just tossed it and didn't make a good faith effort to get in touch with the tenant—or failed to get a witness to testify to its obvious worthlessness—you might have to pay. Check your state apartment association for the proper procedure for selling or disposing of abandoned property in your state.

No candles or kerosene appliances

Tenants who are short of cash may use candles or kerosene lamps or heaters. They are dangerous and should be prohibited. Require tenants to use flashlights in the event they have no electricity.

Locks and alarm systems

"Tenant warrants that he has tested all locks and alarm systems, if any, and that they are all in good working order and that tenant has been instructed as to how to operate the alarm system."

Check your state law

I could have simply given you the John T. Reed approved lease instead of this chapter. I deliberately did **not** because of the variations in state law. The Texas Apartment Association lease that I use would be **illegal** in New Jersey. A lease which would be legal in New Jersey would be pro-tenant to the point of legal malpractice in Texas and would tell the tenant that he has rights under state law which he does **not** have in Texas. You **must** make sure your lease complies with **current** state law.

PART FOUR: <u>EXPENSES</u>

14

Expenses

Reducing expenses

You reduce expenses to increase cash flow. But for **some** expenses, you have a **double** incentive to reduce them. Reducing **those** expenses also increases the value of the building.

Which expense reductions increase the value of the building? Those having to do with **verifiable** expenses.

Two categories of expenses

I divide residential expenses into two categories:

- Verifiable
- Discretionary.

Verifiable expenses are those a prospective apartment building buyer can verify. Namely:

- Utilities
- Taxes
- Payroll.

Discretionary expenses are those which vary from owner to owner. Namely:

- Repairs
- Supplies
- Capital expenditures, etc.

No value increase from reducing discretionary expenses

I doubt that you'll get any value increase out of reducing discretionary expenses. Because the apartment building buyer won't **believe** you.

So you **prove** that you only spent one percent of the gross on repairs for the last three years. So what? If anything, that would make me suspect there was a lot of **deferred maintenance**.

The total spent on repairs is determined by the owner's standards. **Not** by the building. So about all you prove by showing that you spent little on repairs is that you have low standards.

But reducing verifiable expenses *does* increase value

The way I buy buildings is probably roughly the same as the way others do. I get the utilities and taxes amounts from the seller. Then I **verify** them with the appropriate authorities or by inspecting the bills.

I **estimate** all the other expenses using averages from my own experience and/or regional apartment operating expenses figures. Those regional figures are published by the Institute of Real Estate Management. Also, some local organizations like the Apartment Association of Greater Dallas or Cain and Scott, Inc. in Seattle publish their own local studies.

That means I will spot and give you credit for any reductions you achieve in your verifiable expenses. But your discretionary expenses are **invisible** to me. I don't even ask for them, let alone believe them. I just stick in my own figures.

This book is about reducing *both* kinds of expenses

Don't get the idea that I think reducing discretionary expenses is worthless. For value increasing purposes, it is. But you should still try to reduce **all** expenses because it increases your cash flow.

Taxes

Reducing taxes requires you to fight City Hall. But that **can** be done successfully. And since property taxes are one of your **largest** expenses—and are a **verifiable** expense—getting them reduced is very worthwhile.

Utilities

Ever since the first gas lines in 1974, Americans have taken it as an article of faith that you should conserve energy.

I don't.

I'm a businessman. And a believer in the free market. I believe you should do what makes economic sense in your building.

All sorts of companies sell utility conservation devices to landlords. Most are garbage. Including some of the popular ones like separate meters.

Three-year pay back criterion

I have a three-year pay back criterion. That is, if a proposed improvement won't pay for itself in three years or less, I won't do it. That applies to utility conservation devices as well as other things.

I eagerly look for utility conservation devices which **will** pay back in three years or less. And I've found a number of them which I'll tell you about. But most don't make the cut. I'll tell you about them, too.

There is no energy 'crisis'

There is no energy "crisis." Never was. Most people **believe** there was because of the gas lines in '74 and '79. But there were no gas lines in Japan or Germany. Yet those countries were also targets of the Arab oil embargo. And those countries produce little or no oil. The U.S. is the world's third largest oil producer (after Saudi Arabia and the Russia).

The reason we had gas lines when Japan and Germany didn't was because we had a Department of Energy—and they did not. Indeed, an investigation was done by the government into rumors that oil companies caused the "shortage" by deliberately holding back oil. The conclusion: The oil companies did no such thing. The "shortage" was caused by the government's allocation system which, among other things, caused government agencies and resort area gas stations to have surpluses while other stations were overwhelmed with demand and put on reduced allocations.

We now have the oil glut they said we'd never have again. And we have had it for some time.

Little real increase in energy prices

In 1967, the Consumer Price Index was 33.4 for all items. Electricity was 29.9. By 1988, the all items CPI was 118.3 and electricity was 111.5. That's only a slight real (adjusted for inflation) increase. Yet to judge from what you hear and read about the "Energy Crisis," prices have gone up **astronomically**. They have not.

The number of energy savings devices that make sense now—but **didn't** make sense in 1967—is relatively few. Most energy saving devices are much too expensive for what they save.

The squanderers myth

The other notion that inspires people to buy energy saving devices it that we were a nation of idiots before the Oil Embargo. Squandering energy the way drunken sailors spend money.

We were not. Essentially, **everybody** has a three-year pay back criterion—or something similar. Although few think of it in such terms. We weren't idiots in 1967. We bought energy saving devices back then—like Volkswagens and insulation for buildings. If it made sense, we did it.

Since then, we've had a small, **real** increase in energy prices. As a result, a few more energy-saving devices make sense now than then. You must **do the numbers**. You should **not** assume that energy is so godawful expensive that all or most energy saving devices now make sense.

Preventive maintenance

Energy conservation is one sacred cow I do not worship. Preventive maintenance is another. Preventive maintenance is right up there with motherhood and apple pie.

I'm more skeptical.

For example, hot water heater manufacturers say you should drain the hot water heaters once a month. Few owners do though.

I did it once or twice. When I believed preventive maintenance was an unquestionable good. My hot water heaters last about ten years. I've never met a drainer whose hot water heaters lasted longer. I even suspect that the jostling caused by the draining might **shorten** the life. The one hot water heater I drained developed a leaky drain valve. I had to buy a screw-in cap to fix it.

And draining hot water heaters takes time. Time is money. Before you adopt a plan of preventive maintenance, you'd better make sure the value of the time it takes does not exceed the amount saved by extending the life of the equipment. And that it really does extend the life of the equipment as much as you think it will.

Cars and houses

Most people know little about building machinery. So they tend to treat it as a mysterious black box. Preventive maintenance is something the mysterious black box demands. So we'd better give in or the mysterious black box will cause us trouble.

But there are two pieces of complicated machinery which you **do** own and probably regard as less mysterious—your car and your home.

By preventive maintenance standards, I'm probably a bit sloppy in the way I take care of my cars. Average. But sloppy. My '75 Granada had 120,000 miles on it when I sold it. Worked fine. It cost about $5,000 when we bought it. I'd say we got our money's worth out of it. Would I be better off if I had been Mr. Preventive Maintenance regarding that car? I doubt it.

Same goes for refrigerators, houses, computers, etc. that I've owned. I never take care of them as well as the manuals say I should. But I've never had a premature failure as a result.

Manuals often exaggerate

The manuals which come with equipment tell you what preventive maintenance you should do. But me thinks they prescribe too much. Most give you a daunting list of frequent preventive maintenance steps. They have two reasons to exaggerate:

- If they prescribe many steps, you probably won't do them all. Then, if there's a failure, they can blame it on you.
- If they can get you to baby the equipment with tender loving care, the chances they'll have a warranty or other complaint are reduced.

Dry cleaners, for example, have often told me that clothing manufacturers often exaggerate on clothing care labels. They tell you to be far more careful than is necessary with garments. And why not? It's no skin off their nose to have you hand wash everything.

Quantity versus quality

Be careful when you cut expenses. It's the fat versus bone debate you hear between politicians. **Some** expense reductions will make a better building. They do that by reducing the expenses while inflicting little or no detriment to the building. But many expense cuts should **not** be made.

The classic example is the skinflint landlord who replaces the 100-watt bulbs in the hall lights with 40-watt bulbs. That's OK if 40 watts is enough light. But typically it leaves the halls dark, dingy-looking, and less safe. Aesthetics and safety are quality issues which do not appear as line items on your cash flow statement. But they are there. Hidden in your income figures. Dark, dingy, unsafe buildings rent for less than well-lit, clean, safe buildings.

In many cases, the adverse impact on the **top** line (rent income) of an expense cut will more than use up the favorable impact on the expense line. That means a **worse bottom line**.

Don't just measure performance by the numbers

There's a temptation among owners and property managers to measure the performance of a resident manager by the numbers only. Vacancy rates, rents collected, total expenses, etc.

You must resist that temptation. You must also rate performance **qualitatively**. You do that by talking to tenants, inspecting the property, and having others "shop" the complex (pose as a prospective renter and report to you on your manager's performance). I sent post cards to all my tenants quarterly. The post cards will solicit feedback by phone or postage-paid reply card.

Cheapest guy not necessarily the best

You already know this. But it bears repeating. The cheapest supplier is not necessarily the best. You should rent apartments to the highest acceptable bidder. And you should award contracts to the lowest **acceptable** bidder. Not the lowest bidder.

You should rent apartments to the highest acceptable bidder. And you should award contracts to the lowest **acceptable** bidder. Not the lowest bidder.

The big picture

Reducing expenses increases cash flow and—in some cases—raises property value. But don't lose sight of the big picture. **All** operating expenses combined usually total just 55% of the gross.

In other words, if you want to increase your cash flow and building value, it's a lot easier to achieve that through **rent increases** than expense decreases.

Expense decreases are more pleasant. Because you don't have to send out any rent increase letters. But they are also tougher to achieve.

10% expense reduction versus 10% income increase

How much can you expect to reduce your property tax bill in a successful appeal? Maybe 10%. (Although I got a 25% reduction in 1985 on one property.) And how much of your gross income goes for property taxes? 7.6% of the gross income was the median for U.S. garden apartments in 1986 according to the Institute of Real Estate Management. So a 10% reduction in property taxes is typically a .76% increase in cash flow—and a .76% increase in building value. On a building with a $100,000 annual income and a value of $650,000, that's a $760 increase in annual cash flow and a $4,940 increase in building value.

Worth doing? Yes. But I wouldn't spend more than about $2,000 worth of cash and time on it. In contrast, a 10% increase in **rent** would result in a $10,000 a year increase in cash flow and a $65,000 increase in property value.

So you can see that expense decreases warrant **some** of your time and money. But rent increases warrant a lot more. They are much more valuable. And often much easier to achieve.

Expenses notebook

You ought to have an expenses loose leaf notebook on each property.

Initially, you should gather information relevant to each expense. For example, in the property tax section, you should have the lot and block number, the address and phone number of the tax collector, the land and improvements assessments, the current tax rate, etc. Then, whenever anything relevant to property taxes happens, you should make note of it in that section of the notebook. Or three-hole punch the relevant document and put it in the notebook.

Every now and then you should analyze each expense in detail. And that analysis should be put in the appropriate section of the notebook. I suggest the following monthly schedule:

January	electricity	July	insurance
February	property taxes	August	repairs
March	gas	September	capital improvements
April	water	October	telephone
May	trash	November	subcontractors
June	payroll	December	all others

Actually, your schedule should be different because of your climate, insurance renewal dates, and property tax appeal deadlines, and so forth. But the basic idea is that you ought to look for ways to cut each expense at least once a year.

15

Property Taxes

Reducing property tax expense

In some states, you pay just one property tax—a real property tax. In other states, you pay both a real property tax and a personal property tax. For example, I paid only a real property tax in New Jersey. But you pay both real and personal property taxes in California and Texas. Plus, in Texas, the property is taxed separately by the city, county, and school district.

Make sure you're paying the *right* tax bill

Make sure the property tax bill you're paying is the right one. Typically, it's sent to your mortgage lender and some clerk who couldn't care less pays it. In those cases, you often never see the bill at all. You only see an entry in your annual mortgage statement.

I once inquired about my tax bill and learned that the city had sent me the wrong bill. The one they sent me belonged to the biggest apartment complex in town. My building was **half** the size of the other! Does that convince you to make sure you're getting the right bill?

Find out what your assessment is

Find out your assessment. Typically, you can do that by calling the tax office. Better that you should get it **in writing**. You can do that by visiting the tax office. Or, in many places, by visiting the local library. Libraries often have tax books which list ownership and tax assessment on every property in the county. Also, many real estate brokerage offices also have tax books where you can look up assessments. Nowadays, this information is also available on CD-ROM or on-line. Make sure there has not been a recent reassessment before you rely on a book.

Assessments are almost always below market value

In all probability, your assessment will be **below** the market value of the building. Does that reassure you?

The tax assessor hopes that it will. But it should **not**.

Even in states where state law requires properties to be assessed at 100% of market value, most assessments are low. According to a 1981 Census Bureau study, the average assessment is only 37% of market value. Assessors deliberately assess too low to avoid riling the property owners.

A guy who owns a $200,000 property finds that his assessment is only $92,000. He stifles a smile and sneaks out of the tax office before he attracts attention. "Boy, am I getting away with murder," he thinks.

Below market assessment doesn't prevent tax overcharge

Actually, there's a good chance he's getting screwed by the tax assessor. His property is assessed at $92,000/$200,000 = 46% of market value. Yes, he is getting away with murder if the other properties in the community are assessed at 70% or 80% of market value. But what if they're assessed at only 30% of market value?

That means that the average other $200,000 building owners in town are assessed at 30% x $200,000 = $60,000. So our friend who is assessed at $92,000 on the same value, and thinks he's getting away with murder, is really getting murdered himself.

That, sports fans, is **why** tax assessors under assess. If they assessed at market value as many laws require, it would be very easy for property owners to spot over assessments. By assessing at **less** than market value, they lull property owners into a false sense of security.

Commercial property more often overcharged

Assessors tend to **over**charge **commercial** property (anything other than homes) and **under**charge **homes**. There are two reasons for that. One is they don't know what they're doing and assume that commercial is more valuable than it is.

Secondly, they figure it's good for them **politically**. Home owners are more numerous than owners of commercial buildings. And many owners of investment property are **absentee** owners who neither live nor vote in the community. So if you're going to get somebody mad at you, better to get some rich guy who lives 100 miles away mad than the local home owner who lives in the community.

Check the description

There is typically a form describing your property in the tax assessor's file. You should get a copy of it for the tax section of your expenses notebook.

And you should scrutinize it. Your assessment is based on that description. Typically, that description was filled out by a college student. He was hired by a mass assessment company which, in turn, had been hired by your community. The college student was paid a minimum amount and was told to go up and down the streets of the town filling out forms on properties.

He probably was not closely supervised. And he may well have made big mistakes regarding your property. Mistakes which you can cite in any property tax appeal.

The town's average assessment-to-value ratio

To find out if you are paying too much tax, you need to find out the town's average assessment-to-value ratio. In some areas, the state publishes the average assessment-to-value ratio. New Jersey is one. If so, get hold of that state report. Then compare your assessment to your town's average. If yours is higher, you should be able to win an appeal.

If there's no statistical study available, you'll have to do your own. Do that by identifying a bunch of properties like yours and checking their assessments. If the average of that group is lower than yours, you have a case for an appeal. Now that these are generally available in computer form, calculating community averages should be easy.

Computer technology has given rise to a new scam. Dishonest property tax appeal firms send you a computer-generated letter which says that your property is assessed too high and cites nearby "comps" to prove it. Only trouble is, they give you the street but not the address of the comp. In fact, the comps are chosen only because the street is near yours and the assessments are low. Upon closer investigation, you will find that the "comps" are not really comparable. These firms are looking for a front-end fee and will may a perfunctory filing on your behalf. But it is extremely unlikely that they will win a reduction in your assessment. They are just trying to trick people into paying them the front-end fee.

How to seek a reduction

There are two kinds of appeal:

- Informal
- Formal.

Use informal first. You just visit the tax assessor and explain why you think the assessment is too high. If you have a decent case, and he's a decent guy, he may agree to a reduction right there.

I did that with **personal** property taxes on one Texas building. And got a huge reduction.

In a formal appeal, you have to fill out forms, appear at hearings and all that. But if the reduction is significant, it's worth it.

Appealing your taxes is the equivalent of a capital expenditure to improve the property. In fact, the **cost** of appealing taxes must be added to the property's basis and amortized over the life of the property for income tax purposes. That is, it's treated like a capital expenditure.

So you should apply the three-year payback criterion. That is, you should not spend more on appealing the taxes than three times the amount of the tax savings you feel confident you'll achieve.

In deciding whether to appeal, take these things into account:

- The **probability** of success.
- **Value of your time**.
- Any **fees** you'll pay to government, attorneys, expert witnesses, etc.
- **Duration** of the appeal process

Some attorneys, former assessors, appraisers, and others specialize in obtaining tax assessment reductions. Hiring such a person may be wise for you. Whether to do that depends on the person's expertise and fee.

Some work on a **flat fee** basis. Others on a **contingent** basis. That is, they get paid a percentage of the reduction.

How to find a professional tax appealer

The best source is your fellow landlords. Ask at the apartment association meeting if anyone knows a good tax appealer.

Others who might know of someone include:

- Property managers
- Major property owners in the community
- Real estate attorneys

- Larger real estate brokers
- Tax assessor. Try asking him who appears on behalf of the taxpayer most in the tax appeals in this community.

Tax appeal firms are listed in the *Yellow Pages* under "Tax Ad Valorem Consultants."

Best in the state

Since tax appeal laws are generally uniform throughout the state, it might be wise to look outside your own community. Try the state apartment or other real estate-related trade association. Or property managers, owners, etc. elsewhere in the state.

Seminars on tax appeals

State organizations often offer tax appeal seminars. If so, you should take one. At least find out who the instructors were. They are often leading lights in the tax appeal business.

National tax appeal firms

There are firms which do tax appeals nationwide. They advertise in *Multi-Housing News*(http://www.apartmentlife.com/mhn.htm), and *National Real Estate Investor* magazine(http://www.k3.com/media/intertec/trade/NATREINV.HTML). Tax assessors are typically provincial, so any out-of-town firm would be well-advised to have local people dealing with the local tax assessment folks.

My two successful appeals

I bought an apartment building for $835,000 on November 29, 1983. Just thirty-two days later, on December 31st of that year, the city reassessed it to $1,002,505.

I didn't find out about it until the following December—when my mortgage lender billed me $6,573.66 for an escrow shortage.

I hired the Atlanta tax appeal firm of Easley, McCaleb, and Stallings, Ltd. They charged $850. And got the assessment reduced to $718,728. That lowered my tax bill by about $4,500 a year. And thereby increased my property value by about $4,500 ÷ 10% = $45,000.

A year later, the Dallas tax appeal firm of Marvin Poer and Company got the assessment further reduced to $672,882 for a fee of $300. That saved about $500 a year and increased the property value about $5,000.

Unfortunately, the assessor **raised** the assessment again in '87 to $687,206 in spite of my paying Poer another $300 fee. Because of the collapse in the Texas apartment market, the market value of the property had fallen to about $400,000 in 1987. But the revenue-starved local government seemed loathe to acknowledge such tax-decreasing reality.

You can appeal with*out* professional help

You don't need a pro to appeal. But the people who run the appeals process can be tricky and devious. I appealed the taxes on a duplex once. I gathered my evidence—comparable sales with much lower assessments. I took them to the assessor's secretary, Mrs. Smith. She told me to show them to the assessor, Mr. Brown. He said I did not need to submit them until the hearing.

I thought from the instructions that I had to submit them **before** the hearing. But who am I to question the assessor?

When I introduced the comparable sales at the hearing, the appraisal firm representative snapped, "They're inadmissible. You have to submit them in advance."

I pointed to the assessor, Mr. Brown, who was at the hearing and said, "That's what I thought. But he told me I didn't need to submit them until the hearing." Mrs. Smith was also at the hearing. She exploded with, "That's the first time I ever heard that one!" Mr. Brown, the assessor, denied he had told me I didn't need to submit them til the hearing. Although he was clearly uncomfortable about the lie. Result. I had no case. Appeal denied.

Abide strictly by the procedures

My advice? There are a lot of sleazeballs in this world. And many of them work for tax assessment offices. Read the tax appeal instructions carefully. **Do exactly what the written instructions say**. Don't miss any deadlines—not even by an hour—not even if you have a "good excuse." If any official countermands the instructions, make him put it in writing.

When is the best time to appeal?

The best time to appeal is when you have the strongest case. When is that? One example is when you **pay** less than a building than it is assessed for. That rarely happens. But when it does, you've got a solid reduction case. Building values go up and down. When they go down is a good time to appeal your assessment. Values go down when interest rates or expenses or vacancy rates go up.

Prop 13 reassessment

In California, real estate is reassessed when it is sold. That's the rule established by the Proposition 13 tax-cutting initiative. To avoid reassessment, some people do lease options instead of sales. Actually, the authorities know that trick and have declared lease options which involve the lessee/optionee putting up significant equity within a short period of time to be sales which trigger reassessment. (California State Board of Equalization Advisory #80-147) To avoid that, make sure the tenant's equity in any lease option does not cross the "significant" line (whatever that is).

Where to get further information

There are at least three books on the subject:

- *You Can Get Your Real Estate Taxes Reduced*
- *Lower Your Real Estate Taxes*
- *Digging for Gold in Your Own Back Yard*

And there's one periodical: *The Journal of Property Tax Management*. The publishers' names and addresses are in the back of this book. Statistics on property taxes are followed by the Advisory Committee on Intergovernmental Relations in Washington, DC.

Fighting city hall

In some cases, landlords have lowered their property taxes by fighting tax increases on a city-wide basis. For example, in November of 1991, University City, MO landlords campaigned against a ballot measure that would have raised their property taxes 31.4%—and won.

Sales tax

State and local sales taxes vary considerably and change frequently. Some may apply to residential rental properties. If they apply to you, get a copy of the laws and study them for opportunities to lower your taxes.

16

Electricity

Depending upon the metering of your building, electricity could be one of your biggest expenses. Although I almost bought one building which still gives me a chuckle whenever I think about it. It had about 20 units. But the owner's electric bill was **zero**. Everything, including the exterior lights, was on the **tenants'** meters.

Not that the owner had been dishonest with the wiring. Each apartment had one exterior light next to the entrance, for example. And there was no laundry room because a commercial laundramat was within walking distance.

But with most buildings—especially master-metered (owner pays all electric) buildings — electricity is one of the biggest, if not **the** biggest, expense.

Conservation measures

There are a zillion conservation measures you can take. I'll try to identify **all** of them. Although I will recommend **against** many of them. And I'll tell you why.

Your bill

I told you to scrutinize your tax bill and property description. Do the same with your electric bill. And put some of the information in your expenses notebook under "Electricity."

The bill typically contains:

- Rate category
- Description of service (electric, guard lights, etc.)

- Sales tax, if any
- Demand meter reading
- Consumption meter reading
- Meter reading dates
- Rate paid
- Address of meter
- Multiplier
- Fuel charge
- Others like electric company address and phone

Rate category

All electric users are assigned a rate category. Different categories are charged different rates. So you want to make sure the electric category has you in the **right** one.

One of my buildings was in Texas Power & Light's "General" category. The TP&L lady says all master-metered apartment buildings or buildings with demand meters are in the general category. That building is master-metered **and** has a demand meter.

She also told me that I was in the "LP-20" category. That fact was not on my bill. She said that's a cheaper subcategory of the general category. I was eligible for that subcategory because my kilowatt (KW) demand exceeds a specified minimum.

She sent me a copy of the definition of each rate category and subcategory which I put in my expense notebook for that property.

Rate categories in a separate-metered building

My **other** building had **separate** meters. My tenants paid "Residential" rates. So did I on **vacant** apartment electric bills. But the bills for my exterior lights were under Texas Electric Service Company's "General" rate.

I put the manager's house on a separate meter. It was on the same meter as the laundry room, pool pump, and some exterior lights. Looking at the old bills as I write this, I notice that the house was under the "General" rate. The house went under the "Residential" rate when it was separate metered.

So putting the separate meter on reduced the **rate** at which electric is paid on that house over what it used to be—by switching from the "General" to the "Residential" rate. Not to mention the fact that the consumption went down when the manager paid for it himself.

Rearranging might pay

In some cases, you may be able to switch part of your bill to a lower rate by rearranging the metering. In the example I just cited, I had a mixture of "Residential" and "General" on one meter. So it was all billed at the "General" rate. By **separate**-metering the residential and other stuff, I was able to lower the overall **rate** at which that building pays electric.

But I note that it cost $660 to have it done. I did it for administrative purposes. Not to switch rates. So before you add meters to get better rates, make sure the switch passes the three-year payback test.

Another instance where rearranging meters might pay is consolidation or deconsolidation. If the rate structure gives discounts for high **volume** use, and you have multiple meters, you may want to consolidate to just one meter to qualify for the discount.

And if there's a break for **low** volume use, it might make sense to split up circuits on one meter to more than one meter. That doesn't make **common** sense to me. But in the "Energy Crisis" era, utilities commissions are doing some strange things. If your state utilities commission has imposed a "small-is-beautiful" rate structure on your electric company consider splitting up your meters.

Description of service

The description of service on your bill is usually pretty straightforward. Typically, it just says "electric service." Which is self-explanatory.

One of my bills also lists "guard lights." Those are mercury vapor lights on telephone poles owned and erected by the electric company. The electric company assumes that they use 68 kilowatt hours (KWH) per month. That's 68 ÷ 30 = 2.267 KWH/day. They're 175-watt lamps and they're probably lit an average of 10 hours a day or 10 x 175 watts = 1750 watt hours or 1.75 KWH. .

At one point, I could buy a 175-watt, wall-mount, mercury vapor light from Sears for $37.99. If ten hours a day is the correct usage, using my own instead of theirs would have reduced my consumption by 2.267 - 1.750 = .517 KWH per day or .517 x 30 = 15.51 KWH per month. I paid 5.9 cents per KWH at that building at that time. At that rate, putting in my own light would have saved 15.51 KWH per month x $.059 = $.914 per month. That's almost a three-year pay back period. $.914 per month is $10.97 a year. In three years you'd save $10.97 x 3 = $32.90.

The fixture and bulb cost more than that. Plus there's tax, installation, replacement bulbs in the future. I'll stick with the electric company's guard lights.

Sales and other taxes

In some areas, electricity users pay sales tax. That can get a little tricky. In Texas, for example, a change made apartments exempt from paying **state** sales tax on electricity. They still have to pay **city** sales tax. The apartment association told apartment owners to make sure they weren't paying state sales tax. Many were and got refunds as a result.

If you're paying sales or other taxes on your electric, check to see if you're exempt.

Demand meter

The demand portion of the meter measures your peak usage. How that relates to your bills varies from electric company to electric company. Generally, however, if you reduce your peak demand, you reduce your bill.

There **are** ways to reduce peak demand. But none that I've heard of make sense for your average apartment building.

Consumption meter

The consumption portion of the meter measures how much you use. In apartment buildings, it's often a meter with a 10 multiplier. That is, it gives readings in tens of KWH. So you have to multiply the reading by ten to get the actual KWH.

Normally, you can let the electric company do all the meter reading. But if you're having a problem, you might read it yourself or have an employee read it. The purpose of reading it yourself is to find out **sooner** what the consumption is.

You may want to read it yourself

The bigger the bill, the more sense reading it **yourself** makes. If you let the electric company read it, you won't get the reading until about two weeks after the end of the period in question. If a problem which increased consumption began shortly after the last meter reading, that problem would go undetected for about six weeks—if you relied on the electric company's readings. But if you read it yourself every two weeks or so, you'd have spotted the problem within two weeks instead of six.

Possible problems include a central air-conditioner running continuously instead of turning on and off normally, tenants using electric space heaters, ovens used for heating, etc.

Estimated readings

Sometimes, the electric company does **not** read the meter. But they still send you a bill. They **estimate** what the meter reading would have been. Based on past experience.

If they do that more than occasionally, you ought to complain. Sometimes, you find that the meter reader is obstructed. An obstruction which you need to remove. In any event, you are entitled to **real** readings, not estimated ones.

Meter reading dates

We tend to assume these are 30 days apart. But sometimes they aren't. Sometimes they'll **skip** a month. Sometimes the meter reading dates shift around. One will be 30 days from the previous; the next, 25 days; the next, 34 days; and so forth.

You need to keep that in mind when comparing months. For example, you may wonder why the January '85 bill was 20% higher than the January '84 bill. Maybe because the January '85 bill covered a 34-day meter reading period and the January '84 bill only covered a 28-day reading period.

Check the reading dates before you draw any conclusions about electricity use patterns.

Lighting

Part of your electric bill goes for lighting. You can probably reduce that. Here's how.

First do a **lighting survey**. A lighting survey is simply a list of all the lights you pay for. Here's a sample:

LIGHTING SURVEY				
Location	**Wattage**	**Type**	**Number**	**Hrs on/day**
Parking lots	150	I	16	10
Entries	100	I	24	10
Laundry	80	F	2	24

The letters under "Type" stand for Incandescent or Fluorescent. The number is the number of bulbs. This is the lighting survey for my separately-metered building. It's typical of separate-metered buildings.

The parking lot lights are 150-watt flood lights mounted high on the building walls. The entry lights are 100-watt bulbs in large colored globes hanging in the recessed entryways. The laundry has a fluorescent fixture with two 80-watt, 8-feet long, fluorescent tubes.

What can be done to reduce lighting electric

What can you do about lights to reduce their cost? Five things:

1. Eliminate it.
2. Replace it with a window.
3. Reduce the wattage.
4. Shorten the time it's on.
5. Put it on a tenant's meter.

Eliminate it

My Fort Worth building was next to a huge billboard. The billboard is on the property of an adjacent office building. The billboard is lit up at night. So is the office parking lot. On top of that, there are public street lights in the same spot.

I walked the complex at night to make my lighting survey. (You should do the lighting survey once **at night** to spot unnecessary lights and once in daytime to spot lights burning during those hours.) Clearly, in that spot, there was enough light from **off** the property that no on-property light was needed.

So why did my building have two 150-watt spots there? I don't know for sure. Maybe because the building was built before the billboard and office building. Maybe because the builder was just not thinking.

But those spots had been running up the owner's electric bill for fourteen years. I told the maintenance man to remove them. Not replace them with lower wattage bulbs. Just **remove** them.

The savings? The consumption was about 2 bulbs x 150 watts x 10 hours per day x 365 days per year = 1,095,000 watt hours per year or 1,095 KWH per year. The cost was $.121 per KWH on that meter. So taking out those two bulbs saved me $.121/KWH x 1,095 KWH = $132.50 per year.

Don't forget bulb replacement cost

I also saved bulb replacement cost. 150-watt spot (called par floods) bulbs cost $3.87 each from the Maintenance Warehouse (a national supply house for landlords 800-431-3000). Their rated life is 2,000 hours. If they last their rated life, you need to replace them every 2,000 hours ÷ 10 hours per day = 200 days. A two-bulb fixture would have 2 x 10 hours per day x 365 days per year = 7,300 hours per year. That'd require 7,300 hours per year ÷ 2,000 hours per bulb = 3.65 bulbs per year at a material cost of 3.65 x $3.87 = $14.13 per year.

And that $3.87 cost doesn't not include installation. My maintenance man had to go get the forty foot ladder, climb up, unscrew the bad bulb, screw in the good one, climb down, test the new one, take the ladder back to its storage place.

Labor time to change a bulb is probably about 1/4 hour. At $8 an hour that's $8 x 1/4 = $2.00. Doing that 3.65 times per year costs a total of $2.00 x 3.65 = $7.30. Total annual savings for eliminating those bulbs:

Electric	$132.50
Bulbs	14.13
Labor	7.30
Total	$153.93

Cost? Only the labor needed to take them out or $2.00. Payback period? $2.00/$153.93 = .01 years or .01 x 365 = 3.65 days. In other words, taking out those two bulbs paid for itself in four days. And saved me $153.93 a year while I owned the property.

More subtle opportunities for eliminating lights

Not all opportunities for eliminating lights are so obvious. Other areas definitely need some lights. But maybe not as many as are being used.

My master-metered building had a single light outside each tenant's door. Those 60-watt bulbs provided the light for the courtyard. But did we need **that many** lights to get adequate light?

I asked my managers to take some out—like every other one—and see if the remaining lights provided enough light. They fiddled around and were able to eliminate many of the lights without jeopardizing safety or security. And without unacceptable aesthetic effect.

Non-monetary considerations

In your zeal to cut expenses, don't forget why you **have** lights. Lights serve four purposes:

- Safety
- Security
- Aesthetics
- Advertising and directing.

You could eliminate **all** the lights. That would save money. But your tenants would be bumping into things in the dark, suing you for resulting injuries, complaining to the city, and moving out—unless there were adequate lights from **off**-site. For safety's sake, you must have enough lights to prevent injury.

Depending on the local crime rate, you also need enough light to **discourage criminals**. Burglars, car thieves, rapists, and robbers prefer to operate in or near dark areas. Tenants dislike dark areas because they don't care for burglars, car thieves, etc. Although lights to avoid tripping generally also take care of security.

Lights have an **aesthetic effect**. That is, they can make the building more attractive. That's why people install lights in their yard. Sodium vapor lamps provide more lumens per watt than incandescent lamps. But some also have a ghastly, harsh, orange colored light. So by replacing incandescent lights with sodium vapor, you save electric. But you also may make your building look like a state prison.

Finally, lights help people find your building, manager, and tenants. People like prospective tenants and your tenants' guests. If your building is located where traffic passes, you have a free ad. But if the sign is not lit up, you **lose** your free ad when the sun goes down.

Don't be electric-wise but rent-foolish

If your tenant's guests have trouble finding them, you could lose a tenant or three. Vacancies eat up electricity savings awfully fast. For example, in that building where I saved $153.93 by eliminating two spot lights, the rents were $285 for a one bedroom. Had those lights been necessary—and eliminating them cost me a tenant—my savings would have been almost wiped out in just two weeks of vacancy ($285 ÷ 2 = $142.50).

So don't get so psyched up about saving electric that you hurt your marketing effort to either new or existing tenants.

Replace the light with a window

Did you ever buy a door? Notice how some contain "lights?" You've got diamond-light doors. Two-light doors. Three-light doors. The "lights" they're referring to are windows. Because a window lets in light.

Some of the lights on your lighting survey may be there because the room has no windows. By putting in a window—or a door with a window in it—you may be able to eliminate a light. Or at least put it on an electric eye so it only goes on when it's dark.

In some rare cases, when there is a lot of off-site light at night (from billboards, adjacent buildings, street lights, etc.), a window may even provide 24 hours of light. But that's probably stretching it.

Windows may hurt insulation or security

In addition to the cost of installing a window, don't forget the possibility of increased **energy** cost or reduced **security**. Windows, even double- and triple-glazed windows, have a relatively low R-factor. An insulated wall or door has a much higher R-factor than the most energy-efficient window. And windows allow sunlight to pass through which means heat gain which requires more air-conditioning. So if the space in question is heated and/or air-conditioned, installing a window may increase energy costs. And that increased energy cost may exceed the savings in the light bill.

Also, windows present an opportunity to criminals. A determined criminal can get through anything. Including a wall. But most criminals will look for a window. So from a security standpoint, the fewer windows, the better.

What about **skylights**? They're tough to use anywhere but on a cathedral ceiling or a flat roof. They usually leak. And they have the same R-factor problem. Only it's more costly on the ceiling because heat rises, cold air falls, and you get more heat gain from sunlight. Skylights are an irrational fad.

Vacancy electric

When you have a vacancy in a separate-metered apartment building, the electric company puts that meter in the owner's name. I was astonished at how much electric a vacancy could use. In 1985, I averaged $27 a month per unit in vacancy electric bills!

I told the managers repeatedly to turn off the circuit breakers. And they promised they would. But the vacancy electric bills stayed the same. I suspect that I eventually got the cooperation of the managers—but that vendors like carpet steam cleaners and drapes guys would turn the breakers back on.

Steam cleaning guy goes into the apartment and turns on the light switch. No light. He goes to the circuit breaker panel—and turns every breaker on. Thereby turning on the electric heat or air-conditioning, hot water heater, and refrigerator. When he leaves, he turns off the lights.

Anyway, I finally concluded that jawboning the managers wasn't getting the job done. So I set up a carrot-and-stick incentive program. I told the managers I pay 40¢ per day per unit for vacancy electric. If the actual bill was **more** than that, I deducted the excess from their pay. If it was **less**, I gave them the difference as a bonus.

This worked quite well. My vacancy electric cost was a constant 40¢ a day or about $12 per unit a month. The managers usually got a small bonus or get docked a small amount. The lesson learned is that nothing less than docking them provided enough motivation to get the job done.

By reducing my vacancy electric cost by $15 per unit per month I raised my cash flow and building value. With an average 5% vacancy rate in a 33 unit building I should have had 5% x 33 = 1.65 units vacant continuously. At $15 a month savings per vacancy, I saved $15 x 1.65 = $24.75 per month or $24.75 x 12 = $297 per year. That, in turn, raised the building value about $2,970.

Minimum lighting standards

In 1990, I was one of the defendants in a civil trial. One of my tenants said she was raped in her apartment around 2AM and that it was my fault. Among other things, her attorney said my lighting was inadequate. In the course of preparing for the trial, my insurance company hired a lighting expert. He said our lighting exceeded the Illuminating Engineering Society of North America (www.iesna.org) and American National Standards Institute (http://web.ansi.org/default_js.htm) light quantity guidelines for multifamily parking lots—.6 footcandles. You should make sure you exceed it as well.

Deregulation of electricity

There has been much talk about deregulation of electricity in recent years. Pertinent laws have been passed. But I have not seen much action. I signed up to change my home electricity supplier to Enron in response to an Enron solicitation. Later, I got notice that Enron would not be providing electricity to me in spite of my selecting them as my provider. They are not yet ready.

Ultimately, electricty will be like long-distance phone service. When that happens, you should go with the supplier who charges you the least.

17

Lights

Big bulbs cost more than little bulbs.

That's why skinflint landlords have been replacing 60-watt and 100-watt bulbs with 40-watt bulbs since light bulbs were invented.

You should do the same whenever a particular lighting need is overpowered. In other words, if a 40-watt bulb is adequate, by all means use 40-watt bulbs instead of bigger bulbs. But make sure it **is** adequate—for safety, security, aesthetics, and advertising. As a general rule, 40-watt bulbs are **not** adequate anywhere but in a closet or refrigerator.

But you may find 100-watt or 75-watt lights are adequate where 150-watt lights are used.

Fluorescent versus incandescent

All watts are not created equal. Actually, what you want are **lumens**, not watts. A lumen is a unit of **light**. Watt is a unit of **power**.

Fluorescent lights are much more efficient than incandescent lights. In technical terms, they give more lumens per watt—about three times more. That means you can replace a 60-watt incandescent bulb with a 20-watt fluorescent tube—and still have the same light.

Should you?

Only if there's no installation cost, as a general rule.

Fluorescent fixture cost

My master-metered building had incandescent ceiling lights. Each fixture contained two bulbs. The tenants probably put in 100-watt bulbs. And they probably are on twelve hours a day. That's 100 watts x 2 bulbs x 12 hours per day x 365 days per year = 876,000 watt hours or 876 KWH per year.

A fluorescent fixture would need only one third the wattage to give off the same light. That's 200/3 = 67 watts. There is no 67-watt fluorescent tube. But you can get 40 watt tubes. A two-tube fixture with two 40-watt tubes would be 80 watts of fluorescent light which is equal to 240 watts of incandescent. Close enough.

The new usage would be 80 watts x 12 hours x 365 days per year = 350,400 watt hours or 350.4 KWH. The savings would be 876 KWH - 350.4 KWH = 525.6 KWH per year. At that building, I paid 5.9 cents per KWH. So installing a fluorescent kitchen fixture would save me $.059/KWH x 525.6 KWH = $31.01 per year. (My current home electricity rate is 13.737¢/KWH.)

A three-year payback period means I can afford to spend as much as three times that or $31.01 x 3 = $93.03 to have the fluorescent fixture installed. Can it be done for $93.03?

Fluorescent fixture cost

Maintenance Warehouse's cheapest kitchen ceiling fluorescent fixture with two 40-watt tubes costs $39.24. Plus 8% sales tax brings it to $39.24 x 1.08 = $42.38. That leaves $93.03 - $42.38 = $50.65 for installation. Can you get an incandescent kitchen light fixture taken down and a fluorescent fixture installed in its place for $50.65?

Maybe. I doubt an electrician would do **one** fixture for that. But you might be able to get an electrician to a bunch of them at one time for less than $50.65 each. Your maintenance man or some other non-electrician could probably do it cheaper if allowed by local law.

Using non-licensed electricians

I don't mean to wink at it. In the movie "The Towering Inferno," the fire was caused by the builder taking shortcuts with the wiring to save money. The builder was the bad guy of the movie. Now suppose **you** save money by having two-dozen ceiling lights installed by a non-licensed electrician. And suppose there's a fire and someone is hurt. Then **you'd** be the bad guy. Not a very pleasant prospect is it?

Ever been sued for wrongful death? How much do you think the plaintiff's attorneys would ask for? I suspect about three times your net worth. How much would the jury award them if they won. Probably about 90% of your net worth plus the limit of your liability coverage. You want to risk all that to save a couple bucks on light fixtures? I don't.

Replacing *fixtures* is marginal

Generally speaking, you should not replace one working incandescent light fixture with a fluorescent one to save on electric. That is, it's questionable whether the electric saved would be worth the high labor and materials cost for installation.

And remember, the assumptions I made above may be **incorrect**. Maybe the lights are **not** on 12 hours a day. Maybe the tenants only put **60**-watt bulbs in the fixtures. Maybe half the tenants have one bulb burned out and rarely get around to replacing it. With fluorescent tubes, both always draw current or neither does.

Real world may not jibe with the projections

In short, the engineering calculations may show that you'll save $31.01 per unit per year. But after you spend $2,200 putting them in, your electric bill may only go down by $19 a unit a year. That's the real world. It doesn't always jibe with the numbers. The laws of physics always apply. But engineers tend to overlook things.

Like tenants stealing fluorescent tubes when they move. Or increased hours on per day because tenants resent the owner saving money on electric and not passing the savings on to them.

That's why I like to experiment before going whole hog. Put in one or two energy-saving devices—like fluorescent light fixtures—then look at the electric bill. Is there a savings like the one you figured on? If so, proceed with installing the rest of the fixtures.

Screw-in fluorescent lamps

Not all fluorescent lights require a fluorescent **fixture**. Some just screw into an incandescent socket.

Bingo.

No electrician needed. No new fixture needed. No installation cost whatever.

Do **those** make sense?

You're darn tootin'.

For example, Maintenance Warehouse sells a Retrofit 22-watt circline bulb. It screws into a regular socket. It give off light equivalent to two 66 watts of incandescent bulbs. And it costs just $9.80.

I've seen a similar product on sale for $5.97.

There are dozens of similar products with wattages varying from 5 watts up to 20 watts.

Some screw-in fluorescents look ugly. So they need to be inside a fixture cover. But their shape is such that they often will not **fit** into the existing fixture.

PL- and SL- fixtures

PL- and SL- bulbs are a recent innovation. There are about the same size and shape of a regular incandescent screw-in bulb. They have tiny U- or H-shaped fluorescent tubes. Here are some specs from Maintenance Warehouse's catalog:

Wattage	Diameter	Height	$/each	$/12 or more	$/36 or more
5	2 3/8"	4 1/4"	8.81	7.80	7.41
7	2 3/8"	5 1/2"	8.81	7.80	7.41
9	2 3/8"	7 5/8"	8.81	7.80	7.41
13	2 3/8"	8 5/8"	10.01	9.01	8.65

These prices include both a base and a bulb. Presumably, you only have to buy the base once. When the bulb burns out, you use the same base and just get a new bulb. The bulb only costs $3 to $4.

I replaced the incandescent bulbs in the exterior entry lights at one of my complexes with SL-18s. First we tried just one. The manager said the you couldn't tell the difference between a fixture with an incandescent bulb and one with the SL-18. So we replaced the entire complex's exterior entry lights.

The prices of the SL-18s were much higher then. But it was still worthwhile. Here are the numbers.

According to my electric bills, each bulb saved about $2 per month or $24 a year. I paid $24.87 each for the SL-18s. So they have a one-year payback period.

In that complex, there were 32 such bulbs, so my annual electricity savings is $24 x 32 = $768 which raises the building value $7,680.

Non-incandescents last longer, too

You not only save on electric with non-incandescents. You also save on bulbs and labor to change them. I had three two-tube fluorescent fixtures installed in my home office in 1980. When I moved out three years later, I had never replaced a tube. My new home is full of fluorescents (we had it custom built). I only replaced six tubes in 4 1/2 years.

Here are some life comparisons.

Bulb	Life
100-watt incandescent	750 hours
22-watt circline fluorescent	12,000 hours
175-watt mercury vapor	24,000 hours
70-watt high-pressure sodium	26,000 hours

Longer life saves labor and bulb replacement costs. But it also decreases the incidence of burned out bulbs, which are a **safety** hazard. Replace all exterior incandescents with non-incandescents for safety and lawsuit avoidance reasons. You should do that even if there were no cost savings.

Watch out for cold temperatures

One thing about fluorescents, though, they sometimes produce much less light when used outdoors in cold weather areas. Make appropriate inquiries before you buy. And if there's any doubt, install only one or two lights on your property. Then see how they do when winter weather comes. The exterior fluorescent fixtures in the Maintenance Warehouse catalog specify cold weather ballasts.

Big bulbs are more efficient

Big bulbs are more efficient. For example, a regular 100-watt incandescent bulb produces 50% more light than **four** 25-watt incandescent bulbs. So one big bulb in place a two or more small ones can save money.

Watch the **heat**, though. The maximum wattage is usually engraved on the fixture. Look closely to see what it is. If you put a 100-watt bulb in a fixture designed for 60-watt bulbs, you will probably overheat it and be forced to replace the fixture. What's worse, you could start a **fire**.

Do *not* use long-life incandescent bulbs

Every now and then some salesman sells my managers long-life incandescent bulbs. As soon as I find out, I tell the manager to return them immediately. You should, too.

Long-life incandescent bulbs are a scam. Not that I'm disputing how long the bulbs last. I'm skeptical..But I have no evidence that they **don't** last that long.

There are two problems with them.

1. They produce fewer lumens per watt.
2. Cashing in on the guarantee is so hard it's meaningless.

A regular incandescent bulb will produce 17.4 lumens per watt in certain sizes. The same size long-life incandescent bulb will only produce 14.8 lumens per watt. That means you use more electricity to operate long-life bulbs.

Long-life bulbs are typically guaranteed. Wonderful. But how do you know whether a burned-out bulb had been on for the guaranteed number of hours when it burned out? Are we supposed to mark them? If so, where? And with what kind of pen that the marking can withstand hundreds of hours of intense heat?

And even if you wasted time and money marking all your light bulbs, how do you get your money back? Send the bulb to the factory in Tennessee or somewhere?

On top of all that, long-life bulbs cost more than regular ones. Forget them.

Some fluorescents better than others

Sylvania claims their Super Saver Plus fluorescent 34-watt gives off the same light as a regular 40-watt fluorescent bulb.

Fluorescent interior lights also save on air-conditioning

Fluorescent lights run **cooler** than incandescents. That's one reason why they're more efficient— less waste heat. That means less heat which the air-conditioning system has to cool. I will not attempt to calculate the savings, though. Too many variables. (That excess heat **helps** heating expense but air-conditioning is generally the bigger bill.)

The more efficient, the more ugly

One rough rule of thumb in lighting is that the more **efficient** the light is, the **uglier** it is. The most attractive light is incandescent. The least attractive is low-pressure sodium—with it's industrial strength, unearthly, yellow glare.

So don't forget aesthetics in your zeal for energy savings. Remember that electricity is only about 1% to 10% of the gross income. And lights are only about 7% to 27% of the total electric bill. Rents, in contrast, are about 97% of the gross income. Don't harm your efforts to improve the 97% in order to save a fraction of one percent.

Efficiency and lives of various bulb types

Here are some figures on various bulb types.

Light Bulb Comparison		
Type	Lumens/watt	Life in Hours
Incandescent	11-24	750
Mercury vapor	30-63	16,000-24,000
Fluorescent	50-100	10,000-20,000
Metal halide	67-115	7,500-15,000
High-pressure sodium	66-140	20,000-24,000
Low-pressure sodium	80-183	18,000

The high end of the ranges in lumens per watt is for the largest bulbs of that type. For example, the 50 lumens per watt figure is for 22-watt fluorescent lights. But the 100 lumens per watt figure is for 96 inch long, high-efficiency fluorescent tubes.

'World records'

Watch out for ads, books or articles which claim savings of "up to" a certain figure. What that means is that the **world record** savings using this device is such and such.

Furthermore, it probably never happened. To set a world **athletic** record, you must have certain wind conditions, certain certified judges, recently calibrated timing and measuring equipment, etc. But to set a "world record" in energy conservation, about all you need is to **say** that you did it. Many claimants may even be basing their boast on **theoretical** figures. Whichever, the claims are rarely checked by unbiased observers.

You may install a new light which saves "up to 70%" on your building—only to see little more than a 5% drop in your light bill.

This is true not only of advertising, but also of supposedly objective articles and books. Article and book authors may not have a product to sell you. But they **do** want to sell you on the idea that they are very sharp guys. So their story of how much a particular energy-saving device saved may be exaggerated. And probably is.

Experiment, experiment, experiment

When it comes to saving energy, you're from Missouri. That is, you'll believe it when you see it—in your own electric bill—not in some "study" a salesman is showing you.

If you find a light which promises to save energy, run the numbers as I have above. See if there appears to be a three-year or less payback period. If so, buy **one**. That's right, one.

Install it and see how it does. Does it give enough light? (If you really want to get professional, you could measure the light output of the old and proposed bulbs with a light meter.) Does it flicker? Is the light adequately attractive? Is the fixture ugly? Will it stand up to cold weather?

Use your home as a research lab

And look at your electric bill. Is it lower? If you have a master-metered building, you won't be able to see any difference with just one light. So maybe you try it at **home**. Turn off everything in the house. Read the meter twice over fifteen minutes. Then screw in the light you're considering replacing—leaving everything else the same—and read the meter again twice over fifteen minutes. Finally, take out the light you're considering replacing and screw in the new light you're considering and read the meter again.

If that experiment shows a lower KWH consumption for the new bulb over the old one, you've got something. But I **still** wouldn't go whole hog until I'd installed them in the building for a month or so. Just to look for unexpected problems.

It is **possible** to save on your electric bill for lighting without adverse aesthetic, safety, or security effects. But you should approach any product for doing so with **great skepticism**. Do a thorough test before you equip your whole building with any product.

Don't rely on anecdotal evidence

You'll meet some landlords who will brag about energy savings. They'll claim big savings and urge you to do the same thing. Chances are they are telling you **not** what their electric bill showed. Rather they are regurgitating what the guy who **sold** them said. They decided to believe him. And they wanted to believe him. So after the stuff was in, they didn't **really** check to see if the savings were there. So your skepticism should apply not only to ads, articles, and books, but also to fellow landlords who swear on a stack of Bibles that they saved 48% on their electric bill by installing Acme Watt-Savers or whatever.

Recommended plan

In general, you should replace all incandescent bulbs which burn all night or longer with some sort of non-incandescent bulb. Typical places to do this would be

- Hallways and stairwells
- Exterior entry lights
- Laundry room lights

Replace all exterior lights with non-incandescents. Use screw-ins where possible. New fixtures probably make sense but you should do the numbers to make sure before you have them installed.

Motion-sensing switch

The September 1984 *Pacific Gas & Electric Progress* newsletter told of an apartment manager who installed motion-sensing switches in the laundry room. When someone is in the room the lights are on. A few seconds after they leave, the lights go off. Sounds interesting.

Timers versus photoelectric switches

Do **not** control night-time lights with **timers**. They'll drive you nuts. They need to be adjusted monthly to account for variations in sunrise and sunset. And they need to be adjusted every time there is a power outage. As a result, they will frequently be out of adjustment and thereby either creating a safety hazard or wasting electricity. Plus they have moving parts which can and often do malfunction.

Control all night-time lights with photoelectric switches. And don't make the stupid mistake one of my managers did. He put the photoelectric sensor on a wall facing a street light. Think about it.

For further information

The American National Standards Institute
1430 Broadway
New York, NY 10018
212-642-4900

The Illuminating Engineering Society of North America
345 East 47th Street
New York, NY 10017
212-705-7926

The National Electrical Contractors Association
7315 Wisconsin
Bethesda, MD 20814
301-657-3110

The National Lighting Bureau
2101 L Street NW Suite 300
Washington, DC 20037
202-457-8437

The National Association of Electrical Distributors
45 Danbury Road
Wilton, CT 06897
203-834-1908

The International Association of Lighting Management Companies
14 Washington Road, Suite 502
Princeton Junction, NJ 08550-1028
609-799-5501

18

Appliances

The biggest energy user is air-conditioning or heating—depending on your climate and whether your heat is electric. Heating domestic hot water is typically the second biggest user of energy—if you have an electric hot water heater. Then come refrigerators, clothes dryers, and ranges. The TV and other appliances are relatively small potatoes.

My electric bill at my master-metered apartment building ran about $550 a month in the non-air-conditioning months. The building had gas heat and gas hot water. But in the five air-conditioning months, I ran an average of about $1,300 a month. That gives me an annual total of $550 x 7 + $1,300 x 5 = $10,350.

Let's figure $550 a month is non-air-conditioning. That's a non-air-conditioning annual electric bill of $550 x 12 = $6,600. Subtracting that from the total bill we get an annual air-conditioning bill of $10,350 - $6,600 = $3,750. That's $3,750/$10,350 = 36% of the total. The percentage of the total will vary from building to building. But 36% is probably typical for Dallas, Texas area master-metered apartment buildings.

How do you conserve on air-conditioning and heating?

How can you reduce your air-conditioning and heating electric bill? It's **tough**. And the calculations are much "softer" than for lights. Remember how skeptical I told you to be about devices which would save on your light bill? Be **far more** skeptical about devices which'll save on air-conditioning and heating.

Here are some suggestions.

Attic insulation

Here's an insulation map.

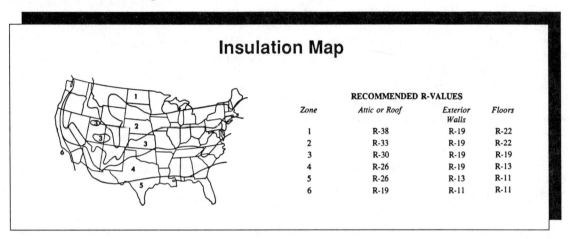

Insulation Map

Zone	RECOMMENDED R-VALUES		
	Attic or Roof	Exterior Walls	Floors
1	R-38	R-19	R-22
2	R-33	R-19	R-22
3	R-30	R-19	R-19
4	R-26	R-19	R-13
5	R-26	R-13	R-11
6	R-19	R-11	R-11

It shows the recommended R-values you should have in the walls, ceiling, and floor in various parts of the country. Take them with a grain of salt. Don't make a change if your R-value is already pretty close to the recommended level. About the only time to insulate an attic is when it is easily accessible and it has little or no insulation at present.

Do not **over**insulate. Do not follow the if-some-is-good-more-must-be-better approach. It's not so. You should **never** exceed the standards in the insulation map.

Insulation is tricky, too. For example, the electrical code prohibits insulating over recessed light fixtures. And it's hard to insulate over the trap door to the attic. But any hole in the insulation has an **exponential** detrimental effect on the overall R-value of the whole attic. That is a hole which is only 4% of the attic surface will cause a **greater than** 4% loss in insulation value.

Awnings

"As much as 14%" savings is what my local utility says in a brochure. That's probably for a treeless house in Death Valley. See if it pays back in three years with a **1%** savings. Then **maybe** do it. Awnings are generally attractive. But some aren't. Also, make sure they physically last as long as the payback period you are counting on.

Deciduous trees

Deciduous trees are those which lose their leaves in winter. Their summer shade can reduce the load on the air-conditioner. "Up to 20%" says Pacific Gas & Electric. Probably also in Death Valley. Trees take forever to grow. Mature trees are very expensive to plant and more likely to die as a result of having been moved.

Replace the filters

Air filters are relatively cheap. But going into occupied apartments to change them is a real pain. Change those in **vacancies** when necessary. Have the maintenance man check the filter whenever he has occasion to go into an apartment for another repair. But other than that, I've never been convinced you should make any great effort on the air filter front.

Tune-up

I'm told an annual tune-up of an air-conditioner—especially those big jobs like you have in a master-metered, central system building—will save electricity.

Maybe.

But I'm skeptical. The air-conditioners I'm most familiar with are those on my cars and home. They've never been tuned up. They just hum along year in and year out.

I can certainly see the **logic** behind the claim that a tune-up will help. And I've had my apartment building air-conditioners tuned up. I just haven't seen any energy saving results. Because they're either too subtle or nonexistent. I have my car tuned up every now and then. That's supposed to improve mileage. But it never has enough to notice.

I suspect that you should just have your air-conditioners fixed when they break. And listen to any recommendations the serviceman offers. But I do **not** recommend the annual tune-up. I think that's a manifestation of the "Mysterious Black Box Syndrome." Not unlike sacrificing a virgin to appease a volcano.

I have tried having a service contract on a big, central air-conditioning and heating system. And I've tried **not** having a service contract. Haven't seen any difference in energy consumption.

Attic ventilation fans

Do **not** get an attic ventilation fan. They are **not** cost effective. The logic of reducing the attic temperature notwithstanding. I was going to write an article on them once. In the course of researching it, I found that the National Bureau of Standards had exhaustively tested attic ventilation fans. And found that they did **not** reduce air-conditioning cost.

The reason is that once you insulate the attic floor to the R-value recommended, it doesn't matter how hot it is up there.

I called the trade association for attic ventilating fan manufacturers to see if they had a rebuttal. They did not. They could only offer anecdotal evidence. "Old Joe got one and he swears by it."

Anecdotal evidence is garbage. Old Joe is full of baloney.

Storm windows

Very expensive. I'd want to see some **real favorable** numbers before I went ahead. I put storm windows on a house once. Saw **no** drop in energy cost. None. Zero. **Big** drop in my bank account though.

Caulking and weather-stripping

Caulking and weather-stripping is said to have a very short payback period—like less than one year. But that only applies when it is **needed**. A building which has pretty good caulking and weather-stripping already should only get a spot check.

Cover air-conditioners during heating season

Many window or sleeve air-conditioners allow cold air in during winter. Covering them can stop that infiltration. The covers are said to have a payback period of less than a year.

I much prefer the prefabricated cover to the piece of plastic for aesthetic reasons. The prefab covers, however, cost about twice as much. That doubles the payback period.

You need to figure labor cost, too. That's especially high when apartments above the first floor are involved.

Apply reflective solar film to windows

I think this stuff is ugly. One source reported a two-year payback period. But I don't believe them. Too many variables.

Day/night thermostats

I have a day/night thermostat in my home. And it worked—there until it broke. But I put one in an apartment once. It did **not** work.

Tenants generally do not like thermostats which they cannot control. And they have infinite ways to control "uncontrollable thermostats." An office building I managed had thermostats which were covered with "tamperproof" clear plastic boxes. Of course, the boxes had air holes so the thermostat could sense the temperature. And laying on top of the box every time I went there was a straightened-out paper clip which the tenants used to adjust the temperature setting.

If the tenants cannot **move** the setting, they can **trick** the thermometer in the thermostat. Want heat? Put an ice cube on top of the thermostat. Want air-conditioning? Put your heating pad or toaster under it.

I **might** go for a day/night thermostat which is **hidden** from the tenants. And/or inaccessible because it's in a locked boiler room or some such. (Such thermostats have remote sensors which sense exterior temperatures or an interior temperature in a hidden or inaccessible location.) Dropping the setting supposedly saves 5% on the heating cost per degree.

Temperature-limiting thermostats

A temperature-limiting thermostat sets an upper limit on heating and/or a lower limit on air-conditioning. Typically, the tenant has his own thermostat which he controls. But there is another, secret thermostat which limits the setting to a certain temperature.

These limiting thermostats are supposedly highly accurate. Sounds interesting. But I'm skeptical. Too many variables. Especially when the device interacts with human nature—which a temperature-limiting thermostat does.

If the existence of the secret, temperature-limiting thermostat gets out, the trick techniques may be employed (ice-cube in winter, lamp or heating pad in summer). And how do you keep it secret? Your manager or maintenance man may tell. Or you may have a knowledgeable tenant who figures it out. Plus, if you don't already have them, you have to **install** them. How you gonna do that without arousing suspicion?

Insulate pipes

One article I saw on this showed a payback period of 2.9 years. I tend to discount published payback periods.

I **do** like pipe insulation for aesthetic reasons, however.

Did he say "**aesthetic** reasons?"

Yes, I did. Most boiler rooms look like Medieval dungeons. The tenants don't see them. But prospective **buyers** do. You can really soup up the appearance of a boiler room with rigid, formed pipe insulation and neat signs that show "Hot Water, "Return," etc. (You can get those signs from Seton Name Plate Corporation, P.O. Drawer DC-1331, New Haven, CT 06505 203-488-0085.)

Button up vacancies

Vacancies consume energy for climate control. It's hard to totally eliminate. Because you need some heat in winter to avoid freezing pipes. And you may need some air-conditioning in summer for painting and cleaning personnel and to make the unit attractive to prospective tenants.

But as much as possible, you should shut down vacancies. Flip all the circuit breakers off if you can. Clean the refrigerator and prop the door open so it won't smell from not running. Set the thermostats as low (in winter) or high (in summer) as you think you can get away with.

Domestic hot water

The classic saving device is the insulating blanket. They're so cheap, I'd say you can hardly lose. Maintenance Warehouse used to sell them for $6.81 to $8.19 each depending on size and R-value.

In my house, summer gas consumption is only for domestic hot water. One August bill was $12.14. That's $12.14 x 12 = $145.68 a year for domestic hot water gas. To get a three-year payback on an $8.19 hot water heater jacket, you'd need to save just $8.19/3 = $2.73 a year or $2.73/$145.68 = 1.9%. Seems like you ought to be able to get a 1.9% savings without too much trouble.

Gas is typically **much cheaper** than electric for domestic hot water. According to Pacific Gas & Electric, it takes about 6,935 KWH to heat hot water for a year by electric in a typical home. And 365 therms of gas. And using some assumptions about rates, they figured the cost as:

Electric $566
Gas $212.

So putting an insulating blanket on an **electric** hot water heater should pay back nearly **three** times as fast as on a gas hot water heater like the one in my home. Some areas of the country with cheap electric rates would have different numbers.

Be careful installing the blanket. The one I installed in my last house stayed on OK. Although it slid down a bit. But the one my apartment manager installed fell off.

Pacific Gas & Electric says insulating blankets save about 30 therms of gas or about 500 KWH per year. That's about an 8% saving for gas and a 7% savings for electric.

Timer on the circulating pump

Many buildings have domestic hot water circulating pumps. These pumps circulate the hot water around the building so that there's little wait when a tenant turns on the hot water faucet. They are necessary. But some say, only during hours when most people are **awake**.

So you may find it feasible and cost effective to install a **timer** or photoelectric switch on your hot-water-circulating pump. The timer shuts the pump down from, say, 11:00 pm to 6:00 am. That will save energy. A little on the pump motor. But more on the cost of heating the hot water. The pump forces you to heat **all** the water in the building. When it's shut off, you're generally only heating the water in the tank.

One article put the payback period at only four months. Timers are cheap, so I'd try this one, too.

Tenants can still get hot water when the circulating pump is turned off. It's just that it takes longer to arrive. If you get many complaints about it, shrink the times period it's off a bit. For example, if you get complaints from early risers, move the "on" time from 6:00 am back to 5:00 am.

Reducing the hot water temperature

Hot water heaters have a thermostat. Actually, it's called an aquastat. It senses the temperature of the water, compares it to the minimum setting on the aquastat, and turns on the electricity or fire if the temperature is too low. Just as you save energy by lowering thermostat settings, you save energy by lowering aquastat settings.

How low can you go? My unscientific but sensible approach is to lower the setting a little bit. Then see if you get any complaints.

If not, lower it a little bit more. Keep lowering it a little bit each week until you get "no hot water" complaints. Then raise it a notch and leave it there.

According to the Institute of Real Estate Management, the minimum temperature when the building does **not** have dishwashers is 125 degrees F and 145 degrees F if the building **does** have dishwashers. How do you tell what the temperature of your water is? Turn on the faucet and stick a thermometer into the water stream. Make sure it's a thermometer which reads up to 150 degrees or so—like a cooking thermometer.

But I wouldn't rely on the IREM figures. I prefer the lower-til-you-get-complaints method.

The payback period on this is instantaneous. Because there's **no cost** to turning down the temperature setting on the hot water heater.

Low-flow showerheads and faucet aerators

Showerheads allow water to flow at rates of from about 2 gallons per minute (GPM) to about 7 GPM. And non-shower faucets run at about 3 GPM. By replacing high-flow showerheads with low-flow showerheads and by installing flow-limiting aerators on faucets, you reduce water consumption.

Part of the water you save is **hot** water. If you save hot water, you also save the energy it takes to heat it. So low-flow showerheads and faucet aerators are gas or electricity savers.

There are also inserts you can buy instead of a low-flow showerhead itself. The insert fits inside the neck of the showerhead. I've heard about two problems with inserts: they result in a **dribble** of water that causes tenants to complain or remove them and they sometimes result in **water hammer**—a banging noise and vibration in the pipes. Experiment before you install them throughout your building.

The inserts and aerators are so cheap it's hard to imagine them not paying back. And the showerheads aren't bad either. Maintenance Warehouse has these prices if you buy more than five.

Insert	$.96
2.75 GPM head	4.15
2.75 GPM aerator	.85

Annual Energy Consumption

Appliance	Electric (KWH)	Gas (Therms)
Air-conditioner	860	283/ton
Dishwasher	363	
Dryer	933-1,170	47-75
Freezer (15 cu ft)	1,195	
Freezer, frostfree	1,761	
Heat lamp, infrared	13	
Microwave oven	190	
Oven & range	1,175	105
Oven, self-cleaning	1,205	
Refrigerator	728-1,095	
Refrigerator, frostfree	1,217-2,190	
Swimming pool pump	2,790	
Trash compactor	50	
TV, color, solid state	350-440	
Washer	103	
Water bed heater, king	1,109	
Water heater	4,219-6,935	316-365

One article I saw showed a **one month** payback period. I'm skeptical because of the labor costs. But I suspect that the actual payback period is much less than three years.

Refrigerators

They say you should vacuum the coils every three months to increase efficiency. I'd ask the people who clean the apartments to do that in a master-metered building. But I wouldn't enter occupied apartments for that purpose.

Appliance power use

For your general information, the annual energy consumption figures on most residential appliances are shown in the chart above.

Service contracts

For years, I bought heating and air-conditioning service on an *ad hoc* basis. That is, when I needed it, I paid for it. I thought service contracts were probably overpriced.

Then, after a series of major outages of my central air-conditioning system, I decided I'd better try the service-contract route before my boiler insurance company terminated my policy. The boiler-insurance company had to replace two compressors. They cost $5,000 to $10,000.

I now believe that service contracts are **best** when you are dealing with large central equipment like central heaters, air-conditioners, and hot-water heaters. Here's what I spent on heating and air-conditioning on my DeSoto, TX, 25-unit apartment building from my purchase at the end of November 1983 until the present (April 1991):

1983	$0.00
1984	$823.32
1985	$3,926.60
1986	$3,715.00
1987	$2,065.00 (Service contract started December 1987)
1988	$3,701.00
1989	$4,828.00
1990	$5,249.00
1991	$5,297.00 (for the twelve months ending April 1991)

On average, I paid less before I started the service contract. But these figures don't show the hassle of having your air-conditioner go out in the middle of a hot summer. Tenants scream. Some move out. You make lots of long-distance phone calls and you worry. Since I started the service contract, I've had no major outages at all. I plan to continue. The lack of emergency hassles is worth the price to me.

Front-loading washers

Front-loading washers use 40% less water than top-loading ones. That saves on the energy to heat the hot water. They also use about 40% less electricity to operate. Pacific Gas & Electric estimates annual savings of about 5,000 gallons of water in the typical home. That, they say, saves $75 to $112 per year. Apartment units, since they have smaller average family size, would save less.

19

Separate Meters

Separate meters and submeters

A great many landlords—maybe most—swear by separate meters. Some apartment lenders **insist** on them.

Not me.

They don't impress me at all.

And I suspect it is almost **never** cost effective to install separate meters or submeters.

Tenants waste energy when the owner pays but...

The whole idea behind separate meters is that tenants waste energy when it's on the landlord's meter.

There's no doubt about that.

In October 1975, Midwest Research Institute did a study of the matter for the Federal Energy Administration. That study concluded that

> *"residential customers whose electrical service is provided through master meters consume about 35% more electrical energy than those who receive electrical service through an individual meter."*

That 35% figure was picked up and bandied about for years. In fact, it is probably the basis for a bunch of laws that were passed prohibiting construction of master-metered buildings. And the basis for the common redlining of master-metered apartment buildings by investors and lenders.

It's not 35%

A 1980 study done by the University of Colorado at Boulder for the Department of Energy said,

"the popularly-used figure of 35% savings due to individual metering is inaccurate."

According to the University of Colorado, the correct figures are

Cooling, lighting, appliances	10%-35%
Electric space heating, cooling, hot water	5%-25%
Heating and hot water only	0%-20%

Why should an owner separately meter?

As I said, it's true that tenants waste energy when someone else pays for it. But what should you **do** about it?

The idea behind separate metering is that the owner can put the savings due to reduced energy consumption in **his** pocket. **Before** separate metering, let's say the apartment rents for $450 a month. And let's say that the electric bill on that unit is $50 a month.

If 20% is wasted, the electric bill on that unit if it were separately metered would be $40 a month. A $10 savings.

So if the owner charged $410 a month rent, and the tenant pays $40 a month electric, the tenant's position is the same as before. But the landlord is $10 a month better off—because he got rid of a $50 a month electric bill—but only lost $40 a month in rent.

That's the theory.

But there's more to it than that.

It's expensive

I had a house separate metered. It cost $660. Plus it flunked electrical inspection forcing us to move the pool pump. And the electrician failed to put the dining room light on the right meter. So we had to hire another electrician to do that for $275. For a total of $935.

According to a Department of Energy study, it cost at least $100 a unit extra to install separate meters **when an apartment building was being constructed new**. So it costs much more than that to separate meter **after** the building is built.

The University of Colorado study in 1980 said it costs from $50 to $2,000 per unit to install various kinds of metering devices on existing buildings.

I can't get much closer to the correct figure for your building. Too many variables. You'd need to get bids from electrical contractors.

The payback period

If you really could save $10 a unit a month, you'd save 12 x $10 = $120 a unit a year. In three years that's $360. So it would make sense to do it if you could get the separate meters installed for $360 or less.

But remember that's only **if** you'd save $10 a month. **Will** you save that much? It's very, very hard to determine how much, if anything, you'd save.

The big question

The big question is how much will you have to **lower rent** when you install separate meters. I've had apartment owners tell me they didn't have to lower the rent **at all** when they installed separate meters.

That is absurd. May be true. But it's absurd for them to expect me to believe the separate meters had no effect on the market rental value of the apartments.

There is only one way you can install separate meters and keep the same rent. If the rent **before** the separate metering was far **below** market.

So the question is really, "How much does the market rental value of the apartments go down when you separate meter?"

The answer is, a bunch.

At one point, I got $385 for a one bedroom master-metered apartment in DeSoto, Texas (near Dallas). That's a 20 year-old building with no pool or tennis court. No cathedral ceilings or washer/dryer hookups. No ceiling fans. No balconies or patios. No fireplaces.

Brand new one-bedrooms with all those amenities rented for $325 to $335 in nearby Lancaster. What do you suppose my 20-year old, few amenities building would be worth if I separately metered it? $285?

Psychology

Earlier, I showed that logic dictates that a tenant paying $450 for a master-metered apartment should be willing to pay $410 for that same apartment separately metered. But are tenants logical?

Is it possible that some tenants would prefer a $450 never-have-to-worry-about-the-electric apartment to a $410 apartment where the electric bill jumps around and in many months **exceeds** $40?

Some people like a steady monthly bill. You can arrange that with most electric companies if you have a separate meter. But tenants sometimes don't know that or don't want to be bothered or don't want to risk getting hit with a lump sum bill if they underestimate the monthly amount.

Hidden costs of switching

There are many tenants who prefer master-metered buildings. If you switch to individual meters, they'll probably **move** to a master-metered building. If you think turnover is costly, move-outs are an additional cost to figure on when you're deciding to convert.

One owner who converted said he discovered another problem. Some tenants who pay their rent on time and otherwise behave have **checkered pasts**—including not paying an electrical bill or two. They **must** live in master-metered buildings.

Because when a building goes separate meters, the tenants have to call up the electric company to arrange for service. The former deadbeats can't do that. The electric company computer knows them. So they move out.

Climate and rate structure

The University of Colorado figures I cited above are based on experience in certain buildings. Your buildings are probably in a different climate. And your electric company probably has a different rate structure.

In the Northwest, for example, electric rates are relatively low. And the climate mild. New York City rates are high and the climate, harsh.

The lower the rates, the less difference between the way master-metered tenants and separate-metered tenants behave. And the more mild the climate, the less effect behavior has on energy consumption (because the heater or air-conditioner will rarely run no matter where you leave the thermostat).

Central systems

So far, I've been talking about separate metering of units which have separate appliances. That's expensive enough. But what about where there are systems which are central to the whole complex?

I managed apartments in New Jersey where the heat and domestic hot water came from a central system (master metered) and the electric was separate units for each apartment and separate metered. That's common in New Jersey—central heat and hot water, separate electric and maybe even gas for a range.

In Texas, my master-metered building had gas central heat and central hot water (and a few gas ranges for some strange reason). And it had one big air-conditioner which served the entire complex.

In order to totally separate meter a building with central systems, you must either get rid of the central systems and replace them with individual air-conditioners, heaters, hot water heaters, etc. Or you must use special meters which measure the **use** of air-conditioning, heat, and hot water in each unit—in addition to separate electric meters to measure use of electric for appliances and lights.

Either way, you're talking about a bunch of money.

Special meters

Many landlords don't know it. But there are meters for virtually every type of system.

Submeters

Submeters for gas or electric work the same as the meters utilities use. The only difference is that you, the owner—or your agent—must install, own, maintain, and read them and bill the tenants and collect the money. There are laws governing these meters. Make sure you are familiar with them before you switch. For example, in Texas you can turn off the electric of a delinquent tenant if you pay his electric but not if you have submeters. (PUC of TX§ 23.51)

BTU meters

These measure the **volume** of water moving through the pipes and the **drop or rise in water temperature** in the apartment. My master-metered building has a two-pipe system. That means two pipes carry water which is either heated or chilled to each apartment. In each apartment is a heat exchanger—which is a set of coils and a fan. The fan blows over the coils to extract hot or cool air depending upon the setting of the tenant's thermostat and the temperature in the apartment.

The more extreme the tenant's thermostat setting, the more the fan blows over the coils. The more the fan blows over the coils, the bigger the temperature change in the water during the time it is passing through that apartment. That's what the BTU meter measures. The reading is used to prorate the building's total energy bill to each tenant according to his use of energy.

Sound complicated? It is. BTU meters are expensive.

Volumetric meters

Measure only water flow. I don't think they'd work in a building like mine. Water flow is exactly the same in everyone's unit. Only suitable where tenant's use of thermostat and/or windows for temperature regulation affects flow of heated or chilled water.

Heat evaporation meters

Small tube of liquid attached to radiators. Read once a **year**. Measures amount of heat used. Big in Europe where tens of millions are in use. I can't imagine them working here. Tenants don't stay that long. And those that do would try to fiddle with the meters.

Electronic heat meters

Measure heat emitted from radiators.

Time meters

Measure the amount of time heat exchanger fans, etc. are on. Readings are used to prorate total energy bill.

Indoor/outdoor temperature differential monitors

These measure the difference between the outdoor and indoor temperatures in each apartment. The bigger the difference, the bigger that tenant's share of the total bill.

Hot water meters

These measure apartment's use of domestic hot water. Total domestic hot water bill is then prorated accordingly.

Use of special meters

Some special meters are expensive. Some cheap. Some are very accurate. Others not. Their durability is open to question. Convincing the tenants that they accurately measure energy use is a whole 'nother matter. In short, these gizmos scare me. I'd want to talk to a local owner who had been using them for some time before I agreed to use them.

Economies of scale

Remember that I told you large bulbs were more efficient than small ones? Do you suppose that's also true of air-conditioners and heaters?

It is.

A 40-ton air-conditioner will cool an apartment building with less electricity that 40 **one**-ton air-conditioners.

The Dallas Apartment Association does an annual study of apartment building operating expenses. In the 1981 study, they found a $.12 per square foot per year difference between two-pipe and separate air-conditioner master-metered buildings. That is, the electric bills were $.12 per square foot of apartment area **less** in master-metered buildings if the building had a central, two-pipe air-conditioner than in master-metered buildings where each apartment had its own air-conditioning unit.

The total utilities (electric, gas, and water) figure that year was 99.9 cents. If half of that was electric, that's $.50 for electric. What percent is $.12 of $.50? $.12/$.50 = 24%.

What'd I say was the percentage tenants waste on cooling when the building is master metered? Between 5% and 35%. That's about a wash isn't it?

In other words, the **bad** news about master-metered central system buildings is that the tenants waste electricity—about 5% to 35%. But the **good** news about master-metered central system buildings is that the air-conditioners are 24% more efficient.

You'd have the best of both worlds if you had a single, big, central air-conditioner—and some metering system which would encourage the tenants to conserve. But I'm not advocating that. Probably best to forget the separate meters or submeters.

So separate meters and separate air-conditioners for each unit reduce **tenant** waste. But those same little air-conditioners increase waste due to **inefficient equipment**. In other words, the legislators who thought they were doing a good thing by prohibiting master metered buildings probably actually even made things **worse**. Not only do those little air-conditioners **use** more energy. But it takes more energy to **manufacture** an air-conditioner for every apartment instead of one for every twenty or so apartments.

We expect government to do stupid things. But don't **you** fall for the separate-meters-are-always-better line.

Rate differentials

You need to consider your local electric rate schedule before you convert to separate meters. In some utilities, **volume** users get a discount. If you separate meter, the discount is lost. In my example above, I said your apartment had a $40 a unit electric bill. And that the tenant would have the same bill after separate metering.

But what if a volume discount applied to your bill? And the tenant doesn't get that after conversion? What if he has to pay $44 for the same quantity of electric you paid $40 for?

That fouls up the savings calculations, doesn't it?

In some cases, the tenant will be **better** off. My own separate metering of that house is a case in point. Not only is the electric company losing the energy they sold due to my managers wasting electric. They're also having to sell the smaller amount of electricity at lower "**residential**" rather than "general" rates.

But on the other hand, in some utilities, a residential building gets a better rate than a non-residential business. But when you separate meter, the remaining owner meters cover only laundry rooms, parking lot lights, pool equipment, etc. The local rate schedules might be such that separate metering will throw your **owner** meters into a **less** favorable category than when you were supplying electric to the units. Check it out before you switch.

Vandalism

If separate meters means separate air-conditioning units, expect vandalism and general cosmetic ugliness to be a problem. Separate air-conditioners means a compressor for each unit. If they are on the roof, the present no vandalism or cosmetic problem. Just a wear and tear on the roof surface problem.

But if they are on the ground, they are ugly at best. At worst, the fins on the compressor inspire children to poke them with sticks. That's even more unsightly. And it reduces the efficiency of the units. And, for some reason, there always seem to be several which have their covers permanently off. If the compressors are on the lawn, the gardener has to trim around them. Large central air-conditioning units which are located in a boiler room present little or no vandalism target and don't clutter up the property.

"But what if utility rates jump?"

The main reason for wanting separate meters is fear of another jump in utility rates like we had in 1974. What about that?

A jump in utility rates directly affects **owners** of **master**-metered buildings. But it also directly affects **tenants** in **separately** metered buildings. For example, a 30% jump in rates raises the master-metered landlord's utility expense 30% and the separate-metered tenant's utility expense 30%.

What will happen? The master-metered landlord will raise his rents. Will that cause his tenants to move out? No. Where would they go? To a **separate**-metered building? Not likely after a 30% increase in utility rates.

If any master-metered owners do **not** raise their rents, they'll find they have a flood of applicants—and they'll fill any vacancies overnight.

Owners of separately-metered buildings may suddenly find they have move-outs—as tenants who just got hit with 30% utility bill increases move to master-metered buildings.

What I'm saying is that it all comes out in the wash. After a big utility rate increase, rents on master-metered buildings rise accordingly. If they didn't, there'd be a mass emigration out of individually-metered buildings into master-metered buildings.

Higher gross rent multipliers on separate meters

Some apartment owners will point out that separately-metered buildings have higher gross rent multipliers. True. They also have lower rents. Like I said, it all comes out in the wash. Separate-metered buildings are **not** more valuable.

RUBS

RUBS stands for Resident Utility Billing System. It means that you bill tenants separately for rent and utilities even though you have a master meter. How do you arrive at each tenant's utility bill? You prorate the big bill according to each tenant's share of square footage.

What do I think of RUBS? I think it's **nonsense**. I tried my own version of RUBS on duplexes and triplexes I owned during the first "Energy Crisis." If it'll work anywhere, it'll work on small buildings like that. It didn't

RUBS is illegal in 16 states. Other states regulate RUBS. Tenants don't like it as a rule. They argue about the proration. They complain that the bill is high because the owner hasn't taken conservation measures—like installing a new boiler. Etc., etc., etc.

I say forget it.

Summary on separate meters, submeters, and RUBS

Contrary to widespread and fervently held belief, there is absolutely no investment reason to prefer separate-metered buildings over master-metered buildings. I prefer master-metered buildings myself.

Contrary to widespread and fervently held belief, **society as a whole** is better off with master-metered apartment buildings. Because it takes more energy and money to manufacture, install, bookkeep, and operate tens of millions of separate meters and heaters and air-conditioners than it does to manufacture, install, bookkeep, and operate millions of master meters and multi-unit central heaters and air-conditioners.

I doubt that installation of individual meters or submeters is **ever** cost-effective—since I see no advantage to having separate or submeters. I invite sellers of submetering devices and services to send me hard facts which prove me wrong. I made that same invitation in the first three editions (17,500 copies sold) of this book. And heard from no one.

De minimus separate meters may pay

One of my subscribers, Ira Serkes, points out that *de minimus* separate meters may make sense. *De minimus* is Latin for triflingly small.

For example, suppose your tenants pay their own gas and electric—except for domestic hot water which you pay for. If you could shift the cost of heating the hot water to their gas or electric bill, they probably would not notice it. (You would **tell** them, of course. But they wouldn't notice it in their **bills** unless they got out a calculator and compared this September's bill to last

September's and so forth.) As I said earlier, it's maybe $12 a month. Few people would move over $12. In other words, if the amount added to the tenant's bill is **small enough**, the rental market value of the apartment will **not** go down as a result of separate metering.

The **tenants** wouldn't notice the $12—but **you** would. In a mere four-unit building that'd be 4 x $12 = $48 a month or $48 x 12 = $576 a year and a $576 ÷ 10% = $5,760 increase in building value.

The problem is that the cost of separate metering a *de minimus* portion of the utilities is probably **not** *de minimus*. In the above four-unit example, you'd have to add three hot water heaters and the related plumbing and/or wiring. With a three-year payback criterion, you'd have to spend no more than 3 x $576 = $1,728 on the labor and materials.

Shifting to tenant's meter

In some cases, you can shift something that's on **your** meter to the tenant's meter. Like the owner I told you about who put the exterior lights on the tenants' meters.

In most residential rental properties, there is an exterior light next to or above each tenant's entrance door and patio door. In many, if not most cases, these lights are on the owner's meter. In most cases, you could probably shift the light to the tenant's meter (again telling them what you were doing) and avoid a rent decrease because of the *de minimus* size of the change in the tenant's bill.

If the light is necessary for safety, etc., you need to require the tenant to keep it lit. As a practical matter, you'd probably have to replace the bulbs yourself and not give the tenant a switch. In other words, the light would be turned on by a photoelectric switch.

If a tenant got their electric turned off for nonpayment of the electric bill—but still lived in the building—you'd have a safety hazard. That would be rare. But since you can't tolerate a safety hazard even for one night, you'd better leave the wiring so that you could switch back a light to the owner's meter if necessary.

A 75-watt bulb burning ten hours a day consumes 10 x 75 x 365 = 273,750 watt hours or 273.75 KWH. At, say 13¢ a KWH, that's $35.59 a year. If you could do the labor of switching for 3 x $35.59 = $106.76 per unit it would meet the three-year payback criterion.

I can't think of any other item you could do this with but exterior door lights. But if your building has one of something else for each unit—and that something is now on your meter—transferring it to the tenants' meters may make sense.

Make sure you tell not only the tenants who are in place when you do it but all subsequent move-ins as well. Tenants who are not told frequently find out. For example, their circuit breaker trips and they notice that the lights **inside** their unit were not the only ones that went out. If they find out **that** way, they'll likely be angry at you and may cause trouble. But if you tell them up front, they'll probably shrug it off as insignificant—which it is—to them.

20

Gas

Gas bills are usually pretty straight forward. As with electric, they have various rates. You should find out the definition of each category to make sure you're in the right one.

And if you're paying sales tax, you should make sure you're not exempt for being residential property. In Texas, for example, residential is exempt but you often have to apply for the refund.

Cubic feet and therms

Some gas meters read in cubic feet; others in therms. There are 1.048 therms per 100 cubic feet in case you need to convert.

Pilot lights and flue dampers

I already covered most of the techniques for saving gas in the section on electricity. One that I didn't cover is turning off the heater gas pilot light in summer. According to PG & E, a gas pilot light on a gas range uses 1/5 therm per day and a pilot light on a swimming pool heater uses 1/4 therm per day. I assume a gas pilot light on a heater uses a similar amount.

I paid about 70 cents per 100 cubic feet in Texas in the late '80s. Let's call it 70 cents a therm, too, since they're so similar. At that rate, a pilot light uses about 1/4 therm/day x 365 days/year x $.70 = $63.88/year.

Cutting it off for, say, five months should save 5/12 x $63.88 = $26.62 a year. The labor of shutting it off and turning it back on again should be about $5 a year. That's a net of $21.62.

The flue or chimney on a gas heater or gas hot water heater must be open when the fire is on for safety. But if it's still open when the fire goes **out**, valuable heat is lost. An automatic flue damper opens whenever the fire is on but closes as soon as it goes out.

Logic dictates that would save energy. Is it cost effective? I don't know. I've seen savings figures ranging from 2% to 15%. Texas's TU Electric says **vent**, not flue, dampers save 6 to 8%.

Carrier offered a flue damper called a "Chimney-Lock" as an option on its gas furnaces. Another was offered by SaVent, 4399 Hamann Parkway, Willoughby, OH 44094. *Consumer Reports* magazine favored one made by Flair Manufacturing Corp., Hauppauge, NY.

Modular boilers

Most furnaces have one flame. It's either on or off. It burns at the same intensity whether the outdoor temperature is 60 degrees or 6 degrees. One way to get around this inefficient on-or-off approach is a **modular** heater. With a modular, you have multiple furnaces. The colder it is, the more of them that light up. That supposedly saves energy on mild but cool days.

Sounds logical. Is it cost-effective? I don't know. Might be worth investigating, though, if your furnace needs replacing.

An IREM booklet suggested the savings might be 9%.

Outdoor reset controls

An outdoor reset control adjusts your boiler aquastat according to outdoor temperature. Just as the flame goes full blast no matter how mild the weather, so does the normal aquastat always ask the flame to stay on until the same water temperature is achieved.

An outdoor reset control lowers the aquastat setting in milder weather so that the water in the boiler is not heated to the same temperature as is needed in the dead of winter.

Sounds logical. Is it cost-effective? IREM estimates a 7 to 15% savings. I'd expect less.

Other gas saving tricks

Some heating boilers also heat domestic hot water. That's efficient in winter when the boiler is running already anyway. But it's **inefficient** in **summer** because you're firing up an oversize boiler for just domestic hot water needs.

As a result, it may be cost-effective to disconnect the domestic hot water portion of the heating boiler and install a **separate** domestic hot water heater. Unlike many of the heat-saving devices above, you can probably get a pretty good handle on the savings this will produce. Because you know you're going to be shutting down the boiler for four or five months. And figures on how much it will cost to heat domestic hot water should be readily available.

According to PG & E, a typical decorative gas light uses about 15 thousand cubic feet of gas per year which cost about $7.20 a year in 1984.

Texas's TU Electric says you save 4 to 6% on your gas bill by having your furnace inspected regularly.

Furnaces need air. They send the air they use up the chimney. Since it costs money to heat the air inside your building, you don't want to be sending any of it up the chimney. To avoid that, your furnace should get its air from **outside**. TU Electric says that will save about 8 to 10%.

Gas pipelines

If you have gas at your building and you don't get it from tanks that are periodically delivered there, you have gas pipelines. You must comply with state and federal gas pipeline safety rules. In Texas, the Railroad Commission publishes the rules. They require tha you have an "Inspection, operation, and Maintenance Plan." The Texas Apartment Association *Redbook* has a fill-in-the-blank plan.

21

Heating Oil

In some parts of the country, heating oil is a common fuel. In other parts, it's virtually unknown. If your properties are in an area where heating oil is unknown, skip this chapter.

Shop for price

Gas and electric rates are set by utilities. But oil prices are set by the **market**. So if you use oil for heating and/or domestic hot water, you have an opportunity to get a deal on price.

When I owned several duplexes, I asked for and got a volume discount from a local oil dealer. He suggested that I get some other people for an even bigger discount. So I got my mother's house and several other duplex owners—and did indeed get a bigger discount for all of us.

You can tell whether you're getting a good deal from *The Wall Street Journal*. The wholesale price of "Fuel Oil No. 2" is listed under "Oil Prices" every day. The closer your price is to that price, the better you're doing.

Flame retention burners

According to an IREM book titled *Energy Cost Control Guide for Multifamily Properties*, you can save on oil by replacing an inefficient old burner with a "high-speed, flame retention burner." Consult your oil man for more information. Savings are hard to predict. Although IREM notes that a well-tuned old-style burner can achieve combustion efficiency of about 75% whereas a newer model may reach an efficiency of 80% to 85%.

22

Water and Sewer

Water bills vary considerably from water district to water district. Two of the three water bills I got also included a charge for sewer. It's common for the sewer bill to be based on the amount of water used. Although I've also owned buildings where the sewer was included in the property taxes and buildings where the sewer bill was a flat rate based on the number of toilets in the building.

Otherwise, my bills just list my consumption in gallons or cubic feet. 100 cubic feet = 748 gallons.

Water consumption

Consumption also varies a lot. For example, in 1987, my house used 1,297 gallons per day; my 25-unit apartment building, 3,942 gallons a day; and my 33-unit apartment building (with pool), 4,210 gallons a day.

My 25-unit used more water per day than the 33-unit when I did the first edition of this book. I suspected leaks. Now that it's less than the 33-unit, that suspicion is probably confirmed. In the interim, one of my resident managers there was a **plumber**. He tightened the place up somewhat. But the main thing was replacing the cooling tower which chronically had standing water in the grass around it.

According to a Department of the Interior study, household water use breaks down this way:

Toilet	45%
Bathing	30%
Kitchen	14%
Laundry, etc.	11%

The U.S. Bureau of the Census tells us that the average household flushes the toilet 19.4 times a day (your tax dollars at work digging up these statistics). A sales brochure I have says the average household uses the shower 3.3 times per day and that the average shower lasts five minutes.

Note that the average **household** is bigger than the average **apartment** household. About two thirds of all Americans live in homes.

What a 'tight' building consumes

My house was brand new when we moved into it on October 14, 1983. So it probably had no leaks. It **does** have low-flow showerheads, low-flow aerators, and low-gallons per flush toilets—all of which are required by California law. At that time, we had no lawn or sprinkler system. So the water consumption then might serve as a gauge of what a leak-free family would use. Our use from October 14 to October 22 (the normal meter reading day) was 281 gallons per day. From October 22 to December 23, it was 241 gallons per day.

That's a husband, wife, and one two-year old boy.

Roughly speaking, it would appear that 100 gallons per day per person is the standard. And it seems to me I've seen that figure somewhere.

In the October 24, 1984 *Wall Street Journal*, there was a story about a Phoenix builder with a water conservation hang-up. That story said the average Phoenix household used 240 gallons per person per day. But that John Long's homes use only 53 gallons per person per day. So it appears that if you pull every water conservation trick in the book, you can get it down to 53 gallons per person. I suspect that might be below the point of diminishing returns.

Average apartment consumption

How many people live in an apartment? One or two in an efficiency or one-bedroom. Two or three although occasionally one in a two-bedroom. If your building is small, you can probably just list each unit and how many people live in it. If your building is large, compute the average of a representative sample and apply that to the whole complex.

Just for talking purposes, I'll use a figure of 1.5 persons per apartment. With that average, you should consume 1.5 persons per unit x 100 gallons per person = 150 gallons per unit per day.

At that rate, my 25-unit should consume 25 x 150 = 3,750 gallons per day—not the 4,943 gallons per day it recently consumed. Assuming the excess is waste due to leaks, they are costing me 4,943 - 3,750 = 1,193 gallons x $.337/100 gallons = 11.93 hundred gallons x $.337/100 gallons = $4.02 a day or $4.02 x 30 days = $120.61/month.

My 33-unit should have consumed 33 x 150 gallons = 4,950. It did better than that at 3,422 gallons per day. In fact, 3,422 gallons per day is 3,422 ÷ 33 = only 103.67 gallons per unit per day. Hmmmm.

Maybe tenants use 100 gallons per person per day—but not all of it is apartment water. That is, they go work and use the toilet there. Seems that if my 33-unit (with pool) could get by on 100 gallons per unit per day, then **most** apartment buildings could do the same.

Checking the bills for a 37-unit building I got rid of in 1983, I find that one month's bill was for 173,200 gallons. That's 173,200 ÷ 37 = 4,681 gallons per unit per month or 4,681 ÷ 30 = 156 gallons per person per day. Bingo.

Based on my experience, it appears that a well-run apartment building should use between 100 and 150 gallons per unit per day. If you're using more than that, you probably have leaks.

Leaks

What leaks? Toilets mostly. And faucets to a lesser extent. Sometimes underground pipes.

A faucet leak can waste up to seven gallons a day. A toilet leak up to hundreds of gallons a month.

Toilets may run continuously. That happens when the ballcock doesn't go up high enough to shut off the refill spigot inside the toilet tank. Or when the valve malfunctions. You can **hear** the water running when this happens. And you can **see** it if you take the top off the tank.

You can sometimes fix it by just fiddling with it. Screwing the float valve rod in a bit so the ball float rides lower. Or bending the rod so the ball float rides lower.

Invisible toilet leaks

The other toilet leak problem is silent and invisible. That's a leaky flapper valve. Take off the toilet tank top. You see that black rubber thingamajig at the bottom of the tank? It has a chain attached to the top of it and to the flush lever. That's the flapper valve.

If it fits tight, no leak. Loose fit, silent, invisible, costly leak. How do you tell if there's a silent, invisible leak? Drop a toilet tank leak detector in the tank, not the bowl. A toilet tank leak detector is simply a tablet of food color. If the tank does not leak, the water in the tank will turn the color of the tablet. But the water in the bowl will not—until you flush it. If the tank **does** leak, the water in both the tank and the bowl will turn the color of the tablet **before** you flush it.

Solution? Replace the defective flapper valve and seat with a Fluidmaster Flusher Fixer. It's made of stainless steel. Fits right over the old one. Maintenance Warehouse sells them for $3.26 in quantity. Figure maintenance man labor at $3.00 (1/2 hour at $6 an hour). That's a total cost of $3.26 + $3.00 = $6.26. To achieve a three-year payback you'd need to save at least $6.26/3 = $2.09 a year. At 15 cents per hundred gallons, you'd need to save $2.09/.15 = 1,391 gallons per year or 1,391/12 = 116 gallons per month. Since I said leaky toilets can waste up to **hundreds** of gallons per month, that's about right.

Do you need a plumber?

You don't need a plumber to fix a leaky toilet tank. So don't get intimidated by the mechanism in the tank. If you take the top off and flush it a couple times, you'll see that it's pretty simple. Your maintenance man or resident manager should fix leaky toilet tanks. Same with leaky faucets.

Underground leaks

Underground leaks are a mess. They are usually caused by **electrolysis**. That is a combination electrical-chemical reaction between the soil and the pipe. When you find the leak and cut the damaged piece of pipe out, you find it's smooth on the inside except for a pinhole. But rough and pitted on the outside around the hole. Water companies sometimes have equipment that can help you detect underground leaks.

One building I managed had a central hot-water heating system. Inside the buildings, the pipes ran between floors. But at the end of each building, the pipes dove down under the slab to go to the next building.

A tenant would call and say, "My living room floor's hot." That meant a pipe had been corroded through and heated water was blasting out into the dirt under that living room.

To repair it, we had to turn off the heat to the buildings on that loop of pipe, move out the tenants in that apartment, take up the carpet, jackhammer a hole in the concrete slab floor, dig down through hot mud until we found the pipe, turn the heat back on to see where the water came out, hacksaw the perforated section out, and replace it with a dresser coupling. Then when we felt confident the dresser coupling was tight and no other leaks were there, we close it up and restore the apartment. Gawd, what a mess!

The cheap solution? Beats me, folks. That's why the question, "Have you had any problems with underground leaks?" appears in my books, *Residential Property Acquisition Handbook* and *Office Building Acquisition Handbook.* If you own a copy of my first book (which was replaced by *Residential Property...*), *Apartment Investing Check Lists*, write it in. Ask it of any of the following:

- Seller   • Previous owner   • Resident manager
- Property manager   • Heating service company.

When it comes to underground pipe leaks, better to buy another building.

Sacrificial anodes

I'm told that you can prevent or reduce the incidence of electrolysis of underground pipes through the use of sacrificial anodes. A sacrificial anode is attached to the pipe to be protected by a wire like a ground wire. The sacrificial anode is buried near the pipe. The theory is that the sacrificial anode is so constituted that the electrolysis happens to it **first**. That spares the pipe. Boat owners also use sacrificial anodes to prevent similar damage to boat hulls.

Do sacrificial anodes works on pipes? After repairing several underground pipe leaks, I'd sure try sacrificial anodes or anything else that might help. By the way, gas companies, for whom avoiding leaks is far more important, are expert at leak prevention.

The 2:00 am leak check

Most people are asleep at 2:00 am. And unless your building has some automatic water user that goes on all hours of the day, there should be no water flowing in your building at that hour.

So you can find out whether you have a leak problem—and how extensive it is—by reading your water meter at, say, 2:00 am and 2:30 am. If it's moving at all, you've probably got a leak. By noting the two readings and the time between them, you can calculate the amount of water lost per hour.

The bigger the building, the less accurate this is. Because even at 2:00 am, some people are getting out of bed to use the toilet, a rare person is actually taking a shower or doing wash, and so forth.

One other warning. Water meters are usually in the side walk or lawn in front of your building. At 2:00 am you need a flash light to read the meter. One of my seminar students told me he was doing just that at 2:00 am one morning. He had to lay on his stomach to read the meter. When he looked up, he noticed that he had been joined by two policemen—who found his explanation of what he was doing suspicious enough to take him "downtown." So you should take adequate identification and money for a phone call when you go on a wee hours meter-reading expedition. And maybe a copy of this book to show this page to the police.

Reducing gallons per flush

Old style toilets use about 6.5 gallons per flush. Newer ones use only 3.5 gallons per flush. At 19.4 flushes per day (the national average), the lower model saves 3 x 19.4 = 58.2 gallons per day or 58.2 x 365 = 21,243 gallons per year.

Should you replace a working toilet to take advantage of that savings? Maybe. At 15 cents per hundred gallons, 21,243 gallons of water is only worth $32. To get a three-year payback, you'd need an installed price of 3 x $32 = $96.

But if you need to replace a tank anyway, by all means get a 3 1/2 gallons per flush model.

The October 24, 1984 *Wall Street Journal* story I mentioned earlier also noted that a Finnish company called Colton-Wartsila, Inc. makes a one-gallon per flush toilet that really works. And that story said that an American company, Eljer, planned to offer a one-gallon per flush toilet, too. A September '87 *Sunset Magazine* story said such ultra-low-volume toilets cost $160 to $300 while conventional toilets cost $35 to $100. Maintenance Warehouse sells a 1.6 gallons per flush Mansfield toilet and tank for $99.00. The California Department of Water Conservation claims that a family of four can save $25 to $50 per year on water bills with a ulv toilet. That'd be $9.38 to $18.75 for our apartment family of 1.5. That's not enough to generate a three-year payback on a $160 expenditure. (In Glendale, AZ, you get a $100 rebate for replacing a regular toilet with a ulv toilet. That's enough to make hitting the three-year payback possible.)

Bricks in the tank

Don't put bricks in the tank. You might drop one. There goes a whole tank and the labor it takes to replace it and clean up the mess.

Bricks are heavier than water. The tank was not designed to handle that kind of weight. So putting bricks in the tank may cause the tank to tilt and leak.

Some bricks dissolve in water. Not good for valves.

Dams and bags

Dams are rubber walls you put into the toilet tank on one or both sides of the flapper valve. When the toilet is flushed, the water on the outer side of the dams remains in the tank. That reduces the gallons per flush.

I don't like the dams. For one thing, it's not good to muck around in the tank—which is what somebody has to do to install these things. One big apartment owner found their water bill went **up** when they installed toilet dams. When they investigated, they found that a few float valves had been knocked askew and were running continuously. Those few had more than wiped out the savings from the ones that were installed without incident.

Not only did the installers foul up some float valves, so did some tenants who felt the dams needed to be adjusted. The dams are simple. But they must be **precisely** installed. Too far apart, and they save too little. Too close to the flapper valve, and there's not enough water for a decent flush. If they're not tight, water runs out under them and there's no savings at all.

If the flush does not clear the bowl, the tenant will flush again. Two 3.5-gallon flushes use more water than one 6-gallon flush. Worse yet is the four-flusher. (I couldn't resist.)

Tenants often resent dams as making their toilet bowl dirtier so the landlord can pinch pennies. So they may adjust or remove them.

Bags are supposed to do what bricks and dams do. Reduce the gallons per flush in an old 6-gallon toilet. The bags hang from the top edge of the tank inside the tank. They hold some of the tank water, thereby preventing it from going into the bowl during the flush. I don't care for the idea for many of the same reasons I don't like the bricks and dams.

As a general rule, I'd say leave the toilet's gallons per flush alone. Best to confine yourself to eliminating leaks.

Pressure reduction

If your water pressure is greater than 40 pounds per square inch, you should consider installing a pressure-reducing valve. Tenants will probably not increase the length of time they run a shower or faucet. So reducing the pressure will reduce the consumption.

Recycling

Some large air-conditioners use large amounts of water. After going through a cooling tower, it runs just down a drain. That clean water could be recycled for lawn watering or to maintain the water level in a swimming pool. A strategically placed pipe and/or storage tank would allow that.

Lawn water

Since the water you use to irrigate your landscaping does not go down the sanitary drains like toilet flushes, showers, dishwashers, etc., an argument can be made that you should not be charged for sewer on that water.

Some **will** agree to leave off the sewer charge **if** you install a separate water meter which feeds **only** the sprinkler system. Is that cost effective?

Possibly. You need to check with your local utility to see what they charge for a new meter. And you need to get an estimate from a plumber. You need to estimate how much the sewer bill on the old water-and-sewer meter will go down. And don't overlook the **service charge** on the new meter. And check whether you'll throw either meter into a different **rate** category. For example, by taking off the sprinkler demand, you may be able to switch to a smaller diameter feed pipe on the old meter, thereby lowering the service charge in some utilities.

Another alternative would be to use **well water** for irrigation. Since it won't be used for human consumption, you can avoid purification expenses, if any. To tell if a well would be cost-effective, you need to find out the cost of creating the well, the cost of the electricity to run the pump, and the amount of water and sewer charges you'll eliminate on your city or utility water/sewer bill.

How one of my readers got an $18,167 refund from his sewer utility

In 1987, Spencer Roane's mobilehome park had a bad leak—a broken elbow in a 1.5-inch water supply line—for an extended period. When he finally found and fixed it, he figured the sewer utility owed him a refund. They charged for sewer based on water consumption based on the assumption that what came out of the tap must have gone down the drain. But the water from Roane's leak ran into a nearby stream—not into the sewer system.

The sewer department offered $5,000. Roane appealed and got $18,167.

Lawn water conservation

We had a drought in California. So our water utility, East Bay Municipal Utility District, sent us a flyer on how to save on lawn watering. Here are its tips.

To determine your lawn watering needs:

1. Set three flat bottom cans or coffee mugs around your lawn
2. Turn on your sprinklers for 15 minutes
3. Measure the depth of water in each can and calculate the average
4. Find that average depth on this table:

Average depth in inches	1/8	1/4	3/8	1/2	5/8	3/4	1	1 1/8

Time in minutes to water every third day in:

	1/8	1/4	3/8	1/2	5/8	3/4	1	1 1/8
Mar thru May	52	26	19	13	11	9	7	6
Jun thru August	86	43	32	22	18	14	11	9
September thru November	42	21	16	11	9	7	5	4

Note that this is only for the East Bay suburbs of San Francisco. Thirty miles away the table would be different. But it gives you a rough idea of a watering scheme. Avoid watering on windy days and at midday. Avoid watering the sidewalk.

Pool evaporation

Fill your pool and note the high water level and the time of day. Next day, measure how far below that line the water has fallen at the same time. Then measure the area of your pool. If it's a rectangle, just multiply length by width. Otherwise, do the best you can.

My 20 x 30 pool lost about four inches or 1/3 of a foot a day in the hottest part of the summer. That's 20 x 30 x 1/3 = 200 cubic feet per day. The pool level may also be falling due to **leaks**. Check it on days when there should be little evaporation.

Submeters and prorating

Your state probably regulates submetering and/or prorating water and sewer bills (e.g., Texas Water Code § 13.501). Find out what the law is before you do either.

23

Telephone

If your building is less than 50 units, you should **not** have a telephone. Your resident manager should be required to furnish a phone as a condition of employment.

The only disadvantage of that is no *Yellow Pages* listing. The advantage is lower phone cost.

At my DeSoto building, I had no phone. I reimbursed the resident manager for long distance calls only. The phone bills for the first eight months of 1984 averaged 20.90 a month. That's for 25 units.

At my Fort Worth building, I **did** have a phone—for the first eight months of 1984. The bill there averaged $40.90 a month. For 33 units.

What was I getting for the $15 extra a month? A *Yellow Pages* listing. Is that worth $180 a year? I think **not** in a 33-unit building. That building grossed about $110,000 a year then. The key question is would a *Yellow Pages* ad increase the occupancy rate by $180/$110,000 = .2%?

Or, to put it another way, would a *Yellow Pages* listing result in renting one apartment about 18 days sooner than if there were no *Yellow Pages* listing? If you think so, have a business phone. My experience has been that the *Yellow Pages* provide few, if any, prospective apartment or house tenants. (Although they are the prime tenant gatherer for miniwarehouses.)

Phone number and marketing

To be sure, **somebody** has to provide a phone. The phone number needs to be in the classified **ad**. And it should be on a **sign** so visitors and passers by can write it down. And the phone number should be on the manager's **business cards**.

Phone frills

Let's say your building is 50 units or more. That's large enough that the expense of a building phone is such a small percentage that it makes sense to have one.

But what kind of phone? There are phones and there are phones. And the phone companies offer many special services. Which, if any, should you get?

Call waiting

Call waiting is available in most, but not all, locations. It allows you to put one call on hold while you answer a second call. You do that by depressing the hang-up button briefly. And you go back to the first call by doing it again. Is it cost effective?

Maybe. Best way to find out is to try it for a while and see what calls you get by using the call waiting. The manager could log in the call waiting calls. Then, after a month or two, you could go over the log to see whether the additional calls obtained through call waiting were worth the extra cost of the call waiting. In my area at present, call waiting costs $3.50 extra per month. That's so cheap, I have concluded it makes sense for my apartments.

Call forwarding

This is an additional $2.50 in my area. Normally, I don't see where it would be appropriate for a resident manager. However, some special situation may make it worthwhile. If the special situation is **caused** by the resident manager, then he or she should pay for this feature.

Answering machine

By answering machine I mean a device which answers incoming calls with a recording which asks the caller to leave a message when he or she hears the beep.

I know that many people don't like to leave messages on these things. But enough are comfortable with them that a three-year payback shouldn't be hard to come by. If you're skeptical, you could probably rent or borrow an answering machine for a while to see if the calls it picked up were likely to meet the three-year payback criteria. I have old answering machines that still work lying around my office. You could probably get such a machine for little or nothing from a friend or relative.

Local phone companies now offer message-taking services. They are probably more reliable than answering machines. Ask what your local company charges.

Cordless phone

A cordless phone allows the manager to put the phone in her pocket and wander all over the complex. She might be cleaning an apartment, or showing an apartment, or just walking the complex to make sure everything's OK. Without a cordless phone, incoming calls are either lost or, if you have an answering machine and the prospect uses it, start a game of telephone tag.

With a cordless phone, the manager can answer the phone while out of her apartment or office.

A cordless phone can also be useful on the rare occasion when a manager is confronting a possible criminal—like an obvious stranger roaming the complex after dark. He may think twice about making a rapid departure if the manager responds to his back talk by whipping out a phone and dialing 911 or whatever.

In many cities, a computer terminal in the police dispatcher's office displays the number and address **from which** a 911 call is coming. That is, as soon as the police answer the phone, your resident manager's phone number and address are displayed on a computer screen. Explaining that to a bad guy should be an effective deterrent in many cases.

Before you buy, you should **test the phone on your complex**. Sears cheapest claims a range of 700 feet. But they add the phrase, "Depending on local conditions." Indeed. If the phone doesn't permit your manager to receive calls while in the units or around the complex, it's of no value.

Is a cordless phone cost effective? I think so. You only need less than $30 benefit a year from Sears cheapest to get a three-year payback period. Same rationale as the answering machine—only a cordless phone is even better for covering times when the manager is out of her apartment or office but not off the complex.

Extensions

As a general rule, the manager should pay for any extensions. That is, any phones other than one. There may be circumstances where a second phone is needed because of something the owner is responsible for. And in those cases, the owner should pay for the second phone.

A cordless phone should eliminate the need for extensions for the most part.

Note that the longer a resident manager stays in one place, the more goodies then tend to talk the owner into. Multiple phones are a typical goody which should be terminated if you have it.

Chimes and other nonsense

Before I bought one building, the managers had somehow talked a previous owner into a chime instead of a bell. That cost extra every month. (Although it probably wouldn't in this day of owning the phone.) If you find any such frills in your building, get rid of them.

The off-site 'on-site' manager

One of the resident managers I had in a past building started out living on the complex. But then she and her husband bought a fixer-upper house across town. Gradually, they moved into the fixer upper and persuaded a previous owner of the apartment building to permit them to get a phone which rang both at the apartment complex and in the home.

There's a one-time charge for setting that up. But if it frees up an apartment to **rent**, it makes sense. You'd need to create a small office in the complex. A desk, phone, and powder room would be about all you'd need. At worst, you could have the manager use one of the smaller apartments for such an office. Resident managers usually occupy one of the biggest apartments in the complex.

In most states, there are laws which say you must have a **resident** manager for complexes bigger than around 10 to 20 units. I think you can ignore those laws—as long as you manage the building well. I'm not ignoring them at present. But there have been times in the past when I owned or managed properties where the "resident" manager spent the night off-site. Never had a complaint about that.

Long distance call log book

You should have the resident managers log in long distance calls.

Owning phones versus leasing

You'll probably find that owning the phone is cheaper than leasing. Use the three-year payback criterion.

MCI, Sprint, and all that

Should you use AT&T, MCI, Sprint, etc. for long distance calls? I don't know. Their rates and quality change too often. You'll have to make your own comparison. I have gone with MCI and Sprint at times. But I always come back to AT&T due to quality and billing problems. One time was when I tried to make a long distance call and got a Sprint recording saying that my long distance service had been temporarily disconnected. When I called Sprint to ask what was up, I got no answer. So within minutes I switched back to AT&T.

More recently, I switched and began to receive a $500-a-month minimum bill from AT&T, whom I was no longer using. They said I had verbally agreed to a long-term contract. I did not and do not recall doing so. I have never had a $500 a month phone bill in my life.

Your phone bill

You should ask the phone company to explain your bill to you at least once. Once a year would be better.

Many new developments

There are a number of new developments in telephony and there are sure to be many more. One is the advent of using the **Internet** to make phone calls. There are two main reasons to do that: it's **free** and you can get **video** as well as audio. Absentee landlords especially should investigate Internet telephone and videophone calls. Videophone calls would be especially useful for interviewing prospective tenants and prospective employees.

A new device, PhoneMiser (www.PhoneMiser.com), connects to a windows-equipped computer. Every time you make a long-distance phone call, it connects you with the long-distance company that has the lowest rate for that call at that moment. If that device becomes widespread, long-distance phone rates will collapse. Furthermore, I suspect that devices like PhoneMiser will not only become widespread, it will become ubiquitous. PhoneMiser costs less than $100 plus a monthly fee of $4.95.

24

Trash Collection

Trash collection companies charge by the **size** container you have and the **number of times** it's emptied. So you want the smallest container and the fewest pickups you can get away with.

But don't go too far. If your container is too small or not emptied often enough, trash will overflow. That makes your complex unsightly. And when the wind starts blowing it around, your neighbors complain to the authorities.

Make a trash survey

To find out how much is enough, you or your manager should make a trash survey. To do that, check each container on the complex just before it's emptied. Note how much air rather than trash it contains. The trash company charges you the same to haul away a cubic yard of air as it does to haul away cubic yards of trash. But you don't need anyone to haul air away.

If there's regularly a cubic yard or more of air in the containers just before they're emptied, consider cutting the size of the containers or reducing the frequency of pick-up. Survey the trash containers more than once before you decide.

Switch to a lower bidder

In some cities, you have no choice as to the trash contractor. But in others, you get to pick him. I switched in Fort Worth and thereby cut my monthly bill from $111 to $94. Won't get rich on that. But every little bit helps.

Note that not all trash companies give the same service. If the low bidder gives you lousy service, he's no bargain. So check **references** before you switch. And don't sign a long-term contract if you can avoid it. And don't sign any contract which doesn't give you an out in the event of lousy service. And watch out for incredibly broad clauses in which you warrant that no one will ever put liquids or other common waste matter in the container and that you will indemnify the collection company from any liability.

Check the rate

When the city or other authority regulates trash collection rates, the possibility that you are being overcharged arises. That happened to a friend of mine. He discovered that the trash collector was charging more than allowed by local regulators. And he got a rate reduction and a refund.

Just for comparison, here's what I'm currently paying.

City	Container	Frequency	Monthly
Danville, CA	2 32-gallon	weekly	$22.61
DeSoto, TX	1 6-yard	twice/week	107.26

My per unit weekly amount is 12 yards at the 25-unit and was 12 yards at my old 33-unit. That's 12/25 = .48 yards per unit per week at one and 12/33 = .364 yards per unit per week at the other. This suggests that you can get by with about .4 yards per unit per week. (We do **not** have trash compactors.)

Reader, Alan Stoff wrote to tell me he saved $53 a month by having his manager take the trash cans up nine steps. Fifty-three dollars was the trash company's surcharge for going up and down those nine steps. Scrutinize your bill and get an explanation from the company if necessary to make sure you aren't paying some similarly ridiculous charge.

Use of containers by non-tenants

My Fort Worth container was almost always used only by tenants. That's because there was a fence around part of the property and the container was in the back of the complex.

But my DeSoto container is on a public alley. There's another complex right next to it. And a single-family home neighborhood across the alley. My managers have seen neighbors using the container. And they've even seen outsiders pull up in cars and trucks and use it.

How do you stop them? If the unauthorized use is routine, you can probably get the users to either stop or contribute to the cost. Try a friendly chat first. If that doesn't work, a return-receipt letter. If that doesn't work, gather evidence that it's going on and file a small claims court suit.

What evidence? Photographs (a telephoto lens would help). A video tape. Statements by more than one witness. Dig out some trash with the name and address of the offender. The fact that the offender does not have a trash container of his own. You've seen Judge Wapner on "People's Court." Take the kind of evidence he'd look at.

About the only way to stop occasional users is to either put the containers under surveillance or make them hard to get to by outsiders. A fence is one way. A long walk is another. That is, move the container to a part of the complex where it's far from non-tenants.

Putting them under surveillance is not as flip as it sounds. If one of your employees has a window, and can see the container out the window, it's under surveillance.

Wheel pad

You need a concrete pad for the trash truck to put its front wheels on while it's emptying your container. If they're on asphalt, they'll gouge it to smithereens. Put some wire mesh or reinforcing bars in before you pour the concrete.

Aesthetics

Trash containers are usually ugly. So if the surveillance method requires places a container in a spot which is prominent to prospective tenants, think twice about it.

Do **not** try to hide the container behind a fence. Tenants and others will then simply throw trash into the fenced area. And the trash truck drivers refuse to pick up trash on the ground.

The best solution is to hound the trash company about dirty or dented containers. If the container needs paint, tell the company to paint it. If it needs cleaning, tell them to clean it. If it needs replacing because it's dented badly, tell them to replace it. If you can't get them to respond or replace them with a company who will, have your own staff paint or clean the containers.

Should you own the containers?

In some cases, you can either supply the container yourself or have the trash company supply it. Apply the three-year payback criterion to that decision. And make sure you check with someone who has owned them for that long. I don't know how long they last. Especially when the guy who's emptying them knows it doesn't belong to his company.

Many jurisdictions require closed lids. That, in turn, requires lids with hinges that work. Hinges are the kinds of things that break down from tenant abuse. And from the open lids getting wedged between the container and the truck during emptying.

Unsightly dents come from being rammed by the trash truck. Part of your three-year payback calculation is the question, "Will these containers last three-years?"

Compaction may save you money

There are regular containers and there are compactor containers. Compactor containers squash the trash with an electrically powered ram thereby reducing the number of pickups necessary.

My local trash company says they charge $942 a month for two 4-yard regular containers emptied daily. But the compactor container that would replace them would only be picked up once a month and would cost $619 a month—a $323 a month savings.

Compactors reduce trash volume by about 75%. But the cost savings is only about 30% because the container costs more.

Compactor containers must be plugged into your electric. But, believe it or not, the electricity cost to run them is negligible. A home compactor uses just one kilowatt hour per month which costs about a dime.

Compactor containers start to make sense when your volume is about 12 yards per week hauled away from a single location.

Individual compactors in each unit do not make sense. They cost about $300 to install so you'd need to save about $100 per unit per year to meet the three-year payback criterion. $100 per unit per year probably far exceeds your **entire** trash removal cost.

Hidden costs of compaction

Writing in his *Mobilehome Parks Report* (916-971-0489), Tom Kerr tells of *Landlording* author Leigh Robinson's experience at one of his mobilehome parks. It reveals some hidden costs.

First the unhidden costs: $11,000 for a Marathon RJ-1835 compactor with a 2-cubic-yard side load hopper. The hidden costs:

• Specially reinforced concrete pad on which to set the compactor
• New 220-volt line to the compactor
• Small size means compactor is often full and residents put trash on the ground until the manager runs the ram. That makes extra work for the manager.
• Container has to be separated from compactor when the trash truck comes to empty it. That requires two men to move the container out of the compactor.
• The design is such that trash spills out of the container when it is moved out of the compactor for pickup. That makes more work for the manager.

Leigh feels the compaction might have worked out if he had bought a bigger compactor. He says it should probably be a top-loading, not side-loading model, and be three yards instead of two (for this 44-pad mobilehome park). In fact, he thinks even two yards might have been adequate if it had been a top-loading container.

Trash containers can kill

Trash containers with wheels can tip over and kill or injure people who use or play on them. I recommend that you **not** have wheeled containers at all.

If you **must** have wheeled containers, make sure they comply with Title 16 Code Federal Regulations, Part 1301 and with American National Standards Institute standard Z245.3 (*Safety Requirements For The Stability Of Refuse Bins*, $8, 1430 Broadway, NY, NY 10018). Generally, these standards require that the container be designed so that it does not tip over when 191 pounds of vertical force is placed on the leading edge when the wheels are in the most unstable position or when 70 pounds of force is exerted horizontally on the top when the wheels are in the most unstable position.

As a general rule, most containers meet the **design** standard these days. But that's not the only standard. ANSI requires that the container be placed on a "**hard level surface**" and that there be signs on the container saying that. ANSI also requires signs that say "Caution---Do not play on or around." I doubt such signs are very effective. But if your container does **not** have them and someone is hurt, the plaintiff's attorney will use the lack of signs against you.

The Consumer Product Safety Commission tells me that children were dying on these containers as recently as the Fall of 1987. The main recent cause is placing the container on the **ground** instead of pavement. If the ground is sandy or soggy, one wheel can sink down throwing the center of gravity past the tipping point.

Side-loading trucks

Most trash trucks are front-loaders or rear-loaders. A side-loader can reduce the amount of parking lot space you need to devote to the trash container.

Common area trash cans

You can get attractive trash cans for pool decks and other common areas from Upbeat, Inc. (800-325-3047) and other suppliers.

PART FIVE:
<u>RESIDENT MANAGERS</u>

25

Recruiting Resident Managers

Recruiting a resident manager

When you acquire a building big enough for a manager, you either keep the resident manager who comes with the building or you get another one. I've done both. Keeping the existing manager has both advantages and disadvantages.

The existing manager knows the complex and the tenants. That's an advantage. But the existing manager has often racheted his or her compensation up too high over the years. That's a disadvantage.

Converting a tenant to manager

One source of new managers is the tenants in the building. I've had several of those who worked out well. But if you offer the job to **all** the tenants in a flyer, those who apply and **don't** get it will resent it. Selectively approaching a few likely candidates is best.

Help wanted ad

The best source of new managers if none of your tenants are right is a classified "help wanted" ad.

You should read Chapter 20, "How To Hire Your Apartment Manager" in William Nickerson's book, *How I Turned $1,000 Into $5,000,000 in Real Estate in My Spare Time*. It has an excellent discussion of the various applicants you get and how to evaluate them. Although it was written in the '50s, it describes some of my manager searches (in the '80s) to a T.

Nickerson recommends asking applicants to write to a box number. I've always had them **call**. I disagree with Nickerson on that. These days, my experience is that it's too hard to find good people to make them write to a box number. I suspect box numbers only made sense in the Depression.

Wording of the ad

My ads are short and sweet.

Resident manager for 33-unit apartment complex in Meadowbrook 214-555-5555.

The ad should tell the applicant **how** to apply—that is a phone number or address to write to. It should tell either the **size** of the complex or whether the job is **full-** or **part-time**. As with an apartment for rent ad, it should tell roughly **where** the complex is located.

I see no need to get into compensation in the ad. In a previous ad I said "compensation depends on experience." But it seems like it goes without saying. The shorter the ad, the cheaper it is, of course.

Category to list the ad under

Look in your paper to see where the other resident manager wanted ads are. And put yours under the same category. In Fort Worth, they are under both the "General Help Wanted" category and the "Managerial-Administrative" category. So I advertised under both. A week to tens days should be enough. Some papers have "Apartment Personnel" or some such category.

Job description

You should write out a brief job description before you get your first calls on the ad. That's not because I think you should behave like some corporate bureaucracy with its job descriptions and policy manuals. Rather you need it to answer applicant questions and to remind you how to describe the job—especially to those who have never done it before.

Here's the one I used recently:

Duties include:

- *Showing vacant apartments*
- *Screening applicants*
- *Collecting rents*
- *Coordinating maintenance work*
- *Depositing rent in the bank*
- *Answering phone*
- *Enforcing leases*
- *Weekend pool care.*

That building had a five-day a week maintenance man who was not being replaced. If the new manager were doing everything, you should add groundskeeping and maintenance to the list.

The outgoing manager said the list was indeed complete but that it sure made the job sound simpler than it was.

That's quite right. And I took pains to explain the following to inexperienced applicants.

Although the actual number of hours worked is fairly small—only about 25 to 40 hours per month in a 33-unit complex—it feels like more. That's because the work comes in spurts at odd times.

Also, some of the work can be unpleasant. Like turning down an applicant, collecting rent from a late payer, telling a tenant to turn his stereo down, or evicting someone. Do you think you can do those things?

Other sources of managers

Apartment association I called both the Dallas and the Tarrant County (Fort Worth) Apartment Associations. I got nothing from the Dallas association. And I got one applicant who needed a bigger complex from Tarrant County. Based on that experience, I'd say contact the association. But don't expect much.

Nearby home owners I've never used nearby home owners. But it seems to me that it would make sense. Especially on a small property. To approach them I'd make a couple dozen copies of a flyer and hang them on doorknobs.

Apartment employment agencies In the Dallas-Fort Worth area, at least, there are several employment agencies which specialize in finding resident managers, leasing agents, and maintenance people for apartment buildings. I told them of my needs and got nothing. I suspect that they only work for larger complexes who need full-time people and pay full-time salaries.

Pirate another complex You could solicit an application from the manager of another complex. You might do this selectively by approaching the manager of a good-looking complex. Or you might send a mailing to all managers of similar size buildings in the area. That's not likely to advance your campaign to be president of the local apartment association. But there's nothing unethical about trying to persuade a competitor's employees to come work for you. Also, you might try local hotel and motel management people. I found that many of my resident manager applicants had hotel/motel rather than apartment experience.

Ask your other managers If you have more than one complex, you might ask the managers at the others if they know anyone who'd be interested. One of them might wish to switch complexes. Or they may know a good prospect.

Ad under "Apartment for rent" On smaller complexes, you may want to advertise for a manager in the "Apartments For Rent" category of the newspaper. I had to do that on a twelve-unit. When the manager gave notice, I told the maintenance man to run an apartment for rent ad and tell all callers that the occupant of that apartment **had** to be the resident manager. I soon got a young couple who originally had no thought of being resident managers but decided it would be OK. They worked out well and were still there when I sold the building.

Hire the first not the best

Most people think the way to hire a resident manager is to interview six or eight people then offer the job to the **best** one. Not according to my experience. If you do that, she'll tell you, "Oh, I already got a job. Thanks anyway."

My experience is that the job market moves to fast for waiting to hire the **best**. You've got to hire the **first**. The first **acceptable** applicant that is.

You should not only have a written out job description or list of duties. You should also have a written out description of the kind of person you're looking for.

Here's what I was looking for last time.

- *Normally home during the day*
- *Enough command presence to run building*
- *Reasonably intelligent*
- *Experience preferred but not necessary*
- *At least $100 a week income from other sources*
- *Well-groomed*
- *Favorable references.*

I insisted on at least $100 a week cash income from other sources because the administrative portion of the manager job on a 33-unit doesn't pay enough to constitute someone's only source of income. So I needed someone whose spouse worked outside. Or who did secretarial work at home or some such. Many applicants had absolutely no source of income and simply wouldn't be able to pay the electric bill and buy food.

I wanted someone who is normally at home during the day because a 33-unit building cannot afford a 40-hour a week leasing agent. Rather the manager must be allowed to come and go as she pleases (to avoid violating the minimum wage law). But she must understand that the building needs to be kept full, too. And that requires answering the phone and the door. The manager can watch TV all day, make handicrafts, take in wash, or do whatever she wants—but she has to be available to answer the phone and door.

No favorable references, no job

Bad tenants don't admit to their poor history. Rather they tell stories which make it impossible for you to check on them. Like, "I've been living at home."

Bad **managers** do the same. Yes, they have wonderful, successful experience. But when you ask, "Who did you work for?" they reply, "Jim Buck. But I don't know how to get in touch with him. The company went bankrupt. And he moved." Or some similar story.

No favorable recommendations, no job. That is, if I can't talk to someone you worked for, and hear that person tell me you did a good job, I will not hire you. That's a **boss** not a co-worker. An **unrelated** boss. It doesn't have to have been in the apartment business. But it has to be a favorable recommendation from a boss.

Do **not** hire someone based on their manner or appearance with no favorable recommendations. No recommendations, no job.

And that's in-person or by phone recommendations. **Not** written letters of recommendation. Seems like every lousy manager on earth has a fistful of letters of recommendation. I once had an applicant whose letter of recommendation was signed by a guy I knew. I called him and he said she was the **worst** manager he ever had and that I should definitely **not** hire her. When I asked why he wrote the letter of recommendation if she was so bad, he said she asked him to do it one day when he was not interested in making her angry.

Leasing personnel must have had successful experience **dealing with the public**. For example, a clerk at a dry cleaners. Experience assembling parts in a factory is an example of a job which does **not** involve dealing with the public.

Immigration Control and Legalization Amendments Act of 1986

For employees hired after November 6, 1986, you must have proof they are allowed to work in this country. Generally that means a filled out and signed Form I-9 and a copy of their drivers license and social security card. That applies to **all** employees, not just those who seem foreign. And you cannot discriminate against foreigners to avoid immigration problems. There are substantial fines for not complying. Call the Immigration And Naturalization Service for details and forms.

When to advertise

Once you offer the job, it will probably take the applicant 24 hours to decide. Then they may want to start immediately. Although some will want to give one or two weeks notice to their current employer. So don't do as I did once and start advertising four weeks before I needed a manager. Advertise only when there are two weeks or less til you need one. Most people who are looking for work are looking for it **right now**. Not next month.

What to ask the applicants

Here are the questions you should ask the applicants:

- What experience do you have?
- Names, addresses and phone numbers of previous supervisors.
- What source of cash income do you have (if part-time size pay at your job)?
- How long do you expect to stay at this job?
- Do you normally spend the day at home (if building is too small to afford office hours)?
- Are you willing to clean apartments (if part of duties)?
- Do you have any apartment management education?
- Do you have a pet?
- Why are you leaving your present job?
- Why did you leave your previous jobs?
- Do you have any questions for me?

Nowadays, a whole lot of once-routine questions are illegal. Sources like your state apartment association can keep you abreast of the latest laws on hiring. Do **not** hire an applicant who previously worked for a **larger** complex. They typically explain that they are tired of large complexes. Then, three months later, they quit to go to a large complex.

The applicant's cash income can't be too small in a part-time job. But it can't be too **big** either. Because if they have a lot of outside income, you will hear the Mating Call of the High Outside Income Manager,

I don't need this job!

You don't need employees who don't need the job. Generally, I avoid people whose outside income is more than three times the income (including free rent) of my apartment manager job. And I avoid people whose net worth exceeds $50,000. That makes sure the job is important to the manager.

If maintenance is included in duties:

- Do you own a truck?
- Can you do the following:

  Carpentry?   Air-conditioner repair?
  Plumbing?   Appliance repair?
  Electrical?   Painting?
  Sheetrocking?   Masonry?
  Taping sheetrock?   Locksmithing?
  Roofing?
- If yes, where did you learn?
- Which of the following tools do you own:

  Hand tools like hammers, saws, screw drivers, etc.?
  Power drill?
  Power circular saw?
  Propane torch?
  Acetylene torch?
  Saber saw?

If the applicant says yes to all the maintenance questions, he's a liar. At least I've never heard of such a person. The ideal maintenance man would be one who possesses a couple skills, a willingness to try new areas like appliance repair, and a recognition of his limitations—like the need for a professional for brick laying or sign painting.

A **truck** is important. Hire a maintenance man without one and you'll find out how many times you need it—as he asks permission to rent one or tells you he needs to buy from Top Dollar Supply because they deliver.

Ownership of **tools** is important for two reasons. First, no apartment owner in his right mind would ever supply tools to his maintenance people. It's impossible to keep track of them. Requiring a maintenance man to supply his own tools (except for lawn mowers and edgers, snow blowers, and pool care equipment) is standard. Indeed, most of the ads for maintenance men will stipulate that. Look at them.

Secondly, a man's claim that he knows how to **use** a particular tool is suspect if he doesn't **own** it.

Meet both the manager and his or her spouse even if the spouse will not be one of your employees. That's because the spouse may be unkempt to the point that it does harm to your marketing effort. I learned that lesson when I found a manager I'd hired had a toothless husband who looked like one of the homeless.

Testing

The National Apartment Association recommends that you test prospective employees. They sell two tests for that purpose:

- The Wilkerson Pre-Employment Screening Audit which tests predisposition to alcohol or drug abuse and
- • The PIC Personality Plus Indicator which tests attitudes.

These both meet Equal Employment Opportunity Commission guidelines according to NAA. To order these tests call NAA at 202-842-4050 or write them at 1111 Fourteenth Street, N.W., Suite 900, Washington, DC 20005.

Questions to ask references

- Are you related to this person?
- Did this person do a good job?
- Would you hire him/her again?
- Can he/she discipline misbehaving tenants?
- What are his/her faults?
- Why did this person stop working for you?

Difficulty getting references

Lawsuits against employers by employees are now the biggest category of civil suits. As a result, many, if not most, employers have adopted a policy of saying practically nothing about former employees.

On the other hand, sound recruiting practice **requires** that you get a detailed, subjective evaluation from previous supervisors. Furthermore, employers are being sued by victims of crimes committed by employees on the grounds that the employer failed to properly check out the prospective employee.

The prospective applicant may have a case against the former employer on the grounds that their unreasonable policy of refusing to give a reference is casting a cloud over the employee or otherwise preventing him or her from getting a job.

You may be able to get a reference from a reluctant former employer if you get the prospective applicant to release the former employer from some of the liability they fear. They should not, and probably cannot, be released from liability for false statements, of course.

Disability discrimination

As a result of the Americans with Disabilities Act of 1990, employers may not discriminate against a "qualified individual with a disability." Indeed, you must make "reasonable accommodations" in order to employ such individuals. There are similar state laws like Texas Human Resource Code § 121.001. The Building Owners and Managers Association offers the ADA Answer Book. You can also get Complying with the Americans With Disabilities Act from Quorum Books at 800-474-4329.

Drug abusers and alcoholics

As a result of the ADA, you may not discriminate against a person who has completed or is still in a supervised drug rehabilitation program and no longer uses drugs. You also may not discriminate against someone who "is erroneously regarded" as using drugs. You are allowed to **test** to see if the person is using drugs as long as you test **every** prospective or current employee for drugs. Furthermore, you'd **better** test every employee for drug use because plaintiff's attorneys use it against you if a someone suffers an injury which might be linked to the employee's screwing up because of drug or alcohol abuse. In other words, you are damned if you **do** test for drugs in a discriminatory way and damned if you **don't** test for drugs as a negligent hirer.

Employee screening

With negligent hiring suits now common, you probably should have all prospective employees checked out by a **screening service**. These services make formal inquiries into criminal records, driving records, credit history, and so forth. Put their report in your files and submit it as evidence when you are sued.

According to Larry Niemann, legal counsel of the Texas Apartment Association, you can get the background investigation done for about $40 to $75. Drug tests are about $20 for each drug. And integrity tests which do not use lie detectors (they are now prohibited by federal law) cost about $40 to $50. That's about $150 total and there are no refunds for people you don't hire. Welcome to the '90s.

When I deeded an apartment building to the Federal Home Loan Mortgage Corporation in 1992, they hired Lincoln Property Company to manage it. The first thing Lincoln did was make my managers take a drug test. There was no evidence of a problem. Drug tests are apparently standard at Lincoln.

You must give **advance notice** of your test requirements. You must get the **consent** of the employee or prospective employee before performing the test. Your procedures must be **reasonable**. The policy must treat **all** employees and prospective employees the **same**. If your employees are **union** members, any drug test must comply with their collective bargaining agreement. You must be extremely careful about what you do with the results of positive tests. You could be sued for **slander, libel, or invasion of privacy** if the results become known to third parties.

26

How Much to Pay Your Resident Manager

How much should you pay your resident manager?

Once upon a time, I had a resident manager who was doing an excellent job. Came with the building. But after I bought it, I checked with the seller to see what he had been paying the old manager. I was **startled** by the answer. It seemed like a lot. But having just bought the building, I was in no mood for the additional hassle of looking for a new manager, so I paid it.

I had not asked about the pay before buying the building. I just assumed that it was either in line or could be brought in line.

But as the months went on, the building was losing money. So I started to look for expenses to cut. Looming large was that manager payroll. But since firing someone who is doing a good job is such a traumatic thing to do, I felt I needed to be quite sure that I was right about the proper pay rate. So I embarked on an exhaustive search for the answer to the question, "How much should you pay a resident manager?" I now feel I've got a pretty good handle on it.

The duties

First we have to establish what we're talking about. The duties included in the resident manager's job include:

- Leasing
- Lease enforcement
- Bookkeeping rents and petty cash
- Groundskeeping
- Pool care (if any)
- Light maintenance

The following are usually paid for **separately**:

• Cleaning apartments
• Painting apartments
• Heavy maintenance.

What's the definition of light and heavy maintenance? Here are some examples of each:

Light Maintenance	**Heavy maintenance**
• Stop toilet leak	• Major roof repair
• Fix leaky faucet	• Extensive wrought iron repair
• Replace door jamb	• Extensive asphalt repair
• Unstop toilet	• Boiler repair
• Repair doorknob or lock	• Major renovation projects
• Fix broken window	• Air-conditioner repair (but not fan motor, condensation pan work)

The line between light and heavy maintenance is not clear. Many maintenance men will tackle some of the jobs I've listed under "Heavy Maintenance" as part of their duties. If you're having trouble deciding whether you're getting all the "light maintenance" you're entitled to, look at the total you're spending on both payroll and repairs. If that total is out of line with regional figures of the same expenses, you probably are **not** getting your share of light maintenance.

Pay rates

Here are the various pay rates I found and their sources:

Resident Manager Pay Rates

How much?	Source
5% of gross	Al Lowry's *How to Successfully Manage Real Estate in Your Spare Time*
$323-484/unit/year	*The 1998 Dupree + Scott Apartment Expense Report* (Seattle)
4.7% to 7.3% of gross	*The 1998 Dupree + Scott Apartment Expense Report* (Seattle)
$321/unit/year	ditto but for Pierce County, WA which is lower rent area
4.6% of gross	ditto but for Pierce County, WA which is lower rent area
9.9% of gross	Median Garden Type Buildings 1997 IREM *Income/Expense Analysis*
8.9% of gross	Median Low-Rise 25 or + units '97 IREM *Income/Expense Analysis*
6.6% of gross	Median Low-Rise 12 to 24 units '97 IREM *Income/Expense Analysis*
9.6% of gross	Median Elevator Buildings 1997 IREM *Income/Expense Analysis*
$.62/sq. ft./yr.	Dallas Apartment Association 1997 *Operating Expense Study*
5% of gross	Duane Gomer's *Creative Apartment Management*
5.2% of gross	Example in Sidney Glassman's *Guide to Residential Management*
4% to 6% of gross	Robert Moore's *Successful Apartment Management*
Apt + $225 for every 20-30 units (1998 equivalent)	William Nickerson's *How I Turned $1,000 Into $5,000,000 in Real Estate in My Spare Time*
5.86% of gross	Average of buildings I managed
$507 to $665/unit/year	*1990 National Apartment Association Survey of Income and Expenses in Rental Apartment Communities*
$.78/square foot	*1990 Apt. Assn. of Greater Dallas Apartment Operating Expense Report*

In its 1997 *Accredited Resident Manager Profile*, the Institute of Real Estate Management found the following compensation levels:

Units managed	Salary	Total Compensation
1 to 100	$23,114	$28,645
101 to 200	$25,919	$30,254
201 to 300	$28,454	$34,678
301 to 400	$31,893	$36,447
401 to 500	$33,351	$37,088
501 to 600	$39,035	$44,050
601+	$43,196	$47,454

Note that complexes bigger than 50 to 100 units generally have more than one employee. This ARM study relates only to the compensation of just one employee—the resident manager.

Here are the Dallas Apartment Association's 1985 and 1987 payroll survey results of total compensation (including cash, free rent, health insurance, bonuses, etc.):

Position	1985 Average Compensation	1987 Median Compensation	1990 Median Compensation
Manager	$1,543 /mo.	$1,800 /mo.	$1,650 /mo.
Assistant manager	1,122 /mo.	1,310 /mo.	1,078 /mo.
Leasing agent	962 /mo.	1,100 /mo.	835 /mo.
Maintenance man	7.64 /hr.	1,444 /mo.	1,400 /mo.
Maid	4.79 /hr.	880 /mo.	954 /mo.
Porter	4.80 /hr.	900 /mo.	867 /mo.
Painter	6.43 /hr.	1,100 /mo.	1,200 /mo.

The average property size in the 1985 Study was 186 units; 1987, 150 to 199; 1990, 100-149. To convert past figures to current dollars,visit the Bureau of Labor Statistics Web site (http://stats.bls.gov/news.release/cpi.t01.htm) for the current Consumer Price Index. Then use this formula:

Current compensation = (past compensation x current Consumer Price Index) ÷ past CPI

For example, 163 was the Consumer Price Index for July, 1998 (1982-4 = 100 base).

I'd say the consensus is 5% or 6% of the gross. Four percent is probably cutting it too close. Note that some of the highest figures are from the Institute of Real Estate Management. Those guys are spending someone **else's** money. Note also that on the smallest buildings, even the IREM guys stay down at 6%.

The above figures include free rent, cash, health insurance, commissions, etc.. You do **not** pay 5% of the gross plus a free apartment. Be careful about using percentage of the gross figures in collapsing markets like the 1980s Mineral Extraction belt (Louisiana, Texas, Oklahoma, Texas, Colorado, Wyoming, etc.). Rents in my Texas apartments have fallen about 20% in the mid-'80s. But I've given my managers **raises** every year. If I didn't, I'd have trouble attracting and keeping good managers.

I'd go to 8% for a good manager. But that's it. The manager I fired for making too much was getting about 12.5% of the gross—**and that did not include maintenance and groundskeeping!** The 5% or 6% figure is the total you should be paying for **both** administrative **and** groundskeeping/maintenance.

I'm not hard to get along with. I'll even "overpay" a little for a top manager. But I ain't paying **nobody** 12.5% of the gross to handle an apartment building's **office** work. Neither should you.

I have given you an overkill amount of data here. The reason is I know what it's like to argue with a manager or other employee over compensation. The more data you have the better. Plus I know how you agonize over whether to fire someone. If there are any studies I have not included here, please let me know about them.

The maintenance/groundskeeping hours required

Let's look at it from another angle. How many hours are required? And how much should the manager be paid per hour? In 1998, I think the answer to the how much per hour question is $8.50.

At my 33-unit, I used to have a maintenance man who worked five days a week. He came in at 7:45 am and quit at 11:45 am. That's four hours a day or twenty hours a week.

As far as I could tell, that was about the right number of hours. Normally we had neither slack time nor a backlog of unfinished maintenance requests. And when I asked him to build a concrete pad for the trash truck wheels, he got behind in his normal duties. So twenty hours a week seemed about right for my 33 units.

There are 52/12 = 4.333 weeks in a month. That means my 33 units needed 4.333 weeks/month x 20 hours/week = 86.67 hours per month of maintenance and groundskeeping. Or 86.67 hours/33 units = 2.62 hours per unit per month.

You should be able to apply that figure to any number of units to come up with the total number of hours of labor needed for light maintenance and groundskeeping.

The administrative hours

Administrative hours can be broken down more predictably into little pieces. Here's my breakdown, again on the 33-unit:

Chore	Hours Per Month
Collect rent 30 @ 2 minutes	1.0
Fill out rent report	1.0
Make bank deposit 2 @ 30 minutes	1.0
Show apartments 20 @ 30 minutes	10.0
Lease apartments 3 @ 60 minutes	3.0
Miscellaneous talks with tenants	10.0
Coordinate maintenance 12 @ 10 minutes	2.0
Miscellaneous projects	4.0
Answer phone 60 @ 5 minutes	5.0
Total	37.0

Rent collection consists mostly of stamping "For deposit only" on the backs of checks dropped through the mail slot. Plus a visit or two to a delinquent. You don't collect rent from vacant apartments or from the manager.

I suspect many resident managers would dispute this breakdown. Fine. Let's hear the specifics. Don't expect to blow me away with that "But I'm on call 24 hours a day" stuff. I've been my own resident manager. I've also been in other jobs where I was "on-call 24-hours a day"—like army officer and father of three small boys. I'm not impressed.

If my breakdown for my 33-unit is correct, it takes about an hour per unit per month to do the administrative work at an apartment building. Or, to combine the maintenance and administrative, it takes a total 2.62 + 1 = 3.62 hours per unit per month for the resident manager to run an apartment building. Call it 4 hours if you want to round it.

Let's check that against some of the other measures. Cain and Scott in Seattle said it took $270 a unit a year in 1988. 4 hours x $6 per hour then = $24 per unit per month x 12 = $288 per unit per year. Close enough.

How about percent of the gross? If $24 a unit is 5% of the gross, what's the gross on that unit? $24 ÷ 5% = $480. Do apartments rent for $480 a month? They sure do.

If there are any resident managers out there who dispute my figures, send your **facts** to me at Reed Publishing, 342 Bryan Drive, Alamo, CA 94507. Remember, that's **facts**. Unsupported opinions I don't need. No one responded to that statement in the first three editions of this book.

Fire them

You say your payroll is higher than my discussion above says it should be? If it's just a **little** bit higher and you're happy with the manager, don't worry about it. But if it's a lot higher— say more than 2% of the building's gross income or $2,000 a year, fire the overpaid manager.

You say your property manager set it up that way. **Fire** him or her, too. Matter of fact, you may have a case for obtaining a refund from the property management company. Property managers hold themselves out as experts. If they then cause you to overpay significantly for staff, they either lack the expertise they claimed—or the motivation to use it. My overpaid manager started out on that property as the employee of a property management company.

I suspect this book's going to get a lot of resident managers and property managers fired. That's because it's the only book that pounds home what the payroll ought to be. The others mention it in passing if at all.

The poor fit problem

One of my new managers angrily cited all manner of inconveniences which the job entailed. Generally, they were **real**. But her solution—doubling her salary—was wrong.

The problem was she was a square peg in a round hole. Some people aren't cut out to be resident managers. She was a prime example. You can have such people in any job. Most have the good sense to just leave. This woman instead demanded that she be paid a premium to compensate her for the aspects of the job which she did not like. I declined. But I've employed resident managers since 1974. And I knew I never had one who complained as much as she did.

Had she been my **first** resident manager, I might have gone along with her demands.

Long-time managers

When I looked at buildings to buy, I was amazed at the compensation packages many long-time resident managers had ratcheted themselves into. One manager of a fourteen unit building had converted one unit into a **full-blown house**. It had two floors, a huge living room with fireplace, washer/dryer, a kitchen with every modern appliance, three bedrooms. The other 13 apartments had none of that. They were just your basic one-floor, one- and two-bedrooms with no special features.

That house had to be worth $800 a month. And we're talking just 14 units. Using the 3.62 hours per unit per month figure I arrived at above, what's that couple making per hour? $800 ÷ (14 x 3.62) = $800 ÷ 50.68 = $15.79/hour. I don't recall for sure. But I believe they were also getting free utilities and some cash.

And I **do** recall what they were paying an outsider to paint apartments. $450!!! You can get an apartment painted for $80 to $100 plus materials. Talk about your sweetheart deals.

Real estate investor Richard Epley says,

> We have found through experience that the last thing we want is a professional resident manager. Our experience has been that these professionals will spend many of their waking hours, not to mention subconscious time, plotting and scheming as to how to milk more compensation out of their job.

Note that the manager I fired for making too much had complained shortly before I fired her that she was the only manager she knew who didn't get free use of the laundry facilities.

Reed's Rule of Resident Manager Compensation says that the longer a manager stays in one building the more space he will occupy and the higher will be his total compensation.

'But how would I ever survive without Bob and Mary?'

There's a reason owners allow long-time managers to push their compensation so high. They believe they can't do without Bob and Mary or whoever.

I've never met Bob and Mary. But I'm darned sure you can do without them. Just as you will if they get run over by a truck—or quit. There are literally millions of apartment buildings which get along just fine without your Bob and Mary. And few go bust because of a manager's leaving. Some have trouble because of bad managers. But there's more than one good manager in the world. And you can get a good manager without paying 10% of the gross or more.

Health insurance and other benefits

The percentages and other figures shown above **include** the cost of health insurance and any other benefits. That is, a health insurance premium you pay on your employee is the same as paying them that much cash.

There are tax advantages to paying part of the manager's compensation in the form of health insurance. If it were **cash** compensation, you'd have to pay social security, federal unemployment, state unemployment, etc. on it. Which increases the cost. Plus, it's tax free to the employee if **you** pay it. Otherwise, the employee would have to pay tax on the income then use what's left to buy a generally non-deductible health insurance policy. The tax law on this is in section 106 of the *Internal Revenue Code*. As an employer, you might be able to buy health insurance for your employees cheaper than they could get the same coverage.

Free rent is tax-free compensation

A free or partially free apartment is a good way to compensate a manager because it's tax-free. So says Section 119(a) of the Internal Revenue Code. You don't have to pay social security tax on the value of the free rent, either. So said the *Rowan Companies* Supreme Court decision. (*Rowan Companies, Inc.*, 101 SCt 2288 The IRS had previously said that the value of the apartment was taxable for social security tax purposes but not income tax purposes.) If the owner pays utilities, those utilities are also tax-free according to Revenue Ruling 68-579.

The manager must be required to live in the apartment as a "condition of employment" in order for it to be tax-free—which is normal in the apartment business. Actually, it's generally required by state law.

So one way to reduce your payroll expense, without reducing anyone's pay, is to make a higher percentage of it tax-free. Do this by paying employees as much as possible in the form of free lodging and/or by paying health insurance premiums. That saves the employee the tax they'd pay if it were in cash. And it saves you all the local, state, and federal add-ons which attach to every dollar of cash compensation you pay.

Wage and hour laws

There's a good book on the subject. It's the *Wage-Hour and Employment Practices Manual for the Multihousing Industry* by Harry Weisbrod.

I'm told wage and hour laws have caused some landlords to lose some large lawsuits. The main problem appears to be managers claiming that they worked forty hours plus overtime but weren't paid the required minimum wage or overtime rates. I surmise that these are ambush suits. Employee never complains about hours or pay or overtime for five years. Then, upon being fired or some such, decides to get back at the owner.

Suing landlords for wage and hour violations is apparently a hot topic of discussion at meetings of resident managers. One of my managers tried to nail me on that. Turned out I was too small to come under the jurisdiction of the Wage and Hour guys. Their minimum was $250,000 in gross rents at all your apartments nationwide. At the time, my gross was about $218,000.

Some state laws, like Texas, now require that employees be paid at least semi-monthly.

Child labor

You should also be aware of child labor laws. You may wonder why. You know that high school kid who cuts your lawn? He's a **child**. In most states, you must have a copy of his **working papers** before you hire him. Furthermore, most states have laws which **hours** he can work on which days of the week and the total number of hours he can work.

Finally, most states prohibit minors under the age of 18 from operating **power equipment**—like power lawn mowers. Which is why no kid mows **my** lawns. And why none should mow yours either.

You think that's a stupid law? Fine. Write your state legislator about it. But don't **violate** it. If nothing goes wrong, there'll probably be no problem. But if the kid is hurt while mowing or going to the gas station to get more fuel, the chances that you'll have a child labor problem go way up. Kid's father mentions to attorney friend that Johnny was hurt while mowing lawn at Woodside Apartments.

- "Oh, really? How old is Johnny?" the attorney asks. "16." *"Did you know that it's a violation of the child labor laws for Johnny to be operating power equipment like a lawn mower?"*

Dollar signs appear in each of Johnny's father's eyes. And in the attorney's eyes. **Your** dollars.

Husband and wife

If a couple perform substantially the same work, you must pay them equally. Furthermore, you cannot reduce the pay of either to achieve equality. You must raise the pay of the lower paid one. That was established in the case of Sandra S. Dean vs. Limited Food Stores as reported in the *Wage and Hour Bulletin*.

Handyman or employee?

Rental owners often use independent contractors. That avoids virtually all the hassles and expenses of employees. But a North Dakota handyman who supplied all his own tools and worked his own hours sued a landlord after two years of working for him. He claimed he was an employee not an independent contractor and wanted back pay and overtime. He won. In a 1993 decision, the North Dakota Supreme Court was impressed by the fact that the handyman did not work for anyone else and was economically dependent on the landlord.

Repair labor times

The following repair labor times were written by D.L. Graham in *The Apartment Owner*. Graham was not identified. I assume he or she is an experienced apartment owner.

Paint room, 2 hours; paint 1-bedroom apartment, 6 hrs.; paint 2-BR, 8 hrs.; replace lock, 1/2 hr.; replace door, 2 hrs.; minor appliance repair, 1/2 hr.; replace hot water heater, 4 hrs.; replace sink parts, 1 hr.; install new sink or garbage disposer, 2 hrs.; repair minor plumbing leak, 2 hrs.; minor toilet repair, 1 hr.; replace toilet, 2 hrs.; replace shower sliding door, 2 hrs.; refinish tub, 4 hrs.; tile floor of one room, 4 hrs.; replace light fixture, 1/2 hr.; replace light switch or outlet, 1/2 hour; install smoke alarm, 1/2 hr.; steam clean carpet in one room, 1/2 hr.; install ceiling fan, 1 hr.; replace screen, 1/2 hr.; replace window pane, 1 hr.; minor furnace repair, 2 hrs.; repair hole in wall, 2 hrs.; replace 4 x 10 porch floor, 5 hrs.

27

How to Supervise Your Resident Manager

Training your manager

Give them a copy of this book and tell them to read it and abide by it. I did that with my managers. And I frequently get orders where an apartment owner will order one copy then later order a half dozen for his employees.

Supervising your manager

Management styles are very personal. I'll tell you what I did. But I'll not say it's the only way. However, there are some underlying principles which should be a part of every owner's supervising style.

I called my manager's once a week and talked for 20 or 30 minutes.

Manager call letter

After each call, I sent a letter summarizing the call. That's easier than it sounds. I printed forms up with appropriate questions. As I talked to the manager, I jotted down their answers on the form. When I was done, I photocopied the form, send the original to the manager, and file the copy in a loose leaf binder.

Following is a sample. The addresses on the form are lined up to fit in a double window envelope.

John T. Reed
342 Bryan Drive
Danville, CA 94526   Address of building

Ms. Manager
123 Elm Street Apt. 1
Yourtown, USA 00000   Date:_____

Vacant apartments: _____

Vacant storage spaces: _____

Late: _____

Ready for occupancy?: _____

Notice: _____

Deposits made: _____

HVAC problems: _____

Roaches, mice: _____

Problem tenants: _____

Laundry equipment: _____

Traffic: _____

Drain stoppages: _____

Landscaper: _____

Roof leaks: _____

Safety hazards: _____

Security problems: _____

Projects: _____

Rent report: _____

Bad checks: _____

Last letter: _____

Excellent record

I keep the letters in a loose-leaf binder. I hope the managers do the same. The letters provide a chronological record of everything that goes on in the building. And a written set of instructions to the managers.

When I replaced two managers a few years ago, I sent the third manager copies of all the letters previously sent. That told her about seven months history of the building—including which tenants had been causing which trouble. Tenants tend to test a new manager. But my new manager knew more than they realized.

Plus the letters showed the new manager **why** the old manager was replaced. That's because they contain many exchanges in which I admonished the old manager to do this or that differently.

In the case of disputes—with tenants, employees, or subcontractors, the letters provide what the law calls a "contemporaneous diary." That is, they have some weight because they were written at the time of the incident in question.

Make sure you write down all the answers you get—even the negative ones. For example, if the manager's answer to, "Are there any safety hazards?" is "No," write down, "no."

Then if someone accuses you of being indifferent to safety or some such, you can point to the fact that you inquired about it every week and were told no problems existed.

Opportunity for compliments

You ought to praise employees for a job well done. You know that. But you probably don't do it as often as you should. The manager letter tends to help you remember. It forces you to stop and think about what you're saying to the employee. I tended to write it once quickly—then go back through it adding compliments where appropriate. As a result, I almost never failed to express my appreciation for good work, no matter how small.

Both praise and courtesy are little things. But they are important. And all too easy to forget in the rush of "putting out fires." The manager letter makes you stop and thereby gives you an extra opportunity to remember the need for praise and courtesy.

By the way, praise and courtesy aren't the only things in the letter. Sometimes my managers screwed up. And I told them. I try to do it tactfully. And softly. "Gee whiz, Trudy. This is the fourth week you've promised to do that."

'X' and 'Y' theories of leadership

You may have heard of the "X" and "Y" theories of leadership. "X" is what we called hard ass at West Point. And "Y" is what we called nice guy.

During our first two years at West Point, most of us decided one or the other was best. And we used to argue about it. But during our **last** two years at West Point, we learned the **correct** answer to the debate. **Both.**

The reason we learned it is that during the **first** two years at West Point, you are almost always a **subordinate**. During the **second** two years, you are almost always a **boss**. And when you're a boss, you find that some subordinates respond to the hard ass approach; and others respond to the nice guy approach. So you use the appropriate approach with the appropriate people. Here's a West Point example.

Sam Brown is a squad leader. He has 9 plebes (freshmen) under him. They live in three different rooms. The Tactical officer announces he will inspect the barracks this coming Saturday. Brown believes in the nice guy approach. He tells his plebes about the inspection and says,

Let's get those rooms looking good, guys.

On Saturday, Room 101 looks great, Room 102 looks mediocre, and room 103 looks terrible.

Brown gets chewed out by the Tactical Officer for room 103 and 102.

If Brown learned his lesson, next time he has an inspection, his instruction will be,

> *Room Inspection this Saturday at 0900. You guys in 101 looked great last time. Do it again. You guys in 102 and especially 103 looked bad last time. So you will have your rooms ready for inspection by* **me** *at 0830—a half hour early. And I'm bringing a quill pad (demerit pad).*

Brown has discovered that 101 responds to nice guy so he has given them nice guy. And he has discovered that 102 and 103 do **not** respond to nice guy, so he is hard assing them. He is probably also accomplishing his mission. That is, all three rooms will look good this Saturday. And 102 and 103 may straighten out permanently. Although I'd probably give them a **second** preinspection at 0845 next time before I'd turn them back to the nice-guy approach.

You'd better have both in your repertoire

If you've never been a manager, you're probably still in the which-is-better-"X"-or-"Y" mode. The answer is that you must have **both** in your repertoire. Same goes for resident managers relations with tenants. You're a nice guy to those who respond to it. And a hard ass to those who don't.

I believe I learned that West Point lesson. Most people think of West Pointers as hard asses. My image of a West Pointer is that if you're a **good** employee or tenant, you couldn't want a **better** boss or landlord. But if you're a **bad** employee or tenant, you couldn't have picked a **worse** place to work or live.

In other words, we recognize the need to treat people well, give them their head, and praise good work. But we also recognize that people sometimes need criticism or being replaced. And we can do that, too. A lot of people, maybe most, don't have the ability to say "no" to a fellow adult—much less fire or evict them. If you're one of them, you better not be an apartment owner or manager.

There's a pertinent paragraph in Martin Mayer's book *The Builders*:

> *Robert Cunningham of HUD's property standards office remembers his days in the field, visiting FHA-insured apartment houses. "If you found a building where the shrubs were trimmed and the lobby was shiny, the halls were clean, all the equipment was polished, you could be sure the first thing the tenants would tell you was that the manager was a son of a bitch. When you went into a building where the shrubs were scraggly and the lobby was run down and the halls were dirty and there was a mess in the basement, you could be sure all the tenants would tell you what a nice guy the manager was."*

You don't have to **be** an SOB to every tenant. But you do have to have the ability to be tough when the situation calls for it. I suspect that if someone contacted my tenants and asked about me, the **good** tenants would say, "Never had any dealings with the man. But the place seems to run OK." To talk to the **bad** tenants, you'd generally have to look **other** than in my buildings—because the bad tenants didn't live there very long. **They'll** probably tell you I'm one of the biggest SOBs they've ever run into. That's as it should be. And I think you'd get a similar response from my good and bad managers—although the good ones would have more to say than my good tenants because the managers **do** have weekly dealings with me.

Show them the books

I sent all my employees the property's books every month. That is the rent report, vacancy report, and full income and expense statement. That's right, the full income-and-expense statement.

My employees knew to the penny how much the building makes or loses each month.

I took a very interesting course at Harvard Business School—called "Labor Relations." It was especially interesting because it was jointly held with a course for labor union leaders. Every other seat in the classroom was filled by a union leader, not students like me **pretending** to be union leaders. I'm talking about **real** union leaders who were at Harvard taking a brief course on running a union.

One day, one stood up and said,

> *I'm going to give you future management guys a quick lesson on how to keep a union out of your company.*
>
> *Number one, fire the slackers. The slackers are the first ones we go to when we try to organize a company. They are the ones who are most attracted to unions. The hard workers are least attracted. If you fire the slackers, it's hard for us to get a foothold. Plus, if you don't fire the slackers, the good workers either leave or say 'to hell with it.'*
>
> *Number two, tell the employees how the company is doing as far as profits are concerned. If you don't, we can stir the employees up by saying that you guys are taking enormous salaries and profits at their expense.*

I never forgot those instructions. And I believe they're as applicable to landlord/tenant relations as they are to employer/employee relations. So when any of my tenants or employees behave in a subpar manner, I get rid of them. And I show my employees the profit-and-loss statements (but I do **not** show them to the tenants—because it would violate my employees' privacy for the tenants to know how much they make).

I know of no other apartment owner who shows the profit-and-loss statements to the employees. I think that's a mistake. If you polled resident managers and asked them what percentage of the rent went into the owner's pocket, they'd probably say, "25%." One apartment owner polled **tenants** on that subject and they said, "30%."

The correct answer to that question is probably **minus 5%** to plus 25% depending on how long the landlord has owned the building. I figure that if the employees are going to **assume** you make far more than you do, you'll be better off if they know the truth.

A tenant once complained to one of my managers that I was making a huge amount of money from his rent. The manager said, "I see the books every month, Fred. I won't tell you how much he makes, but I will tell you that it's darned little. In fact, many months it's a loss."

What would **your** manager say in the same situation?

In 1996, *The Chicago Tribune* wrote about a man named John Case who has a book and a newsletter, both titled *Open-Book Management*, in which he advocates showing employees the books. (www.openbookmanagement.com)

Maximizing the bottom line is the manager's job

There's another reason why I give the employees the books. My goal is to maximize the bottom line—that is, cash flow. My employees' job is to help me do that. How they gonna help me if they aren't allowed to **see** the bottom line and the income-and-expense figures which create it?

Reject the mushroom theory of management

I urge you to reject the mushroom theory of management, that is, keep them in the dark and spread manure over them.

Two guys who sold me apartment buildings led the employees to believe that the buildings were doing worse than they were. One manager found out differently when the building's accountant said, "Boy, the property's really been doing well lately." The owner had recently cried the blues to the manager about how the building was **losing** money.

The other building's manager was getting the same story and believed it. Until I started sending them the books. They asked me if the income or expenses had changed dramatically since I bought it. "No. Why?"

"Because the previous owner said we were losing money."

"No way. My mortgage payment is more than double what his was."

It's not nice to fool Mother Nature. It's also not nice to fib to your employees. Number one, they find out the truth eventually. Number two, if they're so dumb they **don't** figure out the truth, you probably don't want them working for you.

'What if you're making a lot of cash flow?'

Some owners who have owned their building for a long time (and not refinanced) are making a lot of cash flow. Should they disclose that to the employees? Yes. But it would be a good idea to attach a line to the printout which shows the building's **return on current equity**.

Show the building's current market value, the current total debt, and the current equity—which is the difference between the two. Then divide the annual cash flow by the current equity to show the return on equity. And contrast that to what you can earn in a money market fund. It will show a return on equity of about 6% to 9%. Not much considering all the hassles of real estate.

Shoppers

You should have your complex shopped. That is, hire a person to pose as a prospective tenant and evaluate the job your manager does of marketing the building to the shopper. I tell my managers when I hire them that I will eventually have them shopped. But I don't tell them **when**.

In the Dallas/Fort Worth area, the two apartment associations will perform that service. I had it done by the Tarrant County Apartment Association a couple years ago. It cost $45 and I got a 6-page report.

You should either use such an organized service—or just hire someone not affiliated with such a service and tell them what you want.

Courses

I recommend that you **not** pay for formal management training. And if you **do** pay, don't ever pay more than **half**. Make the manager pay for the other half.

I teach seminars. You can spot the people who had been **sent** to the seminar on someone else's nickel a mile away. For starters, they were late. No one else was late. Not after they had paid $445 tuition. Only the paid-by-someone-else folks came late.

Why shouldn't you "professionalize" your staff by sending them to school? After all, the apartment associations hammer away on this theme constantly. I think you should professionalize them **yourself**. **You** might want to attend an apartment-management seminar—although I've taken a bunch and wouldn't recommend any of the ones I took.

I'd like to think that the managers who worked for me are well-trained. In part, because of what I've taught them on-the-job in my weekly phone calls and mail. I've not done any formal teaching to them. Just explaining how and why to handle various situations as they came up.

The courses I'm familiar with seem out of whack to me. Overemphasis on high-pressure selling and legal trivia, and not enough emphasis on income increasing, expense cutting, and problem avoidance.

Evaluation of owner by managers

Every now and then, you should ask your managers how **you're** doing as an owner. Questions like:

• Am I calling you often enough?

- Too often?
- Do you feel you have the necessary tools to do your job?
- Do you feel that you are underpaid?
- Do you like the job?
- Do you feel that you have adequate staff to get the job done properly?
- Do you feel you are getting enough credit for work well done?
- Do you feel you have been unfairly criticized?
- Do you have enough petty cash to do your job properly?
- Do you have enough credit accounts established with local merchants?
- Is there anything you'd like me to do to make your job better?

The more afraid you are to ask those questions, the more you need to?

'Ask if they feel underpaid?'

And what about the question on being underpaid? Isn't that asking for trouble? No. Number one, you'll be surprised how rarely the employee will say they feel they are being underpaid. Number two, if they **do** say they feel they are being underpaid, you don't have to agree with them.

In order to claim underpayment, they must show that the **market value** of their job is higher than you're paying. That is they must prove that you couldn't get someone else to do the same job they're doing in quantity and quality for the same price.

Elsewhere in this book I gave you a whole chapter on how much you should pay. If your manager feels he or she is underpaid—but they're getting what that chapter said they should—they are **not** underpaid. And you should tell them that you disagree with them and why. You should do one of two things with a manager who feels he or she is being underpaid: raise them or replace them. A raise is only appropriate if the manager is correct about the pay. A third alternative would be to convince them that they're wrong. But make sure you **have** convinced them. Because you don't need a resentful manager who feels underpaid.

Bonuses

I like to send flowers to my managers when they do something that's especially helpful. You should, too. I really need to develop some additional rewards. Flowers seem inappropriate for a male employee. And they get repetitive. I've thought about but haven't tried trophies ("World's Best Leasing Agent"), certificates (I Survived the Freeze of '83), gag newspaper headlines (Sandy Warren Named Apartment Manager of The Year), etc.

When to fire

Knowing when to fire someone is probably the biggest difference between a novice and an experienced apartment manager. We all know that all humans are imperfect. So when we are confronted with mistakes or misbehavior by an employee, we wonder is this tolerable imperfection— or **in**tolerable poor performance?

In my early years, I tolerated poor performance because I thought the next manager wouldn't be any better. And might be worse. If I could go back in time, I would now confidently fire those managers within a week of becoming their supervisor. How can I convey that experience to the inexperienced readers of this book? Maybe I can't. Maybe you have to learn that stuff for yourself. But perhaps if I do my best here, you'll learn **quicker** from experience.

The experience you need

I learned who to fire by having many managers. At first, I had no one to compare them to. So I tended to believe what they told me. But each time I had another manager, I learned more what you have to settle for and what you don't.

Manager A misbehaved in manner X, Y, and Z. I thought I had to accept it. But then I met manager B. Manager B didn't do X or Y. Although she did occasionally did do Z. Then I managed manager C. She, too, was never guilty of X or Y. In fact she rarely was guilty of Z.

I have had well over a dozen different managers. That gave me a halfway decent handle on what you have to accept in a manager and what you don't. If you want the same handle, you need to manage that many different managers or more. Each new manager teaches you better the limits of what is acceptable.

Tenant complaints

You should only rarely get a complaint about your manager from a tenant. From 1978 to 1992, I owned between 25 and 58 units. I got about one complaint per year about the manager. That's acceptable. No one can please all of the people all of the time. Some tenants are unreasonable. If your manager is pleasing unreasonable tenants, **that's** a problem.

However, I had one manager who inspired four complaints in one week. For that and other reasons, I fired her. The complaints may be substantive. Or they may not be. I regard **both** kinds as serious. My manager protested that the complaints were vague.

Indeed, if I were trying to get a conviction in court, the complaints would not have been adequate. But managing a building is not a trial. The fact that tenants complain at all is significant. It's like cancelling a TV show. Cancellation doesn't not mean the stars of the show were criminals. It just means they were not popular. It's their **job** to be popular. The same goes for apartment managers.

Tenant complaints indicate a lack of confidence in or feeling of affection for the manager. But an apartment manager **must** be the kind of person who inspires confidence. The kind of person people like. Confucius said, "Man without smiling face should not open a shop." The same applies to becoming an apartment manager.

So if you get more than one complaint per fifty tenants per year **about** the manager, there's a good chance that manager should be fired. **Investigate** the complaints. And try to read between the lines. But I can tell you that tenants generally do **not** complain about **good** managers.

Alcohol or drugs

Fire your employee if:

• He or she is drunk on the job even once.
• He or she is sober during the morning but drinks too much at lunch.
• He or she is unable to respond adequately to an after-hours call as a result of being drunk.
• Tenants accurately report that the employee was drunk on the complex even after hours.

According to a Department of Health and Human Services survey reported in the January 14, 1986 *Wall Street Journal*, 34% of Americans do not drink alcohol at all—including me—and including most of the managers I've had in recent years—although I make no inquiries about drinking habits when I hire. There are also plenty of drinkers who do not drink to excess—like my wife, some of my managers, and millions of others. You do **not** need to tolerate alcohol problems in a manager or other employee.

By the way, drinking problems seem more common among apartment managers than among most other types of work—unacceptable, but common.

Excessive absence

When your manager leaves the complex, your apartments are off the market and maintenance emergencies can cost you more than when she's there.

On the other hand, chaining the manager to the complex is illegal and will hurt your recruiting effort. So what's excessive?

I can't give you a mathematical definition. It's more impressionistic. Here are some impressions.

If I get a no answer when I call during normal hours, I make note of the time and date in my management binder. If it doesn't happen again, I forget about it. But if it happens repeatedly, I ask about it.

If it continues to happen, I call more often. And at more varied hours. Normally, I call before 8:00 am California time; 10:00 am Texas time. Because the phone rates are cheaper. But if I start to wonder about absence, I'll call during the high rate times.

Other indicators of excessive absence are calls from tenants who were unable to get the manager. In many cases they aren't complaining about the manager's absence. It's just that they need help now and he or she's not around.

Post card poll

Send the tenants a quarterly or semi-annual postage-paid, business reply post card asking if they are happy with the management. Here's the card that I use.

You should note that I have received nothing but good cards with no complaints on managers that I had to fire for doing an unsatisfactory job. So the cards are only **part** of the picture.

Since my building has only 25 units, I put the building's mailing list on one sheet of paper. That sheet is laid out to match the layout of the 8 1/2 x 11 Xerox label sheets you can buy in any stationery store. Something like this:

Tenant   Tenant   Tenant
Apt. 101   Apt 102   Apt. 103
123 Elm Street   123 Elm Street   123 Elm Street
Yourtown, USA 00000   Yourtown, USA 00000   Yourtown, USA 00000

And so forth. Whenever I want to send out a batch of post cards, I just make one copy of the mailing list onto a label sheet, peel the labels off, and stick the ones for occupied apartments on the post cards.

Or you could use a computer data base program to keep your mailing list. If it were integrated with your rent reports, you could use the actual tenant names instead of the word "tenant" or "occupant."

No answers

You can have telephone shoppers call about apartments at various times throughout the day.

With some managers, I sometimes got a no answer 20% to 50% of the time. In retrospect, I heard from tenants and others that those managers were "never there."

So if you get a no answer more than 20% of the time during business hours, you've probably got an absence problem and you should investigate further. If your manager won't reduce the absences to an acceptable level, fire them.

Chronic illness is **not** an acceptable excuse for closing the office. That's not to say you should have a sick manager on duty—or that all managers who claim to be sick are lying. Rather, if your manager has a chronic health problem which prevents her from performing her duties, she should be replaced. That includes terminal cancer and such. Sounds hard. But that's life. You can't call in sick to your creditors. The job's got to get done. You have responsibilities to your tenants, to your family, and to yourself. You are not running a nursing home. And you certainly cannot afford to pay someone to neglect your property.

Miscellaneous screw-ups and delays

A good manager makes an occasional mistake. But she does not fail to follow instructions repeatedly. Or fail to do a simple task when told once or twice to do it.

For example, if you tell a manager to call city hall about something, she ought to do it the next day or so. If she fails to do it week after week, she's not a good administrator. And you **can** get people who **will** get things done more quickly.

Managers typically do some bookkeeping. The books should balance. My good managers are out of balance by $5.00 or less about once a year. More frequent out-of-balances or larger out-of-balances are unacceptable.

Missing cash is unacceptable, too. The employee who had custody of the cash when it disappeared will replace it out of his own pocket immediately. Refusal to cover the loss is grounds for instant dismissal. There ought not be any cash on the complex. Tenants should be encouraged to pay by check. And the cash that does come in should be deposited in the bank immediately. Or at least hidden by the manager as she hides her own cash.

You ought not have to tell a manager more than once or twice to do something. You ought not have to explain how to do something more than once or twice. This is not an offense for which you should fire someone as a result of a single incident. But you can get managers who **do** respond to the first or second directive or explanation.

Shying away from **lease enforcement** is unacceptable. Whether it's just not doing it or asking you or someone else to do it.

Taking **kickbacks** is a "fireable" offense. I would define it as accepting a gift or payment worth more than about $25 to $50 from a subcontractor or supplier without getting the owner's approval.

You should make sure your employees know and understand that policy before you fire them for violating it.

Bad grooming

There are some nice people who are nevertheless, slobs. Don't employ a slob—nice or otherwise. Their clothes should be clean and neat. Same with their hair and bodies. Dirt or body odor are "fireable" offenses. I've never had such a manager. You don't need to either.

No leases or leases only to bad tenants

I once fired a very nice lady who seemed to be doing a good job. There was only one problem. She was a weekend leasing agent. And after several months on the job, she never leased a single apartment. I warned her that she needed to start signing some leases. She didn't. So I fired her. She said it wasn't her fault. Maybe so. But the weekday leasing agent was signing leases. And her replacement signed leases.

Same goes for too low a batting average on tenant screening. If more than a small percentage of your manager's tenants turn out bad, tell her to straighten out. If her batting average does not improve, fire her. I'd say no more than one in ten move-ins ought to turn out bad. Of course, even the best can hit a string of two or three bad ones. Just as Babe Ruth could have a slump. But a **consistent** low batting average is unacceptable.

Make sure the lack of leases is not **your** fault. Remember what I said earlier in the book. But in the case I just mentioned, the **other** agent was leasing at the same time in the same complex. So it was clearly not the owner's fault.

Dishonesty

Sometimes managers steal from you. They do this by:

• Lying about move-in and move-out dates and pocketing the rent you don't know about.
• Skimming coin laundry money.
• Stealing cash.
• Hiring someone else to do part of their job and paying them with free rent or a rent discount.
• Stealing supplies.
• Charging supplies for non-apartment purposes to your account.
• Not reimbursing you for personal calls made on your phone.
• Collecting and pocketing unauthorized "transfer," repair, and other fees from tenants.
• Falsely blaming burglaries or robberies for missing cash or supplies.
• Taking kickbacks.

You catch them by paying attention. If you have separate meters, the electric goes into your name when the apartment is vacant. The vacancies are thereby recorded on the electric bills which should jibe with the manager's rent report. If, for example, you got a vacancy electric bill on 103 for March 1 to March 15, the rent report must show that 103 became occupied on March 15th or 16th. If, however, the rent report says it did not become occupied until April 1st, you need an explanation from the manager. If she says the electric company screwed up or that she turned off the electric entirely two weeks early to save money, check with the electric company to see if that's correct.

You could also make up a double post card to send to each new tenant. And include an appropriate lease clause requiring the tenant to fill it out. It would say something like this:

```
    Dear new tenant:

    Welcome to the ABC Apartments. Please take

a moment to fill out and return the attached

post card which we need for audit purposes.

    Thank you,

    Joe Owner
```

The postage-paid reply card would look something like this:

```
    Please tell us the following information:

    Your name _____

    Apartment number _____ Move-in date _____

    Security deposit amount $_____

    Rent amount $_____
```

Or you could fill in the information and ask the tenant to contact you if any of it is incorrect. That's the way most accountant's audit letters are written.

That's one example of how to discover and/or discourage employee dishonesty. In general, you just check up on things. Get corroboration occasionally on how a purchased item was used. Compare what you're spending with industry norms.

No concealed weapons

The Texas Apartment Association says you should prohibit your employees from carrying concealed weapons and put that policy in writing. If you do not, and your employee hurts someone with a gun, guess who will be sued? If the employee says they need a gun because of the neighborhood, you either need to get rid of the building or the employee.

How to fire

Firing for cause should **not** come as a surprise to the employee. If performance is not up to snuff, tell the employee that it's not and what you want. And tell them that the performance **must** be brought up to snuff. One employer did that with white employees, but was reluctant to criticize a black employee before firing her. She sued alleging his failure to criticize her before firing was racial discrimination and won (*Vaughn v. Edel*, 5th Circuit, 1991). If employees fail to straighten out after you counsel them, fire them.

The actual firing should be one sentence. "I have decided to replace you." At that stage, there's no point whatever in discussing why. All you'll do if you discuss why is get into an argument. The employee will typically demand to know why. You should simply refer to that counseling session in which you told them to straighten out and that you do not feel they did. I believe it's dishonest to advertise for a new manager before you have told the old one they're going to be replaced. But you **should** call the help wanted ad in the day before you inform the manager they're being replaced. So that it hits the streets the same day as the old manager.

Get the new manager on board asap. Fired employees are not known for their dedication.

Two weeks notice should be enough. Unless the manager has committed a serious violation of proper behavior such as theft or drunkenness. In that case, you have no obligation to counsel the manager and give them a chance to improve. A person who committed a violation that serious should know that they'll be fired with no notice or severance pay without a counseling session.

'Hostile takeovers'

When you discover an employee has to be fired for dishonesty or incompetence, you have to do a "hostile takeover." That is, you must seize control of your property immediately.

You should do the takeover with a **witness** present. If **you** can't be there, send **two** trusted employees or representatives. Whoever does it should take possession of:

- All keys.
- All rent that was collected but not yet deposited.
- All loose personal property like ladders, supplies, office equipment.
- Leases, receipt copies, and similar records.
- Petty cash and receipts for spent petty cash.
- Vending machine money if you own the machines.
- Phone number and address where the fired employee can be reached.

Immediately notify all tenants and suppliers that so and so is no longer your employee. Do this in writing. Avoid bad-mouthing the fired employee in any way so you don't get sued for slander or libel. In the typical case of this kind, the records will be unreliable so you will have to **reconstruct** them. Generally this requires interviewing tenants and asking them for receipts on recently paid rent. Inspect the property to see if there are any immediate problems. Inventory the personal property.

Gather proof of employee dishonesty and file the appropriate claim with your insurance company. Call the police if you suspect criminal conduct has occurred.

Consider suing the fired employee. Don't overlook the federal racketeering law which allows triple damages and which applies to all sorts of routine business disputes.

Sexual harassment

Ever since Anita Hill and Clarence Thomas became famous, the number of sexual harassment suits and complaints filed has dramatically increased. You need to be careful not to commit or tolerate sexual harassment or get tangled up with someone who falsely accuses you or your employees of it.

I had complaints once that my maintenance man was propositioning female tenants. I got rid of him. No matter how careful you are, you may get in trouble because of a bad employee who violates you policies or because someone fabricates or exaggerates an incident. Sexual harassment violates the Fair Housing Amendments Act [24 CFR 100.65(b)(5)] among other laws. In California at least, you must display a sexual harassment poster on your property.

PART SIX:
FLAT ROOFS

28

Flat Roofs

Flat roofs leak. Frequently, **brand new** flat roofs leak so bad that replacement is the only adequate repair. Because flat roof installation is very tricky—and a high percentage of roofers do a lousy job installing them, Sears Roebuck installs and guarantees **pitched** roofs—but they refuse to get involved in the flat-roof business.

In July of 1987, the San Francisco Better Business Bureau had been swamped with so many complaints about unscrupulous and incompetent roofers that it formed a task force to fight the problem. One inspection company estimated that 25% of all **new** roofs in San Francisco had to be redone in five years because of poor workmanship.

In the June 1985 *Buildings* magazine, Michael Kelleher said about 30% of the new roofs that are installed are not necessary. They should have been **repaired** instead. And he said the vast majority of all new flat roofs only last about **half** as long as they should.

One apartment owner I know of had a complex with 34 flat roofs redone at a cost of $238,000. Within a year, 30 of the 34 new roofs were leaking.

Low incidence of competence

The problem with flat roofs is a low incidence of competence among the installers. If you need carpet, plumbing, electrical work, or even a pitched roof, nine out of ten guys in the *Yellow Pages* will do an adequate job. With flat roofs , however, it's more like **one** out of ten. The reason most building owners get into trouble is that they are used to the "nine-out-of-ten" trades and assume competence among flat roof installers is the same.

How to get it done right

I needed a new flat roof on one of my Fort Worth buildings. As a result of the horror stories I had heard, I called an engineering consultant, Steve Patterson (Roof Technical Services, Incorporated, 817-496-4631, rtecinc@aol.com, www.members.aol.com/rtecinc). He said that if he had to find a good roofer in an area he had **not** worked in, the first thing he'd do is call the major roofing manufacturers and ask for their list of **certified roofing contractors**. Companies like:

- Owens/Corning Fiberglass
- Manville Corporation
- Koppers

Or you could do as I did and hire a local architect or engineering firm. Selecting the contractor is part of **their** job. They have experience working with local contractors so they know who's naughty and nice.

The incidence of competence among architects and engineers is quite **high**. But still make sure you check out the architect-engineering firm. Ask for and call their roofing references. A top firm will have worked for such major flat roof owners as K Mart, Safeway, the federal government, Prudential, and so forth.

Also, get the architect-engineering firm to have their insurance agent send you a certificate of their insurance coverage. If the firm presides over the installation of a **bad** roof, the insurance coverage of the architect-engineering firm may be your main source of corrective action.

Do **not** use a property management firm as a substitute for an architect-engineering firm that specializes in flat roofs. A good property management firm is **less** likely to use a poor contractor—but not **enough** less likely to make it worth the risk.

Architect-engineering firm handles everything

Patterson drew up the **specifications** on my roof replacement, let it out for **bid** to contractors he knew to be reputable and competent, and provided the **contract** they signed (Standard Form of Agreement and General Conditions of Agreement as adopted by the Texas chapter of the American Society of Civil Engineers). Patterson also **supervised** the replacement and made a post-installation **inspection** to tell me whether to pay or not. It turned out new cast iron scuppers (drain entrances) which the roofer had not included in the bid were required. Patterson insisted that the roofer install them at no extra cost to me. I would not have known to ask and, if I had, would have probably gotten talked out of them by the contractor without Patterson.

The roof was completed in the fall of 1985. As of the summer of 1988 it only had one minor leak. (Before I paid for it, there were a couple major leaks and the roofer set the building on fire when applying some hot stuff. This was all taken care of within a couple months of the originally scheduled completion date.)

Converting to a pitched roof

In many cases, the best way to replace a flat roof is with a pitched roof. In one job Patterson did in the mid-80's, the cost to do that was just $2.18 per square foot. Converting works best when there are no air-conditioners or such on the roof. They have to be moved to the ground or to the pitched roof. Air-conditioners on a pitched roof are more dangerous to repair and replace than air-conditioners on a flat roof.

For further information

National Roofing Contractors Association (NRCA) (www.roofonline.org)
10255 W. Higgins Road, Suite 600
Rosemont, IL 60018-5607
847-299-9070

Books:

• *Roofing and Waterproofing Manual* by NCRA (above)
• *The Manual of Built-Up Roofing Systems* by C.W. Griffin, McGraw-Hill, NY
• *Roofs: Design, Application, and Maintenance* by Maxwell C. Baker, Multiscience
   Publications, Ltd., available from NRCA

National roofing consulting firms:

Construction Consultants, Inc.
900 Pallister Avenue
Detroit, MI 48202

CRS, Inc.
P.O. Box 2046
Monroe, NC 28110
704-283-8556

PART SEVEN:
<u>PURCHASING</u>

29

Purchasing

As a landlord, you purchase goods and services. You should purchase them from the **lowest acceptable bidder**. You or your employees sometimes do **not** purchase from the lowest acceptable bidder because of:

• Ignorance
• Laziness
• Kickbacks
• Conflicts of interest.

Ignorance and laziness

You may overpay—but believe that you are getting a good price. William Nickerson tells of an Italian-American apartment seller who was buying refrigerators from a fellow Italian-American. Because of their shared heritage, the seller believed he was getting a good deal. Nickerson knew better—because he knew what refrigerators **could** be bought for.

Many people think that if they buy on the **wrong side of the tracks** they're automatically getting a good deal. Or that if they're told they're getting a "**contractor's price**" or some such—that they're getting a good deal.

The only way to tell if you're getting a good deal is to **shop** around. You should ignore such good deal indicators as your relationship with the seller, the shabbiness of the seller's location, or verbal assurances that you are getting a good price.

Kickbacks and conflicts of interest

I know of a janitorial service owner who was required to pay kickbacks to a property manager. He overcharged for the service. That meant that the building owner was actually paying the kickback to his own property manager.

That same property manager had another subcontractor who overcharged for maintenance work. I had occasion to see a bill for a number of locks which were installed. The price was **triple** what I had recently paid for just one such installation. And this bill was for over a dozen. So there should have been a volume discount. The owner thought he had a good property manager.

Property managers and resident managers frequently give apartment work to friends or relatives. I once hired a guy to paint apartments at a building I managed. He was the lowest acceptable bidder.

But the resident manager complained bitterly about the guy's work. I checked. And I saw nothing wrong with the work. The complaints were baseless. But they continued. Finally, the light bulb went on. I asked the manager, "Who do **you** want to do the painting?" He gave me a name. "Are you related to that person?" He admitted the painter was his out-of-work brother-in-law.

There may be nothing wrong with your manager giving apartment business to a relative. But it makes me nervous. I wouldn't prohibit it. But I watch those prices more carefully than I do others. You should, too.

From time to time, you should ask your manager why they use a particular supplier or subcontractor. You should also ask if they have any non-business relationship with that supplier or subcontractor. That is, is that person a friend or relative?

Heating oil

If you use heating oil, you can and should be trying to get volume discounts. Or at least trying to find the cheapest acceptable supplier. I never found an oil man who didn't give satisfactory service. So price was about the only variable you needed to worry about.

No more than Maintenance Warehouse

I have a Maintenance Warehouse catalog. Virtually everything my managers buy is in one or both. I tell them they can pay **as much as** Maintenance Warehouse, whichever is lower—but **not more**. On the grounds that they can always buy from Sears or Maintenance Warehouse.

And I check the prices on the bills I pay against those in the catalogs from time to time to make sure we aren't overpaying. You should make a game of trying to find prices which deviate from Maintenance Warehouse—in either direction. If you find that the manager paid **more** than Maintenance Warehouse's price, point it out. And if you find that the manager got something for **less** than Maintenance Warehouse, be sure to compliment and thank them.

Also, make sure your managers know that you know that cheapest isn't always best. It's lowest **acceptable** bidder, not lowest bidder. Hold your compliments until you've made sure the good deal the manager got met quality standards.

'The worst crime was to pay retail'

In his movie "Annie Hall," Woody Allen noted that in his family, the worst crime was to pay retail. Don't get into that mentality—the mentality that says paying retail is a disgrace—that you always have to get a deal. There's no prize for that.

You and your employees ought to be price-conscious and shop around—but **within reason**. Remember that time is money—including time spent shopping for the best price. Operating a car also costs money as in driving around looking for the best price and providing your own delivery and moving service.

You and your employees should not waste money by paying too much. Nor should you waste money chasing around after "Superprice."

Volume discounts versus carrying costs

You can generally get a discount for buying in volume. As a result, many apartment managers and maintenance men buy in volume.

Do **not** allow that. Except for heating oil, I know of nothing which residential buildings **use** in volume. If you don't **use** it in volume, don't **buy** it in volume.

That includes light bulbs, washers, carpet, drapes, appliances, etc.

Some owners decide that the complex needs new carpet. And if they get the **whole** complex done, they'll get it cheap. So they do.

Folks, I haven't seen your complex. But I guarantee you the whole complex doesn't **need** carpet—unless there was a flood. At any given moment, 5% of the apartments may need carpet—but not all of them. The amount of wear and stains varies enormously. So what those guys saved in volume discounts, they lost by replacing carpet that didn't need replacing. In fact, they'd almost certainly been better off just replacing carpet when needed on a unit by unit basis.

Store it at the hardware store

My managers frequently complain about lack of storage space. I tell them we store things at the hardware store—by not buying them until we need them. That's not to say we never bought in quantity. We bought light bulbs and such by the case. They don't take up much room and they don't cost much money. And I don't want my managers driving to the store every time they need a light bulb.

The only exception is a hard-to-get part that you can't afford to wait for.

Lost interest, breakage, and 'shrinkage'

When you buy supplies, it's the same as **investing** in them. You were probably earning 5% on the money before you paid it to the supplier. Are faucet washers or light bulbs a good investment? No. They produce no return.

But a $100 tied up in supplies costs you $5 a year in interest. If you didn't get that much saving in the form of volume discounts or trip avoidance, you shouldn't have had so many supplies.

"Shrinkage" means theft. Virtually all employees steal supplies. Although most don't think of it that way. They might use company envelopes to mail personal letters. Or the company photocopier for Junior's resume. Or a company light bulb for a personal lamp. Or a stack of company paper towels for the car trunk.

The typical employee would regard objecting to such things as being unreasonable. "If it's that important to you, here! Here's a penny for the photocopy I made." Of course, if it were only a penny, it wouldn't matter. But it adds up. Especially if you have large stocks of supplies laying around.

Not only do employees take things. So do tenants or plain old climb-through-the-window-at-night thieves.

The best way to prevent shrinkage is to have little laying around to "shrink." In other words, store your supplies at the hardware store or lumberyard. And let **them** worry about shrinkage. You do that by not buying them until you need them.

According to retailers surveyed by Arthur Anderson, "shrinkage" at stores is attributable to:

Employee theft	44%	
Shoplifting	30%	
Poor paperwork	22%	
Vendor theft	4%	(being shortchanged by the guy who sold it to you)

Painting

You can get an apartment painted for about $50 to $80 depending on size. Materials like paint, brushes and rollers are extra. That's a take-off-the-switch-and-outlet-plates job—with no paint on the floor, light fixtures, or bathroom fixtures.

If you're paying more, you're overpaying. Paint one yourself if you haven't done it in a while. I'm told it takes 4 to 8 hours. So $50 is no worse than $6.25 an hour. And can get up to $10 or $12 an hour.

One thing you **do** need is reasonable speed. When a unit becomes vacant, you want it painted within a day or two for rerenting. A painter who's cheap but can't get to it until the weekend is probably unacceptable.

Unless the law requires it, you should **not** paint an apartment or house every time it becomes vacant. Your employees should always try to **touch up** the place if possible. The new tenant should get white walls and a fresh paint smell. But he does not need a full paint job if the last one is largely still intact. Full paint jobs should only be done when the apartment or house has not been painted in three years or more or when the tenants were especially hard on it. And in the case where the tenants were especially hard on the walls, a deduction should be made from their security deposit.

Cleaning

We pay $100 a week for a maid to clean our house. The house is 3320 square feet. That's about $3 per hundred square feet. Apartments typically range from 600 to 1,000 square feet. At $2.71 per hundred square feet, the cost of cleaning them would run from $18 to $30.

However, our maid generally does **not** clean the oven or refrigerator. Ovens and refrigerators are probably the worst part of cleaning a residential unit. Furthermore, our maid comes in weekly. So she's only cleaning one week's worth of dirt. Depending on the cleanliness of the tenant, you may only have one week's worth of dirt, too. But more likely, it's worse than that. Plus, even the cleanest tenants rarely clean under bureaus and such.

Cleaning an oven and refrigerator probably adds about an hour. So figuring $5 an hour, cleaning an apartment is probably worth about $25 to $35 in the typical case. That's about what I paid. And it's what you should be paying.

Heating and air-conditioning service contracts

One of these days I'm going to figure out how to get a handle on heating and air-conditioning repair costs. So far, I haven't. I always feel I'm being overcharged.

It's like maintenance. Highly subjective.

I have tried having a service contract with an HVAC company. And I've tried not having a service contract. I lean toward having one. My numerical analysis shows the comparison to be about six of one and a half dozen of the other.

The company knows far more than you

HVAC companies know intimately exactly what's likely to go wrong with your equipment—and how often. Their service contracts invariably exclude certain things. What do you suppose they exclude? The things most likely to happen. Heating oil service contracts typically exclude the combustion chamber and blower motor. The only things I ever had to replace when I owned oil heated buildings were the combustion chambers and blower motors.

Try it

I suggest that you try getting along without them—and compare your costs for per visit repairs with the cost of a service contract. Make sure you take into account that not everything you paid for on a per visit basis without the service contract would have been done free under the contract.

And when you do this experiment, use a **different** subcontractor than the one you had the service contract with. The service contract guy has an incentive to pump up the bills to show you that he was right when he recommended the service contract.

Assertiveness training

One other observation on heating and air-conditioning service companies. They know that most laymen regard heating and air-conditioning equipment with awe. As a result, they often overcharge.

On the 200-unit I managed, we had an engineering firm make repairs to the huge central heating system. I was impressed at how many of the engineering firm's big shots came to check the work—until I got the bill. All those turkeys standing around watching were **on** the bill. At **higher** hourly rates than the guys doing the work. Apparently the word was out at the firm that we were patsies. And they emptied the office to run up our bill.

I raised heck. And next time they came, I told the first guy who arrived that I'd better not see anyone else on the job. He talked me into one helper. But I pounced on any other engineering firm guys who arrived with, "You aren't planning to bill me for your time are you?" If I got anything other than a "no," I politely told them to take a hike.

Saving $3,000 by asking questions

On another occasion, I had to replace the guts of a large air-conditioner compressor. Beforehand, the engineering firm told me it would cost $5,000 if the problem were X and $8,000 if it were Y. When they opened up, we were relieved to learn that it was X. But the bill which arrived later was for $8,000. I called to ask why and they beat a hasty retreat. $3,000 saved.

Lesson learned? Faint heart never won fair HVAC bill.

Many of these guys figure they can overcharge you because you don't understand the equipment. Don't let them. Ask lots of questions. Especially **before** they begin work. At that stage, they're still afraid that you might use someone else. So you have some leverage.

Beware of time charges for unnecessary people—and unnecessary trips back to the shop. One firm I used in a small town invariably went back to the shop for a tool which they didn't have. That was a **two-hour round trip** back to the big city for which I was charged at air-conditioner repairman rates!

Carpet

Don't replace it until you have to. Try shampooing, steam cleaning, spot remover, dying, you name it. Replacing the darned stuff is very expensive. In a small building, a month in which you replace a carpet is generally a month without positive cash flow.

But when you gotta you gotta. Remember that the name of the game is **rent, not expenses**. When the carpet's condition starts interfering with getting market value rental, replace it.

Neither junk nor the best

At one time or another, most rental property owners have tried to use very cheap carpet. And regretted it.

On the other hand, there's no benefit to using expensive carpet. In residential property, you generally have to replace carpet due to **stains, not wear**. And I know of no carpet that doesn't stain.

So you want the minimum acceptable grade. What's that? Probably FHA specifications. What are they? You could find out. But it's probably not worth the trouble. Just look for the words "FHA approved" or some such. And be careful who you're dealing with. Some sleazeball carpet dealers no doubt sell non-FHA carpet as FHA.

The best advice other than dealing with a reputable dealer is to look at the stuff. Both in the show room and when it arrives—to make sure you're getting what you ordered. Cheap carpet **looks** cheap. That's why you don't want it. You don't have to be an expert to recognize junk carpet. Prospective tenants can recognize it. And so can you.

If you want to save money on carpet, save it by trying to delay replacement—or by suing tenants who cause premature replacement. Not by buying cheap replacement carpet.

Investors meetings

I used to be first vice president of the Delaware Valley Apartment Owners Association. One of the most successful meetings I ran during my tenure is one where I simply went down the list of operating expenses and asked the members what they paid and who they bought from.

Some were shocked to find that they were paying too much for heating oil. We instantly agreed to switch almost everyone in the room to the lowest-priced supplier—and gave the owner who already bought from him a request to see if we could get some sort of additional group discount. He did and we did. That oil supplier was our next speaker as I recall.

On services like plumbing, we asked about standard work like, "What are you paying for replacing a hot water heater?"

Here are the questions I suggest you ask at your meetings:

- What split are you getting from your laundry concessionaire?
- What split are you getting from your other vending machine concessionaires?
- What security deposit are you charging?
- What plumber do you use?
- What outside electrician?
- What outside carpenter?
- What roofer?
- What paving contractor?
- What pool company?
- What painter?
- What are you paying to have an apartment painted?
- What are you paying to have an apartment cleaned?
- What are you paying to have carpet steam cleaned?
- What are you paying for drape cleaning? Drape replacement?
- Where do you get your best ad response?
- What are you paying for new carpet and vinyl? From whom?
- Where do you buy refrigerators? Dishwashers? Disposers?
- How much are you paying for refrigerators, dishwashers, disposers?
- How much are you paying for chlorine? From whom?
- Who do you use for HVAC repairs? Are you happy with them?
- Who's your trash contractor (where private)? How much do you pay?
- Where do you buy paint? How much do you pay?
- Where do you buy supplies?
- Who do you use for locksmithing?

Work done on each unit

I recommend you note on the file jacket of each unit whenever any work is done there. For example:

Apt. 104

3/16/88	replaced fan motor
5/29/88	cleaned
5/29/88	steam
5/29/88	new faucet

That way, if a particular repair is done twice on the same unit, you'll know to ask why. I've caught such problems as double-billing, new faucet to replace six month old faucet, and multiple cleanings that way. When you change managers, the new manager often cleans apartments which the previous manager also cleaned and you end up paying to clean the same apartment twice.

Repeat purchases record

You should also have a record of what you pay for things you buy repeatedly so you can monitor the per unit cost (per bulb, per pound, per bomb, etc.).

Repeat Purchases Record			
Item	Date & $/unit	Date & $/unit	Date & $/unit
Light bulbs, 60 watt			
Par floods, 75 watt			
HTH, 100 lbs.			
Interior latex paint gallons			
Bug bombs			
Disposers			

And so forth.

Computer agents

The most exciting development in the purchasing area is computer agents. Computer programs that search the World Wide Web looking for the best price are becoming available. All suppliers will soon be forced to advertise their products on the Web. Furthermore, they will be forced to do so in a standard format called XML. That will facilitate search programs.

There are also Web sites where you can ask for quotes to provide you with various products or services—what industry calls "requests for bids." Pay attention to these developments and make use of them as soon as they make sense for you.

PART EIGHT: INSURANCE

30

Insurance

Following my advice on insurance may **raise** rather than lower your bill. That's because many landlords are inadequately insured. But if you are adequately insured, following my advice will probably **lower** your premium.

The idea behind insurance

First, you need to understand the basic idea behind insurance. Most people **don't**.

An insurance policy is **not** a lottery ticket. It's not a way of making money by "cashing in" when you have a loss. Insurance has one purpose—to protect you from financial disaster.

Notice that I said **disaster**. Not financial **loss**.

Self-insurance

The cheapest insurance is self-insurance—more commonly known as **no** insurance. You should self-insure whenever possible. The reason self-insurance is cheaper is because you cut out the middleman. Insurance companies have overhead. And they want to make a profit.

It's bad enough when you have a loss that you have to pay for the loss. Having to pay for the insurance company's overhead and profit in addition is the pits. But that's exactly what happens to policyholders as a group when you have insurance.

The total amount of premiums insurance companies collect from their policyholders as a group **exceeds** the amount they pay out in claims. Or at least it better or the insurance companies will go out of business. That means that **on average**, policyholders pay more for insurance than they would have paid for the losses themselves.

You pay not only for the insurance company's overhead and profit, but also for **fraudulent claims** like arson. To an extent, insurance companies try to discourage and discover fraudulent claims. But for the most part, it's easier for them to just pass the cost on to law-abiding folks like you.

One other cost you save when you self-insure is the paperwork of filing claims.

When to self-insure

Can you afford a $1,000 loss? I suspect so. Can you afford a $2,000 loss? I don't mean would you **mind** a $2,000 loss. I know you'd mind. The question is, will a $2,000 loss bankrupt you? I didn't think so.

You should self-insure any loss which would not cause you financial difficulty. For the average real estate investor, that'd probably in the thousands or even tens of thousands of dollars. Landlords who own many properties may even be able to self-insure their entire portfolio—at least for **fire** and such. Juries being what they are these days, they'd better have **liability** insurance no matter how big they are. That would mean they'd have no line for "insurance" at all on their cash flow statement. Although over time their net repairs expense would be higher because they'd also have no "insurance claims" line on the income portion. But the overall net effect over time would be lower cost.

Deductibles

You self-insure at the low end with **deductibles**. When you buy an insurance policy, you can get a low deductible or a high deductible. The lower the deductible, the higher the premium. Don't buy policies with low deductibles. You don't need to pay some insurance company bureaucracy to handle a $400 claim. You can handle that yourself.

I have noticed, however, that after a point, the higher deductibles save very little. For example, I had a $1,000 deductible on my apartment building policy. I wanted a higher deductible. Because a $2,000 or even a $5,000 loss wouldn't bankrupt me.

How much you save

But, according to my one-time agent, George Johnson (512-454-4536), the savings in premium (in Texas—but other states are probably the same) when you raise the deductible from $1,000 to $3,000 is only 2%. From $1,000 to $5,000 is only 4%. From $1,000 to $10,000, 7%.

On the other hand, going from $100 deductible to $1,000 reduces the premium 12%.

My premium was about $6,000 a year. So by raising the deductible to $1,000 from $100 I save 12% x $6,000 = $720. The down side is that if I have a claim which is $1,000 or more, I'm $1,000 - $100 = **$900** worse off than with the $100 deductible. So I'm gambling that I will **not** have a $1,000 loss more than once every two years.

In two years, I save $720 x 2 = $1,440. And if I have that $1,000 or more loss, the higher deductible costs me $900. So I'm $540 better off if I have one fewer $1,000 loss in a two year period.

But to go to $3,000 deductible, the gamble looks less attractive. I save 2% x $6,000 = $120. But if I have loss of $3,000 or more, the higher deductible costs me $3,000 - $1,000 = $2,000. So I'd have to go $2,000/$120 = 16.7 years without more than one $3,000 loss to make the $3,000 deductible worthwhile. Seems to me that the insurance companies should offer more incentive to raise the deductible. I suspect they don't because there's no market for higher deductibles.

No policy

There is another way to self-insure. Don't buy **any** insurance policy. In my case, that'd save $6,000 a year. But if the biggest building I ever owned burned to the ground, I'd have suffered an $800,000 to $1,000,000 loss—depending on what the replacement cost was.

I'd still have the ground. But that was only worth about 10% of the total. Plus I'd have had a cleanup bill. I can **deduct** the loss. But I've never had a taxable income of $1,000,000 a year. So I'd have had to spread the deductions over many years. Although the present value of not paying taxes for many years is substantial. On an after-tax, after land value basis, the loss probably would have netted out at around $500,000 or $600,000. Is that worth saving $6,000 a year? You'd have to suffer a total loss no more often than once every $550,000/$6,000 = 91.7 years.

Rarely a total loss

Actually, buildings rarely burn to the ground. You might have damage to one kitchen—or extensive damage to several apartments. But rarely does the whole complex burn to the foundation—especially if there's more than one building in the complex. Although that **does** happen.

That's why insurance companies only charge $6,000 to cover $1.4 million worth of property. ($1.4 million is the replacement cost of **both** the Texas properties I owned in the mid eighties. I only used the larger one in the example because I figure the 23 miles between them will prevent any fire from spreading from one building to the other.)

In fact, apartment buildings **do** only burn to the ground about once in every 91.7 years or longer. Or to put it another way, if an insurance company insures 91.7 apartment buildings, less than one total loss will occur among their policyholders per year.

The odds are in your favor when you self-insure. For the same reason they're in the insurance company's favor when **they** insure you. If they weren't, insurance companies couldn't make a profit.

But is it worth it?

So it's cost effective for the average guy to have no insurance, because the average guy won't have a loss as large as the premiums he'll save. The problem arises if you turn out to be the one in a hundred or whatever who suffers the big loss.

I'd rather pay $6,000 a year than risk losing $500,000. Even though I know my losses over the years will **probably** be less than my insurance premiums.

But a guy who owns a whole bunch of little properties like single-family rental houses or duplexes might see it differently. The insurance premium on $1.4 million of rental houses would probably be about $6,000 a year. Especially if they were all under one policy.

But if they are 28 rental houses each worth $50,000, self-insurance may sound less threatening. A total loss at one property would cost $50,000 less tax deductions and land value. Let's call it $30,000. And you save $6,000 a year by self-insuring. So you'd need to have no more than one total loss every $30,000/$6,000 = 5 years. That bet I'd take.

But will the lenders let you?

You probably have mortgages on your buildings. Will the lenders let you cancel your insurance? Generally, no. But if you discuss the matter with them as I have here, they may see the light. You could show them your balance sheet and income statement. Get hold of some insurance industry statistics. And perhaps agree to personal liability on any loans on which you do not now have personal liability.

If you've got the wherewithal to cover the loss, they ought to agree to it. Major corporations self-insure. And their lenders agree to it. As long as you have the financial strength to cover the likely loss, it makes sense. If you're big enough, you might even look into starting your own insurance company to insure just your properties. That may involve much red tape, but the logic is there.

Discount for more than one property on one policy

If you have more than one property, you can often get a discount by putting them on the same policy. That's a negotiated discount, not a discount built into state rate schedules.

The theory is that a fire in one building is not likely to spread to another miles away. Although in 1983, my insurance company and I discovered that a **freeze** can hit two properties simultaneously.

They were only able to apply my $1,000 deductible against the **combined** losses (burst water pipes) instead of against **each** loss. So I got $1,000 more from them.

Replacement cost

In general, you should have replacement cost coverage. That is, the amount of the coverage should be enough to rebuild the building at today's building costs. Some companies write "**actual cash value**" insurance—which has a lower premium. Actual cash value means replacement cost less depreciation. In practice, that means you and the insurance company will get into a huge argument if there's a major loss. Actual cash value may be best when the market value of the property is less than 50% or so of the market value—like if the property in question is mostly vacant.

Replacement cost less than mortgage amount

Mortgage lenders generally require that your insurance policy limit at least equal the mortgage amount. But in some cases, the mortgage amount is **greater** than the replacement value. That's been the case with my last two houses. The reason is land values in California are high as a percentage of overall value. And land is indestructible. So it's quite possible for an 80% loan to be greater than the replacement cost where the land value is, say, 30% of the total value.

Insurance companies will write the policy limit at whatever amount you want. And charge you the appropriate premium. But they absolutely will **not** pay more than replacement cost even in the event of a total loss. So the extra premium you pay for the amount by which the limit exceeds the replacement cost is totally **wasted**.

When you are in that situation, you should explain the facts to the mortgage lender and get them to permit you to limit the coverage to the replacement cost—even though it's less than the mortgage balance. I have done that with two different lenders on my California homes.

Two other lenders of mine refused. So I threatened to take them to small claims court—annually. At which point they saw the light.

If they resist, you should insist. If they still refuse, and the amount of wasted premium is significant, sue the mortgage lender in small claims court for reimbursement of the wasted premium. The suit will probably get their attention. And cause a higher-up to agree to the lower coverage. And if the lender **still** refuses, the court will probably see that forcing you to pay for coverage you can't possibly collect on is nonsense.

In 1987, California and Massachusetts passed laws prohibiting lenders from requiring more insurance than warranted by the replacement value of the burnable property. In Texas, insurers will sometimes write separate coverage on the "land and outside improvements." The premiums on such items are quite low—and the lenders are satisfied because the overall **amount** of the coverage equals the amount of the loan.

If for some reason you choose not to fight a lender who makes you cover more than replacement cost, at least tell your insurance company to turn off their **automatic inflation adjustment** machine. Otherwise, you'll have insult added to injury by exacerbating your overinsurance once a year. In fact, you ought to **reduce** your insurance policy limit by the amount of the **amortization** each year as long as the coverage limit is above replacement cost.

Coinsurance

Many hazard insurance policies have a coinsurance clause. It says you must have coverage limits at least equal to 90% or whatever of the replacement value. If you don't, you will have to pay a large penalty in the event of a major loss.

For example, say you have 80% coinsurance. The replacement cost is $500,000. But your policy limit is only $350,000. According to the coinsurance clause, you promised to have a limit equal to at least 80% of the replacement cost or 80% x $500,000 = $400,000. But you didn't keep that promise. You only have $350,000 or $350,000/$400,000 = 87.5% as much coverage as you promised.

So the insurance company will chop 100% - 85% = 15% off any claim they pay. Plus they will not under any circumstances pay more than the amount of the policy limit. So in this example, if you had a $10,000 loss, they'd only pay you 85% x ($10,000 - $1,000 deductible) = 85% x $9,000 = $7,650. If you had been covered for $400,000 or more, you would have received the full $9,000 in the event of a $10,000 loss.

What policies should you have?

So far I've been talking about **fire insurance**. The more accurate name is **hazard insurance**. That's what's usually required by mortgage lenders. And what you ought to have if a total loss would bankrupt your or cause you unacceptable financial loss.

On small buildings, the policy is often called a "homeowners" policy—even if you rent the place out. On my apartment buildings, the policy I had was called a "Texas Commercial Package Policy." You need to talk to agents in your area to find out which policies are appropriate.

Liability

The mortgage lender may not require liability insurance. But you'd better have it. Nowadays, when someone trips on your sidewalk, they think they've hit the lottery. They get some ambulance chaser lawyer to send you a threatening letter. Then, if you or your insurance company doesn't send lots of money quickly, they file a suit—which seeks untold millions for pain and suffering, loss of ability to ever work, etc.

If you don't have insurance, the plaintiff and his attorney will usually try to confiscate your entire net worth and part of your future earning power.

Get liability insurance. $1,000,000 seems to be the most common limit. I don't know what the "right" limit is. No one does. But a million is usually enough to satisfy an attorney working on a 33% contingency basis. There is generally no deductible on liability coverage.

Application for insurance

When you ask for a quote on an insurance policy, the agent will ask you a bunch of questions about the building. "How far to the nearest fire hydrant? The nearest fire house? Are there fire walls?" etc.

Be **careful** how you answer those questions. They determine your rate. Get up off your duff and **find out** how far to the nearest hydrant, fire house, etc. It's in your interest to make sure you answer those questions **accurately** so you don't pay an incorrect, higher rate.

And don't think **in**accurate answers in your favor are even better. Let me quote from *Insurance Principles and Practices* by Riegel, Miller, and Williams.

> *Usually it is the insured's failure to disclose all the facts that is at issue in disputed cases.* **Misrepresentation** *If the insured gives an incorrect answer to a direct question by the insurer, the insurer may accuse him of misrepresentation. If the question was one of fact, all the insurer need prove is materiality...*

What happens if you misrepresent? The insurance company may be allowed to either reduce the amount they pay you or pay you nothing at all.

How a $1,000 expenditure cut the premium by $11,205

Corpus Christi apartment owner, Willard Hammonds cut his insurance premium by $11,205 a year by spending just $1,000 modifying one of his buildings. On the recommendation of insurance consultant Greg Crouch (Austin, 512-473-3602), Hammonds got his property reinspected by a state inspector. The state inspector said he would change the building's "published rate" to a better category if the owner would do three things:

1. Seal, with masonry, a doorway to the attic.
2. Put cement around pipes protruding into the attic from below.
3. Install 1.5-hour, UL-approved fire dampers in air vents leading into the attic.

Hammonds did those things at a cost of approximately $1,000. As a result, his insurance premium on that building dropped $11,205 from $15,346 to $4,231.

'Agreed amount'

Crouch had previously got the premium reduced from $24,314 to $15,346 by persuading the insurance company to reduce the replacement cost from $75 per square foot to $60. There was no danger of a coinsurance penalty because the new policy had an "agreed amount" endorsement. Although $60 per square foot may not be enough to rebuild the place. "Guaranteed replacement cost" means the insurance company will rebuild no matter what it costs. "Agreed amount" just means no coinsurance penalty.

Workers compensation

If you have employees, you need workers compensation insurance. Workers comp is not just another insurance policy. In most states, it is **mandatory** by state law, and **not** having it causes you to lose certain important protection provided by state workers compensation laws.

If you are a small employer, you may have to get worker compensation coverage through the **assigned risk pool**. If no one will write the insurance for you, the state will **force** some company to write it. Your insurance agent or state insurance office can explain how to get coverage this way.

Workers comp premiums are based on the classification your employees fall into and the total payroll. My policy shows a classification of "Apartment House Operation—all employees." You should make sure your classification is the **right** one. Do that by asking to see all the classifications and their definitions. Also make sure they don't overstate the amount of your annual payroll.

A common mistake in Texas, according to Texas Apartment Association legal counsel, Larry Niemann, is lumping clerical workers in the "Apartment House Operation" category. In that state, that mistake would cost you $1,031 per year on an employee who made $10,000 in the late eighties. That was the difference between the $10.77 per $100 rate on "Apartment House Operation" and the 46¢ per $100 rate on clerical workers. Off-site-based supervisors like property managers would typically have qualified for the "Outside Salesperson" rate of 94¢ per $100.

Boiler insurance

Boiler insurance is bit of a misnomer. It covers boilers, air-conditioners and similar equipment.

For a $398 premium, I had $781,000 worth of coverage with a $250 deductible. The policy covered the cost of repairing or replacing the boiler or air-conditioner. The policy also covered "business interruption and extra expenses." I presume that means I get some money if my tenants move out because the air-conditioner isn't fixed fast enough.

Boiler insurance may be partially redundant with a service contract from an HVAC company. If so, get the HVAC company to reduce its coverage and monthly charge accordingly. Boiler insurance, to an extent, is a service contract. The way I read the policy, if my air-conditioner conks out, the boiler insurance company will pay for the repairs and will even pay for replacement if necessary. Service contracts rarely pay for replacement.

You should note one little item I had in one boiler policy. A clause that said,

Our liability under this coverage starts
a. twelve hours after the time of the accident or
b. twelve hours before we receive notice of the accident.

You have to read that a couple times before you understand it. It means that if you don't notify the insurance company of the accident **immediately**, you're not going to get much out of the insurance company. So I've told my manager to send a **telegram** to that insurance company if the boiler or air-conditioner ever stops working.

Employee dishonesty insurance

If your manager handles money, which is likely, you should have fidelity or crime insurance. In my case it's an "Employee Dishonesty" rider to the Texas Commercial Policy. I'm covered up to $10,000 (about one month's rent collections) with a $250 deductible.

If you prohibit your tenants from paying cash in the lease, and pay close attention to any purchasing decisions your employees make, you probably have little exposure to employee dishonesty losses. The big losses in this category come when a manager collects most of the rents in **cash**. Then claims there was a "robbery."

Even with checks, theft is possible though. The manager could gradually get the tenants in the habit of making the checks payable to the manager. A great many tenants think the manager is the owner. Or the manager could get the tenants to pay cash in spite of your policy to the contrary.

Or the manager could open a new checking account in the name of the apartment building and deposit the rents there. If the manager persuaded the bank to accept her signature as valid for withdrawals from that account, he or she could abscond with a month's rent.

Again the question is, would the worst case bankrupt you? You should have the highest deductible which makes sense given what you can afford and what discount you get for raising the deductible. And if you can afford the worst case, don't get the coverage at all.

Rent loss coverage

Fires stop rents from coming in. But they don't stop bills. Fire insurance pays you for the damage to the building. Rent loss reimburses you for the rent you don't get as a result of the damage. It typically stops cold the day the damage is repaired. And you are required to repair the damage with "due diligence and dispatch."

If the number of units damaged is more than a few, you'll probably find that your rent loss coverage stops before the rents resume. Because once the repairs are complete, you have a rent-up situation similar to a newly constructed building. You can get an endorsement from most insurance companies to extend the period of indemnity for loss of rent. It's written for 30, 60, or 90 days. And it generally costs a little extra. At least one insurance company will throw on a 30-day extension for no charge if you ask.

Rome wasn't built in a day, and you don't fill 10 newly constructed or newly repaired apartments in a day either. But the rent loss insurance **does** stop in a day. So **pre**-lease as much as you can.

Flood insurance

There are maps which show flood hazard areas. If the building you want to buy is in a flood hazard area, don't buy it. If you already own it, you should probably get flood insurance. Flood insurance is federally subsidized. So unlike **private** insurance, the odds are in **your** favor with flood insurance. That is the probable claims exceed the premiums.

You need to contact local officials to see if they are participating in the National Flood Insurance Program. Or contact the National Flood Insurance Program, P.O. Box 34294, Bethesda, MD 20034 800-638-6620 (www.fema.gov/fema/finifp.html).

'Claims made' coverage

Your liability insurance has been an "occurrence" policy. Many in the insurance industry want to switch to a "claims made" policy. In an occurrence policy, you are covered **forever** for claims arising out of things that **occurred** during the policy period. In a claims made policy, you are only covered for claims which are **filed** during the policy period.

For example, if a person falls on your steps in November 1988 and sues you in October 1990, you would **not** be covered under a **claims made** policy that expired in December 1988. But you **would** be covered in 1990 on an occurrence policy that expired in December 1988. With claims made, insurance policies that expire before the statute of limitations on filing the lawsuit leave you uncovered for the period between those two dates.

Generally, you would renew the coverage each year so whether it was claims made or occurrence wouldn't matter. But when you **sell** a building, you obviously stop renewing coverage on that building. Coverage on the new building you buy would not apply to claims arising out of the previous property. So when you sell a property which had claims made coverage, make sure you get "**tail coverage**"—a special policy that covers you until the statute of limitations runs out on the period in question.

Other insurance you need

Older buildings frequently violate current zoning and/or building codes. But they are allowed to violate those laws under the doctrine of "**nonconforming use**." That doctrine says buildings constructed before the zoning or building code was changed need only comply with the zoning and building code that was in effect **at the time the building was constructed**.

However the typical zoning law or building code contains a clause saying the building must be brought into compliance with **current** zoning and/or building code if a certain percentage of the property is **destroyed**. My impression is that 50% is the typical trigger point.

As a result of such clauses, you may be required to tear down all or part of the **un**damaged part of your building after a fire or other loss.

The demolition will cost money. And it's **not** covered by the typical hazard insurance policy. (Demolition of the **damaged** part **is** generally covered by hazard insurance.)

To the extent that what you are allowed to restore is less than what was destroyed, you suffer a loss in property value. For example, 51% of a 25-unit burns to the ground. The local law says if more than 50% is destroyed, you must conform to current zoning which only allows twelve units. The hazard insurance company will pay the "**actual cash value**" of what was destroyed. But that will be less than **replacement** cost and may be less than the **market** value of the part of the original structure that was destroyed.

Even if you are allowed to rebuild the same size structure, you may have to rebuild it **better** than the original. For example, you may be required to install sprinklers and numerous energy- and water-saving features—none of which you find cost effective as measured by the three-year payback criterion. Hazard insurance policies generally provide for replacement of "**like kind and quality**." So they won't pay for the **extras** required by the current building code.

Finally, complying with current zoning and/or building codes may take **more time** than just restoring the building as it was. Normal hazard insurance policies don't cover that extra time.

The **good** news is that you can get insurance to protect you from these risks. In Texas, the coverages go by these names:

- Form 290, Contingent Liability From Operation of Building Laws Endorsement
- Form 292, Demolition Cost Endorsement
- Form 293, Increased Cost of Construction Endorsement
- Form 291, Demolition and Increased Time to Rebuild

The **bad** news is that it ain't cheap. My agent quoted a 15% increase in my hazard insurance premium to add these endorsements.

Accordingly, I recommend that you get this coverage only when your local zoning law or building codes contain a percent of destruction clause and your property configuration is such that a fire, tornado, or whatever is likely to trigger the clause. For example, a complex consisting of separate, multiple buildings is **un**likely to be 50% destroyed even in the event of a major fire. But a **single**-structure property **is** far more likely to suffer 50% destruction in the event of a major fire.

So find out exactly what percentage destruction, if any, triggers new, more expensive standards under your zoning and building laws. Calculate what the more expensive standards would cost **you** if they were triggered. Then consider, with the help of an expert like your insurance agent, how likely **your** property is to suffer such a loss. Finally, compare the **risk** to the increased **cost** of the insurance. Use the same kind of analysis I showed you in the discussion of higher deductibles.

How to save mucho by using an insurance consultant

A top notch insurance consultant can save you thousands or even tens of thousands in insurance premiums. The one that I've used, Greg Crouch of Austin, has saved some of his clients hundreds of thousands of premium dollars.

Insurance consultants—**real** insurance consultants—don't sell insurance. They buy it for you. They receive no commission. They are paid solely by you on a fee basis. So the key question to ask someone who says he's an insurance consultant is, Do you ever get a commission for selling insurance? If the answer is yes, he's an insurance **salesman**, not a consultant.

When I called Crouch, I had just been cancelled for the second time in a month—during the 1985 insurance crisis. I called the Texas Apartment Association for help. They referred me to Crouch.

At that point, I was concerned about finding insurance at all—not cutting my premium. For a $2,500 fee, Crouch not only found me a policy with a strong company (State Farm), he cut my premiums on a per-dollar-of-coverage basis. Plus I had more and better coverage when he was done than before. He also was willing to work on a percentage of savings basis but I chose the flat fee option. Here are my before and after premiums:

Policy	Before	After
Hazard	$5,999.00	$4,967.00
Umbrella liability	550.00	400.00
Boiler	498.00	398.00
Non-owned auto	56.00	48.00
Workers compensation	843.00	975.00

But the limits were changed as well:

Policy	Before	After
Hazard	$1,398,000	$1,825,000
coinsurance	90%	none, agreed amount
Boiler	$500,000	$770,000
deductible	$1,000	$250

Before Crouch, I had paid $5,999 ÷ $1,398,000 = 43¢ per $100 of coverage. After Crouch, I paid $4,967 ÷ $1,825,000 = 27¢ per $100.

How consultants can achieve savings

A good insurance consultant gets the results he does because he has expertise and clout. Crouch is a Certified Insurance Counselor (given by the Society of Certified Insurance Counselors). That's a designation which requires considerable education and experience. And insurance consultants who are successful have clout with insurance agents and companies because they control lots of insurance.

In the three months before he placed my insurance, Crouch bought, on behalf of his clients, over $40,000,000 worth of insurance from the agent he bought my insurance from.

When Crouch called him, that agent made an immediate four-hour-each-way drive from his office in Austin to my properties in the Dallas-Fort Worth area. We had to act quickly because I had been cancelled on only ten days notice.

How to find a good consultant

Insurance consultants are listed in the *Yellow Pages* (although many are really insurance salespeople as I said earlier). The ads that use the word "**adjuster**," "agency," or "broker," are salespeople. In addition to the Certified Insurance Counselor (CIC) designation there are also:

- Certified Property and Casualty Underwriter (CPCU)
- Associate in Risk Management (ARM)
- Accredited Adviser in Insurance (AAIC)

There is at least one nationwide insurance consulting company—the Wyatt Company—which probably has an office in a city near you. Wyatt has minimum premium amounts. If yours is less, you're too small for them. Many states, e.g. Texas, now license risk managers. If your state does, you should look for a consultant with such a license. Call the licensing division of your state board of insurance to see if your state has these licenses.

Loss assessment insurance

If you own a property which is part of a homeowners association, you should have a loss assessment endorsement on your policy. It pays off if your homeowners association is sued and settles or has to pay a judgment which exceeds the limit of the association's insurance coverage. For example, let's say your association has $2,000,000 coverage, 150 homeowners, and gets hit with a $5,000,000 judgment. Each homeowner would be assessed his share of the excess of the judgment over the insurance coverage or $5,000,000 - $2,000,000 = $3,000,000 ÷ 150 = $20,000. If you have $20,000 in loss assessment coverage, your insurance company pays. Otherwise, you pay.

It only costs 25¢ per $1,000 on my homeowners policy. That's $5 per year for $20,000.

Premium-reducing actions

There are some actions you can take to reduce your premiums. Like installing:

- Fire resistant roof shingles
- Smoke detectors
- Fire extinguishers
- Pool fences and self-closing gates
- Fire doors
- Correcting aluminum wiring by the "crimp connection" method (For details, contact A.M.P. Special Industries, Valley Forge, PA).

Find out the cost of the installation and the premium savings and do it if there is a three-year payback. In most cases, there is not. I rejected a burglar alarm in one instance because the insurance savings was so small it didn't even cover the cost of the monitoring service.

Shop around

Shopping around is the best way to hold your premium down. It's best to switch policies on the annual renewal date. Otherwise, you have to pay a "short rate" penalty. A penalty for early withdrawal. When my insurance was first cancelled during the 1985 insurance crisis, I shopped around and got the following quotes:

Company	Premium	Best Rating
#1	$13,737.00	A+ 15
#2	24,053.00	C 4
#3	8,460.00	unlisted
#4	5,999.00	A+ 15

"Best rating" refers to the A.M. Best Company's (no street address, Oldwick, NJ 08858 201-439-2200) ratings (probably available in your local library). They rate insurance companies somewhat like Moodys rates bonds. In 1985, A+ was the highest rating; C, the lowest.

The number after the rating is for financial strength. In '85, 15 was the highest and meant the company had at least $100,000,000 in "policy holder surplus plus conditional reserve funds." A 1 rating meant $250,000 or less.

Since 1985, Best has changed their rating scheme. A 15 rating now means $2,000,000,000 in surplus, etc. A 1 rating now means $1,000,000. Unlisted means new and therefore no track record.

You need to check both the premium and the Best rating when you're shopping around. The lowest premium may not be the best deal if it's from Shifting Sands Mutual. Or Bob's Upholstery School and Casualty Company. Those kinds of companies are big on writing insurance and collecting premiums. But they're not too big on paying claims.

In April of 1987—when the insurance crisis ended—you could achieve savings of 25% to 50% on hazard insurance and 10% to 25% on liability insurance by shopping around.

Indiana University insurance professor Joseph Belth says you should get two other opinions in addition to Best's. He recommended the following standards:

- A+ by A.M. Best 908-439-2200
- Moody's aa2 (212-553-0377) or Standard & Poor's AA (212-208-1527) or Duff & Phelps AA (312-368-3157)
- Not rated in any rater's fifth or lower categories.

Computer shopping

You can already shop for some kinds of insurance on the Internet. In the near future, you will be able to shop for all kinds. Current Web sites that you should check include www.safetnet.com, which links to over 300 insurance sites. www.insweb.com covers various types of consumer insurance including homeowners. Since the Internet is changing rapidly, I cannot give you a comprehensive guide to casualty and liability insurance sites. You need to do a search for insurance shopping sites using general search engines.

Earthquake insurance

The State of California took over earthquake insurance in that state. The effect on me of that was I let my earthquake insurance lapse because the new, state insurance was too expensive. Sometimes, it makes sense to self insure, and one of those is when the government gets involved and drives rates up to ridiculous levels.

Require tenants to get renter insurance

You should require your tenants to get renters insurance in your lease. Only 22% of tenants have such insurance. The others will sue you if they have a loss. One of my newsletter subscribers, Bruce Foulk of Westland, WI, requires each tenant to have $6,000 in personal property coverage with a $250 deductible and $300,000 in liability coverage. He says tenants have given no resistance.

PART NINE:
BOOKKEEPING

31

Bookkeeping Techniques

You should produce the following each month.

- Rent report
- Vacancy report
- Deposit report
- Cash flow statement
- Repeat purchases report.

Rent report

I produce my rent report on a computer using a spread sheet program. You probably should, too. Unless you only have a couple units. It looks like this.

Woodside Rent Report

	A	B	C	D	E	F	G
1	Woodside Apartments		Rent Report	Jun-89			
2	Apt.	Name	Potential	Collected	Vacancy	Type	Deposit
3	101	Smith	$340.00	$340.00	$0.00	one bedroom	150
4	102	Jones	$340.00	$252.26	$87.74	one bedroom	150
5	103		$370.00		$370.00	two bedroom	0
6	104	Brown	$360.00	$360.00	$0.00	two bedroom	150
7	105	Johnson	$325.00	$325.00	$0.00	one bedroom	50
8	Totals		$1,735.00	$1,277.26	$457.74		$500.00

I'll stop at 5 units because there are only so many variations. 101 is occupied by a tenant named Smith. The rent is $340 and it was occupied during the entire month of June. It's a one bedroom and the rent security deposit is $150.

102 moved in during June. That's why the amount collected is only $252.26 even though the rent is $340. $252.26 is 23 days rent prorated. The computer calculates the vacancy loss column by subtracting the "Collected" column from the "Potential" column. In the case of 102, there was $87.74 of vacancy loss in June.

103 is a vacant two bedroom apartment. The asking rent is $370.

104 is an occupied two. Note that the potential rent is $360. So the collected rent. If the apartment were vacant, the asking rent would be $370 not $360. But Brown is in the middle of a lease. When the lease is up, he will be raised to market.

105 is also occupied and is below market. Note the low security deposit on Johnson. That's because the tenant has been in the building since the days when much lower security deposits were collected.

Totals

The computer also totals the columns. And counts the occupied units. I use an Excel spread sheet. It has a COUNT command. I tell it to count the number of lines in which there's something in the "Collected" column. In this case, it comes up with 4. No big deal. But the computer can do it so what the heck.

Data entry

Each month I used to get a written rent report from my managers. It was a pegboard style report. They didn't have computers. I then entered the data into the spread sheet shown above.

First I turned on the computer, inserted the appropriate disk, called up the Rent Report, and changed the date. When the report came on the screen, it showed **last month's** report and date. I changed the "June" to "July" and proceeded to enter data.

Enter only changes

Wherever there was been a **change** I typed **over** the old entry. For example, Jones moved into 102 on June 8th. And only paid $252.26 as a result. But in July, Jones will pay the full $340. So I just typed $340 over the $252.26. No need to change the vacancy loss figure. The computer will automatically do that.

Let's also say that Johnson's rent gets raised to $340 in July. You would type $340 over both the old "Potential" and the "collected" column entries. So both the Potential and the Collected would go up from $325 to $340.

And finally let's say that we rent 103. You would type the new tenant's name in the name blank, the amount of rent collected in the "Collected" column, and the security deposit in that column. If the new tenant moves in during the month, the rent will be prorated. You'd enter the prorated amount under "Collected" and again the computer will automatically calculate the vacancy loss for the month.

The security deposit total will change. It's important that you know that because you should have the security deposits in a separate bank account in most states.

Vacancy report

I showed you what the vacancy report looks like in the chapter on setting rents.

Spread sheets versus data base programs

If I had more units, I might use a data base management or filing system program to do the rent report.

With a data base program, you'd set up a separate record for each apartment or rental house. Each record would contain at least the following information:

- Apartment number or address
- Tenant name
- Potential rent
- Collected rent
- Month in question
- Security deposit
- Size of unit.

You could add all sorts of stuff like move-in date, date of last raise, phone number, etc.

Most data base programs have a math feature. So you could have each record calculate it's own vacancy loss by subtracting the collected amount from the potential.

Canned programs

There are a number of companies which sell property management software. I haven't used any, so I can't evaluate any specifically. However, I **have** had experience with some accounting software. I didn't like it.

The problem was that it fit somebody **else's** business. But not mine. And probably not yours. It was like buying a suit in a store with only one size. It might fit. But probably not.

That's why I prefer you-set-it-up programs like spread sheets and data bases. You can customize it to fit your operation. The accounting software I used forced me to enter data I didn't care about, produce reports I didn't want, and failed to give me information I **did** want.

I polled the subscribers to my newsletter, *Real Estate Investor's Monthly*(www.johntreed.com/reim.html), in the fall of 1989 and asked them which real estate software they liked best. The answer, which I published in my 12/89 issue, was what I suspected: **none**. The most votes went to Quicken (www.quicken.com), a check-writing program; then Lotus 1-2-3 (www.lotus.com), and Managing Your Money (www.mymnet.com/retail), another check-writing program. No real estate program got more than two votes.

Use a spread sheet or data base program. You don't have to be a programmer to use it. I'm sure not. You just need to learn some commands and use regular old arithmetic. If you need a lot of help setting it up, hire a 14-year old who knows the spread sheet or data base management program in question.

Deposits

You should get one of the check-writing computer programs like Quicken or Managing Your Money. Use the classes for each property and subclasses for apartment numbers. Use categories to differentiate rent and other types of income. The Quicken manual recommends that you set up a liability account for security deposits.

Cash flow statement

The cash flow statement shows the monthly income and expenses—plus the total for each income and expense item for the last twelve months—and the percentage of gross income represented by each income and expense item. It looks like this:

Cash Flow Statement

A / Item	B Jan-88	C Feb-88	D Mar-88	E Apr-88	F May-88	G Jun-88	H Jul-88	I Aug-88	J Sep-88	K Oct-88	L Nov-87	M Dec-87	N Total	O % of gross	P
Rent	$6,322	$7,236	$7,699	$8,976	$9,153	$9,098	$8,040	$7,736	$8,374	$9,150	$6,979	$6,135	94,896	90.61%	Rent
Laundry	$150	$110	$180	$170	$180	$50	$220	$146	$180	$330	$149	$221	$2,086	1.99%	Laundry
Ins.Clm.											$6,628		$6,628	6.33%	Insur. Claim
Make gd	$0	$0	$0	$0	$0	$0	$0	$0	$0	$0	$0	$0			Make Good
Bad Chk	$0	$0	$0	$0	$0	$0	$0	$0	$0	$0	$0	$0			Bad Chk
Net bad	$0	$0	$0	$0	$0	$0	$0	$0	$0	$0	$0	$0	$0	0.00%	Net Bad
Late chr	$0	$0	$0	$0	$0	$0	$0	$0	$27		$54	$0	$81	0.08%	Late chrg
dep.rec	$340	$220	$550	$0	$25	$0	$25	$425	$650	$125	$200	$0	$2,560		Dep. Rec
Refunds	$100	$170	$0	$0	$0	$0	$20	$104	$286	$54	$758	$25	$1,517		Refunds
Net Dep	$240	$50	$550	$0	$25	$0	$5	$321	$364	$71	($558)	($25)	$1,043	1.00%	Net Dep.Inc.
Income	$6,712	$7,396	$8,429	$9,146	$9,358	$9,148	$8,265	$8,203	$8,918	$9,578	$13,252	$6,331	104,734	100.00%	Income
Payroll	$399	$439	$370	$439	$439	$439	$439	$439	$439	$439	$422	$318	$4,705	4.49%	Payroll
FICA	$179	$0	$0	$98	$0	$0	$217	$0	$0	$221	$0	$0	$714	0.68%	FICA
FUTA	$33	$0	$0	$0	$0	$0	$0	$0	$0	$0	$0	$0	$33	0.03%	FUTA
TX Unem	$14	$0	$0	$32	$0	$0	$35	$0	$0	$31	$0	$0	$112	0.11%	TX Unem
Electric	$596	$933	$607	$736	$935	$1,152	$1,265	$1,361	$1,322	$1,217	$535	$542	$10,659	10.18%	Electric
Gas	$1,150	$840	$602	$0	$849	$306	$235	$198	$208	$239	$285	$602	$4,913	4.69%	Gas
Water	$330	$271	$369	$357	$563	$549	$524		$1,389	$554	$400	$302	$5,307	5.07%	Water
Trash	$96	$96	$96	$96	$96	$96	$96	$96	$96	$96	$96	$96	$1,059	1.01%	Trash
Phone t	$0	$0	$0	$0	$0	$0	$0	$0	$0	$0	$0	$0	$0	0.00%	Phone to
C phone	$0	$0	$0	$24	$0	$0	$0	$0	$0	$0	$15	$15	$24	0.02%	C phone
L Repai	$432			$76				$202					$202	0.19%	L Repair
Repairs	$0	$0	$122	$0	$0	$0	$0	$0	$157	$218	$383	$3,155	$1,266	1.21%	Repairs
Petty c	$404			$298	$43	$33	$31		$52	$36		$189	$1,085	1.04%	Petty c
Taxes	$102												$225	0.21%	Taxes
Insur	$0	$0	$0	$0	$0	$0	$0	$0	$0	$0	$0	$0	$0	0.00%	Insur
Work C	$0	$0	$0	$0	$0	$0	$1,270	$0	$30	$0	$0	$0	$1,300	1.24%	Work C
Dues	$0	$0	$0	$0	$0	$0	$0	$0	$0	$0	$135	$135	$135	0.13%	Dues
Travel	$0	$0	$0	$0	$0	$0	$0	$0	$0	$0	$0	$0	$0	0.00%	Travel
Plumbg	$210	$95	$30	$0	$0	$0	$0	$102	$142	$156	$75	$450	$836	0.80%	Plumbg
Cleanin	$95	$193					$145	$84				$130	$974	0.93%	Cleaning
Steam C	$62	$19		$45		$78	$84	$70	$43	$43	$48	$96	$412	0.39%	Steam Cl
MiscIns	$560	$19		$24			$15			$106		$51	$668	0.64%	MiscIns
Subscrp	$0	$0	$0	$13							$157	$158	$13	0.01%	Subscrp
Advert	$30	$63	$195	$113	$171	$46		$10	$108				$825	0.79%	Advert
Carpet		$1,405			$902								$2,307	2.20%	Carpet
Vinyl	$0	$0	$0	$0	$0	$0	$0	$0	$0	$0	$0	$0	$0	0.00%	Vinyl
HVAC	$262	$528	$262	$262	$262	$262	$262	$262	$363	$250		$262	$3,237	3.09%	HVAC
Drapes	$243	$1,022	$0	$429	$0	$90	$23	$135	$257	$154		$205	$1,512	1.44%	Drapes
Paint	$164	$55	$74	$0	$0	$78	$84	$115					$1,615	1.54%	Paint
Roof	$0	$0	$429	$0	$0	$46	$0	$10	$484	$106		$458	$429	0.41%	Roof
Supplie	$527	$370	$0	$127	$171	$46	$0	$10	$484	$106	$0	$458	$2,299	2.20%	Supplies
Cap Exp	$370	$0	$0	$867					$446				$1,313	1.25%	Cap Exp
Total	$5,484	$6,636	$3,157	$4,013	$4,285	$3,052	$4,627	$3,088	$5,490	$3,813	$2,537	$1,998	$48,180	46.00%	Total
Net Inc.	$1,228	$759	$5,272	$5,133	$5,072	$6,096	$3,638	$5,115	$3,429	$5,764	$10,714	$4,333	$56,553	54.00%	Net Inc.
Mrtge	$6,268	$5,786	$5,786	$5,786	$5,786	$5,786	$5,786	$5,786	$5,812	$5,812	$5,734	$5,734	$69,863	66.71%	Mrtge
Cash flo	($5,040)	($5,027)	($514)	($654)	($714)	$310	($2,148)	($671)	($2,383)	($48)	$4,980	($1,401)	-13,310	-12.71%	Cash flo

Cottonwoods Cash Flow

The reason for the year above each month is that this is a last-twelve-months spread sheet. When the most recent month is, say, September 1988, the year above the September through December columns would be 1987. When you get the September '88 figures, you type them **over** the September '87 figures—and change the year above the September column to 1988. That way the annual totals column at the right side always shows the totals for the last twelve months

Do taxes, insurance, and amortization elsewhere

Some sticklers for detail will want to compute the taxes, insurance, and amortization monthly. I used to try to do that. Forget it. Too much trouble and not worth it. Just list "mortgage payment" as one line item. Even though it contains taxes, insurance, interest, and amortization. The bottom line is before-income tax cash flow. You'll have to break out the property taxes, insurance and interest for your income tax return. So worry about it then. Plus, by then you'll have the lender's annual statement.

Repeat purchases report

The repeat purchases report covers utility **consumption** not cost. Cost is on the cash flow statement. And it covers unit cost of supplies and services you buy regularly like carpet and painting.

The utilities portion of this report should look like the cash flow statement. Only the entries should be gallons, KWH, cubic feet or whatever. Skip the percent of gross column. And put **each year on a separate line**.

You put each year on a separate line so you can compare this March's gas consumption with previous March's' gas consumption. You want it in cubic feet or therms rather than dollars because price changes can conceal changes in consumption. You can't control the price. But you do have some control over consumption. Here's a sample:

Gas in 100 cubic feet

Month	Jan.	Feb.	Mar.	April	May	June
1986	8674	8433	6509	3021	1041	875
1987	9055	8357	6320	3211	1109	903
1988	8523	8015	6581	3105	1002	905

If consumption gets out of line for the month in question, it will show up as a higher number than the ones above. The explanation may be obvious. Like very cold weather. If not, check it out. There may be some correctable problem. For non-utilities, just show the **cost per unit**. Like the cost per gallon of paint every time you pay a paint bill, the cost per yard of carpet every time you have it installed, the cost per bulb when you buy a case of light bulbs.

How to pay your bills

Use the computer programs Quicken or Managing Your Money to pay your bills and keep track of deposits. It writes checks, produces check registers, helps you balance the account, and produces reports like income statements and balance sheets. Quicken also does the extra paperwork required by government on payroll if you have employees.

I use voucher checks printed by a laser writer. Laser printers are the only way to go. I used to use a dot-matrix printer and continuous forms. Those are the ones with the little holes on each side. I wasted much time lining up the first check or other form. And the printer would frequently jam.

After I sign the check, I put it into either the vendor's envelope or one of my double window envelopes. The paid bill then gets dropped into a pocket folder marked "Plumbing 1994" or some such.

When I first got Quicken, I bought their three-to-a-sheet laser checks. They drove me nuts. The voucher checks come one to a sheet with stubs. Now, writing computer checks is so easy that I pay vendors who come to my house, like plumbers, with a Quicken-generated, laser-printed check. It used to be such a pain in the neck that I only paid bills twice a month in batches. I would write manual (old-fashioned) checks if I only needed one immediately.

Memorized transactions

Quicken lets you tell the computer to memorize transactions. After you write a check or record a deposit, you can select "Memorize." When you do, the program remembers that transaction. Next time you begin to enter a deposit or write a check to the same vendor, the entire previously memorized transaction will jump onto the screen after you type the first several letters. If the amount is the same every time, as with a mortgage payment, the computer will change the date to today's date and you simply hit the enter key to do the entire transaction. In other cases, you will only have to change the amount and maybe the invoice number before hitting the enter key.

Elecrtonic payment

Checks are an anachronism. Although they are still the primary way of paying bills, they are clearly on the way out. I have been paying utility bills by authorizing automatic withdrawal from my bank account for years. I have used debit cards to purchase things. Quicken has an arrangement with at least one bank whereby you can pay bills electronically through that bank. That is, you write your "checks" on the computer screen, then, instead of printing them, you transmit them electronically to your bank and they credit the accounts of the payees. No stamps, no checks, no envelopes, no delay while the check is in the mail. Banks charge less for this than for checks. You should pay electronically whenever you can. It's cheaper and uses less of your time.

Check register

When you write a **manual** check, you also make an entry into your check register showing the amount, check number, payee, and purpose. You end up writing some information two or three times—once on the check, once in the register, and, in the case of the payee's name and address, often on the envelope.

A pegboard system will save some of those wasted steps. But a computer's even better.

After I've created my checks, I tell the computer to print a check register. The check register is a report which lists all the records with today's date on them. It puts them in check-number order and shows the payee, amount, category, and class. In the right-hand column, it shows the balance in the account.

Income statement

Once a month, I have Quicken print an income statement. It lists income and expenses by category and class and calculates the net. You can copy the income statement electronically and carry it over to a twelve-month spread sheet program like the one shown earlier in this chapter. But it's a bit tricky. I still do that manually because it's easier. You can also tell Quicken to calculate the income staement for the last twelve months, which gives you the right-hand column of the twelve-month cash-flow spread sheet.

Leigh Robinson, author of the book, *Landlording*, offers a set of word processing and spread sheet templates for real estate investors. It includes 30 word processing templates with landlord letters like eviction notices as well as 14 spread sheet templates:

- Holdings analysis
- Loan payment calculator
- Rent roll
- Rental income record
- Rental income record with occupancy percentages
- Loan table
- Loan table for daily interest rates
- Loan table for variable interest loans
- Financial qualifier
- Depreciation record
- Monthly income/expense analysis
- Financial statement
- Depreciation statement
- Acquisition *pro formas*

There is also a "Quicken Jump Start Kit " on the *Landlording* disks. It has the categories that you would want to use for a rental-property business. That saves you the time to think about and input the categories yourself.

In order to use it, you need an IBM-compatible computer or a Macintosh and a spread sheet program that can read Lotus 1-2-3 or Excel files and any word-processing program. You can order it from me. Specify which type of computer you have an, if IBM, what size disks you use.

PART TEN:
<u>ABSENTEE MANAGEMENT</u>

32

Absentee Management

Absentee is synonymous with bad. As in "absentee management" or "absentee ownership." Or at least that's what you hear.

It's not true.

I used to believe it. Until I became an absentee owner and manager by accident.

I owned 8 units in southern New Jersey. And I had signed a purchase agreement for 12 more there. About that time, I was accepted at Harvard Business School and moved to Boston.

At first, I went to New Jersey once a month—to check on the properties. But after being there twenty minutes, I'd think to myself, "So what's to check? It's the same building it was a month ago."

Gradually, I cut back to every other month. And the world did not come to an end.

Managing New Jersey properties from California

While I was at Harvard, I decided that returning to South Jersey would be anticlimactic. So my wife and I decided to move to the San Francisco area. But I still had my 20 units (in five buildings) in New Jersey.

Obviously, that eliminated my bi-monthly inspection visits. I even had the New Jersey tenants send the rent to me in California. And I called them if it didn't arrive on time. The world still didn't come to an end.

Managing Texas apartments from California

Originally, I planned to exchange my New Jersey properties for one California apartment building. But that was 1978.

Prop 13 passed in June of '78. Tenants had been promised rent **decreases** if it passed. Although nary a landlord who would admit to making such a promise could be found after it passed. In fact, most landlords **did** give their tenants a small rent reduction after Prop 13 passed—under threat of rent control.

But not **all**. The evening news guys had no trouble at all finding little old ladies who had voted for Prop 13 in order to get a rent reduction—and instead got a rent **increase**. In fact, they were able to find a different one each night for weeks.

As a result, Governor Jerry Brown said he would sign a state-wide rent control bill in the California legislature. And Jack Reed (that's me) said "Adios," to California for investment purposes. I exchanged my New Jersey properties for a **Texas** building instead.

Absentee for 17 years

I started my career as an absentee landlord in 1975. In total, I had 17 years experience as an absentee owner. I never had any absentee-caused problems. So I'm long since convinced that there's nothing wrong with absentee management. Absentee is **not** synonymous with bad.

Two tricks

There are two tricks you need to know to succeed as an absentee manager:

• Have more than one employee
• Give the tenants your name, address, and phone number.

More than one employee

If you have only one employee, you'll have to travel to the area in question to hire a new one. That's expensive. And you do have to hire new employees when the old ones quit or get fired.

If you have **two** employees, when one quits, the other can hire the replacement. I've done that many times. In fact, when I wrote the first edition of this book, I had not met either of my resident managers. $1,500,000 worth of apartments and I'd never met the people managing them. Sound crazy? I don't think so.

I had two employees at the 12-unit I owned in New Jersey. A tenant who acted as a leasing agent and lease enforcer. And a fellow owner/member of the apartment association who acted as my maintenance man. The leasing agent got a rent discount. The maintenance man was paid an hourly rate when needed. The tenants had the phone number of the maintenance man. He lived in a house across town.

Replacing managers

On one occasion, my leasing agent quit. So I told the maintenance man to lease their apartment and to insist that the new tenants take the leasing agent job. He did. Then several weeks later, he took a job in Africa. So I called the leasing agent, whom I had never met, and asked her to hire a maintenance man.

"I don't know anything about maintenance," she said. *"I don't even know anything about leasing except what I've learned in the last three weeks."*

"Not to worry," I told her. Then I dictated an ad for her to put in the paper. And I sent her a stack of employment applications and a list of questions to ask the applicants. After she had several applicants, I asked her to read me their applications and to give me her visual impressions. We agreed on one and he was hired. Later I had to replace him and we repeated the process.

More recently in Texas, I had to replace a number of managers. My buildings are 23 miles apart. So I had the manager of the DeSoto building interview applicants for the Fort Worth job—and hired one. Then the DeSoto manager gave two weeks notice that she was quitting. And I had her interview applicants for that job, too. We ended up hiring one of the tenants.

In both cases, the manager did the interviewing. And I checked the references by phone.

Tell the tenants how to get in touch with you

Your tenants should know how to reach you. This is important in **all** cases. And required by law in many, if not most, states. But it's especially important in absentee ownership.

If your manager is messing up, some tenants will probably let you know. Not all of them. Many will just move out. But a small percentage will complain to you before they move. Then you can investigate and take appropriate action.

"Won't the tenants bother me if I give them my number?" you may wonder.

No. I gave the tenants my home address and phone number from 1969 to 1992. I got very few phone calls. And I **wanted** to get the ones I got. Most were from tenants who wanted me to tell the manager to ease off on enforcing some lease provision. My answer was typically a firm no.

On the occasions when I've had a bad manager, the tenants complained about the manager. I investigated. Some complaints were vague. But the very fact that the tenant was complaining was indicative of a problem. If the tenant has confidence in the manager, the tenant will not complain. Lack of confidence—whether based on a concrete incident or a vague feeling—is a serious matter. Resident managers must be the kind of people who win the tenants' respect.

Good management transcends distance

Good management is good management. Absentee owners can be lousy managers. So can local owners. But absentee owners who pay attention can do as well or better than the average local owner.

Earlier in the book, I mentioned that I caught a manager using my electricity. At that time, I was charting my electric consumption. When it jumped one month, I immediately told the two employees to be on the look out for electricity thieves. One confessed.

A local owner might have overlooked that. Because the manager would generally know when to expect the local owner to inspect. And the local owner probably wouldn't chart his electricity consumption.

In other words, being local is no guarantee that you'll manage well. And being absentee is no guarantee that you'll manage poorly.

The full court press

I have an absentee management technique which I call the "full court press." I don't like to use it because it takes too much of my time. So I only use it when I think I have a management problem.

When I'm in the full court press, a leaf will not fall on the property without my being aware of it. That's an exaggeration—but not by much.

The full court press consists of:

- Calling the manager frequently
- Calling the tenants frequently
- Having the property inspected frequently.

Calling the manager

Absenteeism on the part of the manager is a serious problem. And it's exactly the kind of thing a bad manager thinks she can get away with on an absentee owner.

But if I call several times a day at random times, it's hard for the manager to keep her absence a secret from me.

Calling the tenants

Calling the tenants makes for even tighter management. You can call one a month. Or one a week. Or one a day. Or even more.

I did that on one manager I suspected of being bad. One tenant told me there were four newspapers in front of the manager's door. She got the paper free from the publisher because they wanted her to alert them to new tenants and move-outs. As is often the case when people get things for free, she let them pile up for days.

That makes the place look uncared for and unattended.

I immediately called the manager and asked about the papers. Imagine the manager's thought process.

This guy's 1,500 miles away and he knows that I haven't picked up my papers for four days!

If you call a majority of the tenants, you'll know about everything there is to know about the place. It helps if you have a list of questions to ask. Like:

- Are you satisfied with the appearance of the grounds?
- Are you satisfied with the behavior of your fellow tenants?
- Are you satisfied with the maintenance of the complex?
- Are you satisfied with the manager's performance?
- Is the manager available when you need her?

In addition to calling the tenants, it wouldn't hurt to call your other employees, subcontractors, and suppliers. The more calls you make and the more people you talk to about the complex, the less that can occur without your knowledge.

If you think about it, your manager's job is virtually all relating to people: tenants, prospects, suppliers, and other employees. If you **talk** to all those people **about** the job your manager's doing, what wouldn't you know? And all you need to talk to them is a **phone**. You do **not** need to be within driving distance. In fact, the average local owner would probably be so complacent about knowing what's going on that he would **not** make the effort of calling those people.

Have the property inspected

You can have the property shopped by apartment association members posing as prospective tenants in some areas. Or you can hire property managers or real estate agents to do it. Or a friend who lives in the area.

You can hire a photographer to go around and take pictures of the complex including the manager's office and the vacancies. You can hire a video taper to make a video tape of the complex including the manager's office, vacancies and common areas if you want.

I have a unique advantage. I have a mailing list of people who have bought my books. I could contact people on that list in the area in question and probably would find a great many fellow real estate investors who'd be willing to go around and check on my property for an appropriate fee.

If I wanted to, I could probably have the complex inspected every day by a different person. Those of you without mailing lists could probably have it inspected at least every week for a small fee. The cheapest inspector would probably be a home owner who lived nearby.

If I have vacancies, I could have a private investigator move into one in return for rebates of his rent checks. He could put the manager under surveillance. I never did that. But you can see the lengths one can go to in order to make sure no problems go unnoticed.

With a real full court press, an absentee owner can have a manager thinking she'd better clean off her desk, pick up the empty bottle in the rear parking lot, and brush her teeth or the owner will be calling about it the next day. That's too time-consuming for normal operation. But it can be done when you suspect you may need to replace the manager.

Why go absentee?

All things being equal, local ownership and management is best. But things are rarely equal. I live in California. Nice place to live. But I wouldn't want to invest there. At least not in apartments. Too much possibility of rent control. Texas all but prohibits rent control. And the political climate is likewise superior to California's.

Plus, at the time I invested in Texas instead of California, California prices were ridiculous. Ten to twelve times gross. I paid four in Texas. True, the operating expenses are a little higher in Texas. But not that much higher. Texas buildings simply had greatly superior capitalization rates. The mid-eighties collapse of the Texas market does not affect my faith in the wisdom of absentee management. The market collapsed just as much for landlords who were born and raised in Texas as it did for the absentee owners who have property in Texas. Indeed, the devastated Texans now wish **they** had invested absentee.

So if where you want to live also happens to be a good place to invest, great. Don't invest absentee. But if your situation is like mine, don't **hesitate** to invest absentee.

I suspect my properties would operate slightly more efficiently if they were within driving distance of my home. But if the cap rates were lower, that lower return would more than make up for the increased efficiency.

Another way to think of it is that you have to look at a lot more properties to find a decent cap rate (like 10%) in some areas than others. Time is money. So staying local in many cases dramatically increases the amount of time it takes to find a decent deal. That extra time, in turn, reduces the return you get by increasing your "investment" in the property.

PART ELEVEN: LOAD FACTOR

33

Reducing the Load Factor

Load factor is a phrase usually applied to office buildings. The load factor is the percentage of enclosed space which is not rented. Unrented space would be the space used for hallways, lobbies, elevators, janitorial closets, rest rooms, etc.

The lower the load factor, the better.

In other words, if you have to **build** it, you might as well **rent** it.

Reducing the load factor increases both your cash flow and building value.

The partially completed angle

Another way to look at load factors is that they are partially completed parts of the property. For example, the guys who built my Cottonwoods Apartments put thirteen car ports under one of the three buildings. They thought that was an improvement over just a foundation.

But the next owner looked at those carports and saw partially completed garages. By adding just doors and side walls, he'd have rental garages. He already had the land, the concrete floor, the back wall, and the roof of the garages.

Normally, you have to buy the land and pay for the floors and roofs as well as the doors and walls. But here was a situation where the owner could buy garages for the price of doors and side walls alone. That's almost certain to meet the three-year payback criterion.

The underutilized angle

When I bought that building, as I told you earlier, I decided there was too much storage space. So I simply rented it out. No physical changes whatsoever.

Enclosed patios at the Greenbriar

My Greenbriar Apartments was a two-story garden building. The second floor had a balcony running around the entire complex. The balcony had a roof, but it was otherwise open to the weather. Here's a drawing of the second floor of the property including the balcony.

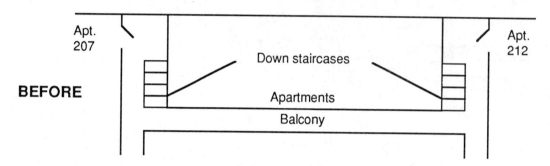

Note that apartments 207 and 212 are at dead-ends of the balcony. Only those tenants would have occasion to use the balcony in front of their apartments. All other apartments face balcony which must be crossed by other tenants.

I noticed on one of my inspection trips that the tenants in those two apartments stored things on the balcony in front of their apartment. Apartment 207 even had lawn chairs out there indicating they used it as a sort of private porch.

I decided it might be worthwhile to make it even more private. So I had my manager install a floor to ceiling wall with a door in it. The wall was made of 1 x 6's standing on end and louvered like a partially opened venetian blind. That allowed any breeze to pass through. But gave the tenants visual privacy. There was already a wrought iron railing where the balcony ended so we did nothing there. Here's a drawing of the what it looked like when we were done.

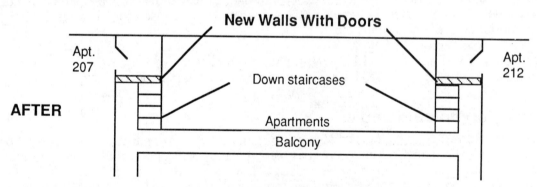

We were able to get approximately $10 or $20 a month more for these two apartments as a result of these enclosed breezeways. I don't know how much for sure because we only had two. We were getting $380 for them when I sold it. Normal two bedrooms were renting for $360 to $370. But the $370s probably moved in after the tenants in 207 and 212 agreed to pay $380.

The wall and door cost us about $300. To get a three year payback, we'd had needed to raise the rent $100 a year or $8.50 a month.

Converting a store room into a bedroom

In that same building, apartment 219 used to be a one-bedroom apartment. It's now a two. That's because it was beside a small store room on another dead end of that balcony. Here are before and after diagrams.

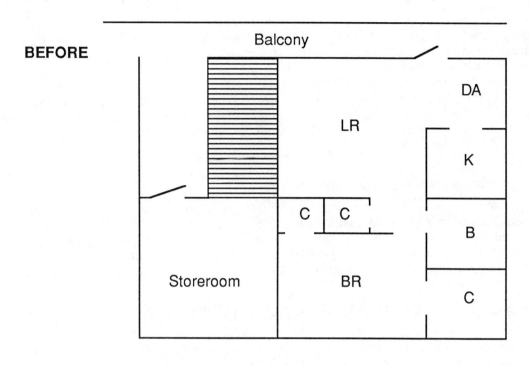

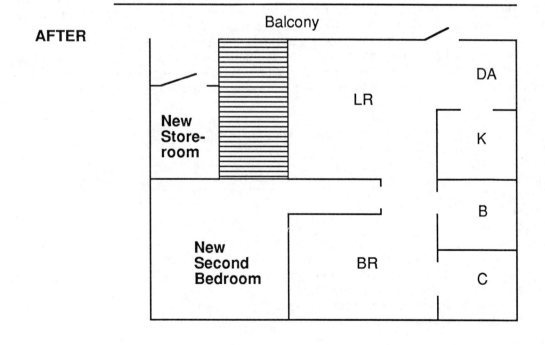

The store room already had one window and a door. The floor was balcony concrete, the walls were open studs, and the ceiling, joists open to the attic. It was big enough at about 12 x 14. All it needed was:

- Carpet
- Sheetrock on the walls and ceiling
- Entrance from the apartment
- Closet
- Electric outlets

In the after drawing below, you can see how we created the entrance and closet. The store room entrance became the doorway between the bedroom and its closet. We even got a store room out of the deal by building one in the dead end space between the stairway railing and the wall on the balcony.

Payback on store room conversion

Converting the store room to a second bedroom on that apartment raised its rental value by $30 a month. I'm absolutely sure of that. Because we had plenty of ones and twos. The twos always rented for $30 more than the ones. And when we offered 219 as a two it rented at a two-bedroom rent.

Making the conversion cost us about $900. So we would have needed a $900/3 = $300/12 = $25 a month rent increase to meet the three-year payback criterion. We did better than that.

Converting a store room to an efficiency apartment

The Greenbriar had another store room. It was 24 feet by 14 feet. It contained one door, one window, the telephone panel, and two flue pipes from the boiler and hot water heater in the mechanical room below. Fortunately, the flue pipes were right next to the walls.

As with the other store room, the walls were open studs and the ceiling joists open to the attic. The floor was concrete.

This store room was too big at 336 square feet to make into a bedroom. Although **two** bedrooms would have been about right. Since this store room was on the corner of the building, we could have added one bedroom to each adjoining apartment. The problem with that was there was only one window in the store room. And one of the adjacent apartments was **already** a two bedroom.

336 square feet was also too small to be a one bedroom apartment. So we made it into an efficiency. That took:

- Sheetrocking walls and ceilings (including boxing the two flue pipes)
- Carpet in the living/bedroom and closet
- Vinyl in the kitchen and bath
- Tub, toilet, and vanity lavatory
- Plumbing for kitchen and bath
- Kitchen sink
- Kitchen cabinets
- Refrigerator
- Range
- Heat pump
- Doors for bathroom and closet
- Lights for closet, bath, kitchen, and dining area
- Wiring for outlets and appliances
- Wall bed.

Wall bed

I had seen the booth of SICO Incorporated (Box 1169, Minneapolis, MN 55440) at the National Apartment Association convention. SICO makes those beds which fold up into the wall. We bought a queen-sized version for this efficiency. In retrospect, I think a sofa bed would have been smarter. In fact, you could probably not supply a bed and leave it up to the tenant to provide either a sofa bed, fold-up bed, or whatever. Here's the **after** floor plan:

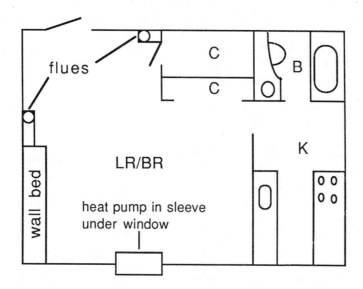

Payback on the efficiency

The efficiency rented for $275 when we got it done. I meant for the tenant to pay the utilities. But the electric company gave us some kind of hard time about it so we didn't.

$275 x 12 = $3,300 a year more rent. The electric bill for that building was about $540 a year per unit the last year I owned it. Subtracting that from the $3,300 leaves $2,760 net. With that much increased net income per year you could afford to spend $2,760 x 3 = $8,280 on the conversion and still meet your three-year payback criterion.

As I recall, it cost us about $5,000. So it paid for itself in only $5,000/$2,760 = 1.8 years.

Converting a three-bedroom to two apartments

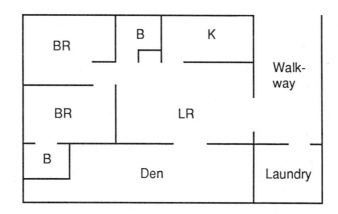

Another corner of that same building originally had an enclosed patio. Enclosed by an eight foot high brick wall. That patio was adjacent to a two-bedroom apartment. It had no roof. The manager moved into that apartment—and asked the owner for permission to cover the patio with a roof—and finish off the resulting space into a family room and second bathroom. When they were finished, apartment 117 looked like the preceding floor plan.

Now that probably added $20 or $30 of value to the apartment. Although I'm not sure what you'd call the finished product. Two bedrooms, two baths, and den? Three bedrooms, two baths? Anyway, our two-bedrooms rented for $370 at that time. So let's say the three-bedroom, two-bath version of 217 was worth $400. I never got to find out because it was the manager's apartment.

Convert to a one and a two

The added space was 14 feet 10 inches x 31 feet 2 inches or 462 square feet. Too small to be a one-bedroom. But it was adjacent to the first floor common laundry room. If you moved the laundry room to the mechanical room, and added the old laundry room space to the addition, the dimensions would be 14 feet 10 inches x 42 feet 5 inches or 629 square feet. That **is** large enough to be a one bedroom apartment.

The addition space already had a bathroom. Although its doorway went into the bedroom of the two-bedroom apartment. And the space already had carpet, sheetrock, and electrical.

The laundry already had plumbing and electrical for a kitchen.

To convert the space to a one-bedroom apartment, you'd need to seal off two doorways, relocate a bathroom plumbing fixture or two, put in some windows, add a couple walls to create a bedroom, install a heat pump. You'd also need to spend some money on the new laundry room. Here's a rough **after** floor plan.

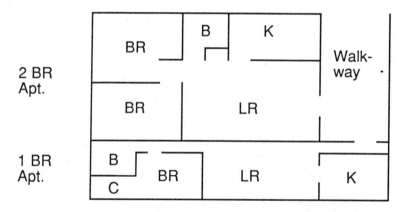

The payback

Then you'd have a normal two-bedroom and an almost normal one-bedroom. Two bedrooms rent for $370 and ones for $340. So the total income on the space would go from $400 as a three to $340 + $370 = $710 for a one and a two.

The increment would be $710 - $400 = $310 a month. Electricity costs would be a little higher. But most of that space is already heated and cooled. So let's say the additional electric would be $400 a year. That gives you a net increase in income of $310 x 12 = $3,720 - $400 = $3,320.

To get a three-year payback, you could afford to spend $3,320 x 3 = $9,960 to make the conversion. Could it be done for that? I suspect so. It's similar in scope to the store room to efficiency conversion. $6,000 or $7,000 ought to do it. I don't know because I sold the building.

Apartment load factors

Look for carports which can be turned into rental garages, store rooms which can be turned into apartments or additional rooms for existing apartments. Look for dead ends in interior hallways which can be converted to rentable apartment space. Here are two drawings illustrating one version of the interior dead-end hallway conversion.

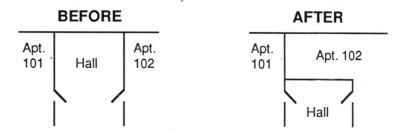

Look for **exterior** dead ends on balconies and on the ground floor.

- If you can't convert the space in question into an apartment, convert it into a room.
- If you can't convert it into a room, convert it into a storage area to be rented to your tenants.

I've thought about but haven't done the following. Build wooden storage lockers with dead bolt keyed locks and rent them to tenants and non-tenants for storage of skis, snow tires, etc. Miniwarehouses typically rent spaces as small as 5 feet by 5 feet (for $22 a month in an example in the book *Self-Service Storage*). You could tuck such lockers in little dead ends and odd space that was too small or too poorly located to become the interior of an apartment.

The basic idea of reducing the load factor is to get the maximum rent out of every nook and cranny in the building. Don't forget that in addition to the three-year payback in the form of additional cash flow, you also get an increase in building value. For example, at a five times gross rent multiplier, my various load factor reductions created the following value increases:

Item	Cost	Increased Rent	Increased Value
Breezeways	$600	$360/yr	$1,800
Bedroom	$900	$360/yr	$1,800
Efficiency	$5,000	$3,300/yr	$16,500
One bedroom	$7,000	$3,720/yr	$18,600

This can be done with single-family rental houses, too. John Beck, editor of the *Distress Sales Report* and author of several books on foreclosure and other distress property investing, says he bought a one-bedroom house in Daly City, California in 1977 at a bargain price—$32,000—because of its only having **one** bedroom. But it had a formal dining room as well as an eat-in kitchen. So he converted the dining room to a second bedroom at a cost of $500 and sold the house two and a half months later for $39,000 **after transaction costs**.

PART TWELVE:
EMERGENCIES

34

Emergencies

Fire

If you or your manager gets a report of **smoke, flames, or fire odor**, call the fire department immediately. Do **not** go investigate to see whether there **really** is a fire. Fire moves unbelievably fast. Seconds really do count. Wasting time to make a preliminary investigation can literally kill people. Preliminary investigations are appropriate for virtually every other human activity. But they are most definitely **not** appropriate for **fires**.

However, **after** you have reported the possibility of a fire to the fire department, it's OK to investigate whether there really **is** a fire—as long as you do not put yourself in a location where you do not have a fast, clear exit if indeed you find a smoke or flames. If you find there is **no** fire, call the fire department again and tell them.

The **second** thing to do when there **is** a fire is evacuate the building. Do that by pounding on doors and windows and telling people to evacuate immediately because of the report of a possible fire. If you **know** there's a fire, say so. The third thing to do is call for appropriate medical help for anyone too **injured** to care for themselves.

If your property is in a high-crime area, you may be found liable for negligence if you do not provide window bars. But if a tenant is injured because window bars prevent them from getting out in a fire, you may be liable for that, too. If you have window bars, they need a quick-release mechanism, which adds about $50 per set of bars.

After the fire's out

After the fire's out and the injured have been taken care of, you have three things to worry about:

- Insurance claim
- Repair
- Possible lawsuits against you.

Public adjuster

I recommend that you hire a public adjuster to handle the claim. Ask for and check their **references** before you hire them. But act quickly.

I had a fire in 1985. And I used a public adjuster (David Hann of the Beneke Company, 214-369-2334). I was surprised at how much I did **not** know about processing a claim. He more than earned his fee. For example, his list of things to claim exceeded what I would have come up with. Here's a partial check list to make sure you don't overlook anything:

- Insulation replacement (it's no good after it gets wet from fire hoses)
- Sheetrock replacement
- Demolition and removal expense
- 10% overhead when you act as general contractor
- 10% contractor's profit when you act as general contractor
- Carpet and pad replacement
- Painting
- Heating and air-conditioning
- Electrical

- Plumbing
- Roof
- Cleaning
- Fire-related phone calls
- Water vacuuming
- Extra water cost due to leaking pipes or water left running to prevent freezing pipes
- Rent loss due to affected tenants breaking leases
- Re-letting fee (if in lease)
- Drapes
- Appliances
- Extra expense to prevent loss of tenants.

Your fire may have other items.

Insurance cost estimates versus receipts

Most property owners use receipts as the basis of insurance claims. That's incorrect. Public adjusters have standard cost figures which they use. Their cost figures are generally higher than your receipts. The difference is that as a landlord, you are sort of an insider in the repair industry and, as such, you can get stuff done more cheaply than normal.

For example, most apartment owners can get apartments painted for $100 or so. But if you call painters out of the *Yellow Pages* and get three bids, the cost would be much higher. Public insurance adjusters use the kinds of figures those *Yellow Pages* advertisers would charge.

The insurance industry figures are higher because:

- You often use your employees or regular subcontractors who work more cheaply for you because of the volume of work you give them.
- You may use lower quality materials than the "like kind and quality" your policy entitles you to.
- General contractor overhead and profit.

You are entitled, under your insurance policy, to hire a general contractor and tell him to take care of the whole mess. Most landlords wouldn't do that because they are used to supervising repairs and don't want the hassle of recruiting and supervising a general contractor. And landlords are typically too cheap to stand by and watch a general contractor do the work much more expensively than they would do it.

If the insurance company's adjuster tries to force you to use a particular contractor, resist. If the insurance company **insists**, scrutinize the specifications with a magnifying glass to make sure you will be getting "like kind and quality." And scrutinize his work before you pay him. You should also insist on:

- A performance bond,
- A certificate of appropriate insurance coverage from his insurance agent, and
- The contract between you and the insurance company's contractor be one recommended by the state society of civil engineers or American Institute of Architects.

In other words, Marquis of Queensbury all the way. Public adjusters typically get from 7% to 10% of the claim check you receive from the insurance company.

Ask major real estate owners in your area who they recommend. Also make sure the guy you hire is state licensed and a member of the National Association of Public Insurance Adjusters (www.napia.com). A license and membership in NAPIA are not proof positive of competence or honesty. But they are a reasonable minimum to set.

Flood

Wet carpet and pad can be salvaged—if you act **quickly**. The action you need to take is water vacuuming. You can rent a water vacuum and do it yourself. But there are so many guys who do it for a living that it's probably better to call one of them. In the apartment industry, the guys who do the water vacuuming are generally the same guys who do the steam cleaning of the carpets on turnover. If the water sits on the carpet very long, it may still be salvageable by a combination of water vacuuming and deodorizing. The pad, however, cannot be salvaged if it is waterlogged. It mildews.

Don't be too sanguine about the flood being your insurance company's problem. Lots of water problems are **excluded** in insurance policies.

Pestilence

I was in the landlord business from 1969 to 1992. For my first 19 years, I never used a pest control guy on a **monthly** basis. Hadn't found it necessary. In the last four years, I did use them. The reason was that I was unable to get rid of tenants' roaches on my own and because so many people nowadays are lawsuit happy. I have not found that professional pest control guys can get rid of roaches. But they seem to be the best available response. I now prefer to have an outside professional rather than my employee apply the chemicals because chemicals are a dirty, litigious word nowadays. In this era of chemicalphobia, it makes more sense to use an outside, trained, certified professional than to try to train your own people. There are also now state laws about who can use insecticides. Doing it yourself or having your employees do it may be illegal.

Lawsuit

Landlords get about one lawsuit threat per 100 tenants per month. When I managed about 300 units, my secretary would get all upset because a tenant threatened to sue us over one thing or another. I finally calmed her down by suggesting that the threat of the moment be entered in our office "Lawsuit-Threat-of-the-Week Contest." That made her realize that we were getting a lot of them and that hardly any suits were ever filed.

When it comes to lawsuits, many are threatened but few are filed—especially when you are dealing with tenants. Many tenants have an Archie Bunker style notion of how the law works. But when they consult with an attorney, they usually learn that they either have no case or, if they have an arguable point, that the probability of victory is far from certain and/or that the possible award exceeds the cost of winning. So they drop the idea when they've cooled off.

But sometimes they **don't** drop it. Sometimes they file the suit.

When you are threatened, you should promptly tell your insurance agent. You should also investigate the facts and preserve the record. **Facts** are what wins lawsuits in most cases. Not law book stuff. And facts are not what you **say** they are. Facts, for litigation purposes, are what you can **prove** in court. That takes: documents, physical evidence, and witnesses.

Having witnesses means more than just noting the names of people with pertinent knowledge. You must **capture** what they know **immediately**. Memories fade quickly. Plus, most people do not want to **get involved** in a lawsuit. So their memory fades even faster—like Washington officials,' "I can't recall."

If you need legal advice, try visiting www.courttv.com/legalhelp/business.

Get a statement

Get a statement from them immediately after the incident if you can. The sooner the better. If possible, type it up and have them sign it in front of a notary. Such affidavits are not admissible in court *per se*—but they **can** be used to impeach a witness (prove he or she is lying). That is, if a witness testifies differently in court than what they said in their affidavit, you can ask in court why they said otherwise on the affidavit. Plus the witness can use the affidavit to "refresh their recollection." That should eliminate the I-don't-want-to-get-involved-and-therefore-don't-remember line.

If there is physical evidence, like a damaged railing, photograph it, measure it, remove, and store it where possible. And if it seems like it might be necessary, have an expert witness examine it before you destroy his ability to do so.

If you are covered by insurance, an insurance company investigator will do the gathering. But they may not do quite as good a job as should be done. And if a judgment is rendered against you— which **exceeds** your policy limits—you'll wish you had preserved the evidence when you could.

Walt Disney Company is apparently a champ at lawsuit prevention and lawsuit winning. An article I read in *The Wall Street Journal* (Couldn't find it in the library to give you the date), said Disney rarely loses a personal injury suit at its theme parks—partly because they're not guilty. The parks are extremely well-designed and maintained—but also due to the fact that whenever an injury occurs, a platoon of Disney employees appears. Call them Mouseka-investigators.

Steno pads in hand they ask everyone on the scene what happened—and their name, address, and phone number. They also write down everything the injured says. Typically, that includes such statements as, "Oh, it was all my fault" or "I told him to watch what he was doing" or "I just took my eyes off him for a minute." You can imagine how those statements sound in court years later when the injured party decides to sue Disney.

Threat of rent control

There are a number of organizations and individuals that have expertise in fighting rent control. In fact, you'd be amazed at their skill level. They are veterans of numerous political campaigns around the country—mostly victorious campaigns for the landlords.

I participated in one in Pennsauken, New Jersey. The town council passed a rent control ordinance on the first reading. But to become law, it had to pass again at a **second** reading. Local landlords not only in Pennsauken but also surrounding areas mobilized. When our representatives first contacted the town council, they laughed in our faces. They apparently assumed that tenants were far more numerous than landlords—therefore voting for rent control was clearly an easy political decision.

Then our guys put a full-page ad in the local newspaper explaining to home owners why they should oppose rent control. We also put out a press release, held meetings, etc. At the second reading of the rent control ordinance, the Pennsauken town hall saw the biggest crowd in its history. The room was filled and a mob of people filled the grounds around the hall.

The crowd consisted largely of outraged home owners. Outraged because we told them, accurately, that rent control would raise their property taxes. (It does that by reducing the value of apartment buildings in the community. Since the local government still needs the same or more tax revenue, they have to make up for the lower apartment building assessments by raising taxes on non-rent controlled property. There are many statistical studies and quotes from tax assessors in rent controlled communities to back up the claim.)

The crowd demanded the ordinance be killed. When a councilman suggested tabling it for further study, home owners accused them of trying to pass it when the crowd was gone and demanded it be killed "now!" It was. A shaken, amazed councilman who had previously scoffed at our representatives said, "Have you guys ever thought about going into politics?"

Who ya gonna call?

Call these guys if you need to fight rent control:

California Housing Council,
  Inc.
1225 8th Street, Suite 330
Sacramento, CA 95814
916-447-3353

National Apartment Association
1111 14th Street, N.W., Suite
  900
Washington, DC 20005
202-842-4050

National Association of Home
  Builders
15th and M Street, N.W.
Washington, DC 20005
800-368-5242

National Association of Real-
  tors®
777 14th Street, N.W.
Washington, DC 20005
202-383-1000

National Multi-Housing Council
1250 Connecticut Avenue,
  N.W., Suite 620
Washington, DC 20036
202-659-3381

Bernard Walp, Political Consultant
430 Point Lobos Avenue
San Francisco, CA 94121
415-386-5013

Your local and state apartment, real estate investor, and builders associations.

Drug dealer

Drug dealers are easy to spot. They have lots of visitors who only stay a minute or so.

Terminate their leases immediately. Call the police. If the police don't respond, call an attorney.

You should come down on drug dealers with every possible legal eviction measure. Some of the ideas I've had (Check with your attorney before you employ them) include:

- Taking the license number of every visitor to the dealer's apartment in a way that the visitor sees you do it
- Photographing or videotaping the dealer's visitors
- Contacting the news media about the guy and the lack of police response
- Contacting the school board if children are among the customers and police don't respond
- Contacting the PTA if the school board doesn't respond
- Contacting the town council and mayor if police don't respond
- Bring the dealer's apartment up to a state of maintenance perfection (which will require your being inside the apartment a lot to work on it)
- File eviction papers on the slightest violation of the lease

- Post signs requiring all visitors to report to the office
- Post signs that non-resident cars who do not have visitor's parking permits from the manager will be towed then have the tow truck standing by and tow the drug buyers' cars instantly
- Make a citizen's arrest.

You may wonder why I tell you what to do if the police don't respond. Because when **I** called, they did **not** respond. The officer asked me to read him the information from the dealer's application. As soon as I said the name, the officer said, *"Oh, yeah. He's a dealer. He's out on bail."*

"So come lock him up again," I said. The police refused. I offered to let them have a vacant apartment to put him under surveillance. They declined. They wouldn't do a thing. We evicted him for non-payment of rent on the second try.

60 Minutes did a piece in which they showed police not only ignoring a neighborhood's pleas that they arrest a drug dealer—but visiting the drug dealer themselves. When it comes to drugs, police corruption is widespread. I doubt it was a factor in my experience. They seemed to just have the attitude that we already arrested and charged him. It's now the court's problem.

To add insult to injury, politicians have lately decided to crack down on the **landlords** of drug dealers. Neighbors are suing in small claims court under nuisance abatement and other laws. Berkeley, CA neighbors banded together and sued landlords in small claims court over drug dealers. They won $155,248 from a rental house owner and $218,325 from an apartment owner. We can't get help on getting rid of these guys—yet we are now to be punished for their being in our building!

What about the danger of retaliation by the dealer?

You may think, "I don't want to take action against a dealer. He might have a hit man get me."

Stay out of the landlord business if that's the way you feel. You can**not** keep drug dealers from moving onto your buildings. I've had **two**. If you do a good job of screening, you'll keep out **most** of them. But some will always get through. And if you get one, you **must** get rid of him or her (I've had one male and one female dealer). Pronto! If you don't, all your good tenants will move out.

You may not knowingly rent to a drug dealer even if he or she does not deal drugs on your property. Just renting to him or her may constitute aiding or abetting a crime (18 USC 2). Or it may be engaging in monetary transactions in property derived from specified unlawful activity (18 USC 1957). Your property could be forfeited to the government if you knowingly receive illegally obtained money or property. (*U.S. v. 92 Buena Vista Avenue, Rumson, NJ*, 97-781)

Graffiti

If graffiti appears on your property, you must remove it within 24 hours. Some cities have laws to that effect. You must remove it regardless of whether there is a law in order to prevent current and prospective tenants from concluding that your property is controlled by gangs. If it keeps coming back and you cannot afford to keep removing it, you made a big mistake when you bought in that neighborhood.

Gangs

If you anger a gang, they will kill you and there is not much you can do about it. But many times you can get rid of gangs by evicting a tenant who is a gang magnet. One of my newsletter subscribers got rid of the gangs infesting his property by getting rid of a resident manager whose daughter was attracting gang members. Later the gang members began visiting another teenage girl in the building and her family was also asked to move, which ended the problem. Some businesses, like 7-11s, have successfully gotten rid of undesirable young people by playing Muzak over public speakers. Mantovani can work wonders with young criminals. Music may not always "have charms to soothe the savage beast," but it can often make him flee in musical disgust.

Gangs generally war on each other, not on law-abiding citizens. That's because citizens are sort of organized into one big "gang" with well-armed police farces and armies if necessary.

Some apparent gang members are really just gang wannabes. They are generally not dangerous and standing up to them will usually work. Local police can probably tell you whether you are dealing with real gang members or gang wannabes.

Dangerously insane tenants

Tenants who are insane sometimes get into your building. And sane tenants change into insane tenants sometimes. For example, I've had two paranoid schizophrenic tenants.

They do things like accuse the maintenance man of stealing light bulbs, play their stereo at top volume, drive east until their car runs out of gas, report that fellow tenants are out to kill them, etc.

You are not allowed to discriminate against the mentally handicapped under the Fair Housing Amendments—unless the individual in question is a threat to the health or safety of others. In that case, get rid of them. Evict them. Terminate their lease. You're not running an asylum for the dangerously insane (although it often seems so).

One of the warning signs of a less than sane tenant is that **another** person comes to rent the apartment. As in "It's for my brother (or son or parishioner or whatever)." It's generally not normal for one adult to look for an apartment for another. It may seem to you that it's not unusual. But I'll tell you from experience that almost every tenant I've had who was helped in the apartment-finding department by a relative or priest or whatever was in some way unable to take care of himself and therefore did not belong in an apartment building. But people try to park these folks with landlords because apartment buildings and rental houses are **cheaper** than the places these people really need.

One of my tenants who was preceded by a "friend" turned out to be a paroled felon who I had to evict for being a general pain in the neck. (Under the Fair Housing Amendments, being a general pain in the neck would not be enough grounds to evict a mentally handicapped person.) Another was a wild-looking horse trainer who looked like he normally slept in the stable. Another was a paranoid schizophrenic medical doctor.

"He's OK as long as he takes his medicine," his father pleaded later. Most paranoid schizophrenics are OK when they take their medicine. And when they are institutionalized, they **do** take their medicine. But in apartments, many tend to **not** take their medicine. And apartment owners and managers can't get into the medicine administering business. If the person who wants to look at the apartment is not the person who will be occupying it, watch out!

You **must** get rid of the crazies. One of my paranoid schizophrenics got to running around with a gun to protect himself from all the people who were out to get him. The police had to remove him from our complex at gun point. If you fail to get rid of a dangerously ill schizophrenic or other insane person—and he or she injures someone—you may be held liable.

Drain backup

Tell all tenants on the same plumbing stack to immediately stop using their plumbing. In a garden building, a plumbing stack is typically two adjacent units and the two adjacent units upstairs. In other words, if sewage backs up into the toilet or bathtub in apartment 101, tell the tenants in 102, 201, and 202 to stop using their plumbing until the drain blockage is cleared. Sewage backups are generally caused by a blockage in the drain line in or below a first floor apartment. Then when another apartment on the same stack uses their plumbing, the drainage flows down and into the lowest apartment's tub or toilet. Call your plumber and a carpet cleaning guy to salvage the carpets.

Insurance cancellation

If calling agents listed in the *Yellow Pages* isn't getting you a new policy, try calling a fee-paid insurance consultant. They often can persuade a reluctant insurance company to cover you.

Late rents

The response of most landlords and managers to late rents is a continuing source of amazement to me. Very simply, you must take **immediate, forceful** action. In my buildings, if a tenant did not pay the rent on the due date, we gave them a three-day notice to quit or pay rent the **next day** (typically the **second** of the month). We also gave them a 24-hour utility turn-off notice. That's legal in Texas when the landlord pays for the utilities in question, which I did.

There was no grace period. We did not listen to explanations about why the rent was late or promises that it would be paid "on Friday." We did not treat "good" tenants any differently. The managers could say, "It's the owner's policy," thereby making me the "bad cop" to their "good cop." But they **had to** deliver the notices.

One late tenant shook off a new resident manager couple I hired by saying in response to their demand for the rent, "I'm going to talk to the owner about it." When they explained that's why they abandoned collection efforts against him, I hit the roof. My managers were to deliver the two notices the day after the rent's due, **period**. There is no explanation or promise which they are authorized to take **instead** of rent.

And they are only to stop their collection/eviction procedure when they have received cash, cashiers check, or money order. Personal checks are OK for on-time rents, but **not late** rents.

The tenant who said he was going to call me about his late rent **did** when the managers resumed their collection activities against him. He asked me if, "...we couldn't come to some agreement like adults." I said, "We already did. It's called a lease and you're in violation of it. If you don't pay your rent today in the form of cash, cashier's check, or money order, we are going to turn off your utilities and evict you."

The managers told me he then paid the late rent. Two weeks later, my bank said the check bounced. They had accepted a **personal** check in spite of my instructions to the contrary.

If the tenant files bankruptcy, immediately file a motion to lift the stay bankruptcy creates.

Skips

Boulder, CO landlord Lowell Campbell rents to students. When they skip owing rent, he sues in small claims court and wins a default judgment. He then sends that to the five main credit bureaus. Later, when the former students apply for jobs and credit, they are embarrassed by the outstanding judgment and pay it off. You can sometimes find skips by:

- Send a letter to their old apartment with "address correction requested" under your return address.
- Contacting their employer (should be listed on their rental application).
- The Department of Motor Vehicles may tell you where they are. It helps to have the drivers license number (you should have written it on the lease or application) and/ or license plate number. Some high school reunion committee got my address from the California DMV and sent me letters urging me to attend their reunion. They had a classmate named John T. Reed.
- If the skip works in a field that requires a state license, the state licensing board can probably tell you where he lives now.

Even if you cannot find them now, you may want to try to obtain a judgment against them. Often, the penniless bad tenant stiffs you, then later becomes more affluent. He may graduate from college and get a job or receive an inheritance or some other windfall. In any event, judgments last for years and can often be renewed. Record your judgment. Check periodically to see if your former tenant has come into some money. If so, take action to put a lien against and execute on (sell) the assets in question.

PART THIRTEEN: HOUSES

35

Rental Houses

Most of the principles in this book apply to all residential rental property whether it be a single-family rental house or a 1,000-unit complex. Indeed, if you have lots of rental houses, you may even have roving versions of a big apartment complex's employees.

But there are a few special tricks to managing rental houses (and two- and three-family properties) which warrant mention.

Leasing

When a building gets too small to have a resident manager, leasing becomes at least a two-location operation. That is, the house is in one part of town and the owner/leasing agent in another.

Beginners typically place an ad with their home or office phone number in the paper offering the house for rent. Then as prospective tenants call, they make appointments to meet them at the rental property.

The problem is that about half the time the prospects don't show. So you waste a trip. And even when they show, you have to make lots of trips to rent a house or small building apartment.

Group showings

Experienced rental house owners like nationally syndicated columnist, Bob Bruss reduce the number of wasted trips by scheduling group showings. That is, they pick a time when they're going to show the property and tell everyone who is interested to be there then. If two or three or more people agree to be there then, at least one will probably show up thereby eliminating the wasted trip problem. Bob generally schedules showings for 5 PM to 6 PM or 7 PM the same night the prospects call. He continues to show the property to groups each night until it's rented.

Group showing is not without cost. Frequently, a good prospect cannot make the group showing—or can't wait until then to find a place—or happens to find another place before your group showing time arrives.

So group showing eliminates part of the market. That, in turn, reduces the rent you get for your property. But if the value of your time is high, the small loss in rent may be worth avoiding wasted or more numerous trips. Bob Bruss also feels the loss of part of the market is partially or completely offset by a sort of auction atmosphere which takes over when prospects see their competition for the house face-to-face.

Bruss also **asks for the prospect's name and phone number** when they call. He feels that by stripping them of their anonymity he increases the probability that they will either keep the appointment or call to cancel.

Meet at your office

Another alternative is to have the prospect meet you at your house or office. Then you drive over to the rental property in separate cars. That way, if they don't show, you haven't lost any driving or waiting time.

Give them the keys

Some owners of multiple rental houses tell the prospects to come to the owner's home or office. Then they

- Look at their drivers license photograph to verify identity
- Note the name, address, and driver's license number
- Take a $20 key deposit
- Get them to sign a receipt in which they agree
    - not to move in
    - not to smoke in the house
    - to turn off all lights and
    - to lock the place when they leave
- Give them directions and the key and
- Send them off to show themselves the house.

The key must be returned within two hours. I'd be afraid the prospect would move in without paying any rent if I did that. The tenant in the movie *Pacific Heights* would have done that. But John Schaub, a Florida real estate author and teacher, has done that for many years says he has never had a problem of that nature.

Keep lienable utilities in your name

In multi-unit buildings, the water and trash collection expenses are almost always sent to the owner. But in **single**-family rentals, it seems logical to have the tenant pay them directly.

Don't do it if the water or trash bill constitutes a lien on your property.

In most jurisdictions where the government supplies water or collects trash, the bill is a **senior lien** against your property—ahead of even a first mortgage. I know of at least one community (Pacifica, CA) where a **private** trash collection company's bills are senior liens. Most utilities with lien power are much more lenient about collecting delinquent accounts than are utilities who can**not** get a lien without winning a judgment in court. And then such court judgment liens are **junior** to all prior liens.

If you let the tenant put lienable utilities in his name, there is a chance that he'll not pay the bill. Unbeknownst to you, those bills pile up. In effect, the tenant is converting the equity in **your** property into **his** cash. By the time you find out, it will probably be too late to do anything about it. (A recent California law makes the tenant, not the landlord, responsible for such bills.)

To look at it another way, if you have the lienable utility bills sent direct to the tenant, you are extending credit to the tenant in the amount of all the bills issued since the last time you made sure the bills were current. At the very least, you should check frequently to make sure a tenant who is supposed to pay lienable utilities bills is doing so. According to the Cincinnati Real Estate Investors Association, one landlord there got stuck with a $6,500 water bill when his tenants spitefully ran the water continuously to stick him with a big bill.

Lawn watering

Rental house landlords typically have a lease clause requiring the tenant to take care of the lawn, including watering. But if the tenant **pays** for the water, he may refrain from watering in order to hold his water bill down. That, in turn, can destroy a lawn worth thousands of dollars.

So if you have the water bills going directly to the tenant, you'd better make sure that he is keeping the lawn watered

- paying the bills and
- watering the lawn adequately.

Neighbor to watch over

In a duplex or larger property, if one tenant skips out or behaves outrageously, another tenant will probably call you about it. But in a single-family house, there is no other tenant. As a result, tenants sometimes skip leaving the door wide open.

That invites vandalism. Or an injury lawsuit if a child playing in the house is hurt or if a criminal uses the house to commit a crime. And in freezing weather, abandonment can cause the pipes to freeze and burst thereby creating a deluge next time the temperature gets above freezing.

So I recommend you tell all the neighbors your name and address and phone number. Also, it's probably a good idea to get **one** neighbor to agree to watch over the place. You might call him weekly or biweekly to ask how things look.

Neighbor to show or lease

Using a neighbor to show or lease makes sense to me. If they just showed the house, you could have them send any prospects who were interested to your home or office. Although I've never done it that way. The neighbor is a sort of resident leasing agent. So he or she does not have to drive anywhere to meet the prospect. And if someone doesn't keep an appointment, it's no big deal because they're can keep on watching TV or reading or whatever.

Plus, as a result of having a stake in the neighborhood, the neighbor is motivated to keep the place occupied and to get a good tenant. Although they may be overly choosy or discriminate illegally, too.

State law may prohibit or restrict how much a person without a real estate license can do in the showing/leasing area. Although that sounds like a law that only a real estate agent could love. And I suspect no real estate agent would complain because they don't want leasing business. In the absence of a complaint, I can't imagine the authorities getting interested in the matter.

The best way to pay such a person is probably by the hour—with $6 to $10 an hour the going rate. When considering using someone else, you should remember that landlords who own three or fewer houses are exempt from the Fair Housing Amendments Act **unless** they use a leasing agent.

Type of tenants

In two-family or larger buildings, the vast majority of apartments have **one-** or **two**-bedroom apartments. They attract single people and couples.

But houses usually have **three** or **four** bedrooms. You'd like them to attract Ozzie-and-Harriet style families. And in many markets, they do. But in most markets, a three bedroom or larger unit will attract groups of **three single people**—students or young working people.

Groups of three single people are more difficult to deal with than singles or couples. They are frequently on their own for the first time and tend to behave at times like children do when Mommy's not watching. Many take pride in their sloppiness and carry deviation from normal housekeeping to extremes. For example, it is common in rental houses to find weeks of dirty dishes in the sink, mattresses on the floor instead of beds, salvaged items used as furniture, and multiple vehicles parked on the lawn.

Group living diffuses responsibility and thereby increases irresponsible behavior regarding lease obligations. The ever-present audience of recent adolescents encourages anti-social behavior. The same three guys who do expensive damage to a rental house would probably do little or no damage if each were living alone in his own apartment.

Tenant mobility

Young people **move** more than older people. And when they move, they move **farther** than older people do on average. As a result, you may get stuck with damage and find that the former tenant you'd like to sue is now in grad school two thousand miles away. Or that the grad student you rented to is now a management trainee on the opposite coast.

Because of their propensity to do more damage than one- and two-bedroom tenants, and their propensity to move beyond your reach when they leave, you should adopt **stiffer credit requirements** with three-bedroom tenants. Like a higher security deposit. And/or co-signers who own real estate in the same county.

Repairs clause

Single-family rental house landlords usually require the tenant to take care of minor repairs. They may set a limit of $50 to $100. It the repair in question costs that much or less, the tenant is to take care of it at his own expense and not even bother the owner about it. That sounds good in theory. But, in practice, it can lead to problems.

The cost of most repairs is arguable. Who's to say what costs less than $100? Virtually every repair can be made to cost more than $100 if you call an expensive outside repairman.

Making the tenant pay for repairs of more than $100 gives the tenant an incentive to make sure any repairs cost more than $100. As a result, the tenant may deliberately damage the broken item further to run up the bill. Or he may conspire with a repairman to charge more than $100 in return for a kickback.

A sliding scale incorporating the insurance principle of coinsurance strikes me as more sensible. For example, the tenant pays

100% of repairs costing less than $100
90% of repairs costing less than $200
80% of repairs costing less than $300
and so forth.

That way, the tenant always has an incentive to prevent the need for repairs or at least to minimize their cost.

But making the tenant pay **anything** for repairs increases the chances that he will let items that need repair go unrepaired. At best, that can result in a deferred maintenance surprise for the owner when the tenant moves out. At worst—if the item needing repair is a stitch-in-time type problem— neglecting it can **increase** the ultimate repair cost. So any lease which discourages the tenant from repairing or reporting maintenance problems must be backed up by a program of **inspections** to make sure the property is not being neglected.

Inventory appliances

Tenants rarely steal appliances from **apartments**. Because there are others around who might notice. But with a house, no one is likely to notice. That's another reason for a larger security deposit and more co-signers. It's also a reason to include in the lease or move-in inspection check list a list of the appliances in the house and their serial numbers. Checking the serial numbers at both ends of the tenant's stay prevents switching of your appliances with cheaper ones.

Appearance for resale

When you sell your house, the buyer will almost certainly not care what the rental income is. And he will probably care little about what the operating expenses are. So, unlike buildings with four units or more, houses do not sell on the basis of their net operating income. Because only a small percentage of the buyers plan to rent the house out. And even the few that do plan to rent the house out are far less sensitive to and sophisticated about its income and expenses than apartment building buyers are.

So the resale game in houses is based almost entirely on the **appearance** of the property. The better it looks when shown to the prospective purchaser, the better the price you'll get for it.

Professional sellers like home builders generally have **model homes** to show prospective buyers. The models are professionally decorated and accessorized (have stuff like towels, silverware, etc. displayed as if someone lived there.) Above all, model homes are in apple pie order. They are cleaned daily. The doors are removed from the bathrooms so that no one uses the toilet.

Now contrast all that with your rental house. If it's occupied by three twenty-year old students who delight in showing the world how pig-like they can be, you will pay a penalty in the form of a lower price when you sell it.

So in single-family rental houses—and to a lesser extent—two- and three-family properties— the housekeeping of your tenants will affect your resale value and therefore your overall return on investment. So you should try to get tenants whose housekeeping more resembles the builders' models than the fraternity's digs in *Animal House*. One way to do that is to charge less than market rent so you can be more choosy as to whom you rent to.

Housekeeping clauses in lease

A rental house lease should require that the housekeeping meet reasonable standards—like beds made when the property is to be shown to prospective purchasers or renters. In general, normal cleanliness standards should be required. Apartment leases generally discuss how the apartment must be on **move-out day**—but not during tenancy. Rental house owners cannot afford to be so unconcerned about how the place looks **prior** to move out.

Inspection and enforcement

With apartments, inspection of the tenants' housekeeping is rarely necessary. But with houses, regular inspection—like annually—may be necessary. And when the house is for sale, you should call every real estate agent who shows it and ask about the appearance of the house as well as the tenants' cooperation with the showing. If you get a bad report, tell the tenants to straighten out. If they fail to straighten out after reasonable warning, terminate their lease.

Bob Bruss says he drives by the property at least monthly, especially in the first months after he rents to a new tenant. He's found that if you gently reprimand them at the start, they usually behave thereafter. But if the tenants neglect the lawn, etc.—and the owner says nothing—they figure neglect is OK with the owner.

Bruss also has a carrot and stick clause in his lease. If a house has a rental market value of say, $1,000 a month, he will advertise it at that rent. But he will list the rent as $1,025 in the lease and put in a clause which says the tenant gets a $50 rent discount if they pay the rent on time and keep the lawn in good condition. If he finds the lawn is **not** in good condition during his driveby, he admonishes the tenant to get to it or "you'll lose your $50 discount."

You cannot afford to let the tenants make your property look unattractive. Nor can you afford to let them take your property off the market by refusing to cooperate reasonably regarding showings.

Cooperation with showings

Earlier in the book, I told you to have a lease clause which gave you the right to show the property during reasonable hours and with reasonable notice and with the key when no one is home. I'll just repeat the importance of having and enforcing such a clause here. A tenant who refuses to cooperate can literally prevent you from selling your own property. And grudging, minimal cooperation can knock thousands or even tens of thousands of dollars off your sale price—and therefore—off your net worth. Don't tolerate either.

Lease-option to increase income

A number of real estate gurus advocate giving the tenant a **lease-option** as a way to increase the income from a rental house. A lease-option gives the tenant the right to not only **live** in the property for a period of time—but also the right to **buy** the property for a specified price during a specified time. The theory is that this makes the tenant willing to pay **more** than market rent and to take care of the place as if it were his **own** home rather than the landlord's property.

Lease-options have potentially dire federal income tax and state law ramifications which you should understand. They also have a serious ethical consideration, that is, the vast majority of the tenants who enter into lease options do not exercise their option. That means they pay $5,000 to $15,000 in extra front money and monthly money above market rental value—and get absolutely nothing for it.

Lease options trigger the vast majority of due-on-sale clauses in conventional mortgages. The way most lease options are written, they could be recharacterized by legal authorities as land contract sales. That is, the courts could say that you did not lease option the property to the tenant—you **sold** it to him—the day the lease option began.

Recharacterization would have numerous consequences which range from bad to disastrous. Those consequences include:

• disqualification of a tax-free exchange
• being declared a dealer who cannot benefit from installment sale treatment
• inability to evict the tenant in the event of default because he is an equitable owner
• loss of interest deductions by tenant
• loss of depreciation deductions by landlord
• payments to landlord would be interest which is not passive income
• possible reassessment of property for property taxes especially in California
• possible violation of state usury law
• possible loss of over-55, $125,000 capital gains exclusion
• possible loss of right to avoid tax on home by buying one of equal or greater value within two years
• liability for failure to make required seller disclosures
• tenant evicted out of lease option may later redeem the property under equitable mortgage laws

The law is not clear on when a lease option which includes payments towards the purchase price will be recharacterized as a sale. So there is no way to draw up the documents to make sure your lease option is not recharacterized as a sale.

Charge extra for credit toward the purchase price

When you lease-option a property, you're actually doing three separate things:

• rent property
• selling the property (potentially)
• selling an option.

So you'd better get **paid** for each. That means

• get fair market rent for the rental
• get a fair price for the sale of the property
• get a fair price for the option.

Only give the tenant/optionee **credit** toward the purchase price of the house for amounts they pay each month in **excess** of the fair market rental value of the property.

And then make sure that the amount of credit you give—and the rest of the money which they have to pay to exercise the option to buy—add up to the fair market value of the property as of the expiration date of the option. For example, if you think the property will be worth $100,000 at the expiration of the option, make sure

• the amount of money they have to pay at closing to exercise the option
• plus the credit they've received for excess monthly payments they've made
• at least equals $100,000.

Many landlords give **too much** credit—like the **entire** amount of the monthly payment—and thereby sell their property too cheap. There is no reason on earth why you should sell your property for **less** than market value. And there is nothing magical about lease-options that changes that fundamental principle.

Charge extra for the option

You also charge extra for the option itself. Above and beyond the monthly fair market rental **and** the purchase price of the house. The option has value because the price may appreciate during the option period to a value **above** the option price. In that case, the tenant/optionee gets a windfall. You don't **give away** that windfall possibility. You **sell** it. And here's an example of how you price it.

Let's say your house is now worth $100,000. It's fair market rental value with no option is $700 a month. You lease-option it with an option price of $117,000 expiring in two years. You figure the probabilities of the property being worth various amounts at or above the $117,000 option price are as follows:

• $117,000   65%
• $125,000   20%
• $130,000   10%
• $135,000   5%
total   100%

To price the option, you compute a weighted average of the lost gain at each value as follows:

Option price	Market value	Lost Gain x	Probability =	Weighted amount
$117,000	$117,000	$0	65%	$0
$117,000	$125,000	$8,000	20%	$1,600
$117,000	$130,000	$13,000	10%	$1,300
$117,000	$135,000	$18,000	5%	$900
		Total	100%	$3,800

So in this example, you would make sure you got

- fair market rent of $700 a month
- $117,000 in the form of excess over $700 a month and/or lump sum payments
- $3,800 for the option.

Dan Kinter, a Sacramento lease option investor says his typical deal is structured like this:

• Value of house	$67,000
• Fair market rental value	$550
• Monthly payment required	$850
• Credit toward purchase price	$100 a month
• Option price	$77,000
• Expiration date	Three years after lease begins—no sooner or later.

He gets $200 a month extra ($850 less $100 credit toward purchase less $550 fair market rental = $200) for giving up the right to any appreciation which exceeds $77,000 (in this example).That $200 is compensation for the option itself like the $3,800 lump sum in my example above.

No matter what happens to the value of the property, Kinter is $300 better off—as long as the tenant continues to pay $850 a month—than he would have been if he had just leased the house for fair market rental value of $550. But the tenant's motivation to pay $300 extra will rapidly dissipate if the value of the property does not move up toward the option price during the option period.

If the value goes up to **less** than $77,000 less 36 months times $100 credit plus 36 months times $200 option compensation or $77,000 -(36 x $100) + (36 x $200) = $77,000 - $3,600 + $7,200 = $80,600—Kinter is also better off than if he had done a regular lease at $550 and sold the property for market three years later.

But if the value **exceeds** $80,600 at the three-year point—and the tenant/optionee exercises the option—Kinter is **worse** off than if he had not done the lease-option. But being **worse** off is not the same as being **bad** off. $80,600 still represents a nice profit on a $67,000 purchase.

Bigger vandalism

One word of management warning on the lease-option. It's **true** the tenant tends to treat the house as if he owned it in a lease-option. Because he's generally building up equity due to appreciation and his monthly credit toward the purchase price.

But if he **defaults**—and you throw him out—he gets **madder** than a tenant who's just losing his security deposit. That often translates into his doing industrial strength vandalism to the property. Five thousand dollars in one example I heard of. So beware of "scorched earth" behavior by the tenant in defaulted lease-options. And keep that possibility in mind when you are screening tenant/optionees, deciding whether to demand a co-signer, and setting security deposit amounts.

Special report on lease options

I wrote a special report on lease options. That report is indispensable to anyone who has already done a lease option or who is considering doing one. See the order form in the front or back of this book or call 925-820-7262 to order it. You can read about it at my Web site www.johntreed.com/reibooks.html.

Homeowners association dues

State laws and CC&Rs often make homeowners dues a lienable debt. As with lienable utilities, you must either pay them yourself or check frequently to make sure the tenants have paid.

PART FOURTEEN:
MAINTENANCE

36

Maintenance

Maintenance expense

Maintenance is one of the toughest expenses to write about. Or control. Because it's highly subjective. Should you replace it or patch it? Should you have your manager do it or bring in an outside contractor? Should we fix it this way or that way? These are the kinds of maintenance decisions you or your staff make every day. What's the **right** answer?

Industry standards

As I told you earlier, there are a number of industry studies on apartment expenses. IREM does one. So does Mike Scott in Seattle (www.dsaa.com)and the Dallas Apartment Association. No doubt there are others. Most of these list maintenance or repairs as a line item. IREM lists the following line items under the subcategory "Maintenance."

- Security
- Grounds maintenance
- Maintenance—repairs
- Painting/decorating

Definition is the problem

It's hard to pinpoint what the proper percentage of gross is. Because each of these studies defines the maintenance category differently. Furthermore, their definitions are less than crystal clear to the people submitting data. So some apartment owners who send their figures in are probably including maintenance expenses which others in the same study are putting under a different category.

Work backwards. Start with those things which are well-defined—like utilities, taxes, payroll, and insurance. Subtract them from the total expense figure (% of the gross, $/sq. ft. or whatever). That leaves you with what everything else should be. Then read the definitions of the other categories like supplies for each study and, if you feel confident about it, subtract those, too.

At best, you'll probably end up with a number which includes not only maintenance but also related stuff like supplies or capital expenditures. At least you can compare it with your operation.

For example, if the IREM study says garden apartments in your area have total operating expenses of 48.9% of the gross—and that 25.9% of that is clearly defined expenses like utilities, taxes, etc.—then 23% are for maintenance and other expenses. If your building uses **more** than 23% for maintenance and those other items, something's probably wrong—perhaps with maintenance. In other words, you can narrow it down. But you probably can't tell from ratio analysis alone whether your maintenance expense is too high.

R.S. Means Company, Inc. (100 Construction Plaza, Kingston, MA 02364, 800-334-3509 www.rsmeans.com) publishes two annual studies which you may want to use to measure your maintenance performance: *Building Construction Cost Data, Repair and Remodeling Cost Data.*

You gotta do what you gotta do

Maintenance is not as smooth flowing an expense as utilities or taxes. When something necessary breaks, you gotta fix it. Doesn't matter whether you'd be over budget for the year or not. So you need to avoid overreacting to a legitimate but unusually large expense. On the other hand, it's more or less normal for one big thing to go each year.

Your boiler needs to be replaced one year. That hurts cash flow. But you dismiss it by saying, *"Well, if the boiler hadn't gone, we'd have done all right. And now that we've got a new boiler, that won't happen again for many years."* Then the next year the asphalt needs major repairs. And you say, *"Well, we'd have done just fine if only the asphalt hadn't gone. Now that it's been resurfaced, we won't have that happen again for many years."* Then the next year the cooling tower goes. Then the roof. Then the compressor. Then the exterior needs painting.

Beginners tend to dismiss such once-every-ten-or-twenty-years expenses as aberrations that don't count. But after you've been in the business for a while, you notice that it's always something. If the asphalt don't get you, the roof will. A year with**out** a major replacement—**that's** an aberration.

In-house versus outsiders

As a general rule, using your maintenance man or manager to do repairs is cheaper. Most outsiders want $30 to $50 just to set foot on the place. And they have to cover their overhead, etc.

So you should encourage your in-house employees to do as much as possible. But be careful that they have both the time and the skill. Bricklaying, for example, looks terrible when done by an amateur. Amateur painting, on the other hand, usually looks pretty much the same as professional painting—assuming proper preparation of the surface was not a big factor in the particular job.

I once had my maintenance man build a concrete pad for the dumpster wheels. He had the skill to do it properly. But not the time. Threw his whole schedule out of whack for weeks. Doing that in-house was a mistake. However, a manager who calls outsiders for **everything** should be replaced.

Outside plumbing expense

Here's what I spent on outside plumbers through 12 resident managers:

Manager	$/unit/year	Manager	$/unit/year
1	$26.33	8	51.68
2	81.29	9	36.77
3	55.42	10	46.54
4	54.57	11	41.42
5	34.38	12	79.79
6	55.78	13	36.76
7	21.46		

There were two major underground leaks on manager #2's watch. Manager #7 was a plumber by trade. So $22/unit/year is about as low as you can get. The average appears to be about $40.

Pay attention

Pay attention to your maintenance bills. Go over them carefully. Ask about anything you don't fully understand. Do not pay **illegible** bills until you get an explanation. Do not pay **coded** bills like "2 zr26c's @ $14.27" without getting an explanation. I once checked on such a bill and the vendor quickly cut the bill down dramatically and seemed to be embarrassed far more than just using a code number would warrant. Compare your maintenance expense with pertinent studies. Talk to other owners and maintenance people about your expenses. Over time, you'll get a feel for what things should cost, when to go outside, the capabilities and limitations of your employees.

Pool expense

Most apartment buildings that have pools have the same size pool—about 20 feet x 30 feet. So obviously, the cost per unit of the pool is higher for the smaller complexes. I estimate that a pool adds about $5 tops to the rental market value of the apartments in the complex that has it. At that rate, the tenant is paying $60 a year to swim or $20 a month if it's a three month swimming season.

34% of tenants said they felt a pool was worthless in an Institute of Real Estate Management study (Nov./Dec. 1987 *Journal of Property Management*). Another 45% said they'd pay $10 to $20 a month extra to have a pool. A complex I used to manage charges $25/year to use the pool.

What's it cost to operate a pool? Past president of the National Apartment Association, Ro Freeman figures about $3,000 without a lifeguard. At $5 an hour, for a three month summer season, an 8-hour-a-day, 5-day-a-week life guard would add about 40 hours/week x 13 weeks x $5 per hour = $2,600. **7**-day-a-week lifeguard service would add 56 hours per week x 13 weeks x $5 = $3,640. I analyzed one of my pool buildings and came up with the following operating costs:

Supplies	$755.89
Electric for light	93.84
Electric for pump	480.00
Permit	127.50
Labor to clean	2,600.00
Water lost	1,116.90
Extra insurance	68.00
Total	$5,242.13

Other expenses that should be considered include:
• Extra property taxes paid because of value of pool.
• Capital expenses which occur from time to time like resurfacing pool.
• Energy to heat pool water if you do that.

Pools are increasingly regulated by local and state laws. Check on them your area. There may now be additional costs not on the above list.

Should you get rid of your pool?

The main way to reduce pool expense is to get **rid** of the pool. Ro Freeman says you get rid of a pool when the complex has less than 60 units. Since he says pools cost about $3,000 a year to operate, he is implicitly saying that the rental market value added by a pool is $3,000 ÷ 60 = $50 per unit per year or $50 ÷ 12 = $4.17 per month. If you use my $5 per unit additional rental market value figure, you could go as low as 50 units. But if local law required a lifeguard, as it generally does in the East, you'd need about $6,000 ÷ $60 per unit per year additional rent = 100 units to justify the expense of a pool. If you are in a year-round hot weather area like Hawaii, Southern California, or Southern Florida, the value added by the pool is probably **higher** than in an area with just a summer season and some chilly summer days.

If you are in doubt, you might figure out how much your pool costs to operate then ask the tenants who want to use it to pay a membership fee. If they are willing to pay enough as a group to cover the cost of operation and a little for your trouble, keep it running. If not, shut it down.

Check with a local pool company as to how to shut it down. The best way depends on your soil, climate, pool configuration, etc. Closing the pool should **increase** the value of your building. Because you wouldn't do it unless the additional rental market value it was contributing was less than the expense of operating it. Since you are getting rid of a big operating expense—but losing a smaller amount of income, your **net** operating income should **increase—and** thereby—your building value.

Written repair requests

Your lease may require written repair requests. If so, abide by it. And keep the requests on file. They may become important in a lawsuit. I lost a suit in which the judge said our failure to insist on written maintenance requests every time was one of the reasons he decided against me.

Playground equipment

Any playground equipment you own must comply with the two-volume Handbook for Playground Safety published by the U.S. Consumer Product Safety Commission, Washington, DC 20207 (www.cpsc.gov). Failure to comply could probably cause you to lose a lawsuit. Having a playground at all is probably a bad idea in this litigious era.

To avoid frozen pipes

- Cover outside faucets in extreme weather
- Insulate exposed pipes in crawl space and attic
- Cover air vents in crawl space and attic during extreme weather
- Insulate pipes in garages and laundry rooms
- Open cabinet and vanity doors which contain water pipes during extreme weather
- Keep minimum heat on in vacant units

Air-conditioners

Real estate guru Jimmy Napier recommends taking broken air-conditioners to air-conditioning and refrigeration schools. They need stuff for their students to work on—like getting your hair cut cheap at barber school. Also, get lots of opinions before you spend big bucks replacing air-conditioners. One of our home air-conditioners stopped working in the summer of 1990. Our regular repair guy said the whole unit had to be replaced at a cost of about $1,000. We got a second opinion. He said the same thing. The unit was unrepairable. It was the end of the air-conditioning season, so we let it go. Then we called a third guy. He was retired and only did repairs—no replacements. He fixed it and charged us $100 in the spring of 1991. As of this writing—September 9, 1998—it still works. Since 7/1/92, repairing air-conditioners has become a big deal because Freon hurts the ozone layer. Do not fool with Freon yourself unless you have the special equipment and training now required by law.

Asbestos, etc.

Rules, regulations, and laws about asbestos, PCBs, etc. are proliferating. Join your local and national apartment association to stay up to date. In general, if you have these substances, you have to take extraordinary steps to notify tenants and employees and when disturbing the substances even for routine maintenance like changing a light fixture or painting. An EPA study in 1993 found that maintenance people, even in buildings with friable asbestos, are not at risk for asbestos-related diseases.

Architectural barriers

State and federal laws now require building features that give access to handicapped people. Examples include ramps and handiapped bathrooms and parking spaces. These are typically required in new construction and **substantial renovation**, especially when government funds are used.

Lead-based paint

Buildings built before 1978 generally contain lead-based paint. Local, state, and federal governments are increasingly regulating it. And tenants are increasingly suing landlords over it. The regulations are so onerous that you should consider selling any pre-1978 buildings you own and avoid buying them in the future. You need to monitor the changing laws and comply with them.

All owners of residential property must provide current and prospective tenants and buyers with a Lead Hazard Pamphlet to be jointly published by HUD and the EPA. Knowing violation makes you liable for attorney and expert witness fees and triple damages.

Owners of buildings built before 1978 that have HUD mortgages or receive Section 8 payments must already tell all tenants and purchasers:
 • The building was built before 1978.
 • The building may contain lead-based paint.
 • Give them a HUD brochure on lead-based paint.
 • The symptoms and treatment of lead-based paint poisoning.
 • Lead-based paint maintenance and removal techniques.

Lead lawsuits are proliferating. New York City had to pay $10 million for not getting lead out of a buildiung it seized for nonpayment of taxes.(*Jose Luis Lugo v. City of New York*, No. 1651/88, NY Sup.Ct. Bronx Co.) A Massachusetts landlord was denied summary judgment in a case where a **guest** of his tenant sued for lead poisoning of their child.(*Preston Ferraro v. Leo Allard*, N, 92-CV-00009, Mass. Hsg.Ct. N.E.) A Maryland landlord had to pay $500,000 plus attorneys fees because he failed to inform a tenant of the danger of peeling paint. (*Richwind v. Brunson*, 625 A. 2d 326, MD. App. 1993) A Brooklyn home owner was ordered to move out of his home and to spend $10,000 to $15,000 to remove lead paint from his home or face fines of up to $8,500. His child had tested near the danger threshold for lead poisoning and the lab had to send the results to the Health Department.

CD-ROM repair guide

I highly recommend the *Reader's Digest Complete Do-It-Yourself Manual*. There is now a CD-ROM version which has the additional features of video and animated how-to demonstrations and an interactive program that estimates the cost of various projects.

Rational diagnosis

People often jump to erroneous conclusions when diagnosing problems, and then implement costly, incorrect "solutions" which leave the problem intact. The best antidote I know of to that mistake is to read and follow the book, *The New Rational Manager* by Kepner and Tregoe. The book sets forward an excellent, logical format for diagnosing complex breakdowns in systems. Kepner and Tregoe, Inc. can be reached at 609-921-2806.

<u>APPENDIX A</u>
Pertinent References
Books

Accredited Residential Manager Profile. IREM Statistics on ARMs.

Aggressive Tax Avoidance for Real Estate Investors by John T. Reed (same author as this book). Reed Publishing. Covers tax-saving ideas for real estate investors.

Alternatives to Master Metering in Multifamily Housing IREM. 1981.

The Americans With Disabilities Act Answer Book. BOMA.

Apartment Investing Check Lists. See *Residential Property Acquisition Handbook.*

Asphalt Pavement Maintenance and Repair: Guide to Specifying and Obtaining Services by Contract by Property Management Association, get from Community Associations Institute.

Best's Insurance Reports, Property-Casualty by A.M. Best Company. Rates insurance companies as to financial strength. Annual.

The Builders by Martin Mayer. W.W. Norton & Company. 1978. Not on property management *per se.*

Building Maintenance by Jules Oravetz, Sr. Theodore Audel & Co. Like the *Reader's Digest Complete Do-It-Yourself Manual* but more oriented toward commercial property and less well done.

Buying Right by John Schaub. Self-published.

The Dupree + Scott Apartment Market Study Dupree + Scott, Apartment Advisers, Inc. Annual study of the Seattle area apartment market including both sale terms and income/expense data.

Complying with the Americans With Disabilities Act by Fersh and Thomas. Quorum Books.

Creative Apartment Management by Duane Gomer. Duane Gomer Seminars. 1978. Your basic apartment management book.

Digging for Gold in Your Own Backyard by Gary Whalen. R.E.I. Press. 1991. How to reduce your property taxes.

Distressed Real Estate Times, Offensive and Defensive Strategy and Tactics by John T. Reed (same author as this book) Reed Publishing. 1991.

Energy Cost Control Guide for Multifamily Properties. IREM.

The Eviction Book for California by Leigh Robinson. Express. How-to-book for evicting tenants in California. Forms, procedures, etc.

Forms for Apartment Management. IREM

A Guide to Residential Management by Sidney Glassman. National Association of Home Builders. Management of huge complexes.

Handbook of Building Maintenance Management by Mel A. Shear. IREM.

Housing Manager's Resource Book National Center for Housing Management, Inc. Written by government bureaucrats.

How I Turned $1,000 Into $5,000,000 in Real Estate in My Spare Time by William Nickerson. Simon and Schuster. Contains some out-of-date numbers. But still the best book ever written on real estate. Excellent sections on apartment management.

How to Buy Real Estate for at Least 20% Below Market Value by John T. Reed (same author as this book). John T. Reed Publishing. 1993.

How to Increase the Value of Real Estate by John T. Reed (same author as this book). John T. Reed Publishing. 1986.

How to Make a Fortune Today Starting From Scratch by William Nickerson. Simon and Schuster. Companion volume to *How I Turned....* Contains questions inspired by his first book—and the answers to those questions. Includes five chapters on improvements and management.

How to Manage an Apartment House California Association of Realtors.

How to Use Leverage to Maximize your Real Estate Investment Return by John T. Reed (same author as this book). John T. Reed Publishing. 1986.

How to Write an Operations Manual: A Guide for Apartment Management IREM. 1978.

Income/Expense Analysis/Apartments IREM. Annual. Contains income and expense figures for apartments of various ages, types, and sizes broken down by major cities and regions in the U.S. and Canada. You get a free copy if you submit income and expense figures from one of your buildings on one of their forms.

Insurance Principles and Practices: Property and Liability by Riegel, Miller, and Williams. 1976. Prentice Hall.

Insurance Repair: Opportunities, Procedures and Methods by Peter Crosa, R.S. Means Co. or available through IREM.

Landlording by Leigh Robinson. Express. Excellent nuts and bolts, practical stuff on managing small apartment buildings.

Lease Options, See *Single-Family Lease Options.*

Managing Residential Real Estate by Paul D. Lapides. Warren, Gorham and Lamont. 1986. Huge (7 lb.), expensive ($68) but full of platitudes and generalities. Also contains numerous forms and full text of some pertinent laws.

Managing Single-Family Homes by Barbara Holland. IREM. 1987. Decent book aimed at Realtors® and apparently edited by committee.

The Manual of Built-Up Roofing Systems by C.W. Griffin. McGraw-Hill.

Means Repair and Remodeling Cost Data: Commercial/Residential. R.S. Means Co. or IREM.

No Cost/Low Cost Energy Conservation Measures for Multifamily Housing IREM. 1981. Pretty good, but overstates the case at times.

Non-Designers Web Book by Robin Williams and John Tollent

Pest Control: Guide to Specifying and Obtaining Services by Contract by Property Management Association. Available through Community Associations Institute.

Practical Apartment Management by Edward N. Kelley. IREM. Management of huge complexes. A bit of IREM's edited-by-committee blandness in this book.

Professional Apartmenteering by C.D. Duke Ellington. National Association of Home Builders. 1979. Lots of practical tips. Some chapters written by others so quality varies.

Property Management by Kyle, Baird, Worsek. Real Estate Education Company. Text book for property management courses.

Property Management Handbook by Cushman and Rodin. John Wiley & Sons.

Reader's Digest Complete Do-It-Yourself Manual Reader's Digest Association. Lots of photos and drawings. Very practical. Now also in a CD-ROM velsion with animations and videos, and interactive estimating worksheets.

Real Estate Investor's Monthly on Investment Strategy by John T. Reed (same author as this book). John T. Reed Publishing. 1991.

Real Estate Tax Appeals by Patrick J. Rohan. Matthew Bender & Co., Inc. Three volume expensive book for lawyers.

Redbook. Texas Apartment Association

Residential Foundations: Design, Behavior And Repair by Robert Wade Brown. 1984. Van Nostrand Reinhold Company, Inc. THE book on the subject.

Residential Property Acquisition Handbook by John T. Reed (same author as this book). Available from Reed Publishing. 1991. Check lists for buying a residential building. Covers physical inspection, financing, closing, etc.

Roofing: A Guide to Specifying and Obtaining Services by Contract by Property Management Association. Available through Community Associations Institute.

Roofing and Waterproofing Manual. Available from NRCA.

Roofs: Design, Application, and Maintenance by Maxwell C. Baker. Multiscience Publications, Ltd. Available from NRCA.

Single-Family Lease Options by John T. Reed (same author as this book). Reed Publishing. 1994.

Self-Service Storage. IREM.

Single-Family Lease Options by John T. Reed (same author as this book). Reed Publishing. 1994.

Successful Apartment Management by Robert C. Moore. Real Estate Investment Publications Company. 1972. Practical, detailed book. Probably out of print now.

The Successful On-Site Manager by King, Langendoen, and Hummel. IREM. Contains a whole lot of IREM written-by-committee, public relations-conscious blandness. Otherwise your basic apartment management book.

Survey of Income and Expenses in Rental Apartment Communities. 1990. NAA

Swimming Pool Management: A Guide to Specifying and Obtaining Services by Contract by Property Management Association. 1987. Available through Community Associations Institute.

Wage-Hour and Employment Practices Manual for the Multihousing Industry by Harry Weisbrod. Harry Weisbrod Associates, Inc. 1979. Very useful.

Periodicals

Fair Housing—Fair Lending by Prentice Hall.

Journal of Property Management IREM. Monthly.

Journal of Property Tax Management. Panel Publishers

Landlord Tenant Law Bulletin. Quinlan Publishing. Monthly.

Mr. Landlord. Home Rental Publishing Company. Monthly.

Multi-Housing News Gralla Publications. Monthly.

Professional Apartment Management. Monthly.

Professional Builder & Apartment Business Cahners Publishing Co., Inc. Monthly.

Real Estate Investor's Monthly by John T. Reed who is also author of this book. Reed Publishing. Monthly. Covers all aspects of real estate investing including residential management and upgrading.

Strategies and Solutions by John Schaub. Monthly.

Weisbrod Wage and Hour News Bulletin. Harry Weisbrod.

Addresses of Publishers

Theodore Audel & Co.
Division of the Bobbs-Merrill Co., Inc.
4300 West 62nd Street
Indianapolis, IN 46268

A.M. Best Company
no street address
Oldwick, NJ 08858

Building Owners and Managers Association
1201 New York Avenue, N.W. Suite 300
Washington, DC 20005
202-408-2662

Cahners Publishing Company, Inc.
1350 East Touhy Avenue
P.O. Box 5080
Des Plaines, IL 60018

Dupree + Scott Apartment Advisers, Inc.
4300 SW Holly Street
Seattle, WA 98136

California Association of Realtors
525 South Virgil Avenue
Los Angeles, CA 90020

Community Associations Institute
1423 Powhatan Street, Suite 7
Alexandria, VA 22314
703-548-8600

Express
P.O. Box 1639
El Cerrito, CA 94530

Duane Gomer Seminars
P.O. Box 3677
Mission Viejo, CA 92690

Gralla Publications
1515 Broadway
New York, NY 10036

Home Rental Publishing Company
P.O. Box 1366
Norfolk, VA 23501

Institute of Real Estate Management (IREM)
430 North Michigan Avenue
Chicago, IL 60611

Matthew Bender
11 Penn Plaza
New York, NY 10001

McGraw-Hill Book Company
1221 Avenue of the Americas
New York, NY 10020

R.S. Means Co.
100 Construction Plaza
Kingston, MA 02364

National Association of Home Builders
15th and M Streets, N.W.
Washington, DC 20005

National Center for Housing Management
1133 15th Street, N.W.
Washington, DC 20005

National Roofing Contractors Association
8600 Bryn Mawr Avenue
Chicago, IL 60631

W.W. Norton & Co., Inc.
500 Fifth Avenue
New York, NY 10110

Panel Publishers, Inc.
36 W. 44th Street
New York, NY 10036

Prentice Hall, Inc.
270 Sylvan Avenue
Englewood Cliffs, NJ 07632

Professional Apartment Management
P.O. Box 4164
Grand Central Station
New York, NY 10163

Quinlan Publishing Co., Inc.
131 Beverly Street
Boston, MA 02114

Quorum Books
88 Post Road West
Westport, CT 06881
800-474-4329

The Reader's Digest Association
no street address
Pleasantville, NY 10570

Real Estate Investment Publications Company
Westgate Station, Drawer 9623
San Jose, CA 95129

John T. Reed Publishing
342 Bryan Drive
Alamo, CA 94507

Real Estate Education Company
500 North Dearborn Street
Chicago, IL 60610

R.E.I. Press
36 South Washington
Hinsdale, IL 60521

John Schaub
1938 Ringling Boulevard
Sarasota, FL 34236

Simon and Schuster
1230 Avenue of the Americas
New York, NY 10020

Texas Apartment Association
606 West 12th Street
Austin, TX 78701
512-479-6252

Van Nostrand Reinhold Company, Inc.

135 West 50th Street
New York, NY 10020

Warren, Gorham and Lamont
210 South Street
Boston, MA 02111

Harry Weisbrod Associates, Inc.
10300 North Central Expressway
Suite 5-350
Dallas, TX 75231

John Wiley & Sons
605 Third Avenue
New York, NY 10158

Organizations
American National Standards Institute
1430 Broadway
New York, NY 10018

Asphalt Roofing Manufacturers Association
6288 Montrose Road
Rockville, MD 20852

Institute of Real Estate Management
430 North Michigan Avenue
Chicago, IL 60611

Multi-Housing Laundry Association
1100 Raleigh Building
5 W. Hargett Street
Raleigh, NC 27601

National Apartment Association
1111 14th Street, NW, Suite 400S
Washington, DC 20036

National Association of Professional
   Insurance Adjusters
1133 15th Street, N.W.
Washington, DC 20005

National Leased Housing Association
1800 M Street, NW, Suite 400S
Washington, DC 20036

National MultiHousing Council
1800 M Street, NW, Suite 285 N
Washington, DC 20036

Apartment House Council

National Association of Home Builders
15th and M Streets, NW
Washington, DC 20005

National Association of Realtors®
430 North Michigan Avenue
Chicago, IL 60611

National Roofing Contractors Association
10255 W. Higgins Road, Suite 600
Rosemont, IL 60018-5607

Roofing Industry Educational Institute
7006 South Alton Way # B
Englewood, CO 80112

Self Storage Association
4147 Crossgate Drive
Cincinnati, OH 45236

Single-Ply Roofing Institute
1800 Pickwick Avenue
Chicago, IL 60025

Urethane Foam Contractors Association (roofs)
4302 Airport Boulevard
Austin, TX 78722

Suppliers
D & G Sign and Label
P.O. Box BB-157
Northford, CT 06472
800-356-9269

Grainger (maintenance supplies)
5959 W. Howard Street
Chicago, IL 60648

Kroy (signs)
14555 N. Hayden Road
Scottsdale, AZ 85260
602-948-2222

Maintenance Warehouse
P.O. Box 20037
San Diego, CA 92120
800-431-3000

Mattick Business Forms, Inc. (petty cash
   envelopes)
333 W. Hintz Road
Wheeling, IL 60090

319-541-7345

NEBS (computer forms and checks)
500 Main Street
Groton, MA 01471
800-225-9550

Peachtree Business Forms
P.O. Box 13290
Atlanta, GA 30324
800-241-4623

Rapid Forms
301 Grove Road
Thorofare, NJ 08086
800-247-8384

Ready Made Safety Signs & Identification
  Products
480 Fillmore Avenue
Tonawanda, NY 14151
716-695-7300

Revere (maintenance products)
P.O. Box 39188
Solon, OH 44139
800-321-1976

Seton Name Plate Company (signs)
P.O. Drawer STD-1331
New Haven, CT 06505
800-243-6624

Ralph Schutzman & Associates, Inc.
    (pegboard rent bookkeeping systems)
1717 Baylor
Dallas, TX 75226
800-972-1074 (In TX 800-441-1459)

Southwood Corporation (signs)
P.O. Box 240457
Charlotte, NC 28224
800-438-6302 (704-588-5000 in NC)

Streamliners (forms)
P.O. Box 480
Mechanicsburg, PA 17055
800-544-5779 (in PA 800-257-6800)

World Division, USA ("Now Leasing"
  banners)
11929 Denton Drive

Dallas, TX 75234
800-433-9843

Consultants
The Beneke Company (public insurance
  adjusters)
P.O. Box 31387
Dallas, TX 75231
214-369-2334

Robert Wade Brown
Brown Foundation Repair and Consulting, Inc.
2614 B Industrial
Garland, TX 75041
214-271-2621

Construction Consultants, Inc. (roofing and
  waterproofing)
900 Pallister Avenue
Detroit, MI 48202
313-874-2770

Carolina Roofing Services, Inc.
P.O. Box 2046
Monroe, NC 28110
704-283-8556

Greg Crouch, CIC
Crouch Insurance Consulting, Inc.
600 Congress Avenue, Suite 1700
Austin, TX 78701
512-467-7299

Steve Patterson
Alexander-Patterson
Roof Technical Services, Inc.
1215 Country Club Lane, Suite 105
Fort Worth, TX 76112
817-496-4631

The Wyatt Company (nationwide insurance
  consultants)
1990 K Street, N.W., Suite 500
Washington, DC 20006
202-857-9200

Appendix B
Definitions

Actual cash value—Fair market value of the building.

Affidavit—Statement of a witness signed in front of a notary public and used in court to prove a witness is lying or to refresh a witness' recollection.

After-tax cash flow—Cash inflows minus cash out flows where cash out flows include income taxes paid on the property's income.

Agreed amount—Insurance policy with no coinsurance requirement or penalty.

Amortization—Principal payments on mortgage.

Appreciation—Increase in property value.

Assessment—Property tax assessor's opinion of the value of your property.

Base date—Date on which all future rents are based in a rent control law.

Before-tax cash flow—Cash inflows from the property minus cash outflows but not including income taxes.

Best rating—Rating of the strength of an insurance company by the A.M. Best Company.

Boiler insurance—Insurance which covers heating, hot water, and air-conditioning equipment.

Claims made insurance—Insurance which pays only if the claim is filed during the policy period regardless of whether the incident which is the basis of the claim occurred during the policy period.

Coinsurance—Minimum percentage of value which insured must have to avoid penalty in the event of a major insurance claim.

Collected rent—Amount actually collected as rent.

Comparable—Apartment building which is similar to yours in location and other features.

Concessionaire—Company or individual who rents space in your building for his vending machines, typically on a percent of gross basis.

Contract rent—Rent stipulated in the lease.

Conversion ratio—Number of leases signed divided by the number of showings.

Co-signer—Individual or organization which signs lease but does not occupy the apartment in question.

Data base program—A computer program which keeps track of files...a sort of electric filing cabinet which does its own filing and retrieving.

Discretionary expenses—Expenses which vary according to the owner's policies.

Diseconomies of scale—Expense increases due to increased size.

Economies of scale—Savings due to increase in size.

Equity—Difference between property value and loans on the property.

Fair market rental value—The highest rent an apartment will bring from an acceptable tenant when competently exposed to the market for a reasonable period of time.

Fidelity insurance—Insurance against employee dishonesty. Sometimes called a "fidelity bond."

First-year expensing—Tax deduction permitted on coin-operated vending machines owned by an apartment owner and rental furniture owned by a non-apartment owner under section 179 of the Internal Revenue Code.

Forfeits—Security deposits forfeited by tenants for lease violations.

"Gouging"—Renting to the highest acceptable bidder.

Increased cost of construction insurance—Insurance to cover increased cost of construction caused by damage which triggers more restrictive building code requirements than in effect when the building was originally built.

Insurance consultant—Insurance expert who advises you on insurance purchases but does not sell insurance or receive a commission from an insurance company.

Kickbacks—Gift of goods, services, or money given by an apartment supplier to an apartment manager to win the building's business even though the supplier is not the lowest acceptable bidder.

Load factor—Space in a rental building which does not produce rental income.

"Lodging"—Internal Revenue Code word which means apartment buildings where the tenant normally stays more than thirty days.

Loss assessment insurance—Insurance against the policyholder being assessed by his or her homeowners association due to a loss suffered by the homeowners association which exceeds the association's insurance limits.

Lumen—Unit for measuring light output.

Master meter—Utility meter which measures the utility consumption of more than one apartment unit. Typically, the building owner receives the bill.

Moving average—Average of the most recent three months, twelve months or other period.

Negative cash flow—Cash outlays exceed cash inflows.

Paranoid schizophrenic—A person who has a psychotic disorder in which the affected person suffers delusions of persecution, retreats from reality, and is torn by conflicting emotions and changing personality.

Payback period—Length of time it takes to pay for an improvement with increased income or savings.

Positive cash flow—Cash income exceeds cash outlays.

Potential rent—The asking rent on a vacant unit or the rent stipulated in the lease on an occupied unit.

Proration—Daily rent charged to a tenant who moves in or out other than on the rent due date.

Public insurance adjuster—Expert in filing insurance claims who represents you with insurance company when you have a significant loss.

Rent concession—Gift of money or goods to a tenant as an inducement to rent.

Rental market survey—List of similar buildings, their features, sizes, and rents.

Rent loss insurance—Insurance against loss of rents due to an insurable accident.

Replacement cost—Cost of replacing a building with one of "like kind and quality."

Separate meter—Utility meter which measures utility consumption by a single apartment unit. Installed, owned, read, billed, and maintained by the utility.

Shopper—Individual who poses as a prospective tenant and gives a report on the manager's performance to the owner.

Soft market—A condition which occurs when fair market rental values drop generally but owners fail to reduce rents as much as fair market rental value has fallen.

Spread sheet program—Computer program which performs mathematical calculations.

Street rents—Rents you are asking new tenants to pay.

Submeter—An electric or other meter which measures utility consumption in a tenant's apartment. Installed, owned, read, billed, and maintained by the owner or his agent. Used to allocate a master meter's bill among tenants according to use.

Turnover ratio—Number of move-ins per year divided by the number of units in the building.

Vacancy rate—Difference between potential and collected rent divided by potential rent.

Vendor—Anyone to whom you regularly pay money.

Verifiable expenses—Expenses which are determined by external factors and by the structure of the building.

Word processing—Computer or computer program which is used to write letters, legal contracts, etc.

Workers compensation—A special type of insurance usually required by law.

Zoning insurance—Insurance against loss of building value caused by damage which triggers more restrictive zoning preventing rebuilding the building to its pre-damage configuration.

INDEX

Newsletter

	Unit Price	Total
_____ one-year subscriptions to John T. Reed's Real Estate Investor's Monthly (12 monthly issues)	$125.00	$_____
_____ back issues (See Web site for list. Minimum order is 3.) 1 to 11 back issues	$ 8.50 ea.	$_____
12 or more back issues	$ 8.00 ea.	$_____

Special reports

_____ Single-Family Lease Options (48 pages)	$ 29.95	$_____
_____ Distressed Real Estate Times: Offensive and Defensive Strategy and Tactics (63 pages)	$ 29.95	$_____
_____ How to Do a Delayed Exchange (40 pages)	$ 29.95	$_____

Books

_____ Aggressive Tax Avoidance for Real Estate Investors— **16th edition**	$ 23.95	$_____
_____ Coaching Youth Football—**2nd edition**	$ 21.95	$_____
_____ Coaching Youth Football Defense—**2nd edition**	$ 19.95	$_____
_____ Football Clock Management	$ 19.95	$_____
_____ How to Buy Real Estate for at Least 20% Below Market Value—**2nd edition**	$ 23.95	$_____
_____ How to Increase the Value of Real Estate (loose leaf)	$ 39.95	$_____
_____ How to Manage Residential Property for Maximum Cash Flow **5th edition**	$ 23.95	$_____
_____ How to Use Leverage to Maximize Your Real Estate Investment Return **2nd edition**	$ 19.95	$_____
_____ Office Building Acquisition Handbook (loose leaf)	$ 39.95	$_____
_____ Real Estate Investor's Monthly on Real Estate Investment Strategy	$ 39.95	$_____
_____ Residential Property Acquisition Handbook (loose leaf)	$ 39.95	$_____

Cassettes   (Two 60-minute cassettes in a binder)

_____ High Leverage Real Estate Financing	$ 29.95	$_____
_____ How to Buy Real Estate for at Least 20% Below Market Value, Vol. I	$ 29.95	$_____
_____ How to Buy Real Estate for at Least 20% Below Market Value, Vol. II	$ 29.95	$_____
_____ How to Buy Residential Property	$ 29.95	$_____
_____ How to Find Deals That Make Sense in Today's Market	$ 29.95	$_____
_____ How to Manage Residential Property for Maximum Cash Flow and Resale Value	$ 29.95	$_____
_____ How to Do a Delayed Exchange	$ 29.95	$_____
_____ Offensive and Defensive Strategy for Distressed Real Estate Times	$ 29.95	$_____
_____ Single-Family Lease Options	$ 29.95	$_____

Software

_____ Landlording™ On Disk software by Leigh Robinson		
IMPORTANT—CHECK ONE: ☐ Macintosh ☐ IBM 5 1/4 ☐ IBM 3 1/2"	$ 39.95	$_____

	Subtotal	$_____
Discount 5% for two or more items totaling over $100	$_____	
California residents: add your area's **sales tax** (except on newsletter subscriptions)	$_____	
Shipping: $4.00 for first item (Except subscriptions)	$ 4.00	
$2.00 for **EACH** additional item	$_____	
(There is **one** shipping charge for any number of newsletter back issues.)		
	Total	$_____

For more information, visit my Web site at www.johntreed.com/realestate.html

Method of Payment: _____ Check enclosed payable to John T. Reed   _____ Visa   _____ MasterCard

Card # _____ Exp. Date _____ Signature _____

Ship to: Name _____Telephone_____

Street Address _____

City _____ State _____ Zip _____ Fax _____

Please mail your order to: John T. Reed, 342 Bryan Drive, Alamo, CA 94507
These prices are effective 10/1/98 and are subject to change.
You can also **fax** your order to 925-820-1259 or **E-mail** it to johnreed@johntreed.com

OR PHONE ☎
925-820-7262

Your Opinion of this Book is Important to Me

Please send me your comments on this book. I'm interested in both compliments and constructive ciriticism. Your compliments provide guidance on what you want. And, with your permission, I'd like to use your favorable comments to sell future editions of the book. Constructive criticism also helps make the book's next edition better.

Evaluation of *How to Manage Residential Property for Maximum Cash Flow and Resale Value, 5th edition*

Circle one: Excellent   Good   Satisfactory   Unsatisfactory

Circle one: Too Advanced   About Right   Too Basic

What part did you like best? _____

_____

What part did you like least? _____

_____

How can I improve the book? _____

_____

My promotional material includes brief comments by people who have read the book and their name, city, state, and occupation. I would appreciate any remarks you could give me for that purpose:

_____

_____

_____

Name _____ Team _____

Address _____

City _____ State _____ Zip _____

Feel free to leave blanks if you prefer not to answer all of these questions. I would appreciate receiving your evaluation even if you only fill out one line.

How long have you been a real estate investor? _____

What is the total value of your investment real estate? _____

What types of property do you own? _____

If your comments will not fit on this sheet, feel free to write them on the back of additional sheets. Please send your evaluation to:

John T. Reed
342 Bryan Drive
Alamo, CA 94507

Newsletter

	Unit Price	Total
_____ one-year subscriptions to John T. Reed's Real Estate Investor's Monthly (12 monthly issues)	$125.00	$_____
_____ back issues (See Web site for list. Minimum order is 3.) 1 to 11 back issues	$ 8.50 ea.	$_____
12 or more back issues	$ 8.00 ea.	$_____

Special reports

_____ Single-Family Lease Options (48 pages)	$ 29.95	$_____
_____ Distressed Real Estate Times: Offensive and Defensive Strategy and Tactics (63 pages)	$ 29.95	$_____
_____ How to Do a Delayed Exchange (40 pages)	$ 29.95	$_____

Books

_____ Aggressive Tax Avoidance for Real Estate Investors— **16th edition**	$ 23.95	$_____
_____ Coaching Youth Football—**2nd edition**	$ 21.95	$_____
_____ Coaching Youth Football Defense—**2nd edition**	$ 19.95	$_____
_____ Football Clock Management	$ 19.95	$_____
_____ How to Buy Real Estate for at Least 20% Below Market Value—**2nd edition**	$ 23.95	$_____
_____ How to Increase the Value of Real Estate (loose leaf)	$ 39.95	$_____
_____ How to Manage Residential Property for Maximum Cash Flow **5th edition**	$ 23.95	$_____
_____ How to Use Leverage to Maximize Your Real Estate Investment Return **2nd edition**	$ 19.95	$_____
_____ Office Building Acquisition Handbook (loose leaf)	$ 39.95	$_____
_____ Real Estate Investor's Monthly on Real Estate Investment Strategy	$ 39.95	$_____
_____ Residential Property Acquisition Handbook (loose leaf)	$ 39.95	$_____

Cassettes   (Two 60-minute cassettes in a binder)

_____ High Leverage Real Estate Financing	$ 29.95	$_____
_____ How to Buy Real Estate for at Least 20% Below Market Value, Vol. I	$ 29.95	$_____
_____ How to Buy Real Estate for at Least 20% Below Market Value, Vol. II	$ 29.95	$_____
_____ How to Buy Residential Property	$ 29.95	$_____
_____ How to Find Deals That Make Sense in Today's Market	$ 29.95	$_____
_____ How to Manage Residential Property for Maximum Cash Flow and Resale Value	$ 29.95	$_____
_____ How to Do a Delayed Exchange	$ 29.95	$_____
_____ Offensive and Defensive Strategy for Distressed Real Estate Times	$ 29.95	$_____
_____ Single-Family Lease Options	$ 29.95	$_____

Software

_____ Landlording™ On Disk software by Leigh Robinson		
IMPORTANT—CHECK ONE: ☐ Macintosh ☐ IBM 5 1/4 ☐ IBM 3 1/2"	$ 39.95	$_____

	Subtotal	$_____
Discount 5% for two or more items totaling over $100	$_____	
California residents: add your area's **sales tax** (except on newsletter subscriptions)	$_____	
Shipping: $4.00 for first item (Except subscriptions)	$ 4.00	
$2.00 for **EACH** additional item	$_____	
(There is **one** shipping charge for any number of newsletter back issues.)		
	Total	$_____

For more information, visit my Web site at www.johntreed.com/realestate.html

---

Method of Payment: _____ Check enclosed payable to John T. Reed _____ Visa _____ MasterCard

Card # _____ Exp. Date _____ Signature _____

Ship to: Name _____Telephone_____

Street Address _____

City _____ State _____ Zip _____ Fax _____

Please mail your order to: John T. Reed, 342 Bryan Drive, Alamo, CA 94507
These prices are effective 10/1/98 and are subject to change.
You can also **fax** your order to 925-820-1259 or **E-mail** it to johnreed@johntreed.com

OR PHONE ☎
925-820-7262

Your Opinion of this Book is Important to Me

Please send me your comments on this book. I'm interested in both compliments and constructive ciriticism. Your compliments provide guidance on what you want. And, with your permission, I'd like to use your favorable comments to sell future editions of the book. Constructive criticism also helps make the book's next edition better.

Evaluation of *How to Manage Residential Property for Maximum Cash Flow and Resale Value, 5th edition*

Circle one: Excellent   Good   Satisfactory   Unsatisfactory

Circle one: Too Advanced   About Right   Too Basic

What part did you like best? _____

_____

What part did you like least? _____

_____

How can I improve the book? _____

_____

My promotional material includes brief comments by people who have read the book and their name, city, state, and occupation. I would appreciate any remarks you could give me for that purpose:

_____

_____

_____

Name _____ Team _____

Address _____

City _____ State _____ Zip _____

Feel free to leave blanks if you prefer not to answer all of these questions. I would appreciate receiving your evaluation even if you only fill out one line.

How long have you been a real estate investor? _____

What is the total value of your investment real estate? _____

What types of property do you own? _____

If your comments will not fit on this sheet, feel free to write them on the back of additional sheets. Please send your evaluation to:

John T. Reed
342 Bryan Drive
Alamo, CA 94507

Newsletter

	Unit Price	Total
_____ one-year subscriptions to John T. Reed's Real Estate Investor's Monthly (12 monthly issues)	$125.00	$_____
_____ back issues (See Web site for list. Minimum order is 3.) 1 to 11 back issues	$ 8.50 ea.	$_____
12 or more back issues	$ 8.00 ea.	$_____

Special reports

_____ Single-Family Lease Options (48 pages)	$ 29.95	$_____
_____ Distressed Real Estate Times: Offensive and Defensive Strategy and Tactics (63 pages)	$ 29.95	$_____
_____ How to Do a Delayed Exchange (40 pages)	$ 29.95	$_____

Books

_____ Aggressive Tax Avoidance for Real Estate Investors— **16th edition**	$ 23.95	$_____
_____ Coaching Youth Football—**2nd edition**	$ 21.95	$_____
_____ Coaching Youth Football Defense—**2nd edition**	$ 19.95	$_____
_____ Football Clock Management	$ 19.95	$_____
_____ How to Buy Real Estate for at Least 20% Below Market Value—**2nd edition**	$ 23.95	$_____
_____ How to Increase the Value of Real Estate (loose leaf)	$ 39.95	$_____
_____ How to Manage Residential Property for Maximum Cash Flow **5th edition**	$ 23.95	$_____
_____ How to Use Leverage to Maximize Your Real Estate Investment Return **2nd edition**	$ 19.95	$_____
_____ Office Building Acquisition Handbook (loose leaf)	$ 39.95	$_____
_____ Real Estate Investor's Monthly on Real Estate Investment Strategy	$ 39.95	$_____
_____ Residential Property Acquisition Handbook (loose leaf)	$ 39.95	$_____

Cassettes (Two 60-minute cassettes in a binder)

_____ High Leverage Real Estate Financing	$ 29.95	$_____
_____ How to Buy Real Estate for at Least 20% Below Market Value, Vol. I	$ 29.95	$_____
_____ How to Buy Real Estate for at Least 20% Below Market Value, Vol. II	$ 29.95	$_____
_____ How to Buy Residential Property	$ 29.95	$_____
_____ How to Find Deals That Make Sense in Today's Market	$ 29.95	$_____
_____ How to Manage Residential Property for Maximum Cash Flow and Resale Value	$ 29.95	$_____
_____ How to Do a Delayed Exchange	$ 29.95	$_____
_____ Offensive and Defensive Strategy for Distressed Real Estate Times	$ 29.95	$_____
_____ Single-Family Lease Options	$ 29.95	$_____

Software

_____ Landlording™ On Disk software by Leigh Robinson		
IMPORTANT—CHECK ONE: ☐ Macintosh ☐ IBM 5 1/4 ☐ IBM 3 1/2"	$ 39.95	$_____
	Subtotal	$_____

Discount 5% for two or more items totaling over $100 $_____

California residents: add your area's **sales tax** (except on newsletter subscriptions) $_____

Shipping: $4.00 for first item (Except subscriptions) $ 4.00

$2.00 for **EACH** additional item $_____

(There is **one** shipping charge for any number of newsletter back issues.)

Total $_____

For more information, visit my Web site at www.johntreed.com/realestate.html

---

Method of Payment: _____ Check enclosed payable to John T. Reed   _____ Visa   _____ MasterCard

Card # _____   Exp. Date _____   Signature _____

Ship to: Name _____Telephone_____

Street Address _____

City _____ State _____ Zip _____ Fax _____

Please mail your order to: John T. Reed, 342 Bryan Drive, Alamo, CA 94507
These prices are effective 10/1/98 and are subject to change.
You can also **fax** your order to 925-820-1259 or **E-mail** it to johnreed@johntreed.com

OR PHONE ☎
925-820-7262

Your Opinion of this Book is Important to Me

Please send me your comments on this book. I'm interested in both compliments and constructive ciriticism. Your compliments provide guidance on what you want. And, with your permission, I'd like to use your favorable comments to sell future editions of the book. Constructive criticism also helps make the book's next edition better.

Evaluation of *How to Manage Residential Property for Maximum Cash Flow and Resale Value, 5th edition*

Circle one: Excellent   Good   Satisfactory   Unsatisfactory

Circle one: Too Advanced   About Right   Too Basic

What part did you like best? _____

_____

What part did you like least? _____

_____

How can I improve the book? _____

_____

My promotional material includes brief comments by people who have read the book and their name, city, state, and occupation. I would appreciate any remarks you could give me for that purpose:

_____

_____

_____

Name _____ Team _____

Address _____

City _____ State _____ Zip _____

Feel free to leave blanks if you prefer not to answer all of these questions. I would appreciate receiving your evaluation even if you only fill out one line.

How long have you been a real estate investor? _____

What is the total value of your investment real estate? _____

What types of property do you own? _____

If your comments will not fit on this sheet, feel free to write them on the back of additional sheets. Please send your evaluation to:

John T. Reed
342 Bryan Drive
Alamo, CA 94507